BUILDING COMPETENCE IN CLASSROOM MANAGEMENT AND DISCIPLINE

FOURTH EDITION

ANNETTE M. IVERSON
University of Northern Iowa

Merrill
Prentice Hall

Upper Saddle River, New Jersey
Columbus, Ohio

Library of Congress Cataloging-in-Publication Data

Iverson, Annette M.,
   Building competence in classroom management and discipline / Annette M. Iverson. —
4th ed.
      p. cm.
   Rev. ed. of: Schoolwide and classroom management. c1999.
   Includes bibliographical references and indexes.
   ISBN 0-13-098175-3
   1. Classroom management. I. Froyen, Len A. Schoolwide and classroom management.
II. Title.
LB3013 .F783 2003
371.102'4—dc21   2002024646

Vice President and Publisher: Jeffery W. Johnston
Executive Editor: Debra Stollenwerk
Associate Editor: Jessica Crouch
Production Editor: Sheryl Glicker Langner
Production Coordination: TechBooks
Design Coordinator: Diane C. Lorenzo
Cover Designer: Jason Moore
Cover Photo: Corbis Stock Market
Production Manager: Laura Messerly
Director of Marketing: Ann Castel Davis
Marketing Manager: Krista Groshong
Marketing Coordinator: Tyra Cooper

This book was set in Life BT by TechBooks. It was printed and bound by R. R. Donnelley &
Sons Company. The cover was printed by Phoenix Color Corp.

Photo Credits: All photos by Annette M. Iverson.

Pearson Education Ltd.
Pearson Education Australia Pty. Limited
Pearson Education Singapore Pte. Ltd.
Pearson Education North Asia Ltd.
Pearson Education Canada, Ltd.
Pearson Educación de Mexico, S. A. de C. V.
Pearson Education—Japan
Pearson Education Malaysia Pte. Ltd.
Pearson Education, *Upper Saddle River, New Jersey*

10 9 8 7 6 5 4 3 2
ISBN: 0-13-098175-3

3/8/04

Preface

Building Competence in Classroom Management and Discipline was written after 15 years of teaching and consulting in the public schools and 10 years of teaching undergraduate and graduate classroom management courses. The title of the fourth edition reflects a commitment to helping educators develop competencies in both collaborative and directive classroom management and discipline strategies. The management approach of the book is based on the assumption that multiple systems influence student development and that school personnel and families need to collaborate in making classroom management and discipline effective supports for all students. Teachers no longer can afford to close their classroom doors and do their own thing. They have a higher calling—to improve outcomes for students by partnering with families and other educators in the school building. Accordingly, ecological theory is integrated throughout the text as the framework for building competencies in classroom management and discipline. Educators are sensitized not only to how micro- and mesosystems influence students' success, but also to the competencies that bridge classrooms with principals' offices and students' homes.

Two major directions in the research literature guided content development of this edition. The first direction comes from the early work of Bronfenbrenner (1979) on ecological theory and his understanding of the complex and multiple systems that impact child and adolescent development. His voice was the first in a long line of scholars and social policy makers that influenced the development of the Eighth National Education Goal (i.e., that schools would promote partnerships with parents that improve the social, emotional, and academic growth of children). Not only is there a national goal for partnering, but there are also federal and state dollars supporting local school districts' partnership initiatives. Early research on collaboration between educators and parents indicates that such collaboration is no easy task (Cibulka & Kritek, 1996). Universities must do their part in preparing educators for the challenge of thinking ecologically and working collaboratively. This textbook is a resource to support that endeavor.

The second major direction of the text is based largely on Kagan's (1992) meta-analytic review of 40 learning-to-teach studies, which culminated in a model of professional growth that concurred with and refined earlier models (Berliner, 1988; Fuller, 1969). One of Kagan's major refinements advised educators to help novices reflect on their own beliefs and behaviors rather than on the moral and ethical implications of classroom practices. Her second refinement advised educators to help novices become competent in the quick, efficient, and directive use of basic classroom management and discipline procedures. Her two refinements of reflection on beliefs and acquiring directive management procedures are reflected throughout the text.

Organization of the Text

In part I, chapter 1 emphasizes theories of human behavior and encourages readers to begin examining their own beliefs. The chapter ends with a description of the IDEAL problem-solving process and a comprehensive application of IDEAL to a student's problem behavior. Chapter 2 contains management procedures for the first weeks of school in each of the three Cs: covenant/relationships, conduct/positive behavior choices, and content/setting and instruction management.

In part II, chapter 3 emphasizes building relationships with students and their families. The chapter provides additional competencies for use throughout the school year. Chapter 4 emphasizes the conduct manager's use of positive behavior choices and provides new information on positive behavior support schools and functional behavioral assessment. In keeping with theoretical changes in learning and instruction, chapter 5 emphasizes the management of teaching/learning activities that are more constructivist based and less direct instruction based.

In part III, chapter 6 focuses on home–school collaboration and on development of appropriate mesosystem competencies. Chapter 7 covers schoolwide discipline. There are two particular strengths of this chapter. The first develops teachers' understanding of their need to consider the limits of principals' options for disciplining students, and the second is the clarification of how, when, and why to use out-of-class consequences in ways that positively affect youth. Finally, chapter 8, with its emphasis on developing competencies in communication, is appreciated by education students, who state that such competencies constitute new and empowering skills not taught in other education courses.

In Appendix A, there are two three-page worksheets that guide readers in the development of a classroom management plan. The first worksheet is for an authoritarian orientation, and the second is for a democratic orientation. Appendix B provides model solutions to three prototypical classroom management problems, one each in the conduct, covenant, and content categories.

New to This Edition

New to this edition are the following:

❑ A schematic drawing of the important concepts of each chapter, located at the beginning of the chapter

❑ A description and time line of the historical events that have led to federal, state, and local emphases on home–school partnerships

❑ A research-based model of home–school collaboration with numerous tables containing collaboration strategies

❑ Schools as positive behavior support (PBS) systems

❑ Functional behavioral assessment (FBA) procedures

❑ New examples to assist students in learning more difficult concepts

Features

❑ Froyen's three *C*s model of classroom management continues to be a conceptual strength of the text.

❑ Chapter 2 can be a short, stand-alone publication of management guidelines for all teachers in the field.

❑ Activities, entitled "Management Challenges," appear in many chapters and encourage reflection on beliefs and problem solving.

❑ Chapters provide opportunities for role-play and practice in implementing management procedures.

❑ Ethical and legal aspects of management are no longer in a separate chapter but are integrated into appropriate chapters throughout the text.

❑ The text has been condensed so that the basic competencies in classroom management and discipline can be covered in a semester or less of university coursework.

ACKNOWLEDGMENTS

The author of the first two editions of this book and coauthor of the third edition, Len Froyen, has retired and generously left the legacy to me. I want to thank him for mentoring my writing of the third edition and trusting me to go solo on the fourth. In particular, I appreciate his conceptualization of classroom management as the three *C*s, and I am pleased to have the opportunity to continue to share them.

I also appreciate and wish to thank the following professors who reviewed the manuscript: Frank Adams, Wayne State College; Karen Bosch, Virginia Wesleyan College; Randi L. Brown, University of Central Oklahoma; Betty Cooper Epanchin, University of South Florida; Warren Schollaers, Armstrong Atlantic State University; and Tim J. Wells, Texas A&M University, Corpus Christi.

Finally, I wish to acknowledge my husband, whose spirit and way of being captures the essence of true collaboration. His partnership greatly facilitated the writing of this book.

Annette M. Iverson, Ph.D.

REFERENCES

Berliner, D. C. (1988). Implications of studies on expertise in pedagogy for teacher education and evaluation. In *New directions for teacher assessment: Proceedings of the 1988 ETS Invitational Conference* (pp. 39–68). Princeton, NJ: Educational Testing Service.

Bronfenbrenner, U. (1979). *The ecology of human development.* Cambridge, MA: Harvard University Press.

Cibulka, J. G., & Kritek, W. J. (Eds.). (1996). *Coordination among schools, families, and communities: Prospects for educational reform.* Albany: State University of New York Press.

Fuller, F. F. (1969). Concerns of teachers: A developmental conceptualization. *American Educational Research Journal, 6,* 207–226.

Kagan, D. M. (1992). Professional growth among preservice and beginning teachers. *Review of Educational Research, 62,* 129–169.

Brief Contents

Contents

CHAPTER 5
Competencies in Content Management: Instruction   *168*

PART 1

Introduction to Building Competence in Classroom Management and Discipline

CHAPTER ONE
Competencies in Classroom Management and Discipline:
The History and the Promise

CHAPTER TWO
Competencies in Classroom Management and Discipline:
The First Weeks of School

Competencies in Classroom Management and Discipline: The History and the Promise

TEXT ORGANIZATION
1. INTRODUCTION
2. FIRST WEEKS OF SCHOOL
3. COVENANT MANAGEMENT
4. CONDUCT MANAGEMENT
5. CONTENT MANAGEMENT
6. HOME–SCHOOL COLLABORATION
7. SCHOOLWIDE DISCIPLINE
8. COMMUNICATION

DEFINITION OF TERMS
CLASSROOM MANAGEMENT
    Discipline

PROBLEM-SOLVING MODEL
NOVICE/EXPERT DIFFERENCES
IDEAL

Classroom Management Introduction

HISTORY
STUDENT POPULATION
DECISION MAKERS
RESEARCH
STUDENT LEARNING
    Academics
    Social
TEACHER EFFICACY
THEORY AND APPLICATIONS
    Ecological
    Behavioral
    Humanistic
    Psychoanalytic
    Personal
        Reflection

ORGANIZATION OF DISCIPLINE KNOWLEDGE
MODELS OF DISCIPLINE
STRATEGIES
FROYEN'S THREE CS MODEL
    Covenant Management
        Relationships
    Conduct Management
        Behavior
    Content Management
        Instruction

An understanding of the material in this chapter will help you do the following:

❏ Define *classroom management* and *discipline.*
❏ Discuss the relationship between classroom management and student learning and teacher efficacy.
❏ Discuss the influence of theories of human behavior on management practices.
❏ Develop awareness of personal assumptions about human behavior.
❏ Appreciate alternative explanations of human behavior.
❏ Summarize the historical events that resulted in an ecological approach to classroom management.
❏ Describe the three conceptual domains of classroom management and discipline used to organize the discipline's knowledge base.
❏ Use a problem-solving process to solve classroom management and discipline problems.
❏ Set personal goals to participate in active learning of management skills.

> All of our children ought to be allowed a stake in the enormous richness of America.
>
> —Kozol, 1991, p. 233.

Jerad was a seventh-grade male student who was upset. He did not want to stay in his classroom. The seventh-grade teacher, Mr. Fix, grabbed Jerad as he tried to run from the room. Mr. Fix held Jerad underneath his arm because Jerad was unruly. The teacher said later that he was trying to keep Jerad "in line," keep other students safe, and keep Jerad himself safe. Jerad was then taken to the vice principal, Ms. Bose, to telephone his mother and explain what he had done.

Jerad's mother, Ms. Barthel, understood her son to say that Mr. Fix had put his hands around Jerad's neck to restrain him, and she immediately came to school with a male friend. Once at school, Ms. Barthel's meeting with Ms. Bose was not private but very public. Students, secretaries, teachers, administrators, and others were on the scene to witness all events.

Ms. Barthel believed that no one was listening to her son's complaints and that she was not being listened to either. When she decided that Ms. Bose was taking the teacher's side, she punched her. Then Ms. Barthel began throwing vases. Hair pulling was also reported. Ms. Barthel and her male friend exited the building. Several school personnel sustained minor injuries, and one required medical attention at a local hospital. Ms. Barthel later told the press that her actions were precipitated by her fear of a teacher in the group who had a pair of scissors.

The preceding scenario is based on a newspaper report of a disciplinary action in a middle school classroom in the Midwest, with names changed to protect identities.

The newspaper quoted the school spokesperson as stating that the student's mother started the fight and that, in fact, the student was treated according to school policy. The insinuation was that school personnel believed they were in the right and had done nothing to cause the problems. The same newspaper quoted Ms. Barthel as stating that she was angry with the school before her son phoned home because the school had done nothing about an incident in which older students had beaten up on Jerad a few days previously. She shared that she was also angry because school officials had Jerad phone her. She believed that the call home was the responsibility of school officials. She expressed sorrow that the confrontation occurred and hoped that matters could be resolved (Iverson, 1996).

Principals, teachers, guidance counselors, school psychologists, school social workers, parents, and community members hope situations like the previous one never happen in their school buildings. Realistically, a whole host of problems will present themselves, some less complex than this and some more complex. How do school personnel prevent such problems? When problems occur, how do school personnel develop solutions that promote students' positive growth? Knowledge of classroom management and discipline principles presented throughout this text will build competencies that prevent most problems and facilitate students' positive growth when problems occur.

DEFINITIONS: CLASSROOM MANAGEMENT AND DISCIPLINE

Classroom management is the act of supervising relationships, behaviors, and instructional settings and lessons for communities of learners. Classroom management typically is preventive and results in decreased incidences of discipline problems. In spite of quality classroom management, a small proportion of students, about 4%, will exhibit behavioral problems that require the development and implementation of specific discipline strategies.

Discipline is the act of teaching students how to behave appropriately. A popular, but incorrect, view is that discipline is the same thing as punishment. Discipline is not punishment; it is the use of specific strategies to instruct students in the how-tos of behaviors that are socially acceptable or valid. In summary, discipline is instructive and rehabilitative. It results in increased incidences of prosocial behaviors.

HISTORY OF CLASSROOM MANAGEMENT: RESEARCH AND THEORY

As early as the mid-1700s, education reformers were asserting that the social stability of the nation and the welfare of individuals required universal access to schools. For many years, it was believed that schools could and should, through appropriate education, solve all of the country's social and individual problems.

Student Population History

In spite of the call for universal access, schoolwide discipline policies from the early 1900s were based on punitive and exclusionary practices. At that time, success in school was not a prerequisite to getting a job. Schools did not have the goal of educating everyone and graduated only 6% of the population. Accordingly, schools were oriented toward children and adolescents who were academically inclined and had socially acceptable behaviors. Discipline policies were based on punishment for breaking the rules and included suspension and expulsion. Such policies were a major way to exclude less able, less motivated, or poorly behaved students.

Decision Makers in History

During the early times of excluding children from school, society was less pluralistic and management was easier. Whole communities tended to agree on expectations for behavior and that teachers were in charge of classes. Teachers were free to teach what they wanted and to discipline children as they deemed fit. At times, discipline consisted of corporal punishment, and few parents objected. When school attendance became mandatory, discipline policies and procedures did not change in significant ways.

It wasn't until the 1960s that the public demanded radical changes in the way decisions were made in schools. In 1966, the Coleman Report brought a great deal of attention to issues of equity in America's schools. This marked the dawning of the early effective-schools research with the goal of helping all children be successful, not just children of privilege. Many poor children were located in large cities. Hence, large city schools became the target of early reform movements. An initial step was the political decentralization of decision making in urban schools, where parents essentially took the management of schools into their own hands. This represented a significant departure from principals and teachers' acting as the sole authority of their respective school buildings and classrooms.

In 1979, Edmonds published his five correlates of effective schools. Because he wanted to emphasize getting schools themselves to change, there was no mention of the need for schools to involve parents and communities. Accordingly, his approach to increasing school effectiveness was short-lived. It already was clear both to educational scholars and to the public that the strategy of having schools change without external support was too simplistic of a strategy in the face of the complex needs of children.

That same year, Bronfenbrenner (1979) published a thorough description of the numerous influences on child outcomes. His ecological theory addressed four levels or systems that greatly impact children's growth and development, in stark contrast to Edmonds' school-only perspective. Bronfenbrenner called the four levels the *microsystem,* the *mesosystem,* the *exosystem,* and the *macrosystem.* The influences of two of the four levels on children—the microsystem (e.g., classroom, home) and the mesosystem (e.g., links between home and school)—are considered with regard to management and discipline throughout this text.

The National Commission on Excellence in Education's 1983 report *A Nation At Risk* (e.g., decreased SAT scores) spurred additional political support for reforms that would guarantee all children's success in school. A year later, Walberg (1984) published his synthesis of thousands of studies that found a decrease in home fostering of learning. Much was known about the positive and significant influence that involved parents have on student outcomes, and Walberg's findings did not go unheeded. By 1988, new school-effectiveness programs included major emphases on parent involvement and on education of parents about their role in supporting the work of the schools. It was in the 1980s that parents and communities across the nation began to question the authoritarian discipline approach (Dornbusch & Ritter, 1992).

The next wave of reform emphasized site-based management that included teachers, parents, and community members' collaborating together on the management of the nation's schools. Following a reexamination of the United States's status as a declining economic power and increasing numbers of children of poverty, a third wave of reform began with a renewed emphasis on collaboration. The African proverb "It takes a village to raise a child" became the language of Hillary Clinton, then First Lady, and was cited in numerous scholarly articles and book chapters (e.g., Berger, 1995; Cibulka & Kritek, 1996). The coordination/collaboration momentum surged with the aid of federal funds flowing to states that had developed initiatives based on collaboration. Success4 initiatives in the state of Iowa are an example. The Success4 Web site describes student outcomes as a result of collaborative goals in school discipline:

> http://www.state.ia.us
> (After this site comes up, browse by topic "Education"; click on featured link
>   "Iowa Department of Education"; click on "Programs and Services"; click
>   on alphabetical listing "Success4.")

In summary, two major developments were largely responsible for the interest in collaboration efforts. The first development was the increase in the incidence of children who are poor, and the second was the U.S. decline in the world as an economic power (Kritek, 1996). By the end of the 20th and the beginning of the 21st centuries, social, political, economic, and educational reformers were asserting that universal access to schools was a necessary, but not a sufficient, condition for resolving social and individual welfare concerns. Rather, collaboration/coordination of schools, families, and communities was required if all students were to attend school successfully.

Research

As noted previously, management in classrooms involves more than disciplining students. It is a process of facilitating positive student achievement and behavior with the ultimate goal of student self-control (McCaslin & Good, 1992). The importance of obtaining classroom management competencies is supported by research on relationships between classroom management and students' academic and social learning and teacher efficacy.

Classroom Management and Student Learning

A meta-analytic investigation of variables that contributed to school learning showed that effective classroom management was more important than student demographics, home support, school policy, curriculum design, classroom instruction, and motivation (Wang, Haertel, & Walberg, 1993). Preparation to manage classrooms has also enjoyed a renewed emphasis because of today's complex social factors (Hyman, 1997).

The sociology of children has changed in important respects and is fraught with numerous problems. Contemporary sociological problems of students stem from a host of interacting variables (Batsche, 1996):

❏ Changes in family structure that result in reduced adult supervision
❏ The effects of television modeling with reduced adult feedback due to inadequate levels of supervision
❏ U.S. economic changes and their impact on education
❏ Discrepancies between the needs of children at the schoolhouse door and the programs that determine what goes on in school buildings

These important sociological changes are associated with various student problems in the schools. Following are examples of problems with which educators contend:

Justin is 14 years old. He has two probation officers. He is able to stay in school only with support.

Darian is 12 years old. At school, he attacks children who call him names.

Karl is 5 years old. He stomps on, pushes down, spits on, scratches, bites, and hits other children in his kindergarten class.

Gabrielle is 5 years old. She is noncompliant with directions and angrily overturns desks.

Classroom Management and Teacher Efficacy

Bridges (1986) found that teacher incompetence could probably be defined as chronic failure to maintain classroom discipline. This is important to note because a high sense of teacher competency has been linked to learning gains in basic skills (Good & Brophy, 1984). Some researchers reported that teachers' feelings of competence or efficacy were enhanced by formal planning (Charles, 1992; Unruh, 1994). Unruh (1994) concluded that, in order to feel competent, teachers need to plan classroom management the same way they plan lessons.

In support of Unruh's position, Kagan (1992) concluded that novices need standardized classroom procedures. They must achieve an integration of management and instruction before they can focus on students' learning behaviors. In addition to the need for standardized classroom procedures, the need to teach prosocial behaviors was clearly shown by Batsche (1996). He asserted that a major flaw in classroom management has been the attempt to erase negative behaviors without teaching prosocial replacement behaviors. On the basis of the prevalence of behavioral concerns in today's classrooms, teachers need both their standardized classroom management procedures and discipline procedures that teach prosocial behaviors.

Preservice teachers are as concerned about their management and discipline skills as their teaching skills during the first years of teaching (Veenman, 1984). Tucker, Plax, and Kearney (1985) found that inexperienced teachers had a meager repertoire of classroom management strategies, regardless of the student misbehavior described. Likewise, Chamberlin and Vallance's (1991) undergraduate students reported that the knowledge gained in university courses did not provide them with practical classroom management and discipline procedures.

Another finding is that classroom realities often do not match novice teachers' images of students. For example, novice teachers often believe that students will respond to innovative instruction with excitement and interest (Kagan, 1992). In actuality, most beginning teachers are faced with students who are not very motivated and often misbehave. Kagan recommended that university course work not only promote preservice teachers' insights into their personal beliefs, but also prepare them for the reality of classrooms by equipping them with standard management procedures. In the next sections, theoretical and personal beliefs are explored. Beginning with chapter 2, classroom management procedures are described.

Educators may be unaware of their basic beliefs about human nature and how those beliefs influence their classroom management actions. They can challenge themselves to do the following:

❑ Become aware of their own basic philosophies
❑ Examine personal philosophies in terms of strengths and weaknesses
❑ Explore other beliefs and philosophies
❑ Select from the various positions what works best in different situations
❑ Ultimately do broad-based planning for competent, flexible classroom management

Theories of Human Behavior and Development

In critically examining an individual's management beliefs, the first step is to investigate a range of diverse theories about the nature of human beings, why they do the things they do, and how they got to be the way they are. Basic assumptions about human behavior can be traced from philosophy to the arts and literature and from the arts and literature to the behavioral sciences. All of these disciplines shape and influence individuals and, ultimately, cultures and cultural beliefs.

Assumptions About the Nature of Human Beings

The beliefs and assumptions that individuals hold about the nature of people have been subtly influenced by their cultural milieus. The beliefs and thoughts that we hold about why other people do the things they do and how they get to be the way they are have a great influence on how we understand and interact with the people around us. In the Western world, there are a number of predominant sets of beliefs or assumptions about the nature of human beings. These assumptions are set forth in the psychological theories of the behavioral sciences but have historical roots in philosophy, art, music, the general culture, and theology (Schaeffer, 1982).

The family and community cultures to which you have been exposed have influenced your beliefs about the nature of humans and their growth and development. Four major psychological theories that span the range of beliefs are described in the following sections. It is likely that one will best match your assumptions about why people do the things they do and why you interact with them in the way that you do. All the theories are based on some common assumptions: All human beings grow and develop continuously; relationships with other human beings are needed to promote optimal growth and development; and environments contribute to the growth and development of human beings in both positive ways and negative ways. The four theories are also different from one another. The differences focus on the assumption of whether individuals contribute anything to their own growth and development and, if so, what the limits of their contributions are.

Ecological systems theory is presented first because it provides the framework for collaborative classroom management and discipline between home and school. Behavioral and humanistic theories both offer numerous strategies that can be helpful in classroom management and discipline. Psychoanalytic theory is presented last. It offers fewer management and discipline strategies for the classroom. However, many people of Western culture have personal beliefs that parallel the assumptions of psychoanalytic theory. It is important to examine psychoanalytic assumptions relative to the other theories and their assumptions.

The extent to which the theoretical assumptions about human beings appear to match your beliefs will influence your commitment to corresponding ways of intervening in classroom management problems. Examine your beliefs as they relate to the following theoretical positions: (a) ecological thought, (b) behaviorism, (c) humanism, and (d) psychoanalytic thought. In terms of ideology, most people lean toward one view more than another. Practically speaking, however, most of us borrow from each view to deal with the complexities of life. Selecting what appears to be the best from diverse theories is referred to as the *eclectic method,* and you are encouraged to do that. Do not be surprised if you find something appealing and convincing about each of the theories of human behavior and development.

In the following sections, each theory is first described in terms of its assumptions about human nature. Second, the importance of the environment and other human beings to a student's growth and development is explained. Third, the theory is used to describe how Mr. Fix might go about classroom management and discipline with Jerad, who was described in the first pages of this chapter. Table 1–1 provides a quick reference and overview of each theory. It can be referred to as you continue, throughout the text, to familiarize yourself with the theories and their assumptions.

Table 1–1
Theories of human development.

Topic	Theory			
	Ecological	**Behavioral**	**Humanistic**	**Psychoanalytic**
Nature of people from birth	Human nature is such that behavior develops as a result of multiple and complex systems-level influences.	Humans are born blank slates. Their contributions to their own development is limited to genetic (e.g., blonde or red hair) and physiological (e.g., fight-or-flight) influences.	Humans are born with their own inner capacity to grow optimally and positively and become all they want to be.	Humans are born with inner drives to meet their own needs and desires first and foremost. The inner drives are referred to as the person's *id*.
Environmental contributions	There are four levels or systems that affect human growth and development in multiple and complex ways: micro-, exo-, meso-, and macrosystems.	Human behavior and development is the result of environmental reinforcements and punishments, paired with genetic and physiological influences.	Optimal human development comes from humans' own inner unfolding in environments that are nondirective and that provide necessary materials and resources.	Human growth relies on the direct input of important others, such as parents, to develop the ego and superego which moderate the id.
Home contributions	The home is one of the most important microsystems in the development of humans. The home as a microsystem is influenced both positively and negatively by other systems (e.g., the microsystems where parents work, the community culture, the state of the nation).	The home is an important environment in the shaping of human behavior because children spend so much time there from birth to school age. Rewards and punishments are a big part of home environments, and children's behavior is shaped almost completely by early home experiences.	Home contributions to human growth and development are of major importance. Optimal homes allow children to explore their environments fully and construct their own meaning. Homes that direct and control children stymie their potential to unfold and be all they can be.	Home or parental contributions to human growth and development are of major importance. The most formative years are from birth to age 5 years. Children spend the most time with their parents, who are responsible for parenting them in ways that help children develop egos and superegos that help control their ids.

Ecological Theory

Bronfenbrenner's ecological theory is based on the assumption that multiple systems in the world around us and the human beings in the systems powerfully influence an individual's growth and development. His ecological perspective is one of the major driving forces behind school reform and funding initiatives focused on collaboration across all systems that impact youth. Classroom managers who consider the multiple levels of influences on students make more effective decisions about how to help them grow.

Classroom managers consider the *macrosystem,* which represents the cultural beliefs, patterns, and institutional policies that affect the behavior of students. The *exosystem* consists of the outside influences and demands in adults' lives that affect students. Parents' work demands, financial stress, or major illnesses influence student behavior. For example, occurrences in teachers' home lives such as marital conflict or alcoholism impact student outcomes. The degree to which the strategies of classroom managers are successful is moderated by macrosystem and exosystem influences. These influences may cause some strategies to be more feasible or effective than others. However, educators have less direct control over macro- and exosystem influences than they do over *meso-* and *microsystem* influences. As classroom managers develop more collaborative partnerships with parents and community members, the influences of macrosystems and exosystems may be more easily addressed.

Ecological Applications in Education.   According to Bronfenbrenner's theoretical model, the systems over which educators and parents have the most direct control are the micro- and mesosystems. The school itself is a microsystem, as are classrooms, playgrounds, lunchrooms, and so forth. The home is another microsystem. Each individual microsystem has its own culture, norms, expectations, and influences on children's growth and development.

Mesosystems consist of relationships between various microsystems (e.g., home–school, classroom–school building). All of these systems constitute students' learning environments (Ysseldyke & Christenson, 1993–1994). Children and adolescents learn in many microsystems. When educators and parents share responsibility, the total learning environment (i.e., school and home) produces powerful, positive effects on student outcomes.

Fantini (1983) labeled the separation of school and home as "miseducative." Hess and Holloway (1984) agreed, stating that collaboration between school and home produced greater gains than either system accomplished separately. Blame is circumvented with the concept of the total learning environment. Educators are unable to point the finger at the other system, "the home," and parents are unable to point the finger at the other system, "the school," when the student is having learning or behavioral problems. Rather, the mesosystem, or home–school partnership, has joint responsibility for defining a common effort toward a common goal (Seeley, 1985).

Teachers who subscribe to the ecological model collaborate with families and other personnel in the building. They make changes in environments, including their own behavior and their instruction, in order to assist children in learning. They do not assume that children's difficulties come from within themselves or are the result of poor parenting practices.

Ecological Applications to Jerad's Case.   What would the application of ecological theory to the case of Jerad have been like? Home–school partnerships may have prevented the situation from occurring, or at least prevented it from escalating once it had occurred. At the beginning of the year, Jerad's mother would have been given the opportunity to indicate that requiring students to phone home and discuss behavioral infractions was unacceptable. The teacher, the mother, and the boy would have developed an acceptable solution. The school would have had a bully–victim program in place, and the services would have been offered to Jerad and his mother earlier in the week.

Mr. Fix would have been aware of how other microsystems in the school and at home could be contributing to difficulties his students might have throughout the year. He would have been fully informed about his own classroom environment as a microsystem and would have known what environmental conditions in his classroom might be contributing to Jerad's upset feelings. For example, he would have known if the upcoming lesson or peer interactions were upsetting Jerad. Mr. Fix would have taken management action on the basis of how microsystems contributed to children's difficulties. He would have had a plan acceptable to others in the various microsystems (e.g., administrators, others teachers, parents, students) for how to handle students who attempt to leave the room without permission.

Educators who ascribe to the ecological model might have helped Jerad in the following manner. He would have known that there was a special place in the building for "cooling down," and he would have been allowed to make his own choice to leave the room and go there. If he had had a history of using the "cool-down" option to avoid an academic task, he would have known that he would make up time in his classroom to work on the task. The teacher would have given him a choice of calming in the regular class or in the special room.

After Jerad was calm, he would have problem solved with adults and shared the source of his agitation. A number of strategies to help Jerad could have potentially occurred in the ecological model. There would definitely have been an appraisal of how family, peer, and classroom cultural factors could be changed to help Jerad. There would have been an educational component, also, that included Jerad and his peers. If the problem was a persistent one, behavior management plans might have been generated (e.g., goal setting and behavioral contracting, structured reinforcement plan) that included skill building in anger control, avoidance of bullying and victimization, conflict resolution, or peacemaking. The school would not have blamed any particular individual or system for the problems. Rather, the participants would have talked about shared responsibility between the home and the school for finding positive solutions. Jerad would not have been grabbed around the neck.

The ecological approach is modeled throughout the text. Three major ecologically based criteria undergird successful classroom management and discipline procedures:

1. *Respect for children.* All children can learn the academic and social–emotional–behavioral skills necessary to be successful in school.

2. *Respect for families.* Families are partners with educators in helping children learn and be successful.
3. *Respect for systems.* Multiple microsystems (e.g., classroom culture, school building culture, family culture, school–home collaboration) make important contributions to students' growth and development.

Implementing the ecological model requires reflection on personal belief systems and flexibility in adopting new assumptions. It requires opening up personal belief systems to critical examination and a willingness to "try on" competing management strategies. Learning to implement various strategies and maximize flexibility is a major aim of this text.

Behavioral Theory

Behavioral theory is based on the assumption that human beings are born with no predisposition toward positive or negative behaviors (i.e., neither "good" nor "bad"). This is the "man is a machine" or "man is a blank slate" belief and is apparent in Skinner's early development of behavioral theory. What human beings become is a direct result of their environment and their biology (e.g., genetic and physiological influences). In other words, they are products of all the positive and negative environmental influences to which they are exposed. They do not contribute anything from themselves to the process of growth other than the biophysical contributions just mentioned.

The assumptions suggest that students who follow classroom rules are reinforced for following the rules. Positive things occur or negative things are withdrawn when they follow the rules. Likewise, students who do not follow classroom rules are reinforced for their behavior. They learn to get what they want by not following the rules. For example, aggressive behaviors get them the ball to play with at recess or result in the removal of an unpleasant task such as seatwork.

Behavioral Applications in Education. Canter and Canter's (1976) model of assertive discipline in education is largely based on behavioral theory. In this model, authority figures continuously direct students in the way they should behave and grow. Rewards and consequences are clearly linked to target behaviors. Educators who hold purely behavioral assumptions see their primary task as controlling, shaping, and directing students to engage in desired behaviors. For example, educators provide much more direct instruction in the classroom and solutions to problems with peers on the playground. They tell students when to go to the rest room, get a drink, and sharpen a pencil. Educators provide rewards and consequences, especially when students are exhibiting problem behaviors that need to be decreased or replaced.

Behavioral theory is foundational to the development of both cognitive-behavioral theory and social learning theory. The latter two theories assume, however, that humans contribute more to their own development than just biophysical influences. An individual's own cognitions and complex, intrinsic motivation factors also contribute to personal growth and development. This growth in behavioral theory has led to well-researched procedures for teaching students self-management.

Behavioral theory and its applications are very different from humanistic theory and psychoanalytic theory and their subsequent applications. Given such differences, it is not surprising that people who hold humanistic or psychoanalytic beliefs may be completely opposed to behavioral strategies in education and vice versa. Classroom management techniques that stem from the presupposition that humans are born blank slates are distinguishable from techniques stemming from the other theories.

What do critics have to say about the weaknesses of behavioral theory and its application in classroom management? First, teachers often do not know how to use rewards and consequences effectively. Effective use of rewards is a science, based on principles gleaned from myriad research studies. The inappropriate use of rewards can cause numerous problems and fail to produce the desired effects. When this happens, teachers become disenchanted with behavioral techniques and turn to more punitive techniques. Punishment strategies are well researched, and they, too, must be skillfully used in order to be effective. In fact, research shows that for punishment to have a beneficial effect, it is to be used very sparingly and in a very narrow range of situations.

Behavioral Applications to Jerad's Case.   Educators who subscribe to behavioral assumptions would have dealt with Jerad in the following manner. They would have planned strategies with both Jerad and his mother in order to have seamless programming across environments. Jerad would have known that there was a special place in the building and at home for cooling down. The teacher would have either told him to go to the special room or given him a choice of calming in the regular class or in the special room.

After Jerad was calm, a number of consequences could have potentially occurred, depending on the home–school plan. Because Jerad, his mother, the teacher, and other school personnel had helped develop the plan, there would have been no surprises when it was implemented. For example, Jerad might have had to call his mother or take a note home to her at the end of the school day. He might have been expected to make up time in the regular classroom for the time he spent in the cooling-down room. If the problem was a persistent one, behavior management plans would have been generated for anger-control training, goal setting and behavioral contracting, structured reinforcement, or a host of other possible strategies. Jerad's mother would have carried out the plan at home because behavior is more likely to change if multiple environments are shaping behavior in the same way. Jerad might have been grabbed around the neck if the teacher thought it would be a punishment that would decrease future attempts to leave the classroom. However, this would have constituted an inappropriate and ineffective use of punishment. School personnel would have talked to the press about what they could do differently the next time in order to prevent such a fiasco.

Humanistic Theory

The humanistic position presupposes that humans are born "good," or with a natural inclination toward positive behaviors that promote optimal growth and development. Positive, supportive, nurturing environments with positive, supportive, nurturing humans help other humans realize their own positive potential. A metaphor of a rosebud's development is often used to explain the tenets of humanism. Every rosebud has potential to unfold and make a beautiful, full rose when in optimal environmental conditions. No one has to help the rose unfold physically for it to become a lovely flower. It will accomplish that on its own as long as the weather is supportive, aphids do not invade, and so forth. Likewise, it is presupposed that human beings will unfold, realize the full potential of their inherent goodness, and be all they can be as long as the environment is supportive (e.g., freedom to explore, adequate materials, unconditional and positive regard from other humans).

The humanistic presupposition further holds that negative behaviors are not humans' natural inclination. They must learn or acquire negative behaviors in order to exhibit negative behaviors. Negative environments, including negative human interactions, teach people to be negative. When human beings have developed in a negative direction, supportive environments and positive human relationships are necessary for those persons to grow in a positive direction. Positive growth still comes from within the individuals; they are responsible and can reach their own potential.

Humanistic Applications in Education. It is from the humanistic theoretical base that Rogerian therapy developed in the field of counseling and that Gordon's (1974) teacher-effectiveness training and Raths, Harmin, and Simon's (1966) values-clarification programs developed in the field of education. Humanism has been a well-received theoretical model by many preservice teachers. The assumptions of the model fit their beliefs that children who are cared for, respected, and taught well will learn and exhibit few or no behavioral problems. The teacher is required to provide the child with unconditional positive regard at all times.

Educators who hold this view see their primary task as creating an optimally positive environment in which they do not interfere with or intrude in students' academic or social growth and development. Rather, teachers allow students to unfold, search, explore, grow, and develop according to their own inner-direction. Examples of humanistic classroom management techniques are relationship building, listening, and allowing students to work together to solve their own problems. Classroom management techniques that stem from the assumptions of humanism are distinguishable from techniques stemming from other theories.

What do critics say about the weaknesses of humanism applied to classroom management? First, when care, respect, and student-centered lessons are not enough to prevent students' misbehaviors, teachers can become disenchanted with the model. They often turn to high-control, punitive management strategies rather than provide unconditional positive regard. Their beliefs about human nature are in conflict with the controlling strategies they adopt. This produces dissonance, and to reduce it, they may completely change their beliefs about children who misbehave.

A second criticism is that teachers who practice from this model think that their role is to be passive. Often they are not equipped with skills necessary to determine when and how to be facilitative in helpful ways with children. A third criticism is that education in the United States is typically structured in a way that does not allow time for the listening, nondirective, child-centered approaches that characterize humanism. A brief example of classroom management and discipline strategies from humanistic theory is applied to Jerad's case in the next section.

Humanistic Applications to Jerad's Case.   Educators who subscribe to humanistic theory would have forged trusting, positive partnerships with families of all students from the first day of school. When older peers picked on Jerad earlier in the week, all involved students would have met with an adult or a peer counselor to develop their own solutions to the problem. All parents and adults would have been involved to the extent that the students' plan would have been enhanced.

The day Jerad became upset, educators would have collaborated with Jerad's mother to provide a supportive and nurturing environment that would have allowed Jerad to resolve his own problems. Jerad would have known that there was a special place in his classroom and in the school building for cooldown, and he would have been allowed to make his own choice to leave the room and go there. After Jerad was calm, he would have had the opportunity to talk with a trained peer counselor or an adult about what he was feeling and thinking. The counselor would have been respectful of the process Jerad needed to go through to calm himself. He or she would have demonstrated unconditional, positive regard for Jerad and offered support when he explored possible solutions and selected one to try.

If Jerad's mother came to school upset, she would have had a private place in which to disclose her feelings to the principal, who would have used listening and communication skills effectively. Jerad would never have been grabbed around the neck, and he would not have been sent to the office to call his mother. All management techniques would have been student centered as opposed to adult directed. The school personnel would have assumed responsibility for the problems with Jerad and his mother when questioned by the press.

Psychoanalytic Theory

A third theoretical position presupposes that humans are born with drives or urges to take care of their own needs, referred to as the *id* in psychoanalytic theory. Humans are assumed to have a strong, inborn urge to take care of their own desires regardless of, and even at the expense of, the needs and desires of others. Psychoanalytic theory, as first constructed by Freud, best represents this view. The entire Western culture has been deeply influenced by Freud's assumptions about human growth and development. Freud argued that his theory was not influenced by the set of Judeo-Christian beliefs that state that humans are born with sinful natures. He further clarified that being born with an id does not equate with being born "bad." The id is present at birth as a biologically preprogrammed safeguard to ensure that our young get their needs met. As youth grow and develop, the id is to be checked or controlled by the development of the ego and the superego.

Freud's assumptions about human nature are not as popular or prevalent as they once were. This is not surprising because humanistic theory developed as the antithesis of Freudian assumptions, and many people were drawn to the attractive set of humanistic assumptions.

On the basis of Freud's worldview, human beings can learn to control their drives in ways that strike a socially acceptable balance between meeting their own needs (i.e., id functions) and the needs of others (i.e., superego functions). Achieving this balance entails a gradual progression of acquiring healthy self- and other-centered behaviors from birth through the early childhood years. The progression occurs if adults, particularly parents, assist children in developing a healthy sense of self, or ego, and a healthy conscience, or superego. Without quality parental assistance, children will continue to follow the natural inclination of their ids, which will result in underdeveloped superegos and egos. This manifests itself as children's seeking first and foremost to get their own desires satisfied and constitutes the undersocialized behavior that creates problems in classrooms.

Environmental variables such as the quality of parenting are believed to be important contributors to children's development in the early years. By the age of 5 or 6 years, environmental influences become less of a focus. Attention shifts to understanding what is within the child, or the structure of the child's personality. Help for children with behavioral problems consists of looking for pathology within the child or the parents and then treating the "ill" child or family.

Psychoanalytic Applications in Education. Psychoanalytic theory and assumptions have implications for education. First, educators who embrace this theory believe that parents are responsible for helping children develop healthy egos and superegos. These educators hold expectations that children will come to school with appropriate social behavior already developed. Social skills are not taught in their classrooms, but such educators give marks for deportment that communicate to parents the areas in which they need to be working with their children. This phenomenon has been referred to as the *hidden curriculum.*

When students exhibit social–emotional–behavioral difficulties, it is believed that the problems come from within the bad ("ill") child or the bad ("ill") family. Educators look less often at what can be changed in the classroom and more often at which families need to seek professional help outside of the school to have their children's behavioral problems "fixed." Psychiatric diagnosis and psychotherapy are dominant approaches to intervention in this medical model approach. In schools, character education programs are often based on psychoanalytic assumptions. These programs include perspective taking, establishing guidelines on right and wrong, and developing moral reasoning. Classroom management techniques based on the assumption that humans are born with drives to meet their own needs while disregarding the needs of others are distinguishable from techniques stemming from the other theory bases.

What do critics say about the weaknesses of psychoanalytic theory and its applications in classroom management and discipline? Most strategies are meant to change basic personality structures and, therefore, take much time and intensive work. In the meantime, critics ask, what are educators supposed to do in the classroom to manage specific behavioral problems? Often, children who misbehave are referred for special education services. The end result often is provision of special education services outside of the regular classroom.

Psychoanalytic Applications to Jerad's Case.   Educators who subscribe to the psychoanalytic theory might have dealt with Jerad in the following manner. He would have been escorted to the office and his mother contacted by an adult. The mother would have been asked to seek outside help in the form of counseling. The mother might have been referred to the school counselor, the school psychologist, or some community mental health center. Jerad might have been referred for special education services that would have placed him in a different setting and provided extra assistance in meeting the expectations of his classroom teacher. In sum, the problem would have been dealt with as a "within"-child or a "within"-family deficit that needed "fixing." The school typically would not have assumed responsibility for the problems that transpired. Jerad would not have been grabbed around the neck.

Personal Beliefs/Theory

Each of us believes in certain assumptions that constitute our basic worldview, the grid through which we see and understand everything that goes on around us. Assumptions are based on what we consider to be the truth of what exists. We live on the basis of our assumptions more consistently than we realize. What we believe is what we do.

This becomes more interesting when the dominant cultural beliefs differ from an individual's basic beliefs. Individuals with beliefs that are quite different from those currently popular will often make culturally (i.e., politically) correct belief statements but may not display espoused beliefs in their behaviors. This mismatch may go undetected by the individuals themselves. If they obtain insight into the discrepancy, it may surprise and dismay them. Mismatches between what a person really believes and what he or she says and does become clear to some students during classroom management role-plays. A particularly good example of how role-play behaviors can provide insight into a person's basic beliefs occurred during a class activity described next.

All of the students in the class had identified what they believed to be their personal assumptions about human beings and their subsequent management approach. Likewise, all had learned the procedure of transitioning students from one place to another in the school (e.g., moving from a large group to small cooperative groups in the classroom, moving from the business classroom to a computer lab). A preservice teacher, who volunteered to play the role of the teacher, had previously identified her management approach as humanistic (i.e., believed in respecting students' abilities to make good decisions and problem solve their own behavioral difficulties in supportive environments).

The teacher was modeling for middle school students the procedure of going quickly and quietly to the library from English class. As she led students from the college classroom and down the corridor to the make-believe library, several of the students began loudly laughing and talking. The teacher turned around and looked at them. When this cue went unnoticed and the students continued to talk and laugh, the teacher said, "Let's keep it quiet in the hall-way." One student continued to talk and laugh, and the teacher, obviously ruffled, grabbed his arm and said, "You need to follow directions."

This was an insightful experience for the preservice teacher, who discovered that she became authoritarian—not humanistic—when she felt she was losing control of the situation. That teacher's behavior did not match her stated beliefs. She did try to maintain a pretense of being humanistic by making the necessity for following directions a desired outcome for students: "you" and "need" rather than "must" or "Be silent or else." Still, the nonspoken accompaniment made the communication a demand. What we say with our nonspoken behavior often speaks more loudly than our words. In this case, overt behaviors, how the teacher acted, helped uncover covert beliefs. A retrospective view often helps detect a person's basic beliefs.

Educators have diverse beliefs about whether all children can learn, whether educators need parents as partners, and whether classroom managers need to consider any variables beyond the classroom walls in order to be successful disciplinarians. One purpose of university courses in education is to help preservice educators examine and change their basic assumptions. However, a number of researchers have shown that students graduate without changing any of their beliefs about these important issues. In the next section, you will review the type of reflection Kagan (1992) found to be helpful in changing beliefs of novice and preservice teachers. You will have opportunities to reflect on your own beliefs about the basic nature of people throughout the course.

Reflection on Management Beliefs.   Kagan (1992) examined 40 studies of professional growth among preservice and beginning teachers. Three studies focused on the impact of preexisting beliefs on new learning early in teacher education programs (Calderhead & Robson, 1991; McDaniel, 1991; Weinstein, 1990). All studies documented that (a) the content of course work was filtered through preexisting beliefs and prior experience and (b) prior beliefs were stable and inflexible.

Six studies focused on novices' changes in their knowledge of teaching as they progressed through the college curriculum (Aitken & Mildon, 1991; Florio-Ruane & Lensmire, 1990; Gore & Zeichner, 1991; McLaughlin, 1991; Pigge & Marso, 1989; Shapiro, 1991). The results of the six studies suggested that, for change to occur, prior beliefs had to be reconstructed. On the basis of these findings, Kagan (1992) recommended that novices be required to examine their prior experiences in classrooms and with authority figures. Ultimately, the examination should include comparisons with the experiences of peers in order to undo tendencies to believe that everyone's experiences are the same. In turn, this reduces the tendency for educators to cling to their assumptions as truth.

Deeply held beliefs about who can learn, what teachers versus parents can teach, and whether problems originate from within the child or from the environment influence a teacher's management of students' behavioral problems. For example, some educators sympathize with Mr. Fix and assert their beliefs that students like Jerad cannot be helped. After all, Jerad has demonstrated repeatedly that he cannot control his behavior and is not interested in being in class to learn. He does not seem to be able to learn. His family cannot be counted on for help. Mom gets upset and aggressive. Why even contact her? Jerad is a rebellious, disrespectful preadolescent who became that way because he had parents who did not teach him respect for authority. He is now a troubled child, beyond any help that the school can give. Because Jerad cannot learn, high control and punishment techniques are necessary to keep him in line. All of these deeply held beliefs will influence a teacher's management style.

Kagan maintains that novice teachers can change their deeply held beliefs if they have repeated opportunities to examine their past experiences in classrooms and their relationships with authority figures. Ultimately, they need also to listen to their peers whose experiences are different in order to see that the way they think and believe is not the only way to think and believe.

Take time to conduct your own reflection on Jerad's case. What approach seemed to be used by the teacher? By the administrator? What do you think each of the two believed about children's learning, about their own teaching, about the importance of partnering with parents, and about discipline? Imagine that you were the teacher or the administrator in this situation. What would you have done when Jerad tried to run out of the room or when he appeared at your administrative office?

On the basis of what you would have done, make a tentative judgment as to your basic beliefs about the nature of human beings. Deeply held beliefs often operate outside of a person's immediate awareness. It is necessary to pay deliberate attention to them for a period of time in order to become familiar with them. Recognition of personal beliefs, a willingness to modify dogmatic beliefs, and appreciation for the diversity of beliefs held by others are necessary precursors to becoming flexible classroom managers who use strategies that help children learn and grow. If your judgments change throughout the course, that is a good sign that you are learning and growing in your personal belief system.

What people *say* they believe may be the acceptable or politically correct thing to say. Students do this in college classrooms, particularly when they believe that they should be humanistic. However, it may not be what they really believe. When push comes to shove, that is, when educators are dealing with a frustrating problem that seems to require immediate action, they will act automatically. Actions during moments of automaticity reflect their most basic beliefs about the nature of human beings. Everyone's beliefs are accepted and acceptable. What is important is recognizing how a person's beliefs can interfere with effective management in some situations.

Assumptions of every theoretical model are rebuttable; they cannot be proven to be true. Rather than cling to a theoretical model as the one true approach to management, an educator would be wise to select interventions from the theoretical model or models that best meet the needs of students' who also have differing views of themselves and the world about them. Meeting students on their terms is likely to strike a responsive chord and produce behavior that is considered more appropriate in the school setting. However, the management and discipline job becomes more complex when strategies are selected to best meet students' needs than it is when strategies are used because teachers are comfortable with them. Therefore, attempts to reduce the complexity have been numerous. In the following section, different ways of organizing the vast knowledge base on classroom management and discipline strategies are described.

ORGANIZATION OF THE KNOWLEDGE BASE IN CLASSROOM MANAGEMENT AND DISCIPLINE

Models of Classroom Discipline

In addition to benefiting from theories of human behavior that inform our classroom management practices, we can draw upon numerous expert models or approaches to classroom management. For example, Charles (1999) described 13 such models. Each model typically focuses on understanding and correcting misbehavior as it relates to one aspect of management. This necessitates learning about numerous models that typically include introductions of their declarative knowledge base and a parallel component of reflection on the moral and ethical implications of classroom practices. They often focus on a body of ideas that enhance understanding of why students behave inappropriately, with less attention devoted to standardized procedures for implementing the various management strategies.

Some educators learn a single model of management and implement it in every situation (e.g., the Canter model of assertive discipline; Canter & Canter, 1976). The weakness of this approach is twofold. First, recall that children's growth and development is influenced by multiple micro- and mesosystems. Their needs are complex and no single theory can offer the variety of strategies a complex situation demands. Second, no single model of discipline comprehensively addresses all three major domains of classroom management: relationships, specific behavioral concerns, and instruction.

Strategies for Classroom Management and Discipline

Teachers must learn the how-tos of hundreds of management procedures and implement them every day. If a student has behavioral problems, teachers rightfully ask, "Which one or two of the hundreds of management procedures would best help the student?" This is the equivalent of putting together a gigantic puzzle of 1,500 or more interlocking pieces. Most people, faced with the task of completing a large and complex puzzle, sort by color or form first. This makes the task easier. Likewise, it is conceptually easier to solve the puzzle of management and discipline problems when all the possibilities are grouped by similarities.

Froyen's Three Cs Management Model

Froyen (1993) analyzed not only the leading models of classroom discipline and management, but also the hundreds of management tasks teachers carry out every school day. On the basis of this analysis, he concluded that there are three basic classroom management domains: relational, behavioral, and instructional. The dozens, even hundreds, of management procedures that teachers use every school day fit into one of the three domains. Likewise, daily discipline problems fall within one of the three classroom management domains. He called the three domains the "three Cs" of classroom management:

> Covenant management—for relationship concerns
>
> Conduct management—for specific behavioral concerns
>
> Content management—for setting and instructional concerns

A brief definition of each of the three domains of management follows; complete descriptions are provided in upcoming chapters. In short, covenant management is the facilitation of trusting, respectful relationships, willingly entered into, that promote optimal school success for all children. Conduct management is the facilitation of positive social–emotional–behavioral growth of children. Content management is occurring when teachers manage space, materials, equipment, the movement of people, and lessons that make up a curriculum or program of studies.

Froyen's three Cs conceptual framework for learning and practicing classroom management procedures is used in this text to organize the competencies described in the upcoming chapters. Ecological theory is used to refine the three Cs model such that each management domain has competencies to build at both the microsystem level and the mesosystem level. Accordingly, chapters are organized by management domains rather than by models or approaches to discipline. As a brief illustration of the use of covenant, conduct, and content management within an ecological framework for decision making, let us think about Jerad and Mr. Fix's interactions presented at the beginning of the chapter.

Covenant Management Applications to Jerad's Case

Covenant Management at the Microsystem Level.   Jerad was upset. About what? Perhaps it was a relationship problem. Perhaps he felt rejected by his peers. Is there any evidence? Yes, Jerad's mother noted that older peers had been picking on him that week. Perhaps he thought his teacher did not like him, was always unfair to him, or did not care about him enough to help him with his problems. What evidence is there that they had an unsatisfactory relationship? First, they had no mutually understood plan for what Jerad should do when he was upset. Second, Mr. Fix attempted to keep Jerad in the room by using physical force. Third, Jerad perceived it as a stranglehold and communicated such to his mother. These happenings imply a lack of a trusting relationship.

Covenant Management at the Mesosystem Level.   Ms. Barthel was upset. About what? Perhaps it was a relationship problem; she felt disrespected. She insisted that no one from the school had told her of a discipline procedure in which children telephoned home to report their own behavioral problems. Maybe she believed school personnel did not care about her son. After all, peers had been picking on him and the school had done nothing to intervene.

If any one of these microsystem or mesosystem level hypotheses about relationship concerns is correct, then the teacher has a covenant management problem to solve. Mr. Fix would have to use covenant management strategies to resolve current problems and prevent future occurrences. If he has basic competencies in covenant management at both the microsystem level and the mesosystem level, he can select strategies from humanistic, behavioral, cognitive-behavioral, social learning, and psychoanalytic theories. Covenant management competencies are introduced in chapters 2, 3, 6, and 8. Chapter 2 describes covenant competencies used in the first few weeks of school. All of chapter 3 is devoted to covenant competencies to be used in the classroom and with parents throughout the school year. Chapter 6 focuses solely on mesosystem management and contains numerous covenant competencies necessary for building home–school partnerships. Finally, chapter 8 provides communication competencies that help build strong, positive relationships with others in the classroom, school building, and home.

Conduct Management Applications to Jerad's Case

Let us say that Mr. Fix is a good covenant manager. He has made superior covenant management decisions and implemented various strategies to build trusting relationships with all students and their families. Still Jerad was upset, attempted to leave the room, and struggled physically with his teacher. Why? What was that all about?

Conduct Management at the Microsystem Level.   Perhaps Jerad's behavior was due to a specific behavioral problem. One assumption is that Jerad responds with significant anxiety to changes in classroom routines and withdraws (i.e., leaves the room). There is no evidence in the story to support this assumption; it is presented here as an example of how divergently we need to think about the nature of students' specific behavioral problems.

Conduct Management at the Mesosystem Level.   A second assumption is that Jerad has witnessed repeatedly his family's way of dealing with emotions. Perhaps they act out their upset feelings by being physically aggressive, and he has learned to do the same thing. What evidence is there? Ms. Barthel came to school upset, punched the principal, and threw vases.

If either the assumption that Jerad responds to change with anxiety or the assumption that Jerad has learned from modeling family members to act out his frustration is correct, then the teacher has a conduct management problem to solve. He will have to use conduct management strategies to prevent future occurrences and resolve current problems. If he has the basic competencies at both the microsystem level and the mesosystem level, he can implement strategies from humanistic, behavioral, cognitive-behavioral, social learning, and psychoanalytic theories. Conduct management competencies are introduced in chapters 2, 4, and 7. Chapter 2 prepares educators in conduct competencies needed in the first few weeks of school. Chapter 4 describes numerous conduct competencies to implement in the classroom throughout the school year. Chapter 7 focuses solely on mesosystem competencies that bridge classrooms with the principal's office and homes.

Content Management Applications to Jerad's Case

Content Management at the Microsystem Level. If Jerad's problem is not due to weaknesses in covenant and conduct management, the final category to consider is content management. Perhaps Jerad's upset feelings and wanting to leave the classroom are related to instructional decisions Mr. Fix made. Examples of this include assigning something that was too difficult, selecting another student to carry out a preferred activity when Jerad had already been told it would be his turn, or moving to a new activity and not allowing Jerad sufficient time to finish the previous one. There is nothing in the newspaper story about academic concerns and, thus, there are no facts or pieces of information to use as evidence in hypothesis building. A common hypothesis in the content management domain is that teachers ask students to do tasks that are too difficult for them or are not interesting. Some students go to great lengths to escape difficult or uninteresting academic tasks. Jerad's upset feelings and attempt to leave class could be the avoidance of an academic task.

Content Management at the Mesosystem Level. Most teachers assign homework and rely on students, with parental assistance, to complete the work accurately and on time. Some students have homes that lack sufficient supports for the successful completion of homework. Perhaps Jerad was upset because students were getting ready to share their homework assignments in class and he did not have his homework done. He had tried every evening that week but the assignment required special supplies and resources that he did not have in his home. If you have not been in many students' homes and observed their home environments, you will be surprised to learn that there are no books, magazines, newspapers, dictionaries, pencils, erasers, or paper. There may not be a quiet space free from distractions. There may not be time to do homework if parents require their children to do household tasks and babysitting. Many homes, even middle-class homes, do not have available supports for homework. Many students do not realize that they should talk to the teacher about the lack of support, or they may be embarrassed about revealing home concerns.

If any one of these microsystem or mesosystem level hypotheses is correct, then the teacher has a content management problem. He has to use content management strategies that will resolve current problems and prevent future occurrences. If he has basic competencies in content management at the micro- and mesosystem levels, he can implement strategies from humanistic, behavioral, cognitive-behavioral, social learning, and psychoanalytic theories. Chapters 2 and 5 focus on content management. Chapter 2 describes content competencies for the first weeks of school, and chapter 5 includes competencies for the duration of the school year, including partnering with families to increase students' academic success.

Covenant/Conduct/Content Interplays

Human behavior is complex. Accordingly, students' behavioral problems can be quite complex. More than one management domain may be contributing to student problems. Likewise, the interplay of these domains may make things worse. In Jerad's case, the teacher, the student, and the mother may not have developed good relationships at the beginning of the year. Jerad and his mother may have difficulty controlling their anger across multiple settings, and this may be exacerbated when they do not have trusting relationships. Jerad may also avoid academic tasks that are too difficult or uninteresting. It may be that Jerad's home lacks supports for completing homework. If he has a strong relationship with his teacher, he may be more likely to seek his teacher's help and less likely to get upset and leave the room. This scenario illustrates the importance of considering contributions from all three management domains during analysis of problems and development of solutions.

The information in this text prepares you to develop basic management competencies that meet the diverse social–emotional and instructional needs of approximately 96% of students (Batsche, 1996). A remaining small percentage of students will not be successful in meeting the expectations of a basic group management plan. It is at these times that educators must be competent in the use of an ecological and developmental approach to problem solving that results in flexible intervention planning. A number of interventions that can be used to assist students with special needs are described in upcoming chapters.

Armed with an ecological perspective and the three Cs management model, educators are ready to practice solving problems like Jerad's. The use of problem-solving processes in the schools has become a prominent trend, with more and more educators being prepared to engage in problem solving. The goal of problem solving is to help students with academic and behavioral problems be successful in regular classrooms. Why do educators need to learn how to problem solve? Aren't all people natural problem solvers?

PROBLEM-SOLVING MODEL

Novice/Expert Differences

All people are problem solvers. For many, the problem-solving process is implicitly known and followed. However, problem-solving processes and solutions clearly separate novice and expert teachers (Swanson, O'Connor, & Cooney, 1990) and suggest that there are aspects of problem solving that can be taught and learned.

Teachers and principals at Price Laboratory School learn how to implement the IDEAL problem-solving model.

A number of problem-solving models are used at an explicit level in schools. All have the same basic steps: (1) Identify the problem, (2) define the problem, (3) explore alternatives, (4) apply a solution, and (5) look back and evaluate progress. The steps are easy to learn. The thinking skills necessary to be expert problem solvers are more difficult to acquire (e.g., working from elaborate systems of knowledge for understanding problems, having integrated sets of principles, using metacognition). These skills develop more slowly as educators gain professional experience.

Professional development in problem solving can be viewed as a continuum of novice-to-expert skills. Professionals who are experts select several complementary strategies to achieve a more lasting solution to a problem. They select quick-fix solutions when something must be done immediately before things get out of hand. However, experts realize that these are temporary and partial solutions.

Novices, when faced with a problem, immediately focus on a quick-fix solution rather than on the systematic hypothesis testing of several possible solutions (Swanson et al., 1990). Experts focus on problem definition and apply thinking skills based on principles, pattern recognition, automaticity, and metacognition. An example of the differences between novice and expert problem solvers follows. A novice observes a student who is not paying attention and immediately decides on a solution:

1. Tell the student to pay attention.

Contrast this with the expert problem solver who thinks through the problem using a prototypical process that emphasizes problem definition and hypothesis testing:

1. Identify that a student is not paying attention to directions.
2. Define "not paying attention" as gazing out the window and not writing down assignment directions.
3. Hypothesize about the reasons why the student is not paying attention:
   • The student has a hearing problem, and the teacher did not provide visual directions.
   • The teacher did not adequately call for the attention of all class members prior to beginning oral directions.
   • The student is having difficulty concentrating on schoolwork because the student's mother is ill and in the hospital.
   • The student would rather be outside: it is spring and the birds are singing outside the window.
4. Select the most likely hypothesis and match the solution to it:
   • The student has a hearing problem, and the teacher determines that a visual prompt is needed prior to giving directions.
5. Evaluate the effectiveness of the visual prompts for obtaining and maintaining student attention and cycle through the problem-solving process again if the solution was not effective.

Novices do not have well-developed pattern recognition skills. Pattern recognition takes experience and practice. When educators do not practice using the problem-solving model, they will continue to be novice problem solvers, jumping immediately into solutions that have a high probability of not working because the solution did not match the actual problem. As my father, a very wise man, often said, "Doing it that way all your life doesn't make it right. If it was wrong when you started, it is still wrong 20 years later." No one becomes an expert problem solver simply by doing the same thing for 20 years. People become expert problem solvers by constant reflection and the accumulation of knowledge, skill, and assured competence.

The IDEAL problem-solving model is frequently cited in education and is shown in Figure 1–1. Study the IDEAL model, and practice applying the steps to classroom management and discipline scenarios during the course of the semester (e.g., the case of Jerad at the beginning of this chapter). The model is described in detail in the following sections.

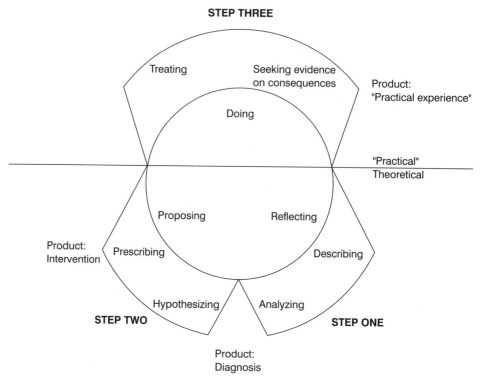

Figure 1–1
Prototypical IDEAL Problem-Solving Model

The IDEAL Problem-Solving Process Applied to Classroom Management

As you proceed through this text, you will acquire the necessary knowledge and skills to help you become a diagnostician and a problem solver. The following example highlights a common type of internal, problem-solving dialogue that produces management insights and interventions.

At the end of the school day, Ms. Harper is preoccupied with thoughts about the way things went that day. She is reminded of an incident that still troubles her. She begins to relive some of the feelings she experienced when Phillip accused her of "always picking on him." This accusation was particularly disturbing because she thinks that she works hard to be fair and considerate. She begins to wonder what is causing Phillip to feel this way.

She cannot easily dismiss this incident because Phillip's behavior—talking during lecture presentations—is unacceptable. She begins to entertain explanations. "Might it be that he feels uninvolved in the class? Is this just one way to get my attention and that of the class? What would happen," she reasons, "if I were to give him more attention when his behavior matches the class expectations?"

Ms. Harper remembers that Phillip usually arrives early for class. She could engage him in conversation then. As the class begins, she might call on him to highlight a point from the previous day's lesson. Questions scattered throughout the lecture, occasionally directed to Phillip, might provide him with another positive source of recognition. "It's worth a try," she concludes.

After a week of using such tactics, Ms. Harper notes that there are no more accusations of being unfair and that Phillip is being quite cooperative. Now he volunteers observations about the previous day's class and/or assigned homework before class gets under way. He still speaks to others during the class but does so when called on to share topically related remarks.

The preceding example shows the complete picture of use of the IDEAL model. However, as a starting point in understanding and using the IDEAL model, let's break down the process and apply it to the previously discussed case of Jerad.

Step 1: Identifying the Problem

Mr. Fix begins by *reflecting* about the characteristics of the situation itself. Jerad has intermittently been the object of teasing by these two boys. They seem to tease him about his reading ability. He struggles more with reading than the others in his group do. He never teases the boys or does anything to get even. He is usually upset by their teasing and tries to get away from them. He is more likely to withdraw than to act out.

Step 2: Defining the Problem

Mr. Fix continues his reflection by analyzing the situation. First, he describes exactly what was going on in the classroom: The students were moving to their cooperative groups, and two boys in Jerad's group seemed to be making teasing comments about him. At that point, Jerad seemed upset and started to leave the classroom.

Personal *reflection* sets the stage for *diagnosis*. Diagnosis helps identify the management function and the form of intervention that would be most appropriate, given the conclusions reached by means of reflection.

Step 3: Exploring Alternative Solutions

Now the teacher begins to speculate about possible courses of action. Given the *diagnosis,* what would seem to be reasonable ways to deal with the possible impact of this condition in the classroom? This textbook is largely a synthesis of answers to this question. Let us conceptualize the situation as one requiring each of the three *C*s of management and the parallel interventions.

At this point we can cast the problem into an *if–then* statement, that is, a *hypothesis*. By hypothesizing about the problem, we establish a connection between a situation and a plausible response to the situation. The hypothesis is a prediction of what we think will happen, given our *analysis* of the problem and our history of dealing with similar problems. We use the *hypothesis* to *select* a specific treatment or intervention.

Hypotheses of Covenant Management.   Notice that most of the hypotheses are based on systems-level changes rather than on changes that only Jerad needs to make.

Example of Microsystem Hypothesis.   *If* all the students practice the social skill of communicating respect, with no put-downs allowed, *then* Jerad will not withdraw and will stay with the group.

Numerous paths are available to a teacher for assisting students in the improvement of their social skills. In this instance, the covenant management *intervention* of teaching and modeling a social skill will help students work cooperatively and contribute to their learning of the subject. The covenant management intervention relies on teaching replacement behaviors or prosocial skills.

Example of Mesosystem Hypothesis.   *If* the teacher and the principal develop trusting relationships with the mother, *then* the mother will collaboratively develop management and discipline strategies to use with her son.

You will learn all the strategies that are available to a teacher for building collaborative partnerships with families. In this instance, the covenant management *intervention* of collaboratively planning management procedures with parents at the beginning of the school year would have established a trusting relationship.

Hypotheses of Conduct Management

Example of Microsystem Hypothesis.   *If* Jerad learns how to cope with peers' teasing, *then* he will use an appropriate strategy to cope with teasing and will stay with the group.

The intervention does not have to involve Jerad alone. Most students could benefit from skill-building lessons in how to cope with teasing. Even though teasing would not be allowed in the classroom, there are numerous unsupervised moments on school grounds when students need the skills to cope with peer teasing. Teachers can ask guidance counselors or school psychologists to team teach the skills in the regular classroom.

Example of Mesosystem Hypothesis.   *If* the mother is provided with the coping strategies for teasing that the class learns, *then* she will assist her son in coping with bullies outside of the classroom.

Parents can receive training at school, or information can be sent home that will help them assist their children with teasing and bullying behaviors. Bullying, harassment, and teasing are being taken more seriously by educators and parents involved in school-improvement planning.

Hypotheses of Content Management

Example of Microsystem Hypothesis. *If* Jerad receives appropriate reading instruction, *then* he will increase his reading fluency and stay with the group.

Any student who has academic delays is to receive appropriate instruction. Academic delays cause students' frustration and upset feelings. The students either withdraw or act out. Seldom are they neutral about being unable to do assigned work.

Example of Mesosystem Hypothesis. *If* the teacher provides the mother with reading strategies to practice with Jerad at home, *then* Jerad will increase his reading fluency.

There are a variety of reading techniques that parents can use to help their children improve reading skills. One strategy is to have a set time at home to read books selected from the library on Saturday mornings. Parents can read the same book and have discussions with their children about the plot or what they are learning.

Step 4: Applying the Solution

We have now constructed a *theoretical* basis for acting. It is theoretical because we have yet to try it out in the classroom. Our plan of action is based on our *diagnosis* of a situation, and our intervention is our best "educated guess" about how to deal with the situation most effectively. The diagnosis is based on *identifying* and *defining* the classroom context of the problem; the intervention is based on a process of *hypothesizing* and *evaluating solutions* based on the context considerations. This suggests a way of *applying the solution* that will increase the probability that students will choose responsible behaviors conducive to learning. You may wish to seek assistance from the special services team, which is prepared to teach prosocial skills and corollary skills.

Some of you using this text will be enrolled in a collateral field experience. Others may be veteran teachers who can draw on practical experience to judge the wisdom of using various treatments presented in this text. Still others will be practitioners who can immediately test various treatments against the daily realities of teaching. In the absence of direct school-related experiences, you may use simulated activities, case studies, or role-playing, or you may even apply these techniques to other situations in your life.

Step 5: Looking Back and Evaluating Progress

By being engaged in the *application* phase of this model, you will be able to *treat* and then *collect evidence* to determine the effectiveness of various techniques. As you try various strategies, you will learn that the success of each depends on many factors. With time, you will develop techniques that are fashioned from decisions that have produced good results for you. The evidence-collecting activities that occur each day will produce the data for revising your theory of management. Generally, success will not be total. To be more successful, you will need to look for flaws in your original identification and definition and for faulty logic that may have contributed to an ill-advised hypothesis and application. Your next intervention will be based on a better conception of the challenge and more refined management skills.

CONCLUSION

Someone once said that there is nothing as practical as a good theory. The wisdom of this observation will become strikingly apparent as you begin to build your theory of classroom management. You have been challenged to reflect on your personal beliefs about why children and youth do what they do and how they get to be the way they are. After you accurately describe your own beliefs and compare them with major theories about the nature of people and how they grow and develop, you will begin to build your theory of classroom management. Your theory will be composed of generalizations that help you make sense of your experiences. These generalizations will shape your decisions and guide your responses to the new and the familiar. Your theory base will grow as your experience suggests pertinent variables and the weight to give them when you are working on the problem definition and prediction. You will begin to see that the process reveals patterns that give shape and substance to classroom events. You will begin to see that management problems are part of a pattern.

Each subsequent chapter will help you understand the patterns or conditions that shape management decisions. This understanding is prerequisite for grasping principles and practices that will enable you to deal with the complex conditions in the nation's schools. In the following chapters, practices are presented as specific techniques and are accompanied by exercises designed to help you acquire the skills necessary to become an effective classroom manager.

SUPPLEMENTARY QUESTIONS

1. Select one or more of the theoretical models discussed in the chapter and identify the underlying assumptions. Do you think these assumptions shape the thinking and practices of most educators, including classroom teachers?
2. Select a problem that you would like to examine objectively and systematically. Prepare an analysis of the problem you have chosen by using the IDEAL steps.

3. The author does not mention specific types of disciplinary problems in this chapter. However, during your reading, specific disciplinary problems may have occurred to you. Brainstorm some common disciplinary problems and determine how different theories might address them.

SUPPLEMENTARY PROJECTS

1. Identify a professional journal read by educators whose professional preparation is similar to your own. Looking at the journal's table of contents for the last year, select an article that deals largely with the classroom management/discipline issues discussed in this chapter. Determine the theoretical model that best represents the author's belief system. Be prepared to compare and contrast the views of the author of the article and those of the other models in this chapter.

2. Check students' views of discipline by asking several students this question: "What is it like being a student?" Extract the statements that describe aspects of classroom management and discipline. What conclusions and implications can you draw from this compilation of statements? Or, check teachers' views of discipline by asking several teachers to describe the good and bad feelings they experience as they interact with students. Isolate the feelings that appear to be associated with classroom management and discipline. What conclusions and implications can you draw from this activity?

REFERENCES

Aitken, J. L., & Mildon, D. (1991). The dynamics of personal knowledge and teacher education. *Curriculum Inquiry, 21*, 141–162.

Batsche, G. M. (1996, October). *Implementing a comprehensive program for students with difficulties with anger control and aggression: Building on classroom strategies.* Paper presented at the Iowa Behavioral Initiative Conference, Des Moines.

Berger, E. H. (1995). *Parents as partners in education: Families and schools working together* (4th ed.). Upper Saddle River, NJ: Merrill/Prentice Hall.

Bridges, E. (1986). *The incompetent teacher.* Philadelphia: Falmer Press.

Bronfenbrenner, U. (1979). *The ecology of human development.* Cambridge, MA: Harvard University Press.

Calderhead, J., & Robson, M. (1991). Images of teaching: Student teachers' early conceptions of classroom practice. *Teaching and Teacher Education, 7*, 1–8.

Canter, L., & Canter, M. (1976). *Assertive discipline: A take charge approach for today's educator.* Santa Monica, CA: Lee Canter and Associates.

Chamberlin, C., & Vallance, J. (1991). Reflections on a collaborative school-based teacher education project. *Alberta Journal of Educational Research, 37*, 141–156.

Charles, C. M. (1992). *Building classroom discipline* (4th ed.). White Plains, NY: Longman.

Charles, C. M. (1999). *Building classroom discipline* (6th ed.). White Plains, NY: Longman.

Cibulka, J. G., & Kritek, W. J. (Eds.). (1996). *Coordination among schools, families, and communities: Prospects for educational reform.* Albany: State University of New York Press.

Dornbusch, S.M., & Ritter, P. L. (1992). Home–school processes in diverse ethnic groups, social classes, and family structures. In S. Christenson & J. Conoley (Eds.), *Home–school collaboration: Enhancing children's academic and social competence* (pp. 111–125). Silver Spring, MD: The National Association of school Psychologists.

Edmonds, R. (1979). Effective schools for the urban poor. *Educational Leadership, 37*, 15–24.

Fantini, M. D. (1983). From school system to educative system: Linking the school with community environments. In R. L. Sinclair (Ed.), *For every school a community* (pp. 39–56). Boston: Institute for Responsive Education.

Florio-Ruane, S., & Lensmire, T. J. (1990). Transforming future teachers' ideas about writing instruction. *Journal of Curriculum Studies, 22*, 277–289.

Froyen, L. (1993). *Classroom management: The reflective teacher-leader.* New York: Maxwell Macmillan International.

Good, T. L., & Brophy, J. E. (1984). *Looking in classrooms* (3rd ed.). New York: Harper & Row.

Gordon, T. (1974). *TET: Teacher effectiveness training.* New York: David McKay Company.

Gore, J. M., & Zeichner, K. M. (1991). Action research and reflective teaching in preservice teacher education: A case study from the United States. *Teaching and Teacher Education, 7,* 119–136.

Hess, R. D., & Holloway, S. D. (1984). Family and school as educational institutions. In R. D. Parke, R. M. Emde, H. P. McAdoo, & G. P. Sackett (Eds.), *Reviewing child development research: Vol. 7. The family* (pp. 179–222). Chicago: University of Chicago Press.

Hyman, I. A. (1997). *School discipline and school violence: The teacher variance approach.* Boston: Allyn & Bacon.

Iverson, A. M. (1996). Management strategies in inclusive classrooms. In B. Stainback & S. Stainback (Eds.), *A handbook of practical strategies for inclusive schooling* (pp. 296–312). Baltimore: Paul H. Brookes.

Kagan, D. M. (1992). Professional growth among preservice and beginning teachers. *Review of Educational Research, 62,* 129–169.

Kozol, J. (1991). *Savage inequalities: Children in American schools.* New York: Crown.

Kritek, W. J. (1996). Introduction. In J. G. Cibulka & W. J. Kritek (Eds.), *Coordination among schools, families, and communities: Prospects for educational reform.* Albany: State University of New York Press.

McCaslin, M., & Good, T. L. (1992). Compliant cognition: The misalliance of management and instructional goals in school reform. *Educational Researcher, 21,* 4–17.

McDaniel, J. E. (1991, April). *Close encounters: How do student teachers make sense of the social foundations?* Paper presented at the annual meeting of the American Educational Research Association, Chicago.

McLaughlin, H. J. (1991). The reflection on the blackboard: Student teacher self-evaluation. *Alberta Journal of Educational Research, 37,* 141–159.

National Commission on Excellence in Education. (1983). *A nation at risk: The imperative for educational reform: A report to the Nation and the Secretary of Education, United States Department of Education.* Washington, DC: U.S. Government Printing Office.

Pigge, F. L., & Marso, R. N. (1989, March). *A longitudinal assessment of the affective impact of preservice training on prospective teachers.* Paper presented at the annual meeting of the American Educational Research Association, San Francisco.

Raths, L. E., Harmin, M., & Simon, S. B. (1966). *Values and teaching.* Upper Saddle River, NJ: Merrill/Prentice Hall.

Schaeffer, F. A. (1982). *The complete works of Francis A. Schaeffer: A Christian worldview: Vol. 1. A Christian view of philosophy and culture.* Wheaton, IL: Good News.

Seeley, D. S. (1985). *Education through partnership.* Washington, DC: American Enterprise Institute for Public Policy Research.

Shapiro, B. L. (1991). A collaborative approach to help novice science teachers reflect on changes in their construction of the role of science teacher. *Alberta Journal of Educational Research, 27,* 119–132.

Swanson, H. L., O'Connor, J. E., & Cooney, J. B. (1990). An information processing analysis of expert and novice teachers' problem solving. *American Educational Research Journal, 27,* 533–556.

Tucker, L., Plax, T. G., & Kearney, P. (1985). *Prospective teachers' use of behavior alternative techniques.* Paper presented at the Communication Theory and Research Interest Group of the Western Speech Communication Association Conference, Fresno, CA.

Unruh, L. (1994). *The effects of teacher planning on classroom management effectiveness.* Unpublished doctoral dissertation, University of Kansas, Lawrence.

Veenman, S. (1984). Perceived problems of beginning teachers. *Review of Educational Research, 54*(2), 143–178.

Walberg, H. J. (1984). Families as partners in educational productivity. *Phi Delta Kappan, 65,* 397–400.

Wang, M. C., Haertel, G. D., & Walberg, H. J. (1993). Toward a knowledge base for school learning. *Review of Educational Research, 63,* 249–294.

Weinstein, C. S. (1990). Prospective elementary teachers' beliefs about teaching: Implications for teacher education. *Teaching and Teacher Education, 6,* 279–290.

Ysseldyke, J., & Christenson, S. (1993–1994). *The instructional environment system—II: A system to identify a student's instructional needs.* Longmont, CO: Sopris West.

Competencies in Classroom Management and Discipline: The First Weeks of School

DEFINITION OF TERMS
AUTHORITY POWER

First Few Weeks of School

COMPETENCIES IN POWER
TYPES/USES OF POWER
Attractive
Expert
Reward
Coercive
Legitimate

PREPLANNING
CONVENANT
Meso-
Phone Contacts
Open House
Micro-
CONDUCT
Micro-
Collaborating on Rules
Dangerous Behavior
CONTENT
Room Management
Instructional Management

An understanding of the material in this chapter will help you do the following:

❏ Describe a teacher who effectively blends the five forms of power to fulfill the three classroom management functions.
❏ Plan for covenant, conduct, and content management of the first weeks of school.
❏ Build positive family, student, and peer-group relationships.
❏ Develop and teach classroom rules and consequences.
❏ Teach students the procedures for managing physically dangerous behavior.
❏ Teach students classroom setting and instructional procedures.

Research on classroom management pinpoints the quality of management during the first 2 weeks of school as a critical indicator of successful management during the rest of the school year (Emmer, Evertson, Clements, & Worsham, 1994). This chapter focuses all your attention on preplanning. First, you investigate the concepts of classroom control and power. Following reflection on how you plan to share control and power with students and their families, you are introduced to preplanning guidelines for covenant, conduct, and content strategies.

COMPETENCIES FOR MANAGING CLASSROOM CONTROL AND POWER

There are many ways to enlist the cooperation of students and families in the affairs of the classroom and the school. Some educators believe that cooperation evolves as students participate responsibly in the decisions that affect their school lives. Students are therefore given an opportunity to talk about the advantages and disadvantages of various educational arrangements and the means to try out promising possibilities. In such schools and classrooms, decision making is collaborative and reveals a respect for both individual preferences and the corporate good. The educator's democratic management style invites involvement, creates a sense of community, and culminates in practices that reflect commonly held expectations.

Other educators are more disposed to set standards themselves and insist on fidelity to them. They believe that students will cooperate because adults can offer a plausible and convincing rationale for the decisions that affect students' educational well-being. Students' allegiance to standards of conduct is a fundamental expectation. Cooperation is not earned; it is expected. This more authoritative management style presumes that just decisions can be rendered, without consultation, and that the compliance of students does not depend on their participation in the original decision making.

These positions represent management style extremes on opposite sides of a continuum. Styles can vary by degree across the continuum such that there is a midpoint at which educators are democratic in their distribution of control and power about half the time and authoritative the other half, depending on the situation. Let's now examine two aspects of control (i.e., authority and power), noting some of their implications for teacher management style.

The Distinction Between Authority and Power

Developing and maintaining classroom control requires both authority and power (Rich, 1982). *Authority* might be defined as the right to make decisions that affect the choices available to students and families. Educators can specify what is right or acceptable in the realm of goals and can select the means for attaining them. This authority is conferred. The state education authority and a local school board delegate the responsibility for educating children and youth to educators and grant them the authority to act in accordance with this responsibility. Thus, authority can be given; it need not be earned by acting in ways that please the group over whom the authority is exercised. In other words, students have little recourse from an educator's authority. In schools that subscribe to ecological approaches to schooling, parents share authority with teachers in setting important educational goals and assuming responsibility for educating youth.

When teachers step into the classroom on the first day of school, they may have already made most of the major decisions about what will be learned and how students will go about learning it. This is an exercise of teacher authority. Teachers whose beliefs are based on the assumptions of behavioral and psychoanalytic theories will be more directive in the learning process than will teachers whose beliefs are based on assumptions of ecological and humanistic theories. Whether less or more directive in teaching and learning in the classroom, teachers have been given the authority at the state education level.

Students seldom object to teacher management decisions as long as they feel that the choices made on their behalf are reasonable. However, if they believe that instruction is uninteresting, requires more effort than they wish to exert, or calls for abilities that they do not have, students may express dissatisfaction with the teacher's choices. In other words, the authority of the teacher and thereby the teacher's control are in jeopardy.

When a teacher's authority is undermined by his or her making choices that ignore expressed student needs, the situation can be corrected. The teacher might ask, "Are there strategies that would be more appealing to students, better satisfy their needs and preferences, and simultaneously serve the interests of society?" or "If I cannot change the strategy itself, can I at least find more palatable ways to help students learn it?" Both questions are aimed at removing an impediment to student motivation.

Not all teachers reexamine goal and method choices when student behavior suggests that these decisions are unacceptable. For example, in the area of curriculum, some teachers feel compelled to operate within the narrow framework of a prescribed curriculum guide or a single textbook because it will prepare students to be successful on high-stake tests. Or, teachers think that their authority has been limited by decisions of the board of education or more experienced colleagues and that they must adhere to the limits set by these groups. It might be said that they have little authority to lead. Their educational choices are curtailed by others; thus, the choices of students are likewise constrained. Rather than seeking greater authority or pressing for more autonomy in making curriculum and methodology decisions, some teachers confronted by this dilemma may resort to the second dimension of management—power—to solve the problem.

Whereas authority can be conferred, *power* must be earned. Although teachers may be given the authority to make choices, teachers cannot be given the power to make students comply with these choices. For example, teachers might employ authority to assign a page of multiplication problems, but they must use power to get students to complete the assignment. On the one hand, authority is of little consequence without power. On the other hand, power seldom becomes an issue when students do not resist authority. If students are willing to accept a teacher's decisions as serving their best interests and are willing to work as though they had participated in these decisions, the need for power becomes merely an academic one (Burbules, 1986).

Types, Acquisition, and Uses of Power

Seldom do educators secure unquestioned obedience to their authority or unconditional commitment to the decisions they make (Reed, 1989). Of course, some educators do have a flair for creating appealing images of the benefits of learning, thereby sustaining high levels of student involvement and minimizing the occurrence of disciplinary problems. In these classrooms students generally do not seek alternative forms of excitement. Nevertheless, even educators who manage to come close to creating the ideal state of affairs sometimes need to resort to the use of power.

Five types of power can be used to get individuals or groups to act in ways that are deemed appropriate (French & Raven, 1959; Raven, 1974; Shrigley, 1986):

1. Attractive (or referent) power
2. Expert power
3. Reward power
4. Coercive power
5. Legitimate power

Attractive Power

To try to influence students to behave acceptably, some educators draw on their *attractive power*. Attractive power is essentially relationship power, the power educators have because they are likable and know how to cultivate human relationships. They do not take the goodwill of students and their families for granted but instead go out of their way to help students feel good about themselves. Peer relationships also flourish; there is a sense of belonging and a mutual sense of purpose. People concerns are always high on the agenda. Students prefer to behave in accordance with educators' expectations because of genuine regard. Simply, attractive power is earned by being personable and hospitable. Humanistic theory embraces the principle of attractive power (see Table 2–1).

Generally, teachers begin with some attractive power because most students start the school year with a favorable disposition toward their teacher. Sometimes called the *honeymoon period,* the first 2 weeks of school are a time of considerable harmony and congeniality. Each party to the relationship is working hard to make the other happy. Some teachers may assume that this is just the way things ought to be and therefore do little to perpetuate this lovely situation. Others do not make the assumption that students are naturally their friends, and they purposely work to build good relationships.

For example, a third-grade teacher reported that, at the end of each school year, she studied her class roster for the upcoming year. Each student who had a history of problems with authority was noted. Prior to the start of the upcoming school year, the teacher invited one of these students and three of his or her peers to accompany her to a fun activity (e.g., a children's play at the community theater, out for ice cream, or to the school to help put up bulletin boards in the classroom). The teacher reported that this attractive power plan had been successful in the initial stages of building relationships with students who did not have a history of cooperating with educators.

Expert Power

There may be some educators who do not have the interpersonal skills or the personal inclination to use attractive power as a basis for influencing student conduct. They may prefer to rely on *expert power,* the power that accrues to educators because they possess superior knowledge in one or more fields. Such educators prize their command of a subject and derive great pleasure in conveying their knowledge to students. They tend to view teaching as the transmission of information and regard their role as being the primary purveyor of cultural ideas and ideals. Behavioral theory values the principle of expert power (see Table 2–1).

Teachers who prefer to rely on expert power to influence student behavior are often characterized as having great enthusiasm for their subject, enthusiasm that is often contagious. Students feel compelled to get involved in the teacher's excitement; they want a piece of the action. Because of their admiration for the teacher, students are willing to embrace the subject. They too would like to experience the exhilaration and joy and the sense of competence the teacher exhibits. Thus, the teacher's power resides not only in an expertise, but also in a companion capacity to unveil it.

There are other educators who believe in sharing expert power with students. They prepare learning environments in which students explore their own interests in and construct their own meaning of a topic. The teacher remains an expert facilitator of student learning but empowers students to be in control of their learning. This is characteristic of teachers who subscribe to cognitive-behavioral and humanistic theories.

Table 2–1
Theories of human development.

Topic	Theory			
	Ecological	**Behavioral**	**Humanistic**	**Psychoanalytic**
Nature of people from birth	Human nature is such that behavior develops as a result of multiple and complex systems-level influences.	Humans are born blank slates. Their contributions to their own development is limited to genetic (e.g., blonde or red hair) and physiological (e.g., fight-or-flight) influences).	Humans are born with their own inner capacity to grow optimally and positively and become all they want to be.	Humans are born with inner drives to meet their own needs and desires first and foremost. The inner drives are referred to as the person's *id*.
Environmental contributions	There are four levels or systems that affect human growth and development in multiple and complex ways: micro-, exo-, meso-, and macrosystems.	Human behavior and development is the result of environmental reinforcements and punishments, paired with genetic and physiological influences.	Optimal human development comes from humans' own inner unfolding in environments that are nondirective and that provide necessary materials and resources	Human growth relies on the direct input of important others, such as parents, to develop the ego and superego, which moderate the id.
Home contributions	The home is one of the most important microsystems in the development of humans. The home as a microsystem is influenced both positively and negatively by other systems (e.g., the microsystems where parents work, the community culture, the state of the nation).	The home is an important environment in the shaping of human behavior because children spend so much time there from birth to school age. Rewards and punishments are a big part of home environments, and choldren's behavior is shaped almost completely by early home experiences.	Home contributions to human growth and development are of major importance. Optimal homes allow children to explore their environments fully and construct their own meaning. Homes that direct and control children stymie their potential to unfold and be all they can be.	Home or parental contributions to human growth and development are of major importance. The most formative years are from birth to age 5 years. Children spend the most time with their parents, who are responsible for parenting them in ways that help children develop egos and superegos that help control their ids.
Control and power in the schools	For optimal student growth, collaboration or sharing of power across systems is recommended. Legitimate power is a goal to be obtained within each system.	School personnel manage the control and power. Students are encouraged to self-manage and are allowed control and power in various situations. Expert, reward, and coercive types of power are emphasized. Legitimate power is a goal to be obtained.	Adults and students collaborate in managing control and power for the common good. Attractive power is emphasized. Legitimate power is a goal to be obtained by each individual, including students.	School personnel manage control and power. Students earn the right to control and power on the basis of adequate cognitive and social-emotional adjustment. Expert power is emphasized. Legitimate power is a goal to be obtained.

Few effective educators do their job without acquiring and drawing on both attractive and expert power. Some students may be reached through attractive power; for others, expert power will be the most appealing. Still others will be captivated by a bold blend of the two. By using power judiciously, teachers can actually add to their power as they expend it.

Reward Power

In some respects the third form of power, *reward power,* is like the joy that students get from a relationship or the inspiration that they get from a subject. In fact, this third form of power often depends on educators' possessing either attractive power or expert power. However, the ability to dispense rewards is not solely dependent on either of those types of power. Praise from an educator who is admired certainly means more to a student than does praise from an educator toward whom the student is indifferent. Praise is positive feedback that affirms the value of a student's effort. Positive feedback does matter, even when it comes from an educator whom the student might not particularly like or admire. In fact, genuine praise, specifically targeted to accomplishment, may gradually lead to a more favorable disposition toward the educator who provided the compliment. Relationships often grow and are nourished by appreciation. Similarly, the seeds of interest in a subject may be planted by praise and nurtured by admiration. Of course, reward power is not limited to social approval. Positive consequences for good behavior is another form of reward power. Educators who subscribe to behavioral theory are the most likely to conscientiously make use of reward power. Educators who subscribe to humanistic theory are the least likely to agree with the use of reward power. (See Table 2–1.)

Coercive Power

When we think of rewards as ways to influence behavior, we are often reminded of the exact opposite—punishments and loss of rights and privileges. The fourth form of power, *coercive power,* is the ability to mete out negative consequences when a student does not comply with a request or a demand. It is often used as a last resort because most educators do not like to make life miserable for students. In fact, most teachers would regard an overreliance on punishment as questionable and regrettable. They reason that educators ought to be able to secure cooperation without resorting to such aversive tactics. They also recognize that punitive tactics often have retaliatory side effects, some active (spite, revenge, vandalism, assaults) and some passive (tardiness, truancy, inattention, restlessness). All of these defeat the very purposes of effective management. Punishment can actually increase resistance to educator influence and create conflict that is not easily overcome by exercising other forms of power.

Despite the drawbacks of coercive power, it is used rather extensively in schools (e.g., time-out, detention, suspension). Educators are not informed about better alternatives and therefore contend that this is the only kind of "treatment" some students understand. The sparing and wise use of coercive power, although unpleasant and often distressing to both parties, can produce positive results when paired with teaching desired behaviors. Educators who subscribe to behavioral theory are the most likely to use coercive power. Those who are humanistic in their beliefs are the least likely to use coercive power. (See Table 2–1.)

Legitimate Power

Finally, the educator might employ *legitimate power* to obtain cooperation with academic and behavioral requirements. Legitimate power emanates from the student's belief that the educator has a right to prescribe the requirements. Similar to authority, legitimate power permits the educator to make decisions because that is the educator's rightful role. The difference lies in the student's acknowledgment of this right; it is not just the conferral of authority by those who hired the educator. In this sense, students accept the educator as leader, even though they had no role in the individual's selection. They willingly follow educator requirements out of respect for the role incumbent. Who happens to occupy the role does make a difference. Not all educators are regarded as having legitimate power and the "right" to make claims on students' time and energy. All theory bases value legitimate power. Humanistic theory values not only educators' legitimate power, but every individual's. In other words, students also have the right to be respected and granted legitimate power by school personnel. (See Table 2–1.)

As noted earlier, it is the coalescence of several forms of power that produces the best results. For example, legitimate power may be more readily accepted if the educator also possesses attractive power. Various combinations or pairings of power geometrically increase the educator's influence (Fairholm & Fairholm, 1984). Imagine a triad of power: The teacher likes, and is liked by, students (attractive); is valued as a resource for the subject (expert); and is sought out as a source of affirmation for personal achievements (legitimate).

PREPLANNING FOR CLASSROOM MANAGEMENT AND DISCIPLINE

Reflective preplanning is a necessary condition for quality management, especially for novice teachers. Do not be misled by the common justification for "winging it": "I do my best work under pressure." There is no empirical evidence that educators do their best work by winging it at the last minute. They may get their work done, but it is rarely their best work. It would be far more accurate for people who wing it to state "I do my *only* work under pressure" rather than "I do my best work under pressure" (Lucas, 1996). People do their best work when they have ample time to develop ideas, lay them aside for awhile, return to evaluate them critically, and refine them. Remember that quality, formal planning is also related to a high sense of teacher efficacy (Unruh, 1994).

Preplanning includes covenant (relationships), conduct (behavior), and content (setting and instruction) management procedures that will be taught during the first 2 weeks. The plan for the first 2 weeks of school can be refined and continually used throughout the school year.

Much of a teacher's effectiveness and credibility is established during the first days of school. The teacher and the students begin to know each other, classroom rules and consequences are defined and practiced, and patterns of lesson presentation and instructional routines are experienced. Let us begin our consideration of the three basic domains of management with an account of how one (fictional) teacher set the stage for a successful school year. Note how the teacher is beginning to develop attractive, expert, and legitimate power.

Looking in on the first day of school, we see Mr. Harmon moving among small groups of students, briefly engaging them in conversation about the previous summer. He recalls something about each one of them that occurred during the summer social events that he used to become acquainted with them prior to school's starting. While doing so, he keeps an eye on the door so he can greet additional students as they enter the classroom. He listens carefully for common summer adventures and privately notes special events on colorful T-shirts.

When the bell rings, Mr. Harmon begins class by using a few common experiences from the small-group conversations as a launching pad for discussing one of his own memorable summer activities. He chooses to tell about a personal experience that involved local family members, was meaningful, and was inexpensive. He does this to encourage everyone to share, regardless of socioeconomic status, which might dictate how students spend their summer days. He tells the class that last June he was ready for a summer break, but now, refreshed after the summer, he is excited about beginning another school year. He relates some of the highlights from the previous school year and shares his optimism about this year's plans. He also confides in students by telling them about a few topics and activities that fell flat last year; this year, he says, he will drop them in favor of some new, more promising possibilities. Mistakes are a source of growth, he tells the class, and they will frequently look for the growth opportunities in mistakes.

Mr. Harmon again uses some of the information he collected during the informal period before class to ask students about their summertime activities. As students volunteer experiences, he asks if there are others who did similar things and invites students to question classmates about their summer adventures. He inquires about unique and first-time experiences. Some of his remarks and observations are meant to establish rapport with students whose cumulative records suggest previous difficulties adjusting to school. Mr. Harmon balances the exciting stories of some highly spectacular trips with accounts of the simple pleasures derived from family gatherings and less costly leisure-time activities. Everyone in the group participates in the conversation.

This get-acquainted activity is followed by a handout designed to find out about student interests and accomplishments, which may later prove useful as subject-matter entry points. Mr. Harmon encourages students to be spontaneous as they respond to each item, and he informs them that their responses will be used to plan individual and group activities. He wants to make the class interesting, one that students will like regardless of their previous experiences with the subject, he explains. Students are encouraged to use the comment section on the handout to describe aspects of school life that they like and dislike.

Examples of instruments that can serve the purposes just described are presented later in this chapter.

Competencies in Covenant Management: Preplanning for Relationships and Attractive Power

The first domain of classroom management that requires preplanning for the first weeks of school is covenant management. Covenant procedures can begin as early as the summer months before school convenes. Covenant management is about managing relationships: school–home, teacher–student, and student–student. Effective relationships rely on communication skills to a great extent. Skills in conduct and content management also strengthen relationships.

Competencies at the Mesosystem Level: Collaborating with Families

Positive and proactive home–school relationships are developed prior to the school year or during the first 2 weeks of school by using at least five basic strategies: telephone calls, letters, home visits, social events, and open houses. These help lay the foundation for positive home–school relationships, which are known to improve students' academic and social–emotional–behavioral success.

Telephone Calls.   Shortly before school begins, telephone calls to the families of each student should be rehearsed for brevity and positive content. The contact is 1 or 2 minutes long, spoken clearly and not hurriedly. Teachers ask no questions and expect no responses. The guardian and/or student may say little or nothing. When the message is concluded, the teacher says "Good-bye" and hangs up.

An example of a script for a telephone call prior to the beginning of school follows. Note the components of the call. The caller greets, identifies him- or herself by name and role, identifies the student by name, invites future contacts, alerts the hearer to the letter, welcomes the family to open house, thanks the hearer for his or her time, and closes.

TELEPHONE SCRIPT FOR TEACHERS' INITIAL CALL HOME

"Hi, I'm [name], your [son's/daughter's] [subject] teacher for the new school year. I look forward to having [student's name] in my class. Feel free to contact me here at school anytime regarding [student's name] progress. You will be receiving a letter that will describe guidelines for the classroom. I also wanted to remind you of our open house on [date, time], and I hope to see you and [significant other] there. Thank you for your time. Good-bye."

Letters.   Phone calls to the home are recommended for building relationships between the home and school. However, when phone calls cannot be initiated, a brief letter can serve a similar purpose. The content of the letter can closely parallel the phone script, as in the following example:

Dear [Guardian's Name],

After several busy summer months with your children, the new school year is approaching rapidly. Your [son/daughter] has been assigned to my class, and I look forward to having [student's name] with us.

You will be receiving a letter that will describe guidelines for the classroom. I also wanted to remind you of our open house on [date, time], and I hope to see you and [significant other] there. Feel free to contact me here at school anytime regarding [student's name] progress.

Sincerely,

[Teacher's Name]

Home Visits.   Brief home visits can also be conducted prior to the beginning of the new school year. The purpose is to communicate the same message as in the preceding phone call script. Visits may last a few minutes while the teacher explains to the family that he or she wants to visit each student's home for brief introductions, before the teacher leaves for the next home visit.

Social Events.   A final covenant strategy for the summer months is to hold a family social event during an evening or a weekend time at a park. Sometimes a family may want to have the event at their home. This can be a potluck meal or dessert only, for which each family brings food and table service. The teacher can make a few introductory remarks prior to eating. Family game activities for 30 to 45 minutes can end the evening event. A variation of this is for the teacher to socialize with groups of four students at a time during the summer months. Teachers have escorted small groups of students to free summer theater productions, had them visit their homes for dessert, played in the park, and so forth. Teachers have found summer social events to be invaluable covenant builders that help everyone get through rough spots during the following school year.

Covenant Activities Once School Begins.   Teachers who engage in covenant activities prior to the start of school have a significant head start in accruing attractive power.

They will continue to engage in covenant-building activities because relationships are so critical and vital to student success. Much energy will be channeled into developing and strengthening them. If phone calls to the home have not yet been made once school begins, however, the following script can be used to talk by telephone to families:

> "Hi, I'm [name], your [son's/daughter's] [subject] teacher for the new school year. I have had [student's name] in my class for only a few days, but I really appreciate how [helpful to others, hard working, etc.] [he/she] is. You will be receiving a letter, if you have not already, concerning the guidelines of the classroom. I wanted to remind you of our open house on [date, time], and I hope to see you and [significant other] there. Feel free to contact me here at school anytime regarding [student's name] progress. Thank you for your time. Good-bye."

Likewise, if home visits were not possible in the summer, they can be conducted once school has begun. Family contacts can also be made by means of the open house.

Open House.   Let us assume that the school year begins with an open house. This activity gives teachers and parents an opportunity to meet one another in the school setting. Generally, teachers provide a brief program that includes a description of their teaching philosophy, the course work objectives, how the class is typically conducted, methods of evaluating and reporting student progress, and the classroom management plan. The session concludes with an invitation to parents to ask questions.

Parents may inquire about the teacher's general educational outlook and the practices that the teacher has found successful for dealing with certain types of learning problems. Someone will generally ask how parents can be helpful. When a parent does not introduce this topic, the teacher may conclude the session by describing ways that parents have assisted at home and school, perhaps by citing specific instances of when parental involvement made a significant difference in the life of a child. Using the account to highlight forms of parental involvement provides parents with specific behavioral targets. Chapter 6 provides additional information on working with parents as volunteers.

Parental Survey.   A general introductory session might be followed by the administration of a survey instrument. Since the teacher cannot possibly meet each parent and acquire information about each child—much less remember details from such conversations—a written instrument might be used. It might employ an open-ended format, or it might be a checklist. The educational backgrounds of parents should be considered when a format is being chosen. Items of information that might be collected include the following:

❑ Qualities of the child that the parents believe to be particularly praiseworthy
❑ Things that the child likes to do in school or areas in which the child has been particularly successful

❏ Things that the child tries to avoid in school or areas in which the child has encountered some difficulty
❏ Impressions of the child's social acceptance at school
❏ Qualities or practices of teachers about which the child comments favorably or unfavorably
❏ The child's reactions to selected kinds of incentives for good work and corrections for unacceptable behavior
❏ Management techniques that work best for parents
❏ Behaviors of the child that they have tried to eliminate at home without much success
❏ Disciplinary measures that the parents prefer to have the teacher use
❏ Receptiveness of parents to jointly applied home–school consequences for appropriate and inappropriate behavior

Parents generally use the informal period that normally concludes the evening to talk about items on the survey instrument. These conversations can alert the teacher to take note of areas of particular concern to individual parents. The conversations may also suggest ways to revise the instrument.

Presentation on Classroom Management.   Silberman and Wheelan (1980, pp. 172–173) offer five observations about classroom and family differences, which are described in Figure 2–1. They can make quite an impact whenever they are presented.

1.   *Classrooms are crowded places.* Parents would be hard pressed to identify another workplace where so many people are squeezed into such a small space. Adults would rebel, overtly or covertly, if they had to work in such close conditions. Yet children are expected to work harmoniously and productively, 5 days a week, in proximity to one another. Obviously, an adult must be present to manage the movement and interactions of students. Without conscientiously enforced rules, student misbehavior would spill out into the aisles of the classroom and into the corridors of the building.
Contrast this crowded setting with the size of many family homes. Sometimes each child has his or her own room. Even when everyone is at home, each person

Figure 2–1

Open House Presentation Outline to Inform Parents of Differences Between Home and School

Source: From Silberman, M., & Wheelan, S. (1980). *How to discipline without feeling guilty: Assertive relationships with children.* Champaign, IL: Research Press. Reprinted with permission.

I. Classrooms are crowded places.

II. Classrooms allow very little privacy.

III. Classroom relationships are not as intimate or close.

IV. The menu of rewards and punishments is not as rich.

V. Teacher authority is more easily undermined.

This classroom is an example of a crowded workplace. Skillful management is required if children are to work harmoniously.

may be able to occupy a different space. In the summer, when children are outdoors much of the time, the amount of space per person greatly exceeds that of the typical classroom. Yet parents find children underfoot. Homes, yards, and neighborhoods are spacious when compared with classrooms, and adults have fewer children to cope with at any one time than teachers have.

2. *Classrooms present little opportunity for privacy.* This point has important implications for dealing with disciplinary problems. The most obvious is that lack of privacy can turn minor incidents into problems. An adult supervising a group of three children, for example, can permit much greater latitude in the behavior of each group member because fewer people are affected when the individual chooses to assert his or her wishes. Each member is also better able to discern the others' wishes and intentions and can better choose compatible behaviors. As the group gets larger and more diverse, it becomes more difficult to express oneself without infringing on the desires or preferences of another person. This is complicated and difficult for the individual who must monitor the differences.

When a disciplinary problem does occur, it is difficult to ignore it as the group size increases. When a person refuses to abide by the rules in a small group, the group chooses either to ignore it or to do something about it. If and when an adult is called on to settle the problem, the adult's actions are more likely to be sanctioned by the other participants in the incident. If the adult determines not to intervene and tells the participants to settle the dispute among themselves, this action is generally not regarded as a failure in leadership. However, when a teacher ignores too many rule violations and does not facilitate student-centered problem solving, students may lose respect and challenge the teacher's leadership. Students are constantly observing the teacher's ability to lead, and from these observations they draw conclusions that govern their subsequent behavioral choices.

The best way to deal with some disciplinary problems is to remove the student from the classroom. Unacceptable behavior is often instigated and fueled by social stimuli. However, where does the student go? Sitting in the hallway, the student may become a problem to someone else. Often the problem is not one the principal needs or wants to handle. The dilemma is finding a place where neither the teacher nor the student feels compelled to save face or play to the crowd. Unlike parents, teachers cannot send the other children away or deal with the offending child in a private place. In addition, because classrooms are crowded places, returning the student to the group can reintroduce the conditions that provoked the original problem. Thus, teachers often create many problems while trying to solve one. One-on-one solutions often occur after school, long after the impact of the situation has diminished.

3.   *Classroom relationships are less intimate.* Parents share so many high and low points of their child's life that these experiences create a common bond transcending momentary disagreements and occasional conflicts. When there is a conflict of wills and the parents decide that they will prevail, there is usually a backlog of goodwill to assuage hurt feelings and reestablish damaged relationships.

Teachers work at building good relationships with students, but they are seldom able to form close attachments like those that bind parents and children. In a classroom composed of 25 to 30 students with whom the teacher is associated for only 1 year, the teacher can hardly be expected to secure from all students the full cooperation and enduring goodwill that parents build during a child's lifetime.

4.   *Fewer means of rewards and punishments are available.* As noted earlier, teachers have very few positive reinforcers at their disposal, and the use of punishment to exact appropriate behavior can have unfortunate side effects. Many high school teachers rely heavily on grades to induce good behavior. Yet a large number of students are indifferent to this form of incentive. Others may be content to "get by" with a grade of C so that they are not subject to most of the demands for responsible behavior. Thus, a teacher's grades are not a very effective form of control.

Teachers often use social reinforcers as an inducement to good behavior. Students thrive on the recognition and approval of their teachers. However, exclusive or extensive use of spoken and nonspoken expressions of approval diminishes their power. Students soon take them for granted or are content to get fewer such rewards. When this happens, they may engage in unacceptable behavior. The teacher must then find other reinforcers to manage student behavior. The options may be more expensive, less acceptable, and difficult to deliver in a consistent and systematic way.

Parents control many more and stronger reinforcers. They also control more powerful aversive consequences and are less subject to public scrutiny when they give consequences to their child. In fact, most parents fully expect other parents to use consequences to manage behavior. Thus, it is not uncommon for parents of teenagers to ground them for a weekend, revoke telephone privileges, or deny them use of the family car. With younger children, parents may remove television privileges and the use of prized toys. Parents provide more things for their children, and they are in a position to determine the use of these things. Parents also have greater control over the way their children use time. Outside-of-school time is not scheduled, or when it is, the schedule often includes privileges that have been given and can thus be taken away.

5. *Teacher authority is easily undermined.* A teacher's authority is conferred and can be taken away by members of the community. When parents make or repeat disparaging remarks about particular teachers or take their child's side in a dispute with a teacher, they diminish the teacher's authority to make and enforce standards. Certainly there are occasions when schools and teachers make mistakes. Education consists largely of making and exercising value judgments, and teachers are not immune from errors in both areas. There are, however, ways to deal with these breaches in confidence that will preserve the teacher's stature and confidence. All too often the ways to adjudicate differences between home and school pit the teacher against the parent. Children can conclude only that the teacher is mistaken, because parents are generally presumed to be omnipotent.

Parents are less likely to undermine another parent's authority. They may disagree with the way other parents fulfill the parenting role, but they acknowledge the other parents' right to be wrong. When their children try to use another family's practices as an argument for why they should be allowed to do something, not infrequently the children are told something such as "I don't care how Mr. and Mrs. Smith handle their children—that's their business. However, as long as you live in this household, you will be at home, and in bed, by 10 o'clock on a school night, and that's final!"

Teachers can introduce these ideas in their open house presentation and later in conversations and conferences with parents, not to evoke parents' sympathy but rather to help them obtain a better understanding and appreciation of a teacher's situation. Parents' expectations of teachers should be shaped by the unique, demanding realities of the classroom. Parents can be helped to understand and appreciate these realities when teachers point out the similarities and differences between home and school management conditions. With their firsthand experience as disciplinarians, parents will be less inclined to be critical of teacher's handling of disciplinary problems and more likely to lend support when called on to do so if they grasp the enormity of the teacher's task.

Competencies at the Microsystem Level: Collaborating with Students

In the development of positive teacher–student relationships, beginning with the first day of school, teachers can concentrate on the following strategies:

- ❑ Greet students at the schoolhouse or classroom door.
- ❑ Have students complete interest surveys and use the results to start conversations and to develop lessons.
- ❑ Demonstrate interest in each student by making one personal comment to him or her each day.
- ❑ Let students know that you see their good efforts in all aspects of classroom life and not just academics.
- ❑ Demonstrate respect by giving them responsibilities (e.g., serve as the runner to the office for delivering notes) and recognition (e.g., selection as student of the week).
- ❑ Present lessons that match the skills of every student (i.e., make accommodations).
- ❑ Develop lessons that will encourage all to participate and have important roles.
- ❑ Monitor favoritism.

Monitoring favoritism is paramount. Brantlinger (1995) interviewed adolescent students from low- and high-income families and asked them about social isolation and relationships with teachers. Although students from low-income families are believed to not care about school and teachers, the findings revealed that such students had strong feelings and cared very much. It was hypothesized that the pretense of not caring was a defensive reaction to possible rejection. In fact, these students were particularly sensitive to teachers' attitudes toward students. Many of these students stated that teachers liked "preppies" (students from high-income families) and disliked "grits" (students from low-income families). They believed that teachers were part of the high-income group and viewed a number of teacher behaviors as snobbish, rejecting, uncaring, and humiliating. Conversely, they expressed appreciation for the few teachers who had been kind.

Teachers can demonstrate interest in all students by asking them to complete interest inventories during the first 2 weeks of school. Interests of students with academic weaknesses or low motivation can subsequently be used to develop lesson plans. Figures 2–2 and 2–3 illustrate examples of interest inventories that can be used at the elementary and secondary levels, respectively.

Competencies in Conduct Management: Positive Behavior Choices

Conduct management strategies for the first weeks of the new school year include establishing explicit rules or guidelines for individual and group behavior while the students are on school property. It also includes establishing positive and negative

What Do You Like?

Name _____ Date _____ Grade _____

Please answer every item completely.

1. When you are not in school, what three things do you really enjoy doing?

   _____

   _____

2. When you cannot watch television at home, what do you most like to do?

   _____

3. If you could do anything that you wanted to do this weekend, what would you

   choose?_____

4. If you could learn about anything that you wanted to learn about, what would it be?

   _____

5. What is your favorite television show? _____

6. Do you like to do your best work in groups or alone? _____

7. Which school subjects do you like best?

   _____

8. What three things do you like to do most in school?

   _____

9. If you had 30 minutes of free time at school each day to do what you really like,

   what would you do? _____

10. What three jobs would you enjoy doing in class?

   _____

Figure 2–2
Elementary Interest Inventory

What I Like

Name_____ Grade_____ Date_____

Complete these sentences to express your own feelings and thoughts.

1. I am very proud that I _____.

2. A reward I like to get is _____.

3. My two favorite television programs are _____.

4. One thing I do very well is _____.

5. My favorite school subject is _____.

6. When I read for fun I like to read stories about _____.

7. One of my better accomplishments is _____.

8. If I had $10 I would spend it on _____.

9. When I have free time I like to _____.

10. I know I can _____.

11. I enjoy _____.

12. Something I want to do more often is _____.

13. One of the things I like best about myself is _____.

14. A good thing my teacher could do for me is _____.

15. In schoolwork my best talent is _____.

16. Something I really want is _____.

17. I feel satisfied when I _____.

18. An important goal for me is to _____.

19. If I did better in school, I wish my teacher would _____.

20. If I could get the chance, I would like to try _____.

Figure 2–3
Secondary Interest Inventory

Figure 2–4
Elementary Classroom Rules

- Be polite and helpful.
- Respect other people's property.
- Listen quietly while others are speaking.
- Respect and be polite to all people.
- Obey all school rules.

consequences for following or not following the rules, respectively. Figures 2–4 and 2–5 show typical lists of classroom rules at the elementary and secondary levels, respectively.

Competencies in Collaborating on Rules

Students come from diverse cultural backgrounds and, consequently, have varied expectations for their own behavior. Not every student will have the same conduct experiences or expectations as those of the teacher. When there is a mismatch between the students' conduct behaviors and the teacher's expected conduct behaviors, conduct management problems are likely to occur. It is the teacher's responsibility to facilitate a better match.

To do so, on the first or second day of class, the teacher can facilitate a student discussion of what the students think appropriate conduct in the classroom should be. The teacher should indicate that the purpose of the discussion is to brainstorm and then define *brainstorming* (i.e., all students' ideas are valued and recorded without discussion or judgment). As the discussion occurs, the teacher should write student comments and input on the board or large sheets of butcher paper taped on the board. Students typically offer similar ideas but use different words to describe them. The teacher should record everyone's comments, even if some seem like duplication.

After the discussion is completed, the teacher and the students should indicate which comments seem to be targeting the same idea. The final group of ideas will probably contain each of the rules in Figure 2–4 or 2–5. The teacher should state the rule tentatively and ask students if that rule seems to represent what they would

Figure 2–5
Secondary Classroom Rules

- Be in your seat with all necessary materials and ready to learn when the bell rings.
- Respect all people and their property.
- Follow directions promptly the first time given.
- Obey all school rules.

like to follow in their classroom. This procedure should continue until all student comments have either resulted in a rule or been set aside as mutually agreed by students. Sometimes students generate a new or different rule than those in Figure 2–4 or 2–5. The teacher should accept and record their rule. Sometimes students do not generate any ideas that could form a rule like those in Figure 2–4 or 2–5. The teacher can determine how important the particular rule is to the classroom and subsequently either lead the students in a discussion about the "forgotten" rule or not do so.

After the list of student-generated rules is finalized, the teacher should direct the class in examining how the rules define appropriate and inappropriate behavior in the class. The teacher should teach by examples and nonexamples. Nonexamples should be close or borderline behaviors that students may have difficulty distinguishing from appropriate behavior. After the teacher models specific examples and nonexamples of a rule, he or she should ask for various students to offer additional examples and nonexamples, respectively.

Some readers may argue that the procedures just described are too time consuming. They are, indeed, time consuming. However, dealing with student behavioral problems is even more time consuming, not to mention frustrating to the point of burnout for many teachers. Cotton (1990) found that approximately one half of classroom time was taken up with noninstructional activities. Disciplinary problems were responsible for a significant portion of this lost instructional time. The collaborative procedures also allow both teachers and students to determine how and when to make use of reward and coercive power.

The value of student collaboration in defining classroom rules is multifaceted. Students feel a sense of ownership and pride when they have a voice in important management decisions. They are more likely to remember the rules, to value the rules, and to adhere to the rules themselves while encouraging their peers to follow the rules. They are more likely to take a positive role in group problem solving should a peer have difficulty following the rules. Finally, they build skills in the democratic process of negotiating behavioral expectations and the use of reward and coercive power for a diverse social group of which they are a part.

Although some preservice teachers will be comfortable with the process just described, other preservice teachers will be uncomfortable facilitating the rules discussion during their first year of teaching. It seems like an overwhelming task for those who express a need for more teacher control at the beginning of their professional careers. It is good to have insight into your own need for control both in this management situation and in all others. A consistent need for high levels of control can be problematic in schools. Educators who are most comfortable under conditions of high control will need to develop leadership skills that give students some sense of control, also. However, it is acceptable to start the first year of teaching with a set of teacher-developed classroom rules and consequences that are taught to students during the first day or two of class. As these teachers grow more comfortable with managing student conduct, they can develop collaborative rules in future years.

Rules

- Act with respect toward all people and property.
- Be on time, ready to learn, with materials.
- Promptly follow directions to the best of your ability.
- Follow all school rules.

Positive Consequences

- Oral and written praise from school personnel to student or parents
- Music during individual work time
- Free time
- Time outside room (library, computer center, outside, hallway, etc.)
- Student choice (soda during video, read on floor, teacher read aloud, games, etc.)

Negative Consequences

- Oral and written reminders or warnings
- Time owed on own time
- Planned discussion on own time
- Exclusion from daily positive consequences
- Other as appropriate (e.g., clean up mess, redo work, apology, school service)
- Parent contact at any time by note or phone call to recognize or alert to student's behavior

---

Figure 2–6
Classroom Rules and Positive and Negative Consequences

Preservice teachers who are comfortable with collaboration can write a script for collaboratively developing rules and practice delivering it. Others who intend to begin their first teaching job with their own rules can write a script for already-developed rules and practice it. An example of a script for collaboratively developed classroom rules follows. See Figure 2–6 for a list of one teacher's possible classroom rules and positive and negative consequences that go with the script. The script, rules, and consequences were developed by an undergraduate student who had completed her student teaching and intended to work collaboratively with students to develop rules and consequences during her first year of teaching.

SCRIPT FOR COLLABORATION ON DETERMINING CLASSROOM RULES

"To start off class today, I want to give you 1 minute of quiet time to think about an important question. There's no right or wrong answer, just your opinion. I'll ask the question, then we'll have one silent minute to think, and we'll discuss our answers. Ready?

"If eighth graders had to live by just one rule, what should that rule be?"

(Encourage all to share ideas, listing them on the blackboard. Note similarities, ask for specifics, and contrast them until all willing students have contributed. Ask students to group the rules that are similar and state the most representative rule from each group. Ask them if these would be acceptable rules for the class to live by during the coming year. When agreement has been reached, post the classroom rules.)

"[Name], will you read rule one for us?"

"Act with respect toward all people and property."

"Can anyone think of an example of someone following that rule?"

(Listening while someone is talking, not touching other people's belongings, using school supplies carefully, talking with words and tone that show respect, etc.)

"How about times when a person might be breaking that rule?"

(Put-downs, writing on the desk, teasing, taking someone's belongings, talking while another person is talking, etc.)

"[Name], will you read rule two for us?"

"Be on time, ready to learn, with materials."

"Most of that rule is self-explanatory; bring your book, paper, and a pen, and don't be late. How about the 'ready to learn' part? Can anyone explain that? [Name]?"

(Read the assigned material, do homework, pay attention, quit talking when class starts, etc.)

"Why is this rule important? What happens when some people are not ready with all their materials?"

(Some people hold back the rest of the class by being unprepared.)

"[Name], please read the third rule for us."

"Promptly follow directions to the best of your ability."

"What does *promptly* mean?"

(Quickly.)

"What are some ways that we work to the best of our ability?"

(Neat writing, staying on task, concentrating, asking questions, using strategies, and following all steps of a task.)

(Do the same teaching activity with the school rules, whatever they may be.)

"Good thinking! I can tell that this class understands the rules. Please ask if you have any questions about the rules or ideas to change or replace the rules we just talked about. When we follow the rules of our class, I know that we can handle more privileges because I can see mature behaviors."

"Positive consequences that might happen after the whole class, a small group, or a person follows the rules consistently might be oral praise or a written note of recognition, listening to music during work time, a few minutes of free time, having class outside our room, or other things you think of, like soda during a video, playing a game, and so on. We will be working on a list of things that you consider positive consequences a little later on."

"We also need to have consequences for someone who chooses not to follow the rules so that they can correct their behavior. If I see students not following a rule, I will remind them of the rule or warn them that they are breaking the rule. The next step could be time owed to me before or after school or a planned discussion about the problem during the student's free time. What other consequences can you think of that would be fair for not following each rule? Let's start with acting with respect. If someone broke that rule, what would be a good consequence?"

(Apologize orally or in writing, fix or replace property, do service in the school, clean up a mess, etc.)

"Those sound pretty logical to me; let's look at the next rule. How about being on time, ready to learn, and prepared? What should we do about breaking that rule?"

(Owe time, redo work, lose points, lose privileges for the day, etc.)

"The last one is a little harder. What do you think I should use as a consequence for someone not following a direction right away?"

(Warn, owe time, etc.)

"I'm happy with the consequences we have thought of—does anyone want to change or add to these?"

"You will be glad to hear that any problems we have with following rules in this class will be resolved by the involved parties in this class—with one exception. If anyone is disruptive to learning and teaching and will not stop, I will send that person to the office. Consequences in the office are determined with the help of the disciplinary officer in charge that day. Here is a list of the consequences that you can expect."

(Give list of out-of-class consequences.)

"The goal of the school is to help you be successful here. Even when negative consequences are used, all of us are committed to carrying out a plan that will help students solve problems in a positive manner. Now that you know what some possible consequences might be, you won't be surprised when I implement one for not following a rule."

"In the next few days, I will be sending a letter to your parents or guardians that explains the rules and consequences this class has developed. I will ask them to discuss the list with you. I want to make sure that everyone understands and agrees to our plan. If parents or guardians disagree with anything, they can complete an attached form and return it. I will give you a copy of the letter in class so you will know what I said in it."

Positive and negative consequences can be brainstormed and determined by using the same teacher–student collaborative process outlined in the preceding script. Emphasize the positive aspects of following classroom rules by brainstorming positive consequences first. Figure 2–7 provides a list of commonly brainstormed positive consequences. Note that students see things that adults call responsibilities as positive consequences. Consequences are presented in categories: classroom and

Positive Consequences

Classroom and schoolwide tasks (social responsibility)
- Special jobs—student helper, peer tutor
- Student teaches a portion of the lesson
- Homework pass (excused from a homework assignment)
- Pass to computer lab, gym, etc.
- Choices in lesson activities

Financial costs
- Food—pizza party, snacks
- Field trip
- Grab bags

Oral and written feedback to students and guardians
- Tell the student what was well done
- Send a special note to the student or present a certificate of merit
- Call the guardian and explain what the student did well
- Send a positive note to the guardian

Freedoms
- Class gets free time
- Computer time
- Free read time
- A few extra minutes of recess
- Hold class outside
- Short class party

- Play music during seatwork
- Movie time
- Learning game day
- Tickets to student lounge, pop room
- Dress up/down day
- Student choice of activity
- Other privileges

Public recognition
- Compliment the student in front of another staff member
- Ask a staff member to acknowledge the student's accomplishments
- Post the student's work in a public place
- Read the student's work to the class
- Shake the student's hand
- Give the student extra adult time

Negative Consequences

- Ignoring
- Gentle oral reprimands
- Oral cues and warnings
- Delaying
- Parental contacts
- Time owed
- In-class time-out
- Behavior improvement form
- Natural consequence (e.g., fix it if you broke it)
- Referral to office

Figure 2–7
Menu of Positive and Negative Consequences for Classroom Use

schoolwide tasks (social responsibility), things that cost money, oral and written feedback, freedoms, and public recognition. Teachers should be prepared in advance to set boundaries on positive consequences and know whether and how they are going to fund positive consequences that cost money.

Cultures go through periods in which it is not acceptable or popular to talk about rules for behavior. Rules may be viewed as oppressive and stripping away the dignity of human beings by indirectly communicating that it is a given that students will do the wrong thing without explicit rules in place. Rules may be viewed as designed to trip up students so that they can be punished. It would be helpful, however, to view rules in a positive manner. For example, rules serve as a common standard to which disparate people can subscribe in order to promote safe, respectful, organized, and efficient environments that are mutually beneficial to all.

An additional reason for rules of conduct is to encourage respectful behavior toward others. Often we do not intend to be disrespectful; we are just busy. In a *Cathy* cartoon, there were rules posted in the employee lounge where she worked. The rules consisted of how to use the coffee room. Why? Isn't that taking a negative view of adults? After all, they are responsible people. Wouldn't it be assumed that adults know the common expectations for behavior in an employee lounge? Perhaps lounges become unkempt because employees are busy. Perhaps they think that one lone cup left in the sink of the coffee room will not matter. After 12 busy workers leave cups scattered around, it becomes a problem for someone (e.g., the secretary, the custodian, colleagues). Rules serve as reminders to busy people with many important matters on their minds and, thus, assist in maintaining respect for others.

If the word *rules* is offensive, call rules by a different name. Try *standards of excellence, policies,* or *guidelines,* but have them, teach them, model them, discuss them, and uphold them. State rules in a positive manner. Contrast the rules about pets in public places that you see in Figure 2–8. Does one manner of stating the rule make you more defensive or rebellious than the other? Does one sound more positive? If you are a pet lover, you may not feel too good about either of the rules. However, if there is going to be a rule about your pet in public places, which one makes you feel more welcome or accepted?

You probably selected the better rule as the one that says "Please have pets on leashes at all times." The rule that stated "No pets without leashes" was probably not your favorite. Note that both rules provide the same boundaries, yet the first rule uses a communication style that is more positive than that of the other.

Albert (1994) suggested that behavioral problems develop when schools rely on rules for managing student behavior. She stated that students tend to see *rule* as a four-letter word signifying "how adults control kids." Her solution is to replace rules with a code of conduct that defines how members of a community are expected to interact with one another. Call it *rules,* call it *code of conduct;* but do it. In studies from the 1960s through the 1990s, researchers found that the active teaching of rules

Figure 2–8
Stating Rules Positively

paired with specific praise and feedback optimally increased appropriate behavior of students (Johnson, Stoner, & Green, 1996; Madsen, Becker, & Thomas, 1968; Paine, Radicchi, Rosellini, Deutchman, & Darch, 1983). A description of one of these studies follows.

Johnson et al. (1996) served as school psychology consultants to a group of teachers dealing with the unruly behavior of a class of seventh-grade students in a rural public school. No individual children were referred as more problematic than others. The focus was on the entire class. Unruly behaviors included students' talking without raising their hands, tripping or chasing each other, throwing paper, engaging in activities other than the one assigned, and leaving the classroom to gather supplies needed to complete classroom assignments. Teachers stated that these behaviors often disrupted classroom activities and decreased the amount of time spent in instructional activities.

Three of the teachers agreed to work on a team and use an experimental school society orientation that emphasized collaboration and data-based outcomes for decision making rather than advocacy of any particular solution. All team members agreed that the interventions should emphasize educating students to prevent problems rather than reacting with negative consequences. Baseline observations of student behaviors in the three classes were completed, and the team met collaboratively to select interventions: (1) use of a class syllabus along with individual student achievement assessment in language arts, (2) active teaching of classroom rules in math, and (3) student self-monitoring of behavior in reading.

None of the teachers believed that active teaching of the classroom rules as an intervention would be successful, especially for an entire class. All three teachers believed that students were aware of their classroom rules and that the rules had been taught sufficiently already. Interventions occurred for 5 days, and student behavior data were collected across all 5 days. The team met to discuss the efficacy of the interventions and concurred that active teaching of classroom rules in the math class resulted in the greatest increase in appropriate behavior. For the next 5 days, the three teachers and the science teacher used the rules intervention. Appropriate behavior reached the 90 to 100% level in all classrooms across the last 5 days.

Proactive approaches (e.g., organizing classroom procedures to promote student-engaged behavior and minimize student misbehavior) have replaced reactive approaches or responding after individual student misbehavior (Gettinger, 1988). Compared with other interventions, the proactive intervention of emphasizing classroom rules was shown to be the most effective, particularly in terms of time and effort for teachers. Actively teaching rules serves two important functions. Rules communicate exactly what is expected, and teachers can attend to students when their behavior is consistent with the rules.

Competencies in Managing Physically Dangerous Behavior

The final stage in preparing for conduct management in the first 2 weeks of school is implementing the crisis management plan for aggressive behaviors in the school environment. A 1995 Midwestern newspaper showed a photo of a middle school teacher carried on a stretcher out of a school building, after he was shot by a seventh-grade student during a social studies class. During 1996 in the northwest region of the United States, a 14-year-old, ninth-grade student came to algebra class and shot and killed a female teacher and two male students. A female student received a gunshot wound that nearly severed her arm and damaged her liver, diaphragm, and kidneys. A rash of school shootings have occurred across the nation since then, resulting in numerous student and teacher fatalities. It is possible to plan ahead by having educators and students trained to respond to crises. More and more school buildings are equipped with their own crisis handbook. All school personnel need to know how to carry out the plan. In the following discussion, you learn how to respond to dangerous behavior in the classroom.

Sprick, Sprick, and Garrison (1993) provided a model for dealing with student behavior that posed threats to another's physical safety—other students, adults, or the dangerous student. Although educators cannot be sure that implementing any one model will successfully resolve all incidents of physically dangerous behavior, a plan of action that is rehearsed can help establish a calmer atmosphere during a crisis. Calm, thoughtful action is always better than panic. Law-enforcement agents in communities are often trained to assist in developing safety procedures to follow during aggressive episodes. Schools can invite such agents to offer staff development courses on managing aggressive behaviors. The Sprick et al. (1993) model for managing physically dangerous behaviors is described here.

Physically dangerous behaviors include fighting, head banging, hitting windows, self-biting, self-pinching, assaulting, engaging in out-of-control behaviors, and issuing verbal threats. The goal of the crisis plan is to help staff respond swiftly and professionally and with objectivity and consistency.

Several principles should guide the implementation of a crisis plan for physically dangerous behavior:

1. Safety is the first consideration. Staff are not required to put themselves in direct physical jeopardy. There are only two options:
   a. Get everyone out of the way.
   b. Have adults physically restrain the student.
2. Intervention must be immediate. There are two priorities:
   a. Ensure that no one is hurt.
   b. Do not reinforce the student for his or her behavior.
3. Follow-up intervention must be intensive, and it will be time consuming.
4. Early intervention has a higher probability of helping to resolve the problem. Do not hesitate to intervene. Many educators think that the first occurrence will be the only one. They "sweep the problem under the carpet" and hope that it is the last they will hear of it. Educators must take every occurrence of an aggressive act seriously and seek professional assistance in carrying out interventions.

Establish policies for responding to physically dangerous behavior:

1. Develop record-keeping procedures for all incidents of such behavior.
2. Involve the student's guardian(s).

Determine whether the student should be referred to special education, and whether other agencies should be involved.

Determine whether there will be consequences for the dangerous student.

Teach the student to manage her or his own behavior.

Safety Procedures

1. Use "room clears."
   - Where will students go and what will they do during a "room clear"?
   - How will the dangerous student be supervised?
2. Use physical intervention with caution.
   - Can students be dispersed so there is no need for physical restraint?
   - Will oral interventions work (before physical interventions)?
   - Did we call for help before beginning physical interventions?
   - Is restraint necessary? Will it be helpful?

Figure 2–9

Classroom Plan for Managing Physically Dangerous Behavior

Source: Sprick, R., Sprick, M., & Garrison, M. (1993). *Interventions: Collaborative planning for students at risk.* Longmont, CO: Sopris West. Reprinted with permission.

Additional truths to be mindful of include these: (a) Nothing can be done to make the situation pleasant. (b) Intense incidents are stressful and exhausting for everyone. (c) Injury has potential legal repercussions. (d) Successful intervention requires the resources and cooperation of many.

Teachers should not be expected to develop or complete interventions alone. Effective interventions include the following five components implemented concurrently: ensure safety, involve guardians, keep records, determine referrals, and instruct students. An abbreviated version of the Sprick et al. (1993) plan is listed in Figure 2–9.

Beginning in the first week of school, teachers typically assist students in drill and practice of safety routines for such things as fire and tornado threats. The same drill and practice must be completed for safety from other threats such as out-of-control behavior of a peer. Teachers should periodically repeat drill and practice throughout the school year. Once a month is not too often to rehearse safety routines when threats occur frequently and students have difficulty remembering or following the procedures. If one time through the routine does not go smoothly, immediately try it again.

An example follows of a script that teachers can use to introduce safety instruction for managing physically dangerous behavior. The script should be followed by role-play or drill and practice of what students are to do in case of a threat. Before the role-play begins, the teacher selects a student who agrees to play the aggressive role. The teacher introduces the safety lesson as in the following script, states the prompt "Students, room clear," tells students to imagine that someone in the middle of the class is angry and turning over desks, and then has students practice clearing the room.

The script includes instruction in how to obey the prompt "Room clear." Teachers will use this prompt to cue students to complete the prescribed safety routine. The prompt can be written on a sign and displayed on classroom walls along with the prompts for tornado and fire drills.

Teachers may determine that they can use variations of this prompt. For example, the prompt "Students, move away" may be used to direct students away from a danger zone when (a) the path to the door and the hall is obstructed or (b) the threat is great enough to necessitate moving students out of the way but not so great that students need to exit the room. For example, if someone is brandishing a weapon in the doorway, students will not be able to escape from the room.

Teachers will often be busy with the out-of-control student or assisting the other students. Therefore, teachers should train two or three responsible and dependable students in how to get help. The teacher may send only one student for assistance, but alternates should be available should a trained student be absent on a given day. Options for getting assistance include directing a student assistant to contact the principal's office by means of the intercom, telephone, or beep system in place in the school. Before teaching the script about physically dangerous behavior, choose the two or three students who will contact the principal for help and train them in their procedures. Select one of them for the role-play when you are teaching the crisis procedure to students.

SCRIPT FOR TEACHING PROCEDURES FOR PHYSICALLY DANGEROUS BEHAVIOR

"There may be times when it is not safe in school, not because of a fire or a tornado, but because somebody is upset and doing unsafe things like fighting and hitting. Can you think of some other unsafe things that somebody might do when he or she is upset?"
(Discuss student responses.)
"When someone is doing things that are not safe, it is very important for the rest of us to act very quickly to keep everybody safe. I am going to tell you the steps to keep safe and then we will practice them. When I notice that somebody, for example, Shawna, is upset and doing dangerous things, I will say 'Room clear.' When you hear me say 'Room clear,' each of you will stay calm and move away from the danger. What does staying calm mean?"
(Discuss student responses.)
"To move away from the danger, you are to leave the room and wait in the hallway for an adult to come. The two steps are (1) the teacher will see the danger

and will say 'Room clear' and (2) students will stay calm and quickly move away from the danger, go out of the room, and wait in the hall."

"Let's practice the 'Room clear' drill. Everyone cannot get out of the door at the same time. I will show you how to take your turn leaving the room and where to stand in the hallway to wait for an adult. When we have finished our first practice, I will answer any questions that you have."

(When the drill is complete and students are back in their seats, Shawna is in the office continuing the role-play. The teacher says the following to the students in their seats.)

"Shawna has had a very difficult time. Shawna will probably feel very uncomfortable about what has happened, and it will be important for all of us to help her feel like a regular sixth grader. Everyone of us will need to continue working as a community/group. Everyone in here has a special goal to work on, not just Shawna. For example, I have to work on being patient. Shawna will be working on controlling her angry feelings."

When a "Room clear" prompt has cleared the room, teachers can step into the hall right outside the door and monitor the disruptive student until help arrives. Sometimes teachers may be able to use their communication skills to calm the student and de-escalate the situation.

School personnel must take steps to ensure the safety of everyone through a well-articulated and well-understood crisis management system. Do not confuse having school rules and policies about violent behavior with having staff trained and assigned to implement a plan and procedures when a rule is violated.

Educators may hold beliefs that practicing safety procedures frightens students unnecessarily and, therefore, no practices are conducted. This is a grievous error when there is a student in the classroom who engages in physically dangerous behavior. Classmates who do not know the steps for keeping themselves safe are at a disadvantage. They are more frightened by aggressive acts when they have not been prepared to keep themselves safe. Practicing together how to keep safe shares the expert power with students. The end result is that they feel even safer.

Guidelines for School Building Policies and Procedures.   In addition to the overall plan shown in Figure 2–9, teachers should receive additional help rapidly. They should use a prearranged signal indicating that a crisis is occurring. School buildings should have a plan for who will respond immediately, a chain of command in case the first person is unavailable, and a communication process to ensure that everyone involved will be kept informed. This plan must be carefully designed and rehearsed occasionally.

Staff must be trained to implement the plan. Training should include which behaviors to ignore and which require intervention. Adults who supervise should be trained to stand at the door, to determine what actions to take if the situation escalates, and to implement proper physical restraint techniques.

It is critical to recognize that consequences for out-of-control behavior tend to have little effect on prevention but may be part of a comprehensive plan. Appropriate consequences include owing time and restitution. Suspension for special education students cannot be instituted without due process.

Guidelines for Location of the Class During "Room Clear" Procedures. Students should go to the hallway and wait for an adult. If dangerous behavior occurs on the playground, students should be taught to move away from the source of disruption. When an adult arrives, the class should go to a predetermined location. Prepared-in-advance, relevant instructional tasks should be stored at the location, and the class should complete them.

Guidelines for Use of Physical Restraint.   There are a number of parameters to keep in mind when you are contemplating the use of physical restraint. The use of a room clear without physical restraint is preferred because it helps ensure everyone's safety more so than physical restraint without a room clear. Furthermore, physical restraint is more likely to result in injury to someone than is a room clear. For some students, physical restraint can result in heightening the emotional intensity. The students are reinforced for out-of-control behavior as a result of the physical interaction with an adult. Use of physical restraint is less likely to teach the student that he or she can control his or her own behavior.

Physical restraint is not an option when the adult is not large or strong enough, the adult is unable to restrain the student easily, there is no other adult to assist, and the adult is not adequately trained or experienced in restraint procedures. Instead, oral interventions should be tried first. Use a firm and loud command. "Roland, stop beating on the window and move to this side of the room, now!" When more than one student is involved, direct each one to a different location. "Roland, move over to the doorway! Aaron, move over to the lockers!"

Guidelines for Working With Guardians.   After the first incident of physically dangerous behavior, request that parents attend a conference. Parents of a disruptive student often do not know what to do, and it will be important for educators to take a positive, problem-solving approach. At the conference, complete four critical activities: (1) Communicate the staff's willingness to help the student, (2) mutually determine the severity of the problem, (3) begin joint problem solving, and (4) involve other social agencies as appropriate.

Home–school partnerships that have already been developed will be a good foundation for crisis work. Phone calls home, letters home, home visits, social events, and open house during the first week of school represent positive contacts that teachers have initiated. On the basis of these school efforts, guardians are more likely to have a sense of a positive relationship with the school should their child exhibit behavioral problems during the school year.

Guidelines for Record-Keeping and Reporting Procedures.   Record keeping is necessary for these reasons:

❏ As a way to assist staff in developing and evaluating interventions
❏ If a special education referral is initiated
❏ If any legal issues arise related to a student's behavior (e.g., assault charges filed by an injured student, school sued for negligence, parents object to confinement, school personnel accused of discriminatory practices if student is of a different ethnic background)

Anecdotal logs should detail all past and current incidents and include the following items:

❏ Date and time of day
❏ Location of incident
❏ Name(s) of adult(s) supervising at the time of the incident
❏ Events that occurred prior to the incident
❏ A detailed description of the student's behavior during the incident, including the duration of the incident and the specific behavior observed
❏ Action(s) staff took to prevent physical injury
❏ Consequences given to the student (if any)
❏ Action(s) taken to minimize future occurrences of the behavior

Administrators should provide teachers with an opportunity to debrief. Logs need to be filed in the central office, and summary records of the number of incidents per week or the number of minutes per week can be used to chart progress.

Guidelines for Teaching Students to Manage Their Own Behavior.   Self-management of behavior typically involves self-control training. Consider implementing one or more of the following interventions: providing academic assistance, restructuring self-talk, using signal interference cuing, mentoring, implementing goal setting and behavioral contracting, teaching self-monitoring, using structured reinforcement systems, teaching stress management, and increasing positive interactions. Several of these are described in chapter 4. All of the interventions are thoroughly described and scripted by Sprick et al. (1993).

School psychologists, special education teachers and consultants, school guidance counselors, and other school personnel with advanced training and expertise in managing severe conduct problems can be used as resources to develop or refine existing classroom and schoolwide plans.

Competencies in Content Management: Setting and Instruction

There is much more to setting and instructional management than is encompassed in the brief episode in Mr. Harmon's classroom presented earlier in the chapter.

However, this episode should help you visualize the way these coordinated functions contribute to effective content management. This episode emphasized (a) typical management demands and decisions that occur prior to and during the first day of classes, (b) a few aspects of management that are common to both elementary and secondary school teachers, and (c) the importance of planning, that is, operating according to a schedule and appropriately distributing activities according to predetermined objectives and allocations of time.

Additional content management functions take up the remainder of this section and chapter 5. Content management includes planning (a) the use of the physical environment, (b) procedures that occur during the instructional day, and (c) instruction.

Many provisions for learning can be made before students are ever assembled for instruction. Teachers characteristically spend several days before school begins readying the classroom, organizing materials, testing equipment, and planning procedures that will support the instructional program. So, what are these important matters that need managing in order for students to get started on the right foot?

Competencies in Room Management

Teachers can make a powerful statement about how they feel about themselves, their students, and their job by the way they prepare the classroom (Grubaugh & Houston, 1990). Obviously, there are some givens, some institutional decisions about what a classroom should look like and how the space should be used, but there are also subtle ways to convey dedication or indifference.

Some teachers will be working in spaces that are already pleasantly painted, well illuminated, and temperature controlled. Teachers might be content with an already favorable setting and do little to add a personal touch. Others will work in buildings in a state of disrepair and in dark, dingy, stuffy classrooms. Teachers might try to transform the dismal setting into an inviting space by using the walls and bulletin boards to display the everyday work of previous students, to generate excitement, and to communicate behavioral expectations. An "at home" atmosphere of warmth and caring is created by displaying plants and personal decorative items that invite inquiries about the teacher's life outside of school.

Teachers can make the classroom a place where children feel at home. The children can be their best and do their best because it is obvious someone feels they are important and wants them to succeed. These are strategies that help build attractive power and invite students to become involved in learning and sharing expert power.

Floor Space and Seating Arrangements. Teaching is a constant quest for student attention. Careful student seating arrangements can maintain attention and facilitate overall monitoring of student behavior. Despite criticisms of neatly ordered rows of seats, this arrangement does provide for a single focal point in the room. Bennett and Blundell (1983) found an increase in work completion with row and column seating, although the quality of work remained the same as for other seating arrangements. Having rows of seats, however, may not be an effective way to

Careful seating arrangements can maintain attention and promote small-group discussions.

promote whole-class and small-group discussions (Rosenfield, Lambert, & Black, 1985). For this purpose, teachers generally design a classroom configuration that permits greater visual contact with speakers (e.g., circle or semicircle).

When teachers are actually making seating assignments, they should remember that school is a social event for most students. Being seated close to a friend can be helpful to some, detrimental to others. It is important to distribute the models of good behavior throughout the class. The social significance of modeling and the powerful effects of imitative behavior have been well documented by Bandura and Walters (1963). Teachers can share expert and legitimate power with students by allowing them to make choices about where to sit. Likewise, if there are students who appear to be socializing too much, teachers and students can collaboratively develop solutions that support improved learning conditions.

Traffic Areas.   Students are not as well coordinated in the classroom as on the playground; they bump into furniture and one another. Clumsiness can provoke laughing and shoving. For these reasons, it is important to plan for heavily traveled lanes to be free of obstacles and wide enough to accommodate the flow.

Teachers can identify the traffic routes by "walking through" the activities likely to occur during the course of a school day. They can plan a typical schedule, list the kinds of behaviors expected of students to fulfill its requirements, and then execute these requirements. A little imagination is also helpful to identify the ways students can deviate from planned procedures. Student behavior can be directed in subtle ways (e.g., arranging space so there is only one way to occupy and use it) or

Management Challenge 2–1

Seating and Socializing

On the first day of school, Ms. Rodriguez prefers to let students select their own seats. She believes that students feel more secure and confident when they are surrounded by people they know and enjoy. This conviction is not without its problems. Some students enjoy one another's company too much. They engage in behaviors that often distract other members of the class. Their socializing also prevents them from getting their own work done.

1. Given Ms. Rodriguez's preference for self-chosen seating arrangements, what might she do to minimize the problems and still maintain the goodwill that often accompanies this practice?
2. When students who are seated by their friend(s) are unable to behave acceptably, what measures might be taken to correct the problem? How might students be involved in solving the problem?
3. Some students have few, if any, friends. They are often viewed as intruders when seated in the vicinity of a friendship group. What can the teacher do to influence the friendship patterns in a class so these individuals feel included?

in more forceful ways (ensuring that traffic proceeds on signal and according to the rules of the road) (Guerney, 1989).

Supplies and Materials

Storage, Collection, and Distribution. The organization of supplies and materials should be directly related to their educational functions. Materials for activities that occur frequently and involve the entire class must be most readily accessible and must be governed by the simplest procedures. For example, elementary teachers might prefer to have students keep selected workbooks in their desks. Secondary teachers might want to store basic or supplementary texts on a shelf just inside the classroom door so that students can select the appropriate book as they enter and exit the classroom each day. In such a case, row dismissals can be used to avoid congestion when students put books back on the shelf at the end of class.

There are never enough closets in a home and seldom enough cupboards in a classroom. Seldom-used materials that serve special learning objectives or are used for short time periods should not occupy prime storage space in the classroom. Supplies that are expensive and might be indiscriminately used by students should be kept out of the room's more public areas.

Many storage problems can be solved by systematic collection and distribution routines. Loading and unloading zones, with "no parking" in either, can reduce student traffic. Teachers should teach students the distribution routines so they can assist. A table at the front of the classroom might serve the functions of collecting and distributing. Teachers who are fortunate enough to have a door at the front and one at the back of the room might choose to distribute materials from the front table and collect them at the back table.

Timing can be an important factor in the collection of materials. When teachers can collect materials on student time, before and after the bell rings, they should do so. When doing this creates other problems, such as delaying the starting time of class or causing congestion that results in ill will, the teacher should try to handle simple management routines either during the downtime just beyond the halfway point in a class session or at the end of a class period. At both of these times, students are least likely to be task oriented. The first suggestion, collecting materials just after the halfway point, is supported by studies of retention, which show that we are less likely to remember things that occur just beyond the middle of a learning sequence or period. The second suggestion takes advantage of a student habit: Students "pack up" their things and shut down their minds just before the class period is over. Of course, teachers can change this habit by the way they use this segment of time.

Teachers should not use the first few minutes of a class session to collect materials. Students are potentially most alert and receptive to instruction when a new activity is begun. Collecting materials at the beginning of a session can cause the informalities

Management Challenge 2–2

Transitions and Socializing

Mr. Greene sympathizes with students who find it difficult to remain quiet for an entire class period. He recalls his own student days when he was always preoccupied with finding opportunities to share important bits of information with others—humorous observations, plans for after school, and choice morsels of gossip.

Mr. Greene believes that students can be so consumed with exchanging social news that they are unable to concentrate on the task at hand. He sees no harm in letting students get these items of social significance off their minds so they can give their full attention to academic work. Thus, he thinks that such conversation might be allowed when assignments are being collected, when materials are being distributed, or when papers are being exchanged for correction.

1. What is your impression of Mr. Greene's analysis of the situation and his justification for permitting students a brief respite from academic concerns?
2. What do you think of his solution?
3. What provisions must his solution include if it is to succeed?
4. What kinds of problems do you think this solution might create? Do these problems more than offset the benefits of the practice Mr. Greene advocates?

that precede the bell to spill over into class time. When there is no clear demarcation between work and leisure periods, there is a tendency for more leisure to creep into each class session. Of course, teachers can pick a point from the social conversation to draw students into the work of the day.

Assessment of Needs, Acquisition, and Management.   Teachers must also conduct an inventory of existing equipment and supplies and the policies for their use. Each instructional activity will require previous arrangements for equipment and materials. Teachers can ensure the availability of these items by examining various activities for common material and equipment requirements.

Generally, most materials are supplied by the school district, with the balance supplied by students. Schools may send home a list of specific items that are students' responsibility to provide. Teachers often keep a small supply of these items on hand for students to "borrow." Loaning and borrowing can become a source of irritation and friction among classmates. Some teachers require collateral (e.g., student's watch, shoe) when supplies are loaned from their private store. When the loan is returned, the student gets the collateral back.

Equipment and materials that students do not purchase may be provided for all classrooms. For these items, the teacher need merely conduct an inventory and replenish the supply as needed. Other items, such as scissors and staplers, that are periodically used by students might be allocated on a so-many-units-per-student basis. Once again, teachers must secure the equipment on the ratio established by the central office.

Teachers are generally given a modest amount of money with which to purchase equipment and materials. This money is used to purchase items that the school does not provide or items it supplies in insufficient quantities. Sometimes teachers will use their personal funds to augment the supply of less expensive items; they find that avoiding the hassle associated with sharing some items is worth the expense. Elementary teachers are likely to use their own money to purchase such items as activity packages to augment a unit of work, holiday decorations, and stickers to reward accomplishments. Secondary teachers are likely to use their own funds to buy products to support equipment acquisitions for an extracurricular program and certificates to recognize meritorious achievements.

Teachers may be asked, on short notice, to identify uses for school district funds unencumbered at the end of the school year. Keeping a "wish list" ready that includes catalog information will put a teacher in a good position to secure part of this windfall.

Generally, the amount of material that teachers can draw from a central supply is restricted. Teachers need to organize their program by units of instruction and ascertain material needs to stay within these restrictions. Whether teachers use learning centers, learning packages, or a wide variety of other supplements to teacher presentations, resourceful and careful management of materials is important. Teachers must devise methods for using materials, prepare written instructions, demonstrate and practice these routines, and assign certain students to assist in their implementation. Careful attention to preplanning the preceding strategies can increase the expert power of a teacher in the first weeks of school.

Competencies in Instructional Management

Instruction during the first 2 weeks of school typically consists of review of the previous year's curriculum. Review is important for a number of reasons. First, review at the beginning of the year serves as an intellectual warm-up, much like calisthenics before strenuous athletic exertion or "ah-h-hing" before a vocal solo. Review "warms up" students' prior knowledge, and they can then hook new learning onto it, organizing and elaborating (Woolfolk, 1995). Academic review gets students ready for more rigorous academic exercises that require new and greater skill.

Second, review serves as informal pretesting and teacher appraisal of skill levels of individual students. Results of this appraisal should be used in future instructional planning. Third, review for students provides an opportunity for immediate success in a new and, therefore, less comfortable or threatening environment. Success leads to a sense of comfort and confidence and subsequent motivation to engage in learning.

Last, review of prior knowledge affords most students the opportunity to function with automaticity in the academic area. This frees them up to process new stimuli (e.g., learning how to relate to the teacher and classmates, how to follow new procedures and rules) (Sternberg, 1985). Careful preplanning of instruction in the first weeks of school is a way for the teacher to share expert power with students.

An additional aspect of content management is managing all the procedures students engage in throughout the instructional day. During the first 2 weeks of school, it is important to teach these classroom procedures. Figure 2–10 provides a relatively thorough checklist of all the procedures teachers must manage during any given school day. To manage procedures effectively, teachers must plan how to carry out each procedure and how to teach it to students. Effective teaching includes direct instruction, modeling, guided practice, independent practice, and corrective feedback.

For example, to teach procedures for appropriate behavior at the opening of class, the elementary teacher might do the following on the first day of class.

SCRIPT FOR TEACHING PROCEDURES FOR APPROPRIATE BEHAVIOR AT THE START OF CLASS

"Students, beginning today we will learn to follow classroom procedures for starting work at the beginning of the class. On the projector screen I'll show a brief assignment for you to complete while I am taking roll and the lunch count. You will have about 3 minutes to work independently on the activity. Your work will typically serve as the basis for the next activity of the day. You are to be on task, doing your best work, even if you are not sure of what you think I want. If visitors walked in at the beginning of this class, they would see you in your seats, writing and thinking on your own. What would it sound like to them?"

(Students should respond that it would be quiet.)

"Let's try it now. When I turn on the projector, read the assignment on the screen and work for about 3 minutes while I take roll and the lunch count. When I am through, I will turn off the screen. I will give you feedback on how I think you did, and you can ask questions

---

Use this checklist to identify classroom management procedures that should be followed in your classroom. To analyze your personal management:

1. Check the space for each item for which you do have a set procedure to teach.

2. Put an asterisk next to those items for which you do not have a procedure but feel you should.

3. Circle those items you feel should be taught in the beginning days of a class.

Beginning Class
___Roll call, absentees
___Tardy students/policy
___Academic warm-ups or getting ready routines
___Distributing materials
___Expected student behavior
___Readmitted students

Room/School Areas
___Shared materials
___Teacher's desk
___Water fountain, bathroom, pencil sharpener
___Student storage/lockers
___Materials needed for class
___Lack of materials procedure
___Seating arrangement
___Location of classroom materials

Setting Up Independent Work
___Defining working alone
___Identifying problems
___Identifying resources
___Identifying solutions
___Scheduling
___Interim checkpoints

Instructional Activities
___Teacher/student contacts
___Student movement in the room
___Signals for students' attention
___Signals for teacher's attention
___Student talk during seatwork
___Activities to do when work is completed
___Student participation
___Laboratory procedures
___Student movement in and out of small group
___Expected behavior in group
___Movement in room/area

Ending Class
___Putting away supplies, equipment
___Cleaning up
___Organizing materials
___Dismissing class
___Chairs up last period

Interruptions
___Rules
___Talk among students
___Conduct during interruptions or delays
___Passing out books, supplies
___Turning in work
___Handing back assignments
___Getting back assignments
___Out-of-seat policies

Figure 2–10
A Checklist for the Beginning of the School Year

Academic Feedback
___Rewards and incentives
___Posting student work
___Communicating with parents
___Students' record of grades
___Written comments on assignments
___Progress reports

Other Procedures
___Fire/tornado drills
___Lunch procedures
___Student helpers
___Safety procedures
___Teacher resource availability

Work Requirements
___Heading on papers
___Use of pen or pencil
___Format for homework
___Neatness, legibility
___Incomplete work
___Late work
___Missed work
___Due dates
___Makeup work
___Supplies
___Lab steps to follow
___Typed or handwritten papers

Communicating Assignments
___Posting assignments
___Orally giving assignments
___Provision for absentees
___Requirements for long-term assignments
___Assignments
___Returning assignments
___Homework assignments

Monitoring Student Work
___Total in-class oral participation
___Completion of in-class assignments
___Completion of homework
___Completion of stages of long-term assignments
___Monitoring all students

Checking Assignments in Class
___Students exchanging papers
___Marking and grading assignments
___Turning in assignments
___Students correcting errors

Grading Procedures
___Determining report card grades
___Recording grades
___Grading stages of long-term assignments
___Extra credit work
___Keeping records of papers/grades/assignments
___Grading criteria
___Contracting with students for grades
___Student-kept grade log

Figure 2–10
(Continued)

about the procedure. Before we begin, are there any questions about what you should be doing?"
(Turn on projector.)

Educators who plan to use cooperative learning structures should also teach students the procedures and skills needed for successful group learning. These skills include appropriate social skills for participating in a peer group.

It may take the entire first 2 weeks of class to teach whole-class procedures and complete reviews of prior learning. Educators may wish to teach cooperative

Management Challenge 2–3

Procedures and Self-Management Skills

Ms. Koch believes in the importance of teaching students the routines associated with various classroom activities. She has established procedures for entering and leaving the classroom, forming small groups, distributing and collecting materials, and a number of other activities that occur during the school day. Whenever a new activity is introduced, she takes time to (a) identify the procedures associated with the activity, (b) specify and demonstrate responsible ways the students are to behave, and (c) have students practice the appropriate behaviors.

The school principal comes to observe Ms. Koch's class the third day of school. On the occasion of her visit, Ms. Koch is introducing the procedures for using a piece of equipment. When the principal meets with Ms. Koch to evaluate the class session, she is quite critical of the time spent introducing students to the piece of equipment. She believes altogether too much importance was placed on discussing and practicing equipment-handling procedures.

1. Speculate about the arguments the principal used to justify her criticism of Ms. Koch's introduction of the piece of equipment.
2. Build a defense for Ms. Koch, and be sure to include what you understand about the teaching of self-management skills.
3. Use this incident and the material generated by your responses to items 1 and 2 as the basis for a role-playing exercise.

learning and social skills procedures after the first 2 weeks. Chapter 5 presents the how-tos of procedures for cooperative learning and social skills training.

As a way to assist yourself in planning procedures for the first 2 weeks of school, recall that a common sequence of classroom instructional activities is as follows:

1. Opening routine
2. Checking
3. Content development
4. Seatwork or discussion
5. (Repeat Steps 2 through 4 for each new content introduced in a single class period.)
6. Closing

CONCLUSION

Management during the first 2 weeks of school emphasizes features of classroom control. Proactive teaching—or the planning that teachers do prior to the resumption of another school year, before and after school, and during free periods and weekends—can have a profound effect on the ecological aspects of developing relationships, positive behavior choices, and instruction. The fact that a circumscribed set of management strategies can be planned before the school year begins and then introduced during the summer months and during the first few days and weeks of school highlights their significance. Few management matters can be dealt with so expeditiously and can have such widespread effects.

If you can successfully respond to any item from the following list, you are well on your way to successfully managing a real classroom during the first weeks of school:

> Do I have every student's name along with the guardian's name(s), address, and telephone number?
>
> Do I have a phone home script prepared to use?
>
> Are my trust-building activities developed?
>
> Am I completely familiar with the school building discipline plan, to the point that I can implement it with integrity?
>
> Are my tentative rules and consequences ready to be disseminated, discussed, taught to students on the first or second day of class, and reviewed throughout the first 2 weeks?
>
> Have I developed the props that I will use for consequences?
>
> Have I developed a letter to send home explaining the classroom rules and consequences?
>
> Are my crisis management plan and tentative classroom management plan approved by the principal and on file in the office?
>
> Have I organized the physical environment of my classroom to prevent content management problems from occurring?
>
> Am I ready to teach classroom procedures to students?
>
> Have I planned lessons for the first 2 weeks of class that review prior knowledge in ways that increase the likelihood of academic and social success for every student?

SUPPLEMENTARY QUESTIONS

1. Incidents of disruptive behavior may peak toward the middle of the week and occur more frequently during afternoon sessions. Given your understanding of setting management, what do you think accounts for these increases? What remedies could you suggest?

2. Persons who observe classrooms with a mind toward the efficient use of time are sometimes appalled by teachers' lack of attentiveness to time management strategies. What aspects of classroom life do you suppose they view as time wasters? What measures would they propose be implemented so that classroom time can be used more effectively?

3. When teachers speak of providing good "structure" so that students feel safe, secure, and purposeful, what do they have in mind? How can structure become so confining or oppressive as to actually constitute an impediment to learning?

4. A student's feelings of security rest in large measure on being able to "read" the environment for cues that certain events are about to happen. Confusion about where things are or when things happen encumbers a student's attempt to make sense of the surroundings. What do you make of this statement? What are the implications for covenant, conduct, and content management?

SUPPLEMENTARY PROJECTS

1. "Settling kids down" is a practical aspect of management. Observe in several classrooms, at different grade levels and across different types of classroom activities, and make a record of the ways teachers typically handle this management challenge.

2. Delays and breakdowns in the flow of events in a classroom are often the precursors to disciplinary problems. These "breaks in the action" are often time-outs from good behavior. Divide a sheet of paper into two columns. Head one column "Delays/Breakdowns" and the other column "Incidents of Unacceptable Behavior." Observe several class sessions and keep a record of instances when interruptions in the flow of events are an invitation to behavioral problems.

3. The tenor of the class period or the school day can be influenced by a teacher's spoken and nonspoken behavior. Make a videotape of the first 5 minutes in several classrooms. List the messages, and speculate about their affective impact on students. Compare your notes with one or more persons who have made a similar critique of the tapes.

4. Design an elementary or a secondary school classroom that you think would be both functional and attractive. Keep a record of the thoughts, particularly assumptions about teaching, learning, and students, that guided your selection and arrangement of furniture, equipment, and materials. Prepare a paper explaining the rationale for your plan and presenting its merits.

REFERENCES

Albert, L. (1994). Discipline tips from the experts: Rule is a 4-letter word. *Teaching Kids Responsibility, 1.*

Bandura, A., & Walters, R. (1963). *Social learning and personality development.* New York: Holt, Rinehart & Winston.

Bennett, N., & Blundell, D. (1983). Quantity and quality of work in rows and classroom groups. *Educational Psychology, 3,* 93–105.

Brantlinger, E. (1995). *Social class in school: Students' perspectives* (Research Bulletin No. 14). Bloomington, IN: Center for Evaluation, Development, and Research.

Burbules, N. C. (1986). A theory of power in education. *Educational Theory, 36*(2), 95–114.

Cotton, K. (1990). *Schoolwide and classroom discipline* (School Improvement Research Series). Portland, OR: Northwest Regional Educational Laboratory.

Emmer, E. T., Evertson, C. M., Clements, B. S., & Worsham, M. E. (1994). *Classroom management for secondary teachers.* Needham Heights, MA: Allyn & Bacon.

Fairholm, G., & Fairholm, B. C. (1984). Sixteen power tactics principals can use to improve management effectiveness. *National Association of Secondary School Principals Bulletin, 68*(472), 68–75.

French, J. R. P., & Raven, B. H. (1959). The bases of social power. In D. Cartwright (Ed.), *Studies in social power* (pp. 150–168). Ann Arbor: University of Michigan Press.

Gettinger, M. (1988). Methods of proactive classroom management. *School Psychology Review, 17,* 227–242.

Grubaugh, S., & Houston, R. (1990). Establishing a classroom environment that promotes interaction and improves student behavior. *The Clearing House, 63*(8), 375–378.

Guerney, M. A. (1989). Classroom organization: A key to successful management. *Academic Therapy, 25*(1), 55–58.

Johnson, T. C., Stoner, G., & Green, S. K. (1996). Demonstrating the experimenting society model with classwide behavior management interventions. *School Psychology Review, 25,* 199–214.

Lucas, R. (1996, September). *Scholarly and grant writing.* Paper presented at the University of Northern Iowa, Cedar Falls.

Madsen, C. H., Jr., Becker, W. C., & Thomas, D. R. (1968). Rules, praise, and ignoring: Elements of elementary classroom control. *Journal of Applied Behavior Analysis, 1,* 139–150.

Paine, S. C., Radicchi, J. S., Rosellini, L. C., Deutchman, L., & Darch, C. B. (1983). *Structuring your classroom for academic success.* Champaign, IL: Research Press.

Raven, B. H. (1974). The comparative analysis of power and power preference. In J. T. Tedeschi (Ed.), *Perspectives on social power* (pp. 172–198). Chicago: Aldine.

Reed, D. (1989). Student teacher problems with classroom discipline: Implications for program development. *Action in Teacher Education, 11*(3), 59–64.

Rich, J. M. (1982). *Discipline and authority in school and family.* Lexington, MA: Heath.

Rosenfield, P., Lambert, N. M., & Black, A. (1985). Desk arrangement effects on pupil classroom behavior. *Journal of Elementary Psychology, 77,* 101–108.

Shrigley, R. L. (1986). Teacher authority in the classroom: A plan for action. *National Association of Secondary School Principals Bulletin, 70*(490), 65–71.

Silberman, M., & Wheelan, S. (1980). *How to discipline without feeling guilty: Assertive relationships with children.* Champaign, IL: Research Press.

Sprick, R., Sprick, M., & Garrison, M. (1993). *Interventions: Collaborative planning for students at risk.* Longmont, CO: Sopris West.

Sternberg, R. (1985). *Beyond IQ: A triarchic theory of human intelligence.* New York: Cambridge University Press.

Unruh, L. (1994). *The effects of teacher planning on classroom management effectiveness.* Unpublished doctoral dissertation, University of Kansas, Lawrence.

Woolfolk, A. (1995). *Educational psychology* (6th ed.). Boston: Houghton Mifflin.

ADDITIONAL RESOURCES

Interventions: Collaborative planning for students at risk, Sopris West, 1140 Boston Avenue, Longmont, CO 80501; phone: (303) 651-2829.

Training in physical restraint, David Mandt & Associates, Richardson, TX; phone: (972) 495–0755.

PART II

Classroom Management Domain Competencies

CHAPTER 3

Competencies in Covenant Management: Relationships

DEFINITION OF TERMS
COVENANT

Competencies in Covenant Management

INDIVIDUAL COVENANTS
POSITIVE INTERACTIONS
PROBLEM SOLVING

MICROSYSTEM COVENANTS
CLASSROOM GROUP
  Four Stages
    Forming
    Storming
    Norming
    Performing
GROUP PROBLEM SOLVING
  Class Meetings
    Social
    Open-Ended
    Educational-Diagnostic

MESOSYSTEM COVENANTS
FAMILY CONTACTS
PARENT–TEACHER CONFERENCES
  Anecdotal Records
  Disagreements
  Assertive Responding

An understanding of the material in this chapter will help you do the following:

❏ Develop trusting relationships with families and students.
❏ Describe the dominant features of the four developmental stages in the formation of group relationships.
❏ Conduct class meetings to prevent and solve classroom concerns.
❏ Describe ways to prepare for and conduct parent–teacher conferences, distinguishing between conferences devoted to student progress and those devoted to classroom management and discipline issues.

> One of the best kept secrets in Washington is that families are educators' most powerful ally.
>
> —Theodora Ooms (Ooms & Hara, 1991)

DEFINITION: COVENANT

A *covenant* is a promise, a binding agreement between two or more persons. It implies that there is a promissory relationship into which persons enter willingly, trustingly, and collaboratively. *Covenant management,* as used in this text, is the facilitation of trusting, respectful relationships, willingly entered into, that promote optimal school success for all children. Specifically, this chapter focuses on what teachers can do to build competencies in managing relationships among students' peer groups, with individual students, and with families throughout the school year. The better the relationships in micro- and mesosystems, the more students will learn and the fewer behavioral problems there will be. Covenant competencies rely on competencies in communication, which are mentioned only briefly in this chapter. All of chapter 8 is devoted to communication competencies.

Recall from chapter 2 the covenant competencies described for getting off to a good start during the first few weeks of school. Specifically, they included establishing contact with families and students prior to the start of the new school year in the following ways: home visits, welcoming messages offered over the telephone, welcoming letters sent to the homes, and back-to-school social events held for entire families and small groups of peers.

Also in chapter 2, you learned how teachers use their covenant management competencies to navigate the first few weeks of school by doing the following: being respectful in all ways and at all times toward every student and family, regardless of race, class, ethnicity, gender, or challenging condition; ensuring that the families of the students in their classrooms obtain necessary community services; holding an open house with an agenda that includes sharing the classroom management plan and volunteer opportunities; having a positive greeting for every student at the door each morning; providing academic lessons that match the needs of every student in order to ensure every student's sense of efficacy; and having every student complete an interest inventory to be used in future lesson planning.

COVENANT COMPETENCIES AT THE MICROSYSTEM LEVEL

With such a quality start in covenant management at the beginning of the year, you might wonder how anything could possibly go wrong. Problems will occur, however, because human relationships are complex and require constant nurturing to grow and thrive under the best of circumstances. Classrooms are especially complex environments in which to build quality relationships and deserve special attention in the classroom management literature.

Unlike the participants of most social enterprises, the participants in classrooms have little recourse if dissatisfied with the program or with one another's company. Teachers and students are assigned to classes, generally with little consideration for individual preferences, and they are expected to get along with one another. Even when students elect to take certain courses, they seldom have the opportunity to choose from among a large number of teachers. When teachers have a chance to participate in the assignment of students to classes, they seldom get a class comprising their first choices. Thus, learning to live together in a classroom, often doing things not of an individual's personal choosing, and interacting with a large collection of persons that an individual might not select as friends are often overlooked challenges of education.

Indeed, it is an enormous challenge, particularly for the teacher leading a disenfranchised and disillusioned collection of individuals. Creating a working unit from such an assortment of students while preserving members' individuality is an awesome responsibility. Accordingly, covenant management requires the application of our highest ideals of how to treat others: respect, compassion, diplomacy, and cooperation, attitudes and skills that characterize democratic interpersonal transactions. Creating and nurturing the arrangements that bring people together in these ways require communication skills, a commitment to egalitarian principles, and caring connections. Most beginning teachers understand and subscribe to the principles, but they have had little experience applying them in a school setting. Some teachers fear that they will lose control of their classroom if they follow their beliefs and are warm, caring, and friendly with students. This fear is apparent in adages such as "Don't smile until Christmas," which some veteran educators share with novices in the building.

Warmth and friendliness, coupled with respectful and collaborative efforts, actually promote positive student behaviors. Persons who go into the field of public education typically have a love for children. It is easy for them to envision themselves as caring, compassionate, patient, and giving adults. They have a dream that two main ingredients will make them happy and successful teachers and make children happy and successful students. The first ingredient is caring about their students, establishing kind and patient relationships with them. The second ingredient is quality and enthusiastic teaching. They should hold onto that vision because it is correct. With some building of additional competencies and a little tweaking of previous competencies, educators, students, and families can have the happy and successful classroom experience of their dreams. Educators can acquire new competencies and refine old ones, first with simulated practice and then in real-life classroom situations.

Covenanting with the Classroom Group

A group takes on the personality of its individual members, some of whom will have a more compelling impact on the group than others. The power aspects of the "hidden curriculum" can shape much of classroom life. For example, a nightly television news program broadcast an exposé on bullies and their victims. Four middle and high school students who had a long-standing history of being victimized at school by their peers were interviewed. One male student reported that he had been popular as an elementary student and had had many friends. However, in middle school another male student who was a bully repeatedly harassed him. Soon the victim had no friends. His former pals joined in the harassment tactics of the bully in order to escape being bullied themselves. Teachers shut their eyes to what was transpiring and provided no help.

On the same television program, a single mother reported that her middle school daughter committed suicide by hanging herself in her bedroom soon after the mom left for work one morning. The mother stated that her daughter had had no friends at school during the past few years. The daughter had been bullied and harassed by numerous classmates for being different (i.e., she wore black clothing and expressed an interest in witchcraft). The principal and teachers reportedly told the mother that there was nothing they could do if they did not personally observe the harassment. Consequently, school personnel did nothing to alleviate the situation. The mother showed the interviewer many notes from students who, after the funeral, wrote apologies for the way they had treated their now-dead classmate.

Could things have been different for these young victims? What could have been done at school to help them be accepted by the group, to achieve that all-important positive identity or role in their class?

Incidences of violence, bullying, dropping out of high school, and other destructive behaviors in schools have turned the national spotlight on potential solutions to these problems. Many of the solutions fall within the category of covenant management, particularly as it applies to relationships among peers. Breakdowns in group functioning are generally due to identity or rationality problems. Students who cannot find a significant role in the group (identity) or who persist in believing that the goals of the group make no sense (rationality) gradually withdraw from full participation. Identity problems become behavioral problems when students who lack social and academic connections to the group feel that they do not belong. Rationality problems become behavioral problems when students see no connection among the present demands of living, their aspirations for the future, and the curriculum. Once the harm is done, the group only marginally influences role and goal decisions of students who see no connection. It is teachers and other adults in the building who must be vigilant about students who fail to identify with the group or to believe in its goals and who must take appropriate steps to help these students.

Peer relationships in classrooms form throughout the school year, going through some predictable phases or stages. In fact, the same group formation process occurs across all groups that are coming together, including adult groups. It might be helpful to reflect on groups in which you experienced the formation process as you read about the stages of classroom groups. When you connect your prior experiences to what you are learning about classroom group formation, it will be more meaningful. You are more likely to have some "ah-ha" moments. Following is a description of a group formation process. Note the important role of teachers in facilitating positive, supportive group formations.

The Four Stages in Group Formation

Mauer (1985) described the four stages of group formation as follows:

1. Forming
2. Storming
3. Norming
4. Performing

The four stages are discussed next to highlight changes in the teacher's management functions throughout the school year. Emphasis is on typical student behavior and the teacher's orchestration of the psychosocial dynamics of group formation in ways that promote every student's positive group identity or role.

The Forming Stage.   The *forming* stage can be characterized as the "honeymoon" period. This is the stage when students are generally on their best behavior. They tend to be task oriented and to look to the teacher for structure and direction. Because they are often uneasy about their relationships with other members of the class, they also look to the teacher to structure these relationships. This is an important time for teachers to begin monitoring their own relationship competencies for signs of bias. The way teachers should relate to students of diversity (e.g., race, class, gender) is integrated throughout the text. A few examples from the research literature are listed next to illustrate how important it is that teachers treat all class members equally from the forming stage of group development through the performing stage.

> Teachers have more contact with males than females during science classes (Jones & Wheatley, 1990). Spread contact out evenly across all students.
>
> Teachers have a tendency to favor high achievers (Allington, 1991) unless they are Black (Leacock, 1969). Treat all students equally, regardless of achievement level or race.

Teachers demonstrate a higher rate of behaviors that communicate rejection toward Black, male students (Ross & Jackson, 1991). Communicate acceptance to every student.

During this stage, leadership is largely a matter of engaging students in the three activities of (1) linking, (2) establishing roles and procedures, and (3) information seeking. These activities generally occupy a significant portion of the school day during September and part of October.

Linking activities are designed to help students see connections between what was learned last year and what will be learned this year. It is particularly important that teachers match the demands of lessons to students' skill levels. This requires accommodations and adaptations of lessons for some students. Teachers who need help in making appropriate accommodations should immediately seek it from the building assistance team. Students need to begin the year experiencing a high sense of self-efficacy. Students' confidence will grow as they realize that prior learning has set the stage for success. They will also view the teacher positively because he or she is experienced as an encourager and enabler.

A natural outgrowth of linking activities is *establishing roles and procedures.* As students engage in academic activities that ensure high levels of success, they can turn some of their attention to finding their place in the social group. Likewise, students will begin to value one another and allow one another to find a positive place in the group. After all, that is what the teacher is modeling. As the teacher makes provisions for various types of group activities, sometimes assigning roles and other times allowing roles to emerge, students will gradually get a clearer sense of what they can do and what others think they can do. It should be clear how important it is for the teacher to make group decisions that facilitate students' respect and positive regard for each of their peers.

Information seeking can be carried out in a mutually advantageous way during the early weeks of school. Free of the more involved management responsibilities associated with teaching new material, the teacher can thoughtfully observe and record the distinctive characteristics of each student. Similarly, when students initially spend a large portion of their time with independent work assignments, they can seek information peculiar to their needs.

During the forming stage, covenant management begins. This is the time to build a firm foundation of trusting relationships. Content management considerations are numerous also. This is review time and it is important to make the review of prior knowledge an exciting event. Teachers have long proclaimed that the best hedge against behavioral problems is an enticing curriculum taught by an enthusiastic and well-prepared instructor. There are fun, creative ways to conduct reviews of prior learning.

The Storming Stage.   Testing the limits is a common way to characterize the *storming* stage. Students begin to create some social distance from their studies and from one another. The stability of the forming stage has provided them with a secure base of operations. They are now willing to take a few risks. A teacher not attuned to this natural dynamic, which often occurs between October and December, might overreact to this change in what has been quite a cooperative atmosphere. Teachers may become concerned and upset. They may seek someone out and talk about their discomfort, wondering outloud what to do about the recent, worrisome changes in their classrooms. This is the time that their confidants might say, "I told you that you would get into trouble being nice. Don't smile until Christmas!"

Rather than becoming upset, a teacher should see the storming stage as a reasonable "setback." It happens in every new group formation and provides the opportunity to restructure and renegotiate relationships. It can be used to clarify expectations, help students grow through conflict resolution activities, and reestablish the teacher's leadership role.

During the storming stage, the teacher must pay more attention to conduct management, as presented in chapters 2 and 4. Conduct management substitutes reasoned and impartial judgment for some of the emotionality of the storming stage. Expectations are made more explicit and are consistently enforced. As a result, there is some distancing from the teacher, who is becoming the focal point for group norms. Teachers who have developed trusting relationships with each member of the group will find students counting on them to be fair when managing individual and group behavioral problems. Even though students do not like the consequences of their actions, they are more likely to accept them and learn from the experience because they believe the teacher has their best interests at heart.

The Norming Stage.   The *norming* stage, which often extends several months after the Christmas break, is dominated by *orienting* and *fueling* activities. Students have begun to accept both content and conduct standards and use these standards to *orient* themselves. They can figure out what is expected by relying on an internal set of cognitive maps.

Just as students engage in more subject-orienting behavior, they also begin to acknowledge and accept the roles they were working out for themselves earlier in the school year. There is less conflict between and among students as role-appropriate behavior becomes stable and predictable. A few individuals may try to assume roles that are neither personally fulfilling nor helpful to the group. It is important for the teacher to collaboratively problem solve positive solutions with them. Individual problem-solving procedures are presented later in the chapter.

Fueling activities are designed to garner the energy to meet academic and social demands. All too often, students will compromise their aspirations because they feel as if they cannot muster the strength and energy to keep marching toward their goals. Remember what those long second-semester days of school were like? They went on week after week in endless procession without so much as a holiday break. As students survey a task, it seems like one more impossible hurdle to jump.

A few students are contemplating not trying to learn anything in school for the rest of the year. Most students assess their abilities and their chances for success. They set a tentative goal based on their past performance. In some cases, they may find that they are not expending enough energy. In other instances, success that comes with a modest expenditure of energy may result in elevating expectations. It is noteworthy that the source, amount, and distribution of energy become important features of this stage of development. Teachers should not assume that tasks are left undone because of a lack of ability. Sometimes unfinished work results from an inability to harness the needed energy and deploy it in an efficient and effective way. This is a time for teachers to introduce novel, fun, and creative methods of encouraging students to keep moving toward their goals.

Remember the math teacher who could read your minds on a basketball game day. She knew that all you really wanted was to be at the game. Forget math class! First, she would show you how fit she was by doing calisthenics in front of the class, bending to touch her toes at the ripe old age of 62 (at least then it seemed like a ripe old age to you and the rest of the class). You secretly admired her and wondered if you would be able to do the same when you reached old age. Then she would turn her entire lesson into the mathematics of basketball. Voilà! Novel, fun, and creative learning opportunities!

Similarly, fueling is important in social relationships. Whereas the energy of some students is depleted by social situations, others find social interactions energizing. The former must find ways to compensate for the tendency to withdraw from relationships. Sometimes these are task-oriented students who will be rejuvenated by success in the academic realm. The latter, whose task batteries are recharged by social activities, may need more help in containing their tendency to "waste" task time. Help in fueling activities is equally important in either case because the social aspects of fueling often determine the direction of a student's academic decisions and performance.

Students who are fueled by working alone can be encouraged to first do their own work, second share their products with peers in order to obtain feedback, and third refine their products on the basis of peer reviews. Students who "waste" task time socializing can be encouraged to use their time in peer groups more effectively. When they demonstrate quality use of peer time, they can be granted the opportunity to select peers with whom they want to complete a classroom activity in which socialization is more acceptable.

For teachers, the norming stage is the most productive period in the school year. During this stage, the relationship between the teacher and the students is grounded in mutual respect. They share common aims and aspirations, and when differences do arise, they work them out in mutually acceptable ways. Communication is an important element in the process of establishing norms and negotiating changes in them (see chapter 8). Everyone in the class is engaged in a process that builds and depends on trust. This process results in a covenant that expresses the class members' faith in common purposes and in one another.

At its best, the norming stage culminates in a bond based on a promise to make the most of a relationship, a relationship that orients an individual to academic possibilities and fuels a personal commitment. Although these are lofty aims not easily attained, this process can set the outer limits for the performing stage.

The Performing Stage.   The *performing* stage is the coalescence of the three previous stages and can be very satisfying for both the teacher and the students. In the parlance of classroom management, students are now more self-reliant, self-controlled, and self-disciplined than at the beginning of the year. They are capable of working independently and in groups. They can rely on the teacher and their classmates when they lose their sense of direction or need an emotional lift. This period of productivity occurs within the other three stages and reaches its zenith during the final months of the school year. The extent to which the performing stage is distributed throughout the school year depends on the eclectic management abilities of the teacher.

Synthesis of the Group Process

Effective group managers must be concerned about all three of the management functions: covenant, conduct, and content. Figure 3–1 graphically depicts this idea and illustrates the relationships among the three management functions and the stages of group formation. Conduct and content considerations, presented in chapters 2, 4, and 5, form the base of the triangle. These functions set the stage for learning. Without a planned and organized program of studies and an orderly way for people to conduct themselves, little teaching and learning will occur. Both of

Figure 3–1
Eclectic Management Model

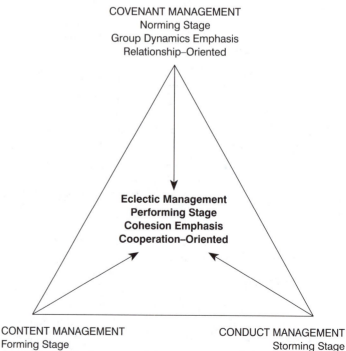

COVENANT MANAGEMENT
Norming Stage
Group Dynamics Emphasis
Relationship–Oriented

Eclectic Management
Performing Stage
Cohesion Emphasis
Cooperation–Oriented

CONTENT MANAGEMENT
Forming Stage
Instruction Emphasis
Task–Oriented

CONDUCT MANAGEMENT
Storming Stage
Individual Behavior Emphasis
Order–Oriented

these functions are heightened by covenant competencies. Students' receptiveness to the curriculum and their willingness to abide by the rules can be greatly increased by the communication-fostering qualities of the teacher and his or her relationship with the students. Thus, this eclectic management triangle reveals a triad of functions that affect the way a teacher views the work of teaching and suggests ways to best perform the work requirements.

The effective classroom manager must be able to perform all three functions and meld them to maximize the contribution of each. Teachers are generally more proficient in the execution of content competencies. Teachers tend to view themselves as well endowed with human relationship skills, but the primary skills that remove barriers and build commitment to learning demand attitudinal underpinnings and a technical facility that a person is unlikely to acquire in the normal course of life events. Teachers can acquire and refine these communication and problem-solving skills if they are more conscious of how they influence student behavior. When it becomes apparent that they are relying on "I said so" and "you ought to" communications, it is time to look for alternatives that invite agreement.

Glasser (1969) offered a pathway to teachers and students that provided an alternative invitation for striking agreements. In making their way along his alternative path, students can achieve a sense of identity and an outlet for their need for self-worth. Glasser referred to this path as the *class meeting*. Feelings of self-worth originate in responsible, respectful involvement with significant people, and the class meeting can be a vehicle for promoting these feelings. Such meetings provide a safe setting where events and concerns can be discussed and examined without fear of failure. Students can resolve classroom concerns in mutually agreeable ways. The teacher's sole responsibility is to facilitate the class meeting.

Group Problem Solving by Means of Class Meetings

Class meetings offer students an opportunity to entertain issues and think about problems that defy singular and simple answers. Students can pose their own questions, examine one another's answers, gain new insights, and mediate their own disputes (Koch, 1988). There is a place for everyone in a class meeting because these meetings emphasize, seek, and value involvement in matters that touch the lives of the participants. Let us look at three types of meetings and the purposes served by each.

Types of Class Meetings

Social Problem-Solving Meetings.   Social problem-solving meetings serve a socialization function. They help students deal with social–emotional dilemmas and peer conflicts associated with growing up (Opotow, 1991). Friendship, honesty, success, fear, disabilities, belonging, respect for differences, harassment, bullying, social skills or life skills, or conformity might serve as pivotal topics. There are also many group management problems that could serve as the basis for social problem-solving meetings. Lack of unity, nonadherence to behavioral standards and work procedures, negative reactions to individual students, class approval of misbehavior, being prone

Social problem-solving meetings in a quality school generated these random acts of kindness.

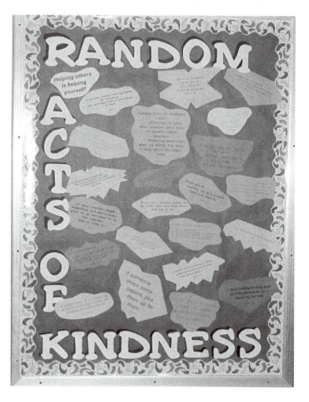

to distraction and work stoppage, low morale, resistant and aggressive reactions, and the inability to adjust to environmental change are cited by Johnson and Bany (1970, pp. 304–305) as common group management problems.

Open-Ended Meetings.   Open-ended class meetings are probably the cornerstone of relevant education (Glasser, 1969). Students are asked to discuss thought-provoking questions that link their lives with the curriculum. They are encouraged to ask questions that deepen their understanding of a subject and to relate the subject to their personal worlds. A social studies class studying the Civil War might consider questions that connect the contemporary experiences of a student with that historical period, as illustrated by the following examples:

> "What change in the conduct of the Civil War would you have made to shorten the duration of the war, alter the outcome of a single battle, or change the outcome of the war itself?"

> "What one 20th-century instrument of warfare, other than nuclear weapons, do you think would have made a decisive difference had it been in the possession of one side in the struggle? Why?"

"What person who has lived during your lifetime might have been able to prevent the civil strife that led to the war?"

Open-ended meetings need not be confined to questions associated with school subjects. They can also be devoted to speculative questions, such as the following, that help students develop the insights and criteria for making more effective personal decisions:

"What would you do if other students made insulting remarks about your parents or friends?"

"When something—an idea, an event, a material object, a preference for behaving—is terribly important to you, what is the best way to get your way?"

Each question sparks differences of opinion, generates varied lines of defense, and is likely to provoke multiple and divergent answers. Yet every student is better informed, is likely to have found the basis for reaching an answer, and has acquired skills for tackling similar issues.

Educational-Diagnostic Meetings. Educational-diagnostic, sessions are directly related to what the class is studying or to ways to improve students' learning abilities. For instance, teachers might use these meetings to solicit student opinions about an upcoming unit of study, baffling and troublesome problems that students have encountered in learning fractions, or an alternative form of evaluating English compositions. These meetings give students an opportunity to enter into a partnership with teachers as the latter search for answers to perplexing problems. Finally, these meetings may be used to find out what students would like to study and what they already know about the topic.

Purposes and Benefits of Class Meetings

Glasser has recommended frequent use of these three forms of class meetings, which are discussed at length in his book *Schools Without Failure* (1969, pp. 143–169). He believes that 20 to 30 minutes should be allotted to class meetings every day in the elementary grades and at least one class period per week in secondary school.

Glasser's rationale emphasizes the need for a sense of identity and the importance of making education more relevant by making it more responsive to the realities of daily living. According to Glasser, classroom meetings should do the following:

❏ Provide a stable bridge across the gap between school and life.
❏ Help students believe that they can control their own destinies and that they themselves are a vital part of the world in which they live.
❏ Keep a class together because the more and less capable students can interact.
❏ Promote involvement because students can always succeed in a meeting—no one can fail.

❏ Help motivate students to do some of the less exciting fact finding necessary to make the judgments and decisions that may evolve from the meetings.

❏ Reduce isolation and failure so that a spirit of cooperation can arise.

❏ Help students gain confidence when they state an opinion before a group, which thereby helps prepare them for the many opportunities in life to speak for themselves.

❏ Increase responsibility for learning and for the kind of learning that is fostered by and shared with the entire class.

❏ Provide for the kind of involvement, value judgments, plans, and commitments that produce changes in behavior.

Discipline problems are less likely to occur in a classroom in which students are disposed toward school, toward one another, and toward the teacher. Everyone has a stake in making the classroom a good place to be.

Procedures for Conducting Class Meetings

Class meetings are more likely to succeed if 10 certain procedures are adhered to:

1. All problems relative to the class as a group and to any individual in the class are eligible for discussion.
2. Discussion is to solve problems, not to find fault or to punish, because both those actions serve as an excuse for not solving the problem.
3. The teacher, but not the class, must be nonjudgmental. The class makes judgments and works toward positive solutions.
4. Teachers can evaluate group processes and how well the procedures are working, but not the ideas of the participants.
5. Meetings should always be conducted with the teacher and all the students seated in a tight circle, with the teacher sitting in a different place in the circle each day.
6. Meetings should be 30 to 45 minutes in duration, although the length of the meeting is less important than its regular occurrence and the pertinence of the problem discussed.
7. Meetings should be held daily in the elementary school classroom and at a regularly scheduled time. Meeting less often than once a week in a secondary school classroom provides neither enough continuity in the discussion nor an opportunity to build group rapport and open communication.
8. Students seem to respond best if they are given an opportunity to raise their hands.
9. It is all right for the leader to call on students who do not raise their hands, usually with a remark such as "You have been listening very carefully; I wonder if you would like to contribute something?" or "I'm sure you have an idea about this, and I would like to hear from you."
10. A teacher never interrupts students to correct an idea or challenge a position, because when students are desperately struggling to express an idea or think through a problem, such a put-down discourages further participation.

Preparation for Class Meetings

Class meetings, like any other activity that produces desirable results, require judicious planning. Students should not be given free rein and permitted to take the discussion in any direction personal whims might suggest. Class meetings should be structured, even though they may be more open ended than class recitation periods, and they should be sufficiently flexible to entertain an unexpected turn of events.

After a topic has been selected, the leader can best prepare for the session by writing questions that can be used to direct the discussion. *Resource Book for Class Discussion** (Educator Training Center, n.d.) is an inexpensive and useful resource booklet for elementary and secondary teachers. It is a compendium of topics, each developed according to a single format, that provides an easy and effective way to prepare for a classroom meeting. Basically, the procedure provides for the progressively more thoughtful and insightful development of a topic in three steps: define, personalize, and challenge. Table 3–1 presents an example of a question and its development according to this format.

Teachers who have used this planning guide have generally felt more confident about their leadership role and have reported being able to develop effective questions without a great expenditure of time. As with all skills, practice both increased the caliber of the questions and reduced the time required to prepare them.

Facilitator Skills for Class Meetings

Class meetings require some group interaction skills that teachers do not ordinarily use in classroom recitation sessions. Class meetings cast the teacher in the role of a facilitator. The session is intended to help students identify, examine, and understand personal frames of reference and to assist them as they apply these ideas to school and nonschool aspects of living. The teacher is challenged to help students expand on their ideas, make connections between their contributions and those of another class member, and examine the implications of their views. So how does the teacher prepare for this new challenge?

Experimentation has always been an exciting way to learn anything. At the outset, the teacher can tell the students of his or her apprehension about leading class meetings, the basis for that apprehension, and why, despite these misgivings, the teacher has decided to proceed with this experiment. The reasons can emphasize the potential benefits of the class meetings for students. Teachers who approach the situation in this way get all kinds of help from students, largely in the form of responsible participation, which in turn helps put the teacher at ease.

Much has been learned in recent years about effective group leaders and the skills that seem to characterize their approach to group problem solving. Individuals with a psychotherapeutic background, such as Glasser, have no doubt influenced the transformation of ideas from the counseling literature into classroom principles and practices. Dinkmeyer, McKay, and Dinkmeyer (1980) adapted the work of Dreikurs and Soltz (1964) and Gazda (1973) to create group development training

---

*Available from Educator Training Center, 100 E. Ocean Boulevard, Suite 908, Long Beach, CA 90801.

Table 3–1
What would happen if we did not have rules?

Define

1. What is a rule?
2. What are some types of rules?
3. Where do rules come from?
4. Why do we have rules?
5. Who uses rules?
6. What are some uses for rules?
7. What is an important rule?
8. How do rules become important?
9. What does it mean when someone says, "Those are the rules of the game"?
10. Does everyone have to agree before something is a rule?

Personalize

1. How do rules affect your life?
2. When are rules most important to you?
3. When do you want to make rules?
4. Have you ever seen rules broken?
5. Have you ever been harmed when rules were broken?
6. How do you feel when you break a rule?
7. Have you ever been happy after breaking a rule?
8. Have you ever heard of a person called a *ruler*?
9. What are the rules at your supper table?
10. Have you ever tried to get someone to break a rule?

Challenge

1. When is breaking a rule very dangerous?
2. What would happen if we didn't have rules?
3. What is the color of a good rule?
4. Is there anything that can be done to reduce the need for rules?
5. If we could make just one rule for good living, what would it be?
6. Do you have a responsibility for enforcing the rules?
7. Why do some people disobey the rules more than others?
8. What would a classroom be like if everyone obeyed the rules?
9. Are there times when rules should be broken?
10. How can we tell a good rule from a bad rule?

materials for classroom teachers. The teacher's handbook for their training package, *Systematic Training for Effective Teaching,* discusses the differences between democratic and autocratic leadership styles and describes the skills that democratic leaders use to maximize student involvement in their classroom.

A list of essential classroom discussion leadership skills is given in Table 3–2, and chapter 8 is devoted entirely to the development of communication skills used to

Table 3–2
Group leadership skills.

Skill	Purpose	Example
Structuring	To establish purpose and limits for discussion	"What's happening in the group now?" "How is this helping us reach our goal?"
Universalizing	To help students realize that their concerns are shared	"Who else has felt that way?"
Linking	To make verbal connections between what specific students say and feel	"Bill is very angry when his brother is late. This seems similar to what Joan and Sam feel about their sisters."
Redirecting	To promote involvement of all students in the discussion and to allow teachers to step out of the role of authority figure	"What do others think about that?" "What do you think about Pete's idea?"
Goal Disclosure	To help students become more aware of the purposes of this misbehavior	"Is it possible you want us to notice you?" "Could it be you want to show us we can't make you?"
Brainstorming	To encourage students to participate unhesitatingly in generating ideas	"Let's share all our ideas about this problem. We won't react to any suggestion until we've listed them all."
Blocking	To intervene in destructive communication	"Will you explain your feelings?" "I wonder how Stanley felt when you said that."
Summarizing	To clarify what has been said and to determine what students have learned	"What did you learn from this discussion?" "What have we decided to do about this situation?"
Task Setting and Obtaining Commitments	To develop a specific commitment for action from students	"What will you do about this problem?" "What will you do this week?"
Promoting Feedback	To help students understand how others perceive them	"I get angry when you talk so long that the rest of us don't get a turn. What do others think?" "I really like the way you help us get our game started."
Promoting Direct Interaction	To get students to speak directly to each other when appropriate	"Would you tell Joan how you feel about what she said?"
Promoting Encouragement	To invite students directly and by example to increase each other's self-esteem and self-confidence	"Thank you for helping us out." "What does Carol do that you like?" "Who has noticed Jamie's improvement?"

Source: Reproduced by permission of American Guidance Service, Publishers Building, Circle Pines, MN, from *Systematic Training for Effective Teaching* by Don Dinkmeyer, Gary D. McKay, and Don Dinkmeyer, Jr., © 1980.

encourage others to share. Some of these skills are those that teachers already use in conducting class discussions and can be transferred to their class meetings. Other skills will expand teachers' ability to draw students into the classroom meeting and to promote critical and divergent thinking, respectful interactions, and group cohesiveness. By practicing one or two new skills each week, a teacher can gradually acquire the entire set of skills. Each of the 12 group leadership skills is designed to help students become more reflective and to help them clarify their thoughts and feelings. Individuals who might find remembering and learning the 12 skills a rather imposing task may want to concentrate simply on becoming an active, or a reflective, listener (see chapter 8).

COVENANT COMPETENCIES AT THE MESOSYSTEM LEVEL

Keeping in Touch With Families

Teachers can continue to maintain communication with parents by sending them letters after the open house at the beginning of the year. Immediately following the open house, a letter can be sent that simply says, "Thanks for attending; it was a pleasure to meet you. Your responses on the survey instrument will be very helpful." You can add a few sentences about how much you are enjoying having their son or daughter in your class and the progress the class has made in becoming a respectful community of learners. Similarly, a letter expressing hope to meet soon in the future to those who were unable to attend, informing them of what was accomplished at the meeting and the accomplishments of the class, is a good way to open communication. Thereafter, occasional positive notes to the home build the relationship and establish the foundation for parental cooperation. Parents are more likely to ask their child about events at school when they are periodically reminded that the teacher takes their child's work seriously.

Notes home can be brief. They may merely repeat a positive exchange that took place between the student and teacher that day or make an observation that confirms a point made on the parental survey instrument. Some schools encourage notes home by using an attractive certificate-of-achievement format, including a picture of the school emblem or mascot and space for a brief statement. For example, a principal at McKinstry Elementary School in Waterloo, Iowa, printed an attractive memo form that included spaces for the names of the parents and their phone number. He called parents, read the message from the teacher, and offered his own congratulations before giving the memo to the student to take home. Parents appreciate calls from the main office that are not a signal of trouble.

Teachers who present their management plan at the open house may want to send a letter home to introduce the plan to parents who did not attend. Teachers who use the survey instrument during the open house might indicate that parents' suggestions at previous meetings have been incorporated into the plan.

Parent–Teacher Conferences

The parent–teacher conference has been the mainstay in programs of parental cooperation (Rotter, Robinson, & Fey, 1988; Wolf & Stephens, 1989). Many schools

Management Challenge 3–1

Caught Between Dissimilar Parental Expectations

Carla is copying other students' work and has cheated on several tests. During a meeting with Mr. and Mrs. Harrelson to discuss the problem, it becomes apparent that Carla's mother and father do not share similar views of her abilities, character traits, and responsibility for creating and solving the problem. You believe that solving the problem depends on common perceptions in these three areas.

1. Why do you believe it is essential for her parents to share similar views of Carla before embarking on a solution to this problem?
2. What would you do to secure similar perceptions of Carla and the situation in question?
3. Would you work toward a common view similar to your own? Why or why not?
4. Given a common basis for working on the problem, what role would you see for these parents? How might your expectations differ because the parents did not share similar viewpoints at the outset?

schedule one or two student-progress conference days each year. The sessions are devoted to brief descriptions of a student's adaptation to the social dimensions of schooling and his or her academic achievements. Contemporary parent–teacher conferences are student led. Students present portfolios of their work and showcase what they have learned.

During the course of the conference, the teacher draws parents into a discussion about the student's progress. The teacher may lead with questions that seek the parents' input before disclosing his or her own assessments. Playing off the parents' observations can keep the conference targeted to their interests and concerns. Some parents, however, feel less anxious and are often more talkative if the teacher and student take the lead and they are able to react to the report. Regardless of the teacher's procedure, successful conferences require conscientious preparation and communication skills.

A teacher might want to begin preparing for the conference by referring to the survey instrument completed at the open house. Discussing the survey information during the conference shows parents that the survey was not just an exercise and that the teacher has a genuine desire to provide for individual differences. This approach can increase the parents' willingness to share additional information about their child. If the teacher then shares insights about the child's attitudes and actions in school, again revealing a personal interest in their child, parents will be more accepting of and responsive to the achievement report. If the report is likely to be less favorable than the parents would like to hear, it is particularly important to use the rapport-building measures just described.

Keeping Anecdotal Records

It is beneficial to try to anticipate what parents will want to know about their child's performance in the school program. Most parents share the same anxieties and common concerns and desires for their children. Teachers can reduce the time required to prepare for conferences if these considerations are used as the backdrop for looking at children throughout the school year. One convenient way to maintain this focus is to keep a folder of work samples, test results, and anecdotal notes for each student. This may be done in addition to the student portfolio. Anecdotal notes, which are periodic entries summarizing significant incidents, are an invaluable tool for building rapport with parents and demonstrating an appreciation for a child's unique characteristics and activities.

Figure 3–2 provides a sample anecdotal entry for a student, Myrna, whose performance is being affected by the home situation. For the moment, the teacher has decided to seek a solution that can be implemented without the mother's participation. However, should the problem persist, documented by additional anecdotal entries, the teacher has the basis for initiating a parent–teacher contact. A contact at this stage is more likely to produce a jointly sponsored home–school plan because the teacher can cite specific instances of the problem and can describe the measures that have produced only modest success. Myrna's mother would surely be favorably disposed to a teacher who has taken such a personal and active interest in her daughter.

Anecdotal reports are often used to make note of the following:

❑ Marked and unexplainable changes in a student's behavior
❑ Reactions to typical classroom events such as examinations, homework assignments, and discussion periods
❑ Interactions with classmates
❑ Reactions to praise and correction
❑ Glimpses of the student in informal situations

As an observational system, the anecdotal report may serve as an account of any significant episode in the life of a student. However, it is important that these entries be divided into the four parts illustrated in Figure 3–2. Hence, the actions that occurred are kept separate from the interpretation and recommendation.

Anecdotal notes taken during a period of time provide a cross section of the student's life at school and provide clues about ways to help the student make the most of school experiences. Entries are used to report on a student's progress, note praiseworthy attainments, and select future goals. When it comes time to report to parents, a wealth of information will have been collected from the teacher's daily observations. A simplified version of this record-keeping strategy has been proposed by Levin, Nolan, and Hoffman (1985, pp. 14–15).

Anticipating Disagreements

Parents and teachers will not agree on all matters reported in a conference. They are less likely to agree when the conference is scheduled to deal with a series of

Identifying Information:

Date: <u>Friday, September 6, 2002</u>   Time: <u>9:48 a.m.</u>

Activity: <u>Prior to bell to begin class</u>

Persons Present: <u>Teacher, student, classmates</u>

Incident Observation:

Myrna entered the room and came directly to my desk. She asked if we were "still going to have the test today." I indicated that the test would be given as scheduled. As I spoke, I could see tears beginning to form in her eyes. I said, "You seem troubled." She said, "I am not ready to take the test." I said, "Sounds like we have a problem. What do you suggest?" She went on to say that she wasn't ready for the test because she had taken care of her baby brother and younger sister until her mother returned from shopping. She said after helping put the children to bed she had to help with the housework. She said she was just too tired to study after finishing household chores. I asked Myrna if she could see me after school so that we could discuss the matter further. She said she had to go home right after school so her mother could take a nap before going to work. She said she could see me during her fifth-hour study hall. I agreed to meet with her at that time. I told her to take her books to the school library and to use the time to prepare for the examination. She thanked me and left the room.

[The foregoing statement provides an objective and brief "word snapshot" of a single incident. The observations, confined to a description of the setting and the behavior of the two parties, exclude all evaluative terms.]

Interpretation:

I believe Myrna desperately wants to succeed in this class. I think she believes that acceptance by other students hinges on being an academic success. She does operate at the fringes of the group and seems to have a very tentative hold on her own sense of self-esteem. Her anxiety contributes to a tentativeness in class discussions and a reluctance to contribute unless called upon. However, her contributions are sporadic, often brief answers, so she does not draw much favorable attention to herself.

[This section includes subjective judgments. The teacher treats the situation as a social adjustment problem and begins to formulate explanations for Myrna's behavior. These tentative interpretations are used to devise an intervention that might help Myrna deal with more than the immediate problem. Another party encountering the same incident might arrive at different conclusions and other remediation procedures.]

Recommendation:

Plan some cooperative problem-solving activities in the class. Pair Myrna with Shelly G. Shelly is a mature and popular student who will be helpful while taking a personal interest in Myrna. Working with a highly visible and well-respected person may draw favorable attention to Myrna and might give her a little more self-confidence during the discussion sessions that follow small-group exercises.

[The teacher decided upon a course of action based on her interpretation of the problem. Another teacher might agree that social acceptance and self-esteem needs lie at the root of the problem but might select other means to alleviate or remediate the condition.]

Figure 3–2
Sample Anecdotal Entry

disciplinary incidents. Even if the teacher has followed all of the foregoing suggestions, some parents may be annoyed or angry about being called to school. Some of their feelings may be based on the handling of the problem, but often they are upset because the child has created problems in public settings. They may not be able to separate the two sources of their negative feelings. This condition might be exacerbated by the ripple effects of divorce, separation, and single-parent situations (see chapter 6).

Teachers may experience some frustration directed at them. This can be quite uncomfortable for teachers, and they often begin to second-guess themselves. They question whether they were right about what they shared and, even if they were right, they question the wisdom of sharing the information. This often results in teachers' adopting a nonassertive response style as a way to sidestep the possibility of conflict and confrontation. Canter and Canter (1976) noted that under these circumstances, teachers are likely to apologize for bothering the parents, downplay the problem, belittle themselves, let the parents off the hook, or downgrade the consequences of the child's behavior. In each of these instances, the teacher will probably come away from the conference feeling even more responsible for the problem and more burdened by the solutions.

A teacher well prepared for the conference and well prepared in communication skills is less likely to slip into the nonassertive response style or, worse yet, to exchange hostility with hostility. Anticipating parents' problems, parents' feelings, and the arguments that they frequently advance can be one useful form of preparation. Dreikurs, Grunwald, and Pepper (1982) developed an exhaustive list of arguments that parents use to support their position. Gordon (1974) also devised a list of problems that come up during parent–teacher conferences. These are problems that might catch teachers unprepared, leaving them stunned and helpless or defensive and hostile. Finally, a practical guide for helping parents of a misbehaving high school student can be found in Hall (1982); the guide can be readily adapted to the parent-teacher conference format.

Using the Assertive Response Style

Another useful step in preparing for the conference is provided by Canter and Canter (1976), who recommend that the teacher have a clear idea of how to present the following five points:

1. *Goals for the conference.* "I need your cooperation to deal with the following problem."
2. *Objectives for the conference.* "I specifically want you to do the following things at home."
3. *Rationale for the conference.* "I am asking you to assist me because I need your help in meeting your child's best interests."
4. *Consequences for the child if the parents do not cooperate.* "I am convinced that if you do not take steps to resolve this problem, your child will fall even further behind in his work or will be even less acceptable to his peers."
5. *Documentation for your assertions.* "I have come to these conclusions after receiving about half of the homework assignments, getting test scores at the bottom of

the class, and hearing him joke about it when I talk with him about my concerns." (pp. 161–162)

The statements following each of the five categories illustrate the assertive response style. The teacher can temper the authoritative role illustrated in the preceding list by inviting parental reactions after presenting materials for each of the five categories.

Neither party should be intimidated by the other, and the child's best interests should be the primary focus of the conference. However, when a conference is required to resolve a discipline problem—whether the problem is one of having to give constant reminders to remain seated during seatwork assignments, provide periodic reprimands for using harassing language toward peers, or deal with occasional acts of insubordination—it is imperative that the teacher and the parents develop a solution collaboratively. In addition, parents should be included in implementing the solution and kept apprised of the results of any interventions.

The assertive approach advocated by Canter and Canter (1976) is but one way to work with parents to solve children's difficulties. Some teachers may prefer a problem-solving approach that invites even greater parental involvement in defining the problem, generating and evaluating solutions, determining how to implement the chosen solution, and helping evaluate the solution's success. The guidelines for conducting a parent–teacher conference, summarized in Figure 3–3, may be a useful adjunct to the foregoing preparation suggestions.

COVENANTING WITH INDIVIDUAL STUDENTS

Positive Interactions

When students are asked to account for their motives for learning, they frequently cite their admiration and respect for a particular teacher. They express their desire to please this individual and often attribute their effort to an affinity for the teacher rather than for the subject. They report never caring much for history until they took it from Mr. Lincoln. Such students' commitments to learning are founded on a relationship that means something to them. The relationship provides both the inspiration and an incentive to learn.

In *The Identity Society,* Glasser (1972) highlighted the powerful impact of personal relationships on an individual's aspirations and achievements. According to Glasser, today's society is role oriented rather than goal oriented. In a role-oriented, or identity, society, people place more importance on being respected as human beings than on being valued for what they can do. They believe that a person's worth should not be measured by accomplishments but by that person's membership in the human family. An individual can be somebody without proving his or her worth in the marketplace. In other words, the student is saying, "I can insist that I have a right to respect and dignity apart from what I am able to do. As a student, I want to be treated kindly and considerately, not just because I fulfill teachers' and institutional expectations, but because every person has a right to such treatment.

The situation is warmer and easier when the teacher sits away from his or her desk (the symbol of authority or position). Parents can also be put at ease if the meeting takes place in a small conference room rather than a classroom, if possible. If such a room is not available, the teacher could arrange chairs at the back of the room for a more informal setting.

Don't rush the interview. It will probably take time for parents to relax, tell what they are really worried about, and express their real feelings and fears.

Be willing to agree with parents whenever possible. When the answer must be no, take a long time to say it, and say it softly, without hostility. When there is agreement on a hundred small things, it is easier for both parent and teacher to state their differences frankly if a difference of opinion does exist.

Listen with enthusiasm. Parents should be encouraged to do the talking, telling, and suggestion making. Give parents a chance to "sound off," especially if they are angry or upset. After they have let off steam, you will find it easier to discuss the problem calmly. Try not to argue with them. Control your facial expressions of disapproval or anger. A wince or frown at a parent's comment or revelation may embarrass him or her or put him or her on guard.

Examine your own emotional reaction to criticism. Do you dislike people who give you new ideas or who disagree with you? If so, you may be getting this message across in subtle, unspoken ways.

Decide in advance what is to be discussed during the parent conference. Assemble a folder of the student's work, and jot down a checklist of the various problems to talk about.

Use the simplest and clearest words you can find to explain what you and their child do in school. Gear your talk to the parents' interests and avoid "pedagese" at all costs. At the same time, don't talk down to parents. They are not children, and they resent being treated as such.

Don't let comments about other children creep into the conversation. Avoid making comparisons with the student's brothers and sisters or with his or her classmates.

Provide parents with at least one action step—one thing they can do at home to help their child overcome a particular problem you've been discussing. Help them understand that their child's success in school must be a joint project of home and school.

Begin and end the conference with a positive and encouraging comment about the child and his or her school activities.

Don't take notes while talking with parents. They may feel intimidated and afraid to speak up.

Don't forget the follow-up. The first step is to write down the gist of what was discussed, so you won't forget it when you are writing the child's next report card or when your are preparing for the next parent conference.

Figure 3–3
Guidelines for Conducting a Parent–Teacher Conference (Author Unknown)

Management Challenge 3–2
Role Versus Goal Conflicts

According to Glasser (1976), role-oriented students personalize everything. When Bill gets a failing grade on a math paper, he regards it as a statement about himself. His teacher insists that the grade merely indicates the quality of his work in mathematics, but Bill insists it reveals a personal shortcoming or is at least a judgment about his worth.

Many teachers claim that the majority of students, despite Glasser's observations to the contrary, are still goal oriented. These students work hard and strive to get good grades. They would like to be favorably regarded by their teachers and their peers, but their sense of self-worth is tied to accomplishment rather than acceptance.

Glasser would undoubtedly agree with this observation but with a disclaimer: These students already have a role. They see themselves as good students, a role reinforced at home and by their success in school. They go for goals because they have found a role. However, what about individuals who lack the home and school support for the role of student? They need first to feel worthwhile as human beings. Then they can muster the courage to take the risks inevitably associated with learning.

1. What side of this argument makes the most sense to you? Why?
2. Can you envision an instance or cite a particular case in which a student personalized a teacher's judgments about his or her work and concluded that he or she was inadequate and unworthy of respect? How might this individual express disappointment and discouragement? Are these behaviors ordinarily treated as disciplinary problems? Should they be?
3. Assuming role precedes goal, how would you go about helping a student whose role is that of a failure and whose goal is to make you feel as miserable as he or she does?

What I am is the true measure of my worth; what I can do, the measure of my generosity of spirit."

Teachers can do a number of things to communicate to individual students that they are respected for who they are rather than for what they do. Respectful communication competencies are described in chapter 8 and are to be used with all students. Some students require that teachers employ additional competencies. Students who are diverse in terms of race, ethnicity, class or socioeconomic status, relocation status, and challenging conditions deserve particular attention during relationship-building processes with the teacher. Chapter 8 includes information that will help teachers be more sensitive to such students' needs. In addition, teachers should access support services (e.g., guidance, school psychology, school social work) for assistance in meeting the needs of diverse students as soon as possible at the beginning of the year.

Students want teachers to draw on their interests as the teachers make curriculum decisions.

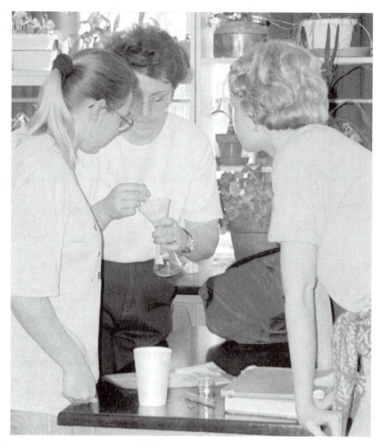

Teachers can focus on accomplishing the following tasks with the entire class or with individuals who need special attention:

❏ Confer with students when deciding about the work to be done, setting up a schedule for doing it, and establishing quality standards.
❏ Model the job and seek student input about better ways to achieve a quality product.
❏ Invite students to evaluate their own work for quality.
❏ Provide the tools and setting that promote self-confidence and congeniality among students.

In contrast, teachers who do not attend to relationship management do not consult students about what work needs to be done. Instead, such teachers tell students what to do, seldom ask them how things might be done better, set the standards for quality, evaluate student work without ever involving them in the process, and rely heavily on coercion to secure compliance.

Clearly, when school personnel focus on building relationships, students will feel good about school and about themselves.

Relationship Management as a Solution to Behavioral Problems

Teachers recognize that a renewed focus on relationship building can help resolve difficulties of individual students (Glasser, 1990). Thus, teachers sometimes have to set aside their emphasis on getting assignments turned in and concentrate on regaining the trust and confidence of the student. They realize that what a student needs most is reaffirmation as a person, and so they spend time establishing a relationship that will enable the student to disclose fears and vent frustrations. One method of strengthening relationships and resolving classroom difficulties is through a series of teacher-led problem-solving meetings with the student. This may or may not include the parent, but it is more often a good decision to include the parent who will support the school-based plan by carrying out a similar plan at home. The teacher and parents may want to meet with the problem-solving team assigned to the building. This is an important consideration when the teacher, parents, and student have already tried solutions without success.

Problem Solving with Individual Students

When students choose to dissociate themselves from learning, the problem is often attributed to a lack of motivation. It is reasoned that given a sufficiently interesting environment and a reasonably challenging task, students will choose to participate in classroom activities. However, what about students who persist in actively disrupting the class? The teacher cannot dismiss behavior that severely disrupts the learning environment. In such instances, involvement with the student as a person is only the first step in a problem-solving process designed to help the student select more responsible behavior.

Chapter 8 presents a planned discussion format that teachers may wish to use. A more involved problem-solving procedure was developed by Glasser (1977). Drawing on concepts from his book *Reality Therapy* (1965), he described a problem-solving process that has produced good results with a wide variety of discipline problems. The following discussion of his ideas focuses on problem-solving techniques.

According to Glasser (1969), discipline problems are simply irresponsible choices. Their recurrence can be reduced by helping students participate in a self-development program of gradual growth toward more responsible behavior. As students assume a more responsible role, they become less of a problem to themselves and to others. How does the teacher go about helping students become personally and socially responsible individuals? What can be done when students make choices that reveal an irresponsible attitude toward themselves or others? Each step in Glasser's (1977) eight-step problem-solving conference strategy, discussed next, illustrates the techniques that make it work. Note that the process is designed to help students regain control.

Management Challenge 3–3

Using Glasser's Problem-Solving Process

Four problem vignettes are listed next. Demonstrate your ability to use the first five steps of Glasser's problem-solving strategy by role-playing a solution for any one of these four problems. Use as the student a class member familiar with the problem-solving process. Then find a person who is not familiar with the strategy and role-play another of the four problems. After each role-playing episode, make a record of your experience, noting the ways that the strategy worked, the difficulties you encountered, and your feelings about the technique. Be prepared to describe what you liked and did not like about this approach to solving behavioral problems.

The Norming Stage: Instructional Concerns

It is the second semester of the year and Jules appears to be giving up. He dawdles on his assignments, if he makes any attempt at all. He seems capable because he can provide correct work if called upon in class, but he thinks of himself as not a very good student. During the first portion of the school year, he performed better, but later he began claiming that the work was too hard. He seems loathe to accept responsibilities. You want to hold a problem-solving meeting with him. You anticipate that he will shrug you off and say that he cannot do the work.

The Storming Stage: Aggressive Behavior Concerns

A teacher and some students tell you that during lunch break from your class they saw Lizzie leading some of her classmates in harassing Jennie. Lizzie is beginning to look like a bully because she has done things like this several times before. The students will soon return for the second half of the class.

The Forming Stage: Hyperactive Behavior Concerns

Jed is extremely active, more active than any student you have ever had in your classroom. He cannot remain in his chair or keep his shoes on. He slides around the room in his stocking feet to sharpen his pencil, get a drink, and a zillion other things—it seems. Literature is just ending and you direct the students to line up to go to PE. Jed zooms for the line and runs into several of his classmates, who fall into one another, knocking their heads together. Tears flow, along with accusations. It seems everyone is immediately upset with Jed and one girl pushes him back. As you head for the scene, Jed turns to you and earnestly tells you that he didn't mean to run into people, he was just trying to get in line.

The Storming Stage: Peer Rejection Concerns

Judgie is not liked very well by her classmates. Today she has been trying to get some of the girls to play a particular game with her during free time. She repeatedly asks them to stop what they are doing and join her in a board game. She wears the girls down, but instead of playing with her, they pick up the pieces of the game and head for the corner to play among themselves. Not easily daunted, Judgie follows them and insists that they let her play. Although it is difficult to ignore her determined attempts, the girls continue to play while she hangs around the outskirts and advises her peers how to play when it is their turn. In spite of their obvious rejection of her as a partner in play, she persists in staying close by.

Step 1: Get Involved with the Student.   The teacher should be friendly toward the student, express concern for him or her as a person, and express the belief that things can be worked out. The teacher works at building a relationship with the student. Only when the teacher has a meaningful relationship with the student can the teacher influence the student in making changes. Students are much more willing to look at what they are doing and make changes when a teacher accepts them for who they are.

Glasser emphasized the importance of helping students get attuned to the reality of the world around them. Their pain and suffering can be alleviated only by first helping them compare the reality of what they actually do with what they say they do. They must see how they delude themselves and the price they pay for evading responsibility.

The teacher creates this readiness to face irresponsible choices by asking the student, "What is it you want?" or "What is it you need?" These questions call up the images that are guiding student choices. The teacher must show an interest in the things that matter to the student.

When teachers at North Cedar Elementary School in Cedar Falls, Iowa, asked students, "What do you really want to happen at school?" the responses included the following points:

Owning my problems	Being responsible for my own actions
Being noticed	Asking for help when needed
Winning	Success
Losing respectfully	Feeling good about myself
Being a leader	Self-control
Being a follower	Confident decisions
Following rules	Self-reliance
Being worthwhile	Alternatives
Being understood	More or better friendships
Understanding others	Acceptance
Talking respectfully	

Teachers found that helping students reflect on their goals contributed to an understanding of the choices that students made, choices that sometimes produced failure or, at least, ineffectual behavior.

Step 2: Deal with the Student's Present Behavior.   The teacher must avoid being a historian who talks about how many times the student has transgressed in the past. A student who has just behaved irresponsibly needs to acknowledge the infraction before there can be any change in behavior. Reminding a student of past transgressions is more likely to produce regret and promises than to result in responsible behavior. When these reminders are experienced as criticism, the student is likely to be more defensive and regain control by justification rather than change.

Teachers take this second step by asking the student, "What were you doing?" Why should the student give the teacher an honest answer? Step 1 laid the groundwork for honesty. Facing reality honestly is easier when you trust another and trust yourself. Under some circumstances, a student might refuse to accept responsibility for a transgression by assuming an air of silence or by hiding behind an "I don't know." In such instances, the teacher can respond, "I thought I saw you [name the behavior]" or "It was reported to me that you [name the behavior]. Unless you indicate otherwise, we will proceed as though this is how you acted."

Generally, students will not hedge when teachers ask what they were doing. The "doing" component of a total behavior is the easiest to accept responsibility for. However, they will hedge and make excuses if asked, "Why did you do it?" Students should never get the idea that they can be irresponsible if they can produce a good justification for being so. The sooner students learn what they are choosing and that they are responsible for their choices, the better.

For example, a teacher catches Don shoving John and disciplines Don, who protests that John shoved him first. Don needs to learn that shoving back was only one way to respond to a provocation. He is responsible for the behavioral choice of shoving back. Don needs to learn other ways to deal with combative behavior at school, but he must also be prepared to accept the consequences that attend unwise choices.

Step 3: Get the Student to Make a Value Judgment About the Behavior. Once students know what they are choosing, it is time to get them to make a judgment about their choice: "Is what you did against the rules?" When rules have been explicitly stated and are consistently enforced, students know whether they have violated a rule. Sometimes the "doing" behavior consists of doing little or nothing. Indifference, rather than disobedience, is the problem. "Are you doing as well as you would like?" might be the value judgment question in this case.

Some students believe that rules are made to be broken or that rules are for others. The teacher may want to establish responsibility by asking, "Is what you did helping you?" Quite often, the student will recall the short-term benefits and respond in the affirmative. When asked, "Is what you did helpful to others?" students are not likely to be so blatantly selfish. They must acknowledge that their behavior is self-serving and that it disregards the general welfare. This is an important step toward responsible problem solving.

Students who are called on to make a value judgment begin to see the social and long-range ramifications of their choices. They begin to realize that what seemed like a perfectly reasonable thing to do has repercussions that were not immediately apparent. They begin to sense that the power to change resides within them. Without a value judgment, students have no need to change. As long as they believe that they made the right choice, that the choice is a consistent expression of their values, there is little reason to change.

When students persist in defending their behavior or refuse to make a value judgment, the teacher might say, "I don't see how your behavior is helping" or "I am having trouble seeing how what you are doing is helping. This is the way it looks to me." Without judging or moralizing, the teacher can provide a value stance that students can examine. The teacher does not impose a value, only offers another way of looking at the behavior and its consequences. Generally, students are prepared to take the next step.

Step 4: Help the Student Develop a Plan to Change the Behavior. The value judgment sets the stage for making things better. The student's internal dialogue might go like this: "If the behavior that got me in trouble isn't really helping me and isn't helping others, I should begin to think about other alternatives. What have I got to lose? My teacher seems to believe we can work this out together. Maybe things don't have to be the way they have been. There might just be a way to work things out."

The teacher once again translates the problem-solving process into pertinent questions, such as "What kind of plan can you make to follow our rules? What kind of plan can you make to make things better for you and for others?" Basically, the teacher is asking, "May I help you work things out?" because this step is designed to help students regain control of their lives. The plan is a management solution that puts the student in charge. Rather than offering solutions, the teacher asks questions to help students identify and judge the effectiveness of their behavioral choices. The teacher is asking the student to come up with a better way, not a perfect way, to act. Feeling better and thinking better are by-products of the process.

Students, often preoccupied with the bad behavior, tend to focus on stopping something rather than doing something. Thus, the teacher must stress building a plan that concentrates on constructive or responsible behavior. "What will I see you doing when you are behaving responsibly?" keeps the conference targeted on positive alternatives. The plan should be simple; it can be extended and expanded after the student has had some initial success. Plans that provide for increments of progress are best. Keep in mind that the need to love and be loved as well as the need to feel worthwhile must find expression in the plan.

Some students find plan building difficult and are unable to suggest ways to deal with a problem. In this case, the teacher might say, "Here are some ways I have seen other students, in similar circumstances, deal with this problem. Do you think any of these solutions might work for you?" The suggestions are not the teacher's, so the student need not feel obliged to accept any of them. The teacher might just omit an obvious option, thereby leaving an opening for the student to offer another alternative. Helping the student evaluate the options and look at advantages and disadvantages of each choice increases the chances of a suitable selection and deepens commitment to see it through. The student gains strength and confidence as one workable option emerges. This final option should not, however, depend on the cooperation of a third party, a feature that decreases the student's control and can provide an excuse for not following the plan.

Step 5: Get a Commitment from the Student to Stick to the Plan.   The plan might be considered a contractual arrangement because both parties have something at stake. Students find the contract a secure reference point; they know more precisely what needs to be done and how to go about doing it. Resolve can still be a problem, but it is easier to muster when the direction and destination are clear.

Teachers concerned with the matter of resolve might ask the student, "Do you think you have a workable plan? Are you going to be able to see it through?" These questions also give the student an opportunity to discuss any misgivings or reservations about the plan. It's a good idea to clear up second thoughts before beginning.

There are no guarantees or assurances the plan will work. Nonetheless, seal the agreement with a handshake or a signature on a written contract. The agreement is more a pledge than an obligation, but a handshake or a signature may prompt a more earnest effort. The student should leave the conference feeling that this is serious business.

Having reached an agreement, the student should get started immediately. The teacher may agree to check periodically with the student to see how the plan is working. There should generally be some objectives en route and some reinforcement points in a plan that cover a period of several days or weeks.

Step 6: Do Not Accept Excuses for a Failed Plan.   Excuses are used to absolve a person from blame, to find fault elsewhere. The teacher is trying to teach students that they can take control of their own destiny, that they can learn to manage their affairs by creating conditions and managing choices that increase the likelihood of attaining their own goals.

Teachers are partial to excuses. We know how difficult it is to be responsible; we are well aware of our own indiscretions. "Let's get on with living, just don't let this happen again" is a convenient way to dismiss a problem and hope it will go away. It seldom does go away; it merely reappears in another form. Therefore, it is important to be tough minded in Step 6 and to accept nothing short of another plan better designed to achieve the original objective. The teacher's attitude should be "I am disappointed, but not discouraged. You blew it today—how about tomorrow? What kind of plan can you make to live within the rules, to make things better for you and for others?" Students should learn that in this classroom incompetent "doing" behaviors will not be accepted.

One other cautionary note. Just as teachers may ask "why" when students misbehave, they are also inclined to ask "why" when students fail to keep the plan. A teacher should not be concerned with why but with "what" the student is going to do and "how" he or she is going to go about doing it. Even valid excuses should not be considered. Instead, the focus should be on the objectionable behavior and beginning the process anew. Accepting anything less than good behavior is a disservice to the student.

Step 7: Do Not Punish or Criticize the Student for Broken Plans. Teachers should not punish or criticize the student for failing to follow the plan, but they also should not interfere with reasonable consequences. This advice might be difficult to follow. Teachers may be inclined to be punitive when students fail to live up to their agreements and responsibilities. The plan, possibly the result of a negotiated settlement, took time to develop, and the teacher expects a good-faith response. In the absence of responsible follow-through, some teachers are likely to look for ways to seek amends or secure compliance through coercive measures. These measures, which represent a teacher's efforts to gain control, contribute to the student's feeling a loss of control. This divisive dilemma poses a problem for both parties. Particularly during adolescence, punitive controls "fuel the fires of rebellion" (Nelsen & Lott, 1990).

Some teachers have found Dreikurs et al.'s (1982) concept of logical and natural consequences to be a useful way to think about and resolve this dilemma. *Natural consequences* are after effects that occur without the intervention of a second party. The consequence is delivered impartially in accord with the setting in which the behavior occurs. A student running down the hall, in violation of a school rule, stumbles and falls headlong down a stairway. Pain and bruises are a natural consequence of the student's choice to run on a recently waxed floor. Another student might be caught taking two stairs at a time in a last-minute dash to a class. A teacher observing the rule violation politely asks the student to come back down the stairs and walk up them. The delay results in the student's being tardy for the next class and automatically receiving a time owed.

The two teachers' interventions in the latter example, one requiring the appropriate behavior and the other imposing a penalty for interrupting the class by being a late arrival, are logical consequences. They are related, respectful, and reasonable (Nelsen, 1985). In the first intervention, the student was asked to negotiate the stairs properly (related), was confronted with the violation politely (respectful), and was asked only to engage in a behavior that served the student's best interests and those of others on the same stairway (reasonable). Similarly, making up lost time, the second intervention, is a fair exchange of a similar commodity (time) and does not embarrass the latecomer.

When we speak of no punishment, we mean no external imposition of pain to rectify a wrong or to deter the repetition of the unacceptable behavior. Proponents of natural and logical consequences point to the detrimental by-products of this use of aversive control (Dinkmeyer et al., 1980; Dreikurs et al., 1982; Nelsen, 1987). They contend that punishment does not set easy with some students, who may choose to express their discontent through passivity (tardiness, truancy, inattention, restlessness, forgetfulness) or with aggression (impertinence, rudeness, defiance, profanity, physical attacks, and vandalism). Although these behaviors are self-defeating, they may seem reasonable to someone who has lost control and wishes to strike back at the person whom they perceive as the cause of their predicament. Building a new plan keeps the focus where it belongs—on students' irresponsible choices and how students can choose more responsible alternatives.

Students can be taught to use the questions that compose the problem-solving sequence; a form can be prepared to guide their thinking and writing. "What is it you want? What were you doing? Is what you are doing helping you and others? What kind of a plan can you make to make things better for you and others?" After looking at the plan, the teacher might ask, "Is this plan going to get you what you want? Tell me this is going to get you what you want." Then go for the commitment: "If this is going to get you what you want, are you going to be able to do it? Are you going to be able to follow through with this plan so that you can get what you want?"

Mutual agreement on the "terms" of the contract allows students to return to the group in good standing. The teacher's attitude should be one of "We cannot accept what you are doing; let's look at your behavior and make another plan within the rules." The teacher should not criticize, because criticism focuses on failure. Building a plan that has a good chance of succeeding is a good investment in the student and in the class.

Step 8: Never Give Up—Return to Step 3 and Start Again.   Because so many well-intentioned plans fail, teachers are often tempted to give up. Problem solving can seem like an exercise in futility. Students can come up with good plans because they know what to do, but they often lack the desire or determination to follow through. As with people who try to stop smoking, students know what they should do, but the substitutes are not equally satisfying.

Some students expect the teacher to give up. Why not? They have often given up on themselves, and other teachers and adults have given up on them. However, to have a chance to succeed, students must believe that their teachers will never give up. Teachers must be viewed as persons who are not easily discouraged, although they are occasionally exasperated. They must assume the stance "If this was a good plan, let's get it done."

Summary of Problem Solving.   Our attention has been devoted to the development of social responsibility and to the procedures that decrease loneliness, isolation, and failure. Less intense "feeling" behaviors can contribute to more manageable, stable, and rational "doing" behaviors. The student experiences greater control and confidence, which gradually help increase his or her repertoire of "doing" behaviors.

OBSERVATION OF A TEACHER'S COVENANT MANAGEMENT

There is no better way to learn about covenant management than to watch a teacher in action. Through a field-placement experience or some other means, ask a teacher for the opportunity to observe in the classroom. In Table 3–3 there is a list of covenant management indicators that can be used to structure your classroom

Table 3–3
Covenant management observation protocol.

Climate Characteristics

1. Class members are invited to participate in goal setting.
2. Freedoms are expressed within explicitly stated and consistently enforced limits.
3. Students choose from a wide variety of activities to achieve common goals.
4. Students progress, as much as possible, according to individual interests and abilities.
5. Group cohesiveness and cooperation are stressed over competition.
6. Democratic practices are used to maintain order and secure compliance with reasonable limits.

Relationship Qualities

7. Teacher and students can be direct and honest with one another.
8. All members of the group feel they are valued by the other members.
9. There is a sense of interdependence; common bonds define group expectations.
10. Each person is encouraged to make the most of unique talents and interests.
11. No one individual's needs are met without regard for the needs of others.
12. Faith and trust are built from a sense of community and shared purpose.

Communication Characteristics

13. Conversations are positive, constructive, and aimed at understanding one another's point of view.
14. Blame-free messages, "I" messages, are used to convey a teacher's emotional reactions to a student's objectionable behavior.
15. Corrective measures are not accompanied by sarcasm and ridicule.
16. Disciplinary actions are aimed at the situation, not at the student's personality or character.
17. Communications safeguard self-esteem, convey respect, and encourage students to take charge of their lives.
18. Appreciation is expressed as descriptive rather than evaluative praise.
19. Diagnostic and prognostic statements that classify and categorize students are avoided.
20. Economical messages, oral and nonoral, are used to deal with minor incidents.

Forms of Assistance

21. "Why?" questions, which evoke defensiveness and deceit, are avoided.
22. The temptation to reassure students or offer them solutions to their problems is resisted.
23. Problem-solving methods are used to place power in the hands of students and increase their sense of self-efficacy.
24. Reflective listening is substituted for giving advise so students can formulate solutions to their problems.
25. Class meetings are used to provide students an opportunity to examine the ideas and feelings that influence value judgements and decisions as well as the ways chosen to fulfil them.
26. Building confidence and fostering involvement are viewed as primary and enabling objectives.
27. Lesson content and activities help students link school and life outside of school.
28. Duties and responsibilities are delegated in such a way that all students succeed and become fully functioning members of the class.

observation. Try to observe every criterion on the list. If any cannot be observed, ask the teacher for the opportunity to conduct a brief interview and ask about the remaining items.

On the basis of what you learned from your observation, the text, class discussions, and your own real-life experiences, construct your own covenant management plan. Appendix A offers a form that can be used for this purpose.

CONCLUSION

Covenant management is concerned with facilitating trusting, respectful relationships that result in caring classroom communities. Lack of acceptance of others and of self is at the root of many behavioral problems. Students who fail at school, or whose successes do not match their own expectations, are likely to harbor feelings of inadequacy. Consequently, many of these students choose to behave irresponsibly, although such behavior can further alienate them and eventually contribute to a sense of hopelessness and despair.

To help such students, teachers can look for role-oriented solutions. Class meetings, by providing all students with an opportunity to participate in meaningful problem resolution, can foster student involvement in school and with one another. School becomes a good place to be; students feel good about themselves and about one another.

Collaboration with families continues throughout the year and supports trusting relationships in the classroom. Letters, notes, and telephone contacts continue the pattern of collaborative communication. Developing competencies for conducting successful parent–teacher conferences continues to strengthen covenant management.

Class meetings will not be a preventive measure for all behavioral problems. Glasser's eight-step problem-solving process can be used to teach individual students responsibility during problem solving. Problem-solving meetings can involve a host of individuals as deemed necessary by the teacher, parents, and student.

SUPPLEMENTARY QUESTIONS

1. Consider how two teachers—one you liked and one you disliked—approached the management of the unique characteristics of groups. How have their approaches shaped your experience as a student?

2. During any one of the four developmental stages of group formation, what have you observed teachers doing or neglecting to do that had a beneficial or a detrimental effect on esprit de corps?

3. Allowing children and young adults to assume increasing responsibility for their own behavior requires considerable trust from adults.
   a. Why might teachers be reluctant to entrust students with the freedom to become responsible persons?
   b. What are the characteristic beliefs and behaviors of adults who trust students to make responsible choices?

4. Some people would criticize Glasser's problem-solving solution for correcting discipline problems as impractical because it requires too much time. When used to deal with minor discipline problems, it is too mechanical; that is, using standard questions to implement Steps 2, 3, 4, and 5 becomes repetitive. How would you answer these two charges?

SUPPLEMENTARY PROJECTS

1. Ask a couple of teachers to describe the personality characteristics of their classroom group. Then ask them to speculate about how the group developed this personality. Keep a record of their remarks, then list them as examples of the three role categories presented in Figure 3–1.
2. Prepare a brief description of each of the four stages a group undergoes during a school year. Ask a veteran teacher whether these stages provide a realistic way to think about management priorities during the course of a school year.
3. Most prospective and veteran teachers have had experience with some type of extracurricular activity, whether a club, an athletic team, a dramatic production, or a musical program. Prepare a paper describing the way in which the developmental growth stages discussed in this chapter can help a person understand the psychosocial formation of extracurricular groups.
4. Interview several teachers about "breakthrough" experiences with hard-to-reach students. Prepare a paper summarizing the sequence of events or the single episode that made a difference. Try to abstract some principles of human interaction and use them to make recommendations for dealing with difficult students.

REFERENCES

Allington, R. (1991). Children who find learning to read difficult: School responses to diversity. In E. Hiebert (Ed.), *Literacy for a diverse society* (pp. 237–252). New York: Teachers College Press.

Canter, L., & Canter, M. (1976). *Assertive discipline: A take charge approach for today's educator.* Los Angeles: Lee Canter and Associates.

Dinkmeyer, D., McKay, G. D., & Dinkmeyer, D., Jr. (1980). *Systematic training for effective teaching.* Circle Pines, MN: American Guidance Service.

Dreikurs, R., Grunwald, B. B., & Pepper, F. C. (1982). *Maintaining sanity in the classroom: Classroom management techniques* (2nd ed.). New York: Harper & Row.

Dreikurs, R., & Soltz, V. (1964). *Children: The challenge.* New York: Hawthorne.

Educator Training Center. (n.d.). *Resource book for class discussion.* Long Beach, CA: Author.

Gazda, G. (1973). *Human relations development: A manual for educators.* Boston: Allyn & Bacon.

Glasser, W. (1965). *Reality therapy.* New York: Perennial Library, Harper & Row.

Glasser, W. (1969). *Schools without failure.* New York: Perennial Library, Harper & Row.

Glasser, W. (1972). *The identity society.* New York: Perennial Library, Harper & Row.

Glasser, W. (1977). Ten steps to good discipline. *Today's Education, 66*(4), 61–63.

Glasser, W. (1990). *The quality school: Managing students without coercion.* New York: Harper & Row.

Gordon, T. (1974). *TET: Teacher effectiveness training.* New York: David McKay Company.

Hall, J. P. (1982). A parent guide for the misbehaving high school student. *Adolescence, 17,* 369–385.

Johnson, L. V., & Bany, M. A. (1970). *Classroom management: Theory and skill training.* New York: Macmillan.

Jones, M., & Wheatley, J. (1990). Gender differences in student–teacher interaction. *Journal of Research in Science Teaching, 27,* 861–874.

Koch, M. S. (1988). Resolving disputes: Students can do it better. *National Association of Secondary School Principals Bulletin, 72*(504), 16–18.

Leacock, E. (1969). *Teaching and learning in city schools.* New York: Basic Books.

Levin, J., Nolan, J., & Hoffman, N. (1985). A strategy for classroom resolution of chronic discipline problems. *National Association of Secondary School Principals Bulletin, 69,* 11–17.

Mauer, R. E.(1985). *Elementary discipline handbook: Solutions for the k–8 teacher.* West Nyack, NY: Center for Applied Research in Education.

Nelsen, J. (1985). The three R's of logical consequences, the three R's of punishment, and the six steps for winning children over. *Individual Psychology, 41*(2), 161–165.

Nelsen, J. (1987). *Positive discipline.* New York: Ballantine Books.

Nelsen, J., & Lott, L. (1990). *I'm on your side: Resolving conflict with your teenage son or daughter* (Chap. 8). Rocklin, CA: Prima Publishing & Communications.

Ooms, T., & Hara, S. (1991). *The family–school partnership: A critical component of school reform.* Washington, DC: The Family Impact Seminar.

Opotow, S. (1991). Adolescent peer conflicts: Implications for students and for schools. *Education and Urban Society, 23*(4), 416–441.

Ross, S. I., & Jackson, J. M. (1991). Teachers' expectations for Black males' and Black females' academic achievement. *Personality and Social Psychology Bulletin, 17,* 78–82.

Rotter, J., Robinson, E., & Fey, M. (1988). *Parent–teacher conferences* (2nd ed.). Washington, DC: National Education Association.

Wolf, J. S., & Stephens, T. M. (1989). Parent/teacher conferences: Finding common ground. *Educational Leadership, 47,* 28–31.

CHAPTER 4

Competencies in Conduct Management: Positive Behavior Choices

DEFINITION OF TERMS
CONDUCT MANAGEMENT
POSITIVE BEHAVIOR SUPPORT
FUNCTIONAL BEHAVIORAL ASSESSMENT

Competencies in Conduct Management

LEGAL COMPETENCIES
DUE PROCESS
CORPORAL PUNISHMENT
ASSAULT AND BATTERY
DETENTION, SUSPENSION,
    AND EXPULSION
SEARCH AND SEIZURE

DIRECTIVE COMPETENCIES
RATIONALE
BASIC PLAN
    Acknowledging Responsible
        Behaviors
    Correcting Irresponsible
        Behaviors
        Ignoring
        Proximity Control
        Gentle Oral Reprimands
        Oral Cues and Warnings
        Delaying
        Preferential Seating
        Time Owed
        Time-Out
        Parental Contact
        Behavioral Contract
    Outside Classroom Limits
    Choosing and Using
        Consequences

SEVERE BEHAVIOR COMPETENCIES
TEACHING DESIRED BEHAVIORS
REINFORCEMENT SYSTEMS
    Implementation
    Example
SELF-MANAGEMENT
OBTAINING ASSISTANCE

An understanding of the material in this chapter will help you do the following:

❏ Commit to sustaining a school environment characterized by positive behavior supports.
❏ Conduct simple functional behavioral assessments that guide intervention selection.
❏ Distinguish between minor and moderate/severe behavior concerns and select appropriate interventions.
❏ Develop a home–school contract that combines behavioral expectations and consequences in both settings.
❏ Access building assistance teams to resolve behavior concerns.
❏ Monitor progress in order to evaluate the success of a behavior management plan.

DEFINITION: CONDUCT MANAGEMENT

Conduct management is the facilitation of positive social–emotional–behavioral growth of children. It requires the following:

❏ School and classroom environments characterized by positive behavior support
❏ Teachers equipped with directive competencies for assisting students in correcting day-to-day minor misbehaviors
❏ Building assistance teams with severe behavior competencies to help students replace significantly negative and chronic behaviors that get them into trouble at home, at school, and in the community

Positive behavior support (*PBS*) traditionally was a systems-level model for promoting the social, behavioral, emotional, and academic growth of students with disabilities. Research of the model supported a shift to applying PBS to all school systems in order to reach the goal of social and academic success for all students. It is a range of systemic and individualized strategies for facilitating social and learning results and preventing problem behavior (Sugai & Horner, 2001). PBS typically consists of four key elements:

1. The facilitation of social–emotional–behavioral and academic growth is founded on the science of human behavior and the belief that all children can be successful.
2. Research-based interventions or those that use data, from functional behavioral assessments, are used to construct learning environments that are (a) supportive of appropriate behavior, (b) less likely to trigger problem behavior, and (c) more likely to teach adaptive behavior.
3. Behavior change must be socially significant.
4. Attention is on the entire system, and practices are prevention based.

The goal of PBS is to help schools and families design positive, effective learning environments. Although the name *PBS* may be new to you, the conceptual model and its applications should sound familiar. Everything you have read in the text so far has been focused on creating PBS environments for students. For additional study of PBS, Table 4–1 includes a list of web sites and journal articles focused on PBS and functional behavioral assessment.

PBS efforts call for the use of *functional behavioral assessment (FBA)*. FBA is a systematic process for gathering information that helps determine the relationship between a student's problem behavior and his or her environment. It is possible to identify events in the environment that maintain problem behavior and, subsequently, to design a support plan for the student or students. FBA methods include reviewing student records, interviewing students and teachers, and conducting direct observations of student behaviors. FBA methods range from highly precise

Table 4–1
Positive behavior support resources.

Web Sites

www.pbis.org	OSEP Technical Assistance Center on Positive Behavioral Interventions and Supports
www.colorado.edu/cspv	Center for the Study and Prevention of Violence
www.uoregon.edu/~ivdb	Institute on Violence and Destructive Behavior
www.oslc.org	Oregon Social Learning Center
www.ori.org	Oregon Research Institute
www.edjj.org	The National Center on Education, Disability and Juvenile Justice
www.air.org/cecp	Center for Effective Collaboration and Practice
www.nichcy.org	The National Information Center for Children and Youth with Disabilities
www.ideapractices.org	The IDEA Local Implementation by Local Administrators (ILIAD) and The Associations of Service Providers Implementing IDEA Reforms in Education (ASPIIRE)
www.fape.org	Family and Advocates Partnership for Education
www.ideapolicy.org	The Policymaker Partnership for Implementing IDEA

Journal Articles

Horner, R., & Sugai, G. (2000). School-wide behavior support: An emerging initiative [Special issue]. *Journal of Positive Behavioral Interventions, 2,* 231–233.

Nelson, J. R. (1996). Designing schools to meet the needs of students who exhibit disruptive behavior. *Journal of Emotional and Behavioral Disorders, 4,* 147–161.

Sugai, G., & Horner, R. (1999). Discipline and behavioral support: Preferred processes and practices. *Effective School Practices, 17*(4), 10–22.

Sugai, G., Lewis-Palmer, T., & Hagan-Burke, S. (1999–2000). Overview of the functional behavior assessment process. *Exceptionality, 8,* 149–160.

techniques to relatively informal ones. Precise techniques can be conducted by support personnel; informal ones can be conducted by teachers.

In fact, the problem-solving process demonstrated in chapter 1 constituted an informal FBA and is the recommended FBA process for teachers. Problem solving includes all the important features of an FBA: identify the problem by reflecting on the events or history of the student; define the problem by recalling the events right before the problem occurred and the events immediately following the occurrence; form your best-guess hypothesis as an *if–then* statement; select an intervention that can test your hypothesis; graph the baseline information about the problem, set a goal, and implement the strategy; and measure progress. If the student is progressing toward the goal, your hypothesis and solution were good choices. If the student is not making progress, cycle through the problem-solving process again.

COMPETENCIES IN CONDUCT MANAGEMENT

What teachers believe about the basic nature of people affects their conduct management. Before continuing in this chapter, consider reexamining your personal beliefs about the nature of human beings and your philosophy of management. Have you developed more insight into your beliefs and philosophy? Are you talking or writing about them in ways that indicate more flexibility on your part? Are you finding yourself to be more student centered and collaborative or more directive in your beliefs? Can you be collaborative sometimes and directive at others and not confuse students? Are you confused about when to be collaborative and when to be directive yourself?

In chapter 1 you read about theories of human growth and development that varied in beliefs about how much direction and control adults need to provide children in order for them to grow optimally. The popular theory of humanism yielded strategies based on respect for students' potential to solve their own problems. Yet, in the same chapter, research in classroom management indicated that successful, expert teachers took quick and direct action to stop behaviors that were disrupting the teaching and learning process. Why the contradictions? How do you make sense of them and know which direction to go?

In chapter 2, you learned how to collaborate with students to develop classroom rules and consequences. You were a facilitator who was student centered. You were not in control and directive unless you opted to teach your own rules and consequences without student input. In the final portion of chapter 2 you learned how to be directive in implementing a "room clear" procedure during a crisis. There was no listening and collaborating during room clears. Then, again, in chapter 3 on covenant management the entire focus was on using covenant strategies? Why the seemingly disparate management styles? Are guiding principles emerging that help you know when to use humanistic and ecological strategies that tend to be more collaborative compared with when to use behavioral, cognitive-behavioral, and social learning strategies that tend to be more directive?

To answer the questions, let's think about educational goals in terms of desirable student outcomes. Student self-management in the context of schools characterized by PBSs, is the goal of conduct management. Research has shown that directive strategies are less likely to produce students strong in self-management. Therefore, collaborative, student-centered strategies must be selected and implemented the majority of the time. Directive strategies are appropriate for two types of conditions. The first condition is when instructional time would be jeopardized if the teacher took time to collaborate on minor misbehaviors in the classroom. The second condition is when severe misbehaviors are threatening the safety of individuals or totally disrupting the learning environment.

In the following sections, quick and efficient directive strategies are described in detail. These basic teachings and enforcement of rules and consequences are sufficient for managing about 96% of all students displaying inappropriate behaviors. More complex techniques are needed for the remaining 4% of students who exhibit severe misbehaviors. There are numerous severe behavior competencies; only a few are described as examples. Suggestions for accessing building assistance teams with behavior specialists are given so that teachers will seek help to manage severe problems. It is time, now, to develop competencies needed for managing the inevitable infractions of the rules committed by the 96% and for managing the severe behaviors of the 4%.

Research Support for Directive Conduct Management

Many frustrated preservice and novice teachers comment that they cannot present the high-quality lessons they prepared because students are "out of control." Research supports the preceding comments of preservice and novice teachers. Doyle (1986) developed a basic premise in his review of classroom management. His premise was that the teacher's management task is more one of maintaining work systems than remediating misbehavior. Order is not achieved once and for all. The teacher continually protects the work systems by using quick, efficient, nonintrusive directive techniques. He suggested that teacher preparation programs need to prepare student teachers with directive techniques that will protect the work system (i.e., presentation of high-quality lessons).

McNeely and Mertz (1990) found that secondary student teachers had a high sense of efficacy and spent a great deal of time planning lessons that had more than one activity at the beginning of their student-teaching experiences. By the end of student teaching, they spent their time on classroom control and planned lessons with single activities in order to reduce disruption. These student teachers obviously were not prepared to implement quick, efficient, nonintrusive directive techniques as recommended by Doyle. In another study, Hoy and Woolfolk (1990) also concluded that student teachers grew more controlling. However, they became more controlling in social problem solving, one area in which students should participate fully with one another while teachers facilitate the problem-solving meetings.

Swanson, O'Connor, and Cooney (1990) focused their research efforts on analyzing differences between expert and novice teachers' problem-solving approaches to classroom discipline. Expert teachers were master teachers identified by building principals, and novices were beginning teachers. As noted in chapter 1, expert teachers were significantly more likely to place a priority on defining and representing the problem prior to intervening. Novices tended to represent problems in terms of possible solutions. Expert teachers also were more likely to solve discipline problems by using direct or external controls (e.g., establish and enforce rules, end action immediately, separate students, use proximity control, modify instruction, model behavior, implement a time-out, confront students, use contingencies). Novice teachers' solutions were more likely to rely on internal decisions of students (e.g., provide maximum freedom, counsel students, encourage, reason, empathize, discuss, involve students more).

Kagan (1992) suggested that preservice teachers need to come to student teaching already equipped with basic procedural skills and strategies in classroom discipline. Only then would they be able to teach high-quality lessons while using external, teacher-directed, high-control techniques appropriately. In other words, preservice teachers should continue to plan and deliver high-quality lessons, which should be paired with competently delivered directive management techniques.

In summary, numerous researchers have concluded that it is possible to teach high-quality lessons with the appropriate use of external, directive behavior techniques. In preparation for learning appropriate use of directive techniques, study the following vignettes and use them as pretests to evaluate your skills in problem solving behavioral problems. At the end of the chapter, you will return to these vignettes and problem solve again to see if you would manage them any differently.

> You walk into your first-hour class several minutes before the bell rings and see a group of students who have arrived early. Several of them are teasing a lone student who is crying. This student has never been a problem for you. What would you do? Is this a condition that calls for collaborative or directive strategies? How would you solve this problem?

> You have a student who spends a great deal of class time either joking around or debating the inherent value of your lessons and assignments. Classmates laugh at his jokes and seem to enjoy his debates with you. Today is no exception. During the first few minutes of the lesson, he first cracks a joke about it and then remarks that it is a waste of time and has no relevance to life outside of school. Collaborative or directive? Which one should you be? How would you solve this problem?

> You are leading the students in a review of some difficult course material. Two students seated toward the back of the room are quietly talking to each other. You have already asked them once to stop talking. Now they are talking again. What strategy should you use? Is it going to be collaborative or directive? How did you decide?

> You are explaining the distribution of grades on the exam you just passed back to students. You describe how this one grade for the class fits into your grading

system. One bright student begins to criticize your grading policies, saying that they are unfair. What do you do now? Does this situation call for a collaborative or a directive strategy? How would you solve this problem?

Class is over and students are exiting the room. Two students begin to argue and one pushes the other with enough force that the student falls into nearby desks. You are tired and the class period is officially over. You are tempted to turn your back and act like you didn't see what just happened. However, you don't. What do you do? How would you solve this problem?

Record what you would do for each of the scenarios. As you study the content of this chapter, revise your solutions if you think of better ones. Compare your responses at the end of the chapter with your current responses as a check of what you already knew and what you have learned.

Directive Conduct Competencies: The Basic Classroom Management Plan

Dreikurs and Cassell (1972) rely on the use of logical consequences, which are impersonal and not based on personal authority, and on encouragement to assist students in displaying positive behaviors. Their approach assists educators in using democratic principles in democratic schools while remaining assertive and directive according to the demands of each situation. This section prepares you to assertively, yet democratically, and competently manage classroom discipline plans.

Sprick, Sprick, and Garrison (1993) described the basic conduct management competencies as follows. The essence of the first competency is this: Know at all times what you want your students to do. In chapter 2 you learned to set the limits—and involve students in doing so—by stating schoolwide and classroom rules in explicit terms so that everyone knew at all times what to do. The more precisely stated and taught the rules are, the less room there is for error. The more latitude there is with respect to what is acceptable, the more students will seek clarity by testing the full range of possibilities. Teachers should restrict the possibilities when there are certain behaviors that they want without exception.

Note that some of the rules leave room for interpretation. For example, how can the teacher be certain students know precisely what is meant by "Be respectful of all people and property"? Planning and review sessions that teach examples and nonexamples can help clarify behavioral standards. This increases the probability that teachers will act assertively with respect to these standards. Students are not sure when teachers are not sure. Students who are not sure test the rules to ascertain teacher intentions; teachers who are not sure tend to be too lenient. Thus, the teacher may have to teach a rule by correcting instances of unacceptable behavior. Of course, it is better to teach the meaning of a rule by means of a preventive or prosocial approach (Schloss, 1983) rather than with a corrective strategy. In addition to the teaching and reteaching of rules, there are additional procedures for specific activities that are in effect at different times of the day (see chapter 5, which covers content management). You are already acquainted with the basic procedures in chapter 2 used to minimize disruptions and maximize time on task when, for example, students are asked to exchange papers for grading purposes. Procedures also need to be taught and retaught.

The essence of Sprick et al.'s (1993) second competency is this: Teachers' control and administration of consequences (Rich, 1988) are important features in a conduct management plan. Educators and students typically manage behavior by managing consequences and implementing educational interventions. Both positive and negative consequences and education are used to increase the probability that students will exhibit rule-governed behavior. When students need additional support beyond the use of the groups' generated list of positive and negative consequences, interventions that emphasize the teaching of desired replacement behaviors are used to support students. Teachers are to work with building assistance teams to implement such interventions.

Acknowledging Responsible Behaviors

Consequences for misbehavior are needed but rarely turn behavior around without acknowledgment of responsible behavior. This is the most powerful element of the basic classroom management plan: It must include both positive interactions and other structured procedures for acknowledging responsible behavior.

Positive interactions are the warm, caring, supportive oral communications you have with students throughout the day. They are noncontingent on students' behaviors. In other words, words that communicate care and support are stated to students about themselves rather than about the situation. For example, Ms. Jones greeted Tanya in the morning with, "It is so good to see you this morning. I hope you have a good day." Later in the morning before drama class, Ms. Jones said to Tanya, "I know you are going to enjoy your part in the skit." Following drama class,

Responsible behaviors are posted in a middle school classroom.

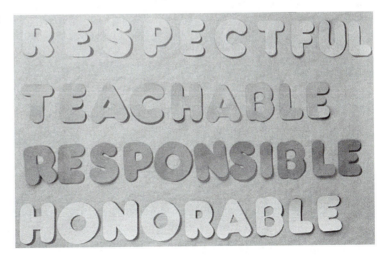

Ms. Jones asked, "Tanya, how did you feel about your role today?" None of the interactions are dependent on Tanya's demonstrating some preferred behavior. Rather, all of them are positive and focus on Tanya alone, and they are occurring at a relatively high rate. Research indicates that positive interactions should occur at a ratio of 3 positives to 1 negative for students who do not experience significant behavioral problems and at a ratio of 10 positives to 1 negative for students who do have serious behavioral problems.

Although it is difficult to maintain high levels of positive interactions with students who have significant behavioral problems, it is absolutely necessary. Teachers must be observant to catch those neutral moments in which to have a positive interaction. The important point to remember about positive interactions is that they occur at the specified ratio regardless of whether or not the student is demonstrating high rates of appropriate behavior. These and similar efforts to provide PBSs for students will increase your success rate with students who have severe behavioral problems.

To be able to acknowledge appropriate behavior, you must monitor whether students are meeting expectations. Visually scan the room on a frequent basis. Move about the room during independent and cooperative group work times. Some teachers like to take notes on a record form. Notes can be used to identify students who deserve recognition for special or sustained efforts. You can acknowledge appropriate behavior by observing, smiling, and nodding. Notes can also be used to identify problem areas. For example, when several students have similar problems on activities, teachers may need to clarify their instructions to the entire group (see chapter 5). Notes can be used to identify students who have problems that require minor interventions. Finally, notes can be used to provide documentation of problems that may require referral.

Oral praise for successful behavior can be used and should be relatively brief, age appropriate, and frequent. The following examples are for a first grader and an eighth grader, respectively.

❏ "Jasmine, you are being responsible for your behavior. I can see that you are listening and watching."
❏ "Ray, your contributions to our discussion really added to our understanding of the issues."

You can also acknowledge responsible behavior with written feedback to a student by sending a "Special Note From Your Teacher's Desk." You can use a phone call or written feedback to parents or guardians for responsible behavior, a job well done, or general appreciation. Certificates of merit can be used intermittently throughout the year or be given to a few individuals each week in a regularly scheduled 5-minute ceremony. These need to be used equitably by acknowledging all students for their merits, not just high-achieving or popular students.

Educators seldom give responsibility to students who have difficulties, but meeting a responsibility yields a greater sense of responsibility. Look for ways to give students additional responsibilities. Figure 2–7 includes a number of activities and social responsibilities that can be used as positive consequences. The following comment shows how a social responsibility could be used to acknowledge responsible behavior for an elementary or a middle school child. The second comment would be better for a high school student.

- ❏ "Nasha, you have turned in your homework for 3 days in a row. How would you like to be my homework checker this week? During attendance and lunch count, you would collect the papers and check them off."
- ❏ "Lars, the coach is looking for a responsible student to set up equipment for the student pep rally. You have been doing excellent work in class this week. How would you like to leave class 10 minutes early to help the coach?"

Finally, it is important to remember that infrequent, major rewards given to a few students tend to be less effective than frequent recognition of daily efforts.

Correcting Irresponsible and Inappropriate Behaviors

Misbehavior is generally a mistake and constitutes a learning opportunity. When you treat misbehavior accordingly, students will also begin to view mistakes as learning opportunities. A first step in managing inappropriate classroom behavior is to brainstorm a list of all potential misbehavior that could occur in a day's time. Make sure each item on the list is an observable behavior (e.g., being disrespectful to each other is observable in terms of putting each other down or making sarcastic comments).

The second step is to determine whether brainstormed misbehaviors should be handled with ignoring, consequences, and/or corrective education. The third step is to brainstorm all possible negative consequences and determine which of these you feel comfortable using. Mentally or orally rehearse how to handle different situations by using various negative consequences. That way you can base your decisions on some experience before you prematurely determine that you will always or never use certain negative consequences.

To be effective, consequences must be implemented consistently, fairly, and calmly. Students must also be informed in advance that certain behaviors will lead to predetermined consequences. Some in-class consequences that teachers can choose from include ignoring, using proximity control, giving gentle oral reprimands, using cues and prompts, providing instructions for positive practice, giving time owed, giving time-out, implementing a behavioral contract, and engaging in goal setting. These strategies are described on the basis of Sprick et al.'s (1993) work.

From the following menu of consequences, select those that you think you would be most comfortable using to teach students to behave responsibly. The consequences should also be the least intrusive in the classroom. Select mild classroom consequences for mild misbehavior that cannot be ignored. The consequence should have some logical association with the inappropriate behavior. Stay calm and consistent when you use the consequences.

Ignoring.   Sometimes students engage in misbehavior because they need attention. Any correction at all from the teacher serves as a form of attention and actually increases the misbehavior. This is because some students find negative teacher attention just as reinforcing as positive attention. It is possible to determine whether misbehavior increases as a result of ignoring by taking the following steps of FBA:

Step 1:   Count the number of misbehaviors that occur at three different time periods. Put the results on a graph on which the x axis is the time periods and the y axis is the frequency of behaviors. These are your baseline data.

Step 2:   Begin the procedure of giving gentle oral reprimands when misbehavior occurs and continue to count every occurrence of misbehavior. After three to five time periods have passed, graph the results. These are your intervention or reprimand data.

Step 3:   Compare the reprimand results with the baseline results.

If the behavior decreased in frequency, gentle oral reprimands worked as an appropriate intervention. You are now fairly certain that the student was not trying to get your attention by misbehaving. In other words, ignoring the behaviors would not have been an effective intervention. The behaviors probably would have increased had you ignored them. Conversely, if the behaviors increased in frequency when you used reprimands, the misbehavior may be an attempt to get your attention. Ignoring is more likely to be an effective intervention. You may decide that you need help collecting observation data and implementing interventions. Most school buildings have assistance teams with members who are available to help teachers with situations such as this that profit from FBA.

Sprick et al. (1993) suggested the following guidelines when a teacher is using ignoring as a conduct management technique. First, if misbehavior increases with oral reprimands, ignoring should be considered. Another rule of thumb is to ignore student misbehavior that does not get in the way of teaching or in the way of students' learning.

Ignoring is the only response to misbehavior that does not require teacher time. If you plan to use ignoring with a student, hold a planned discussion and collaborate with the student. The teacher must also seek opportunities to interact positively with the student. Therefore, tell the student that you will pay a lot of attention to him or her when he or she is following the class rules but that you won't be able to see or hear him or her when he or she engages in irresponsible behavior. Be sure to give examples of responsible and irresponsible behavior. Consistently ignore misbehavior in both body language and talk. Do not interrupt instruction. Keep teaching. Student behavior will get worse before it gets better. Plan to give ignoring 2 weeks before you judge its effectiveness.

Proximity Control.   Proximity control occurs when the teacher moves into the space of a student who is not following the rules. This may be sufficient to assist the student in monitoring his or her behavior. Good times to use proximity control are when students are not paying attention to the lesson and are engaged in talking to a neighbor, playing with objects, daydreaming, or being off task in some other type of mild misbehavior.

Oral proximity control can be used by the teacher to invite a student to participate when he or she appears to be off task. Rather than walking close to students who are talking to each other when they are supposed to be listening, the teacher gets them back on task by asking them a question about the lesson.

Gentle Oral Reprimands.   According to Sprick et al. (1993), gentle oral reprimands are to be used when students do not know that a behavior is inappropriate. These reprimands are also to be used when students are unaware that they are engaging in inappropriate behavior. Teachers can give gentle oral reprimands alone or follow them with instructions that provide positive practice of an alternative behavior. A suggested script follows that can be used at the beginning of the school year when you are teaching students the rules and consequences. This script can be embedded in scripts from chapter 2.

When you are reading scripts, they will tend to sound stilted and unnatural. Give them a try. Change the words slightly to match your style of speaking. You will be pleased with how well they work for you after some practice.

Elementary through high school teachers have used these strategies and scripts successfully. For instance, Ms. Owens, a high school teacher, turned every student misbehavior into a teachable moment by using scripts such as the one that follows. She was a warm, caring, supportive teacher who did not hesitate to use quick, efficient, directive strategies to help her students learn and grow. Students loved her, and she helped some of the "toughest kids" in school turn their behavior around at school and in the community. I will never forget the end-of-the-year award assembly when the biggest, tallest, toughest boy in high school was called up to the stage to receive recognition for being the student who worked the hardest and made the most personal growth as a student that school year. He owed most of it to Ms. Owens' efforts.

Following is the script for teaching the class about the consequence of gentle oral reprimands:

> "The class seems to agree that an appropriate consequence for not following the class guidelines is for the teacher to give a reminder. Let's talk about how this consequence will be used. For instance, one student may make a sarcastic remark to another person or about another person. First, I will quietly tell the student that the comment may have been meant to tease and have fun but it felt hurtful to the peer. Second, I will remind the student of the class rule 'Treat everyone with dignity and respect.' Then I will suggest a different comment to make in the future. For example: 'Cora, that comment was hurtful. It would be better to tell Ben thank you for the assistance he was giving you or not to say anything.'
>
> "What do you think, class? Now that you have heard an example of how this consequence will be used, does it seem acceptable to you?"

When you give a gentle oral reprimand, go over to the student; do not give reprimands from across the room. Use neutral or supportive tones. Avoid increasing the emotional intensity if feedback is repeated.

Oral Cues and Warnings.   Often a teacher deals with a minor incident such as this:

"Harry, what are you doing?"
"What are you supposed to be doing?"
"Well, why aren't you doing it?"
"What if everyone were to behave that way when they wanted to be first?"
"Harry, you know better than that."
"How many times do I have to tell you?"

The teacher wants Harry to change his behavior. She has already tried using eye contact and proximity control. A brief assertive statement will suffice if she does not think that Harry knows what he is doing or what he is supposed to do: "Harry, I need you to follow our rule of being respectful to all people." A statement like this will probably be unnecessary after a few planning and review sessions. Harry will know what he is doing and what he is supposed to be doing.

Oral cues and warnings are appropriate consequences prior to giving a more severe consequence such as in-class time-out. For example, the teacher might say, "Sonya, your tone of voice is starting to sound impatient. Taking a deep breath and lowering your voice would be helpful."

Note that the cue makes allowances for misbehavior but does not excuse it. The teacher does not sanction the unacceptable behavior, but there is no retribution.

Delaying.   Delaying is used when a student engages in excessive misbehavior to get attention. For example, Sonya may be getting attention from her peers, and taking up class time, by repeatedly asking her high school teacher to explain the directions that were given for yesterday's assignment. Rather than continue to explain, the teacher might say, "Sonya, that is disruptive. We can talk about it after class." An elementary school example is, "Monny, you are starting to tattle. Remember you are to write it down, place it in the box, and wait until Response Time." In both examples, students are cued immediately about their unacceptable behavior, but the teacher's full attention is delayed and the conditions are made explicit to students.

Preferential Seating.   Preferential seating is a favorite strategy of teachers and is often used as one of the first interventions. It involves assigning the student to sit in a different section of the room. Often students are seated close to the source of instruction when they have hearing or visual problems and when they have difficulty paying attention or need more teacher assistance to be successful. Seat students away from peers with whom they get in trouble and with peers that have good classroom social skills. Many times this is a weak stand-alone intervention, and it will work best when it is paired with another intervention that matches the particular problem a student is having.

Example of Using Negative Classroom Consequences.   To illustrate how educators can use in-class consequences to manage behavioral problems, let's look at Sprick's (1985) plan to reduce swearing. Students need to learn that swearing is unacceptable in some settings and will be offensive to many people. Sometimes swearing is against the rules. Some people are not offended by swearing but others are. In the teaching process, teachers should not make a big issue of swearing, but they do need to help students see that swearing is not acceptable in a number of environments, including most school environments.

Students swear for a number of reasons: They hear swearing a lot in their environment; it is a habit and is hard to break; swearing makes students feel more sophisticated or tough; students swear to antagonize adults; and students are hooked on the emotional conflict that parallels swearing. It is recommended that the teacher first discuss the problem of swearing with his or her class. The discussion might go something like the following:

> "I am concerned about the amount of swearing that I have been hearing throughout the building. My own feelings about swearing are irrelevant; they don't count. What does count is that many people believe that swearing in a public setting is not okay. Public settings are schools, places of employment, and so forth. Swearing is offensive to many people and these people will judge you solely on the basis of your language. If you choose to swear, other people will conclude that you are a 'bad' person, that you have no regard for others, or that you are illiterate. You may not be welcome in their homes. If you are a male who swears, they may not want you to date their daughter. You might not be selected to represent the school or a club. Many opportunities will be given to others and not you because people will be afraid that you will embarrass them. You could lose a job opportunity because of your swearing, especially if it becomes a habit. I am telling you about this so that you can work on changing. If everybody works on it on their own, great. If not, we can have a class meeting and decide whether you want to set up a consequence for swearing."

When the situation begins to improve, tell students, "I am pleased that you were able to handle the problem of swearing. It's great that the class did this and never needed to discuss using consequences." If the situation does not improve within a week, consider using a mild consequence. You do not want to make a big deal out of swearing. An example of a mild consequence would be owing 3 minutes from lunch period, break, after school, or any enjoyable activity. The amount of time does not need to be excessive. Another example would be filling out a behavior improvement form. Provide students with examples of exclamations that are acceptable by generating them with the students. Tell students that any questionable comments will be considered swearing.

It is critical that you stay calm, unemotional, and consistent when you are giving consequences. Do not argue or debate with students. Tell students to talk with you after class. Praise the class for their self-control if swearing has been a large-group problem. Praise individuals if only a few students have been a problem. When a large number of students are unmotivated to meet expectations, or if only one or two students are unmotivated, it may be time to have another class meeting to support students in the process of solving their own problems.

Time Owed.   Time owed communicates to the student that misbehavior wastes class time and needs to be repaid during a time that is valued by the student. High school teachers really appreciate using the option of time owed rather than detention. It is recommended that you set up small amounts of time owed for each infraction. For example, do not have students owe an entire recess for each infraction. Instead, keep a student in from recess, 1 minute per infraction. Teachers need to decide what the student should be doing during time owed. There are two basic options: Discuss the problem or sit doing nothing. The more boring, the better. Following is an example of what teachers could say when they are giving a student time owed for chronically being off task by talking to others:

> "Your talking is an example of not listening. You owe 1 minute of after-class time."

Secondary teachers and librarians, physical education teachers, or music specialists who have the student for only one period may want to consider in-class time-out as another option.

Losing minutes from recess, eating lunch alone, and having to remain after class or school are social deprivation consequences. Time owed is a natural consequence for not using time in class well. At the beginning of the year, teachers need to talk to students about the times of the day that they can return to their classrooms to pay back the time owed.

Let's consider how time owed would work with Vanessa, a student who talks when she shouldn't. The teacher first uses eye contact. She then moves to proximity control. If neither of these consequences is effective and Vanessa continues to talk, the teacher gives a gentle oral reprimand: "Vanessa, I need you to follow our rule of listening when someone else is speaking." This does not stop Vanessa either. Soon she is whispering to the boy next to her. The teacher now says, "Vanessa, you owe 2 minutes." The amount of time owed generally depends on how much time the teacher thinks Vanessa has been off task. Sprick et al. (1993) recommend starting quite small. For example, 2 minutes of time owed could be completed between classes at the middle school and high school levels. This is enough time to be an inconvenience for students and gets their attention that you are serious about following classroom rules.

For some students, staying in the classroom and missing several minutes of recess or staying after school may not be a negative consequence. They like teacher attention and do not have to compete with others for it during these times. If this appears to be the case, select a different negative consequence. During very hot or cold days elementary students may also prefer to lose recess time and remain indoors. Teachers can manage these situations by arranging for students with time owed to sit quietly in their seats doing nothing or to stand outside by the school building wall during recess for their minutes of time owed.

Some people would argue that a student who has to do assignments during time owed will be less favorably inclined toward the area of study because of the emotional distress associated with the situation. However, the time-owed penalty should be evaluated by looking at the circumstances that provoked it. Insisting that the student use the time to work on missed assignment time in class would be a logical consequence (Dreikurs & Cassell, 1972) if the rule infractions had prevented the student from completing the assignment in class. The logic: If students choose to spend class time unproductively, then the lost time will be recouped on the topic that suffered because of the irresponsible behavior.

Staying after school, even for a few minutes, takes away a precious commodity from most students; after-school time includes a great variety of options, which have to be temporarily set aside. Worse yet, the student is left behind. After the allotted time, friends may have already left the customary gathering place; even if everyone is there, the latecomer has already missed all of the preliminary excitement associated with after-school activities. Penalties imposed by coaches and extracurricular activity sponsors can also increase the inducement to follow the rules.

Time-Out

In-Class Time-Out. Time-out is to be used with care. It is typically reserved for students who engage in misbehavior frequently (Sprick et al., 1993). Time-out serves essentially the same purpose as a warning. Students are removed from the social stimuli that most students want and are seeking. Forms of time-out vary according to the developmental stage of the students. Even high school students can benefit from a time-out, but it is typically given a different name, such as cool-down time, and is implemented in a room separate from the classroom. Time-out may consist of any of the following:

> Student sits with head down on desk for the allotted time.
>
> Student is unable to participate in a group activity.
>
> Student is seated toward the back of the room and turned away from the group.
>
> Student is seated in an area of the room that is screened or partitioned so that the student can hear but not see the events taking place in the classroom.
>
> Student goes to a separate room from the classroom, usually to calm him- or herself.

The duration of time-out is 1 minute for each year of age, with no more than 5 minutes total. Some teachers have students set a timer when they enter time-out. Other teachers prefer to have the student return to class when he or she is ready to follow the rules. The open-ended time frame puts the student in control; the door is always open to those who are prepared to return and act responsibly.

Determine the length of time in advance. Five minutes total for sixth grade and above is recommended. Five minutes or less is recommended for younger students, according to age and sophistication. Kindergartners and first graders should be given 1 minute. Use a timer so that you do not forget the student in the time-out location. Some students do not go to time-out immediately but dawdle, argue, and even refuse to go. Escort younger students to time-out. Tell them that the timer begins when they are in time-out and quiet. Inform older students that the amount of time they take to get to time-out will be recorded and they will owe that time after class. If students misbehave after returning from time-out, calmly send them back. Students with serious behavioral difficulties may need to return to time-out repeatedly during the same morning or afternoon. This is not something that many educators experience but, if you do, stay calm and consistent. Consider these scripts:

- ❑ "That was an example of not following directions. Go to time-out and think about other ways you might have handled that situation. You may return to your seat when the timer rings."
- ❑ "That was an example of not following directions. Go to time-out and think about other ways you might have handled that situation. You may return to your seat when you have filled out a Behavior Improvement Form."

The teacher can facilitate students' use of time-out for reflection on their behavior by preparing a form for students to fill out before returning to class. The form can simply ask the student to state the unacceptable behavior (What were you doing?), the desired behaviors (What should you have been doing?), and the consequences of future misbehavior (What will happen if you continue to misbehave?). The student can return with the form when the time elapses. Nothing is said when the student returns. Later, it is advisable to hold a planned discussion. Most students who need a time-out also need ongoing problem solving to help them learn replacement behaviors.

Time-Out in Another Location.   Time-out in a place outside the classroom is reserved for behavior that is highly disruptive (Sprick et al., 1993). Examples of this include overt defiance toward adults, noncompliance, loud sustained disruptions, highly aggressive behavior, and sustained screaming. As you write your plan for the use of time-out outside of the classroom, determine what behaviors will result in removal from your classroom. Decide where the student will go, how long the student will be there, what the student will do there, who will provide supervision of time-out, and what the student needs to do to reenter your classroom.

Some teachers seat students in the hall or send them to the principal's office for time-out. Neither of these settings is as desirable as an isolated place in the classroom. There are just too many interesting things happening in the halls and the principal's office. There is no incentive to behave acceptably when a student is singled out for attention and becomes a party to events that may be a sharp and interesting contrast to the classroom. Keeping a student just out of reach of an enticing classroom activity, without his or her being able to participate, is much more effective. That means that teachers need to have a backup supply of enticing classroom activities from which to select.

Contacting Parents or Guardians.   The purpose of a parental or guardian contact is to keep parents or guardians informed and to have them encourage the student to behave more responsibly. Educators can request that parents talk to their children, but, at the same time, educators must make it clear that the school will take care of the consequences. Do not lead parents to believe that they should be the individuals responsible for carrying out appropriate consequences. Parental contact should occur for chronic misbehavior but never be considered a sufficiently effective consequence in and of itself. However, parental contact is often effective when the student rarely engages in misbehavior and is from a home with firm but supportive parents.

It is no surprise that very few students want their parents or guardians notified of problems in school. Parents generally tell their children to mind the teacher and generally feel let down when they do not. A parent may not always agree with the teacher's rules or their application, but most parents want their children to be respected and respectful. When a parental or guardian contact is used as the consequence of choice, the student should immediately go to the principal's office, as in the case of Jerad from chapter 1. In Jerad's case, arrangements for this contingency should have been made collaboratively with parents and been built into the management plan so that the consequence could be carried out without delay. This seems to have been a step that was skipped at Jerad's school. His mother seemed unpleasantly surprised that Jerad was asked to phone home.

When the teacher and student arrive at the office, the student should be asked to name the behaviors that have made this call to the parents necessary. The response is corrected for accuracy, if needed. Having reviewed these matters, the student will be prepared to answer the two questions almost any parent will ask: "What did you do?" and "What will you do to follow the rules next time?" Parents want to understand the magnitude of the problem and to know how subsequent plans might involve them.

Unless the parents have already indicated that they disagree with the procedure, the student should be the person who places the call, for a number of reasons. First, the teacher will not absorb the parent's initial displeasure. Second, many children come from single-parent homes or from homes in which both parents work, and a student is more likely to get through to a parent at work. The person who receives the call, when hearing a student's voice, will be much more likely to interpret the situation as an emergency and bring the parent to the phone. Third, the student will begin the conversation with a description of the problem and what he or she contributed to it. The parent will be less likely to come to the student's defense under these circumstances. When the student talks about what he or she will do the next time, it serves as an oral rehearsal and commitment to the parent.

The parent is then a part of helping the student be accountable. Parents are likely to influence their children and say, "I expect you to go back to class and follow the rules. I don't want to have to come to school to pick you up." Requiring students to call parents should not mean that educators expect them to solve problems alone. Problem solving is expected to be a collaborative effort between parents and educators. Educators with knowledge and skills in schoolwide and classroom management have many interventions to try. They realize, though, that ecological theory suggests that partnering with the home increases the success of school-based interventions.

Implementing a Written Behavioral Contract.   The written behavioral contract illustrates a collaborative solution to a behavioral problem. The contract is often used when the regular classroom rules and positive and negative consequences do not work. The teacher, the parents, and the student develop the plan together. Teachers can increase the power of their management plan by joining forces with parents. Sometimes the solution is merely a matter of intensifying the effects of an already-desirable consequence. Attempts to change behavior may mean more when followed by the elementary child's favorite dessert at dinner. A reinforcer, such as a teacher compliment for an improvement, can be strengthened by making more of it at home. The price of a movie, an extension of the Saturday night curfew, or an unexpected, favorite pizza can be incentives for high schoolers to make additional progress. Both elementary and high school students have benefited from home–school partnership consequence plans in which students earned highly coveted, more expensive items by accruing points at school and taking them home. At home, the elementary child's "new bicycle" or the high schooler's "mini stereo" was built by earning it a "wheel" or a "speaker" at a time and pasting pictures of the earned parts on the refrigerator door. Likewise, parents can help strengthen negative consequences with reneged television privileges or the loss of recreational time with friends. When home and school act in concert, students are more likely to get the message and act on it.

Conferences at which the teacher, the parents, and the student are present can be an effective way to produce a behavioral contract. Differences about the behavioral problem or how to handle it should be discussed with the student present. As long as there are differences about what has happened, there will be differences about the need for change as well. Without a student's acknowledging that a change in behavior is needed, it is futile to make a contract. A contract should represent a genuine intent to change and include specific ways to bring about the change. A contract may include any number of provisions and may cover differing periods of time (Lehman, 1982, pp. 35–38; Welch & Tisdale, 1986, pp. 35–40). Figure 4–1 presents an example of a typical teacher–parent–student contract that lists home consequences to deal with a student's behavior in school. All of the consequences are external forms of control and are introduced in the absence of self-control.

Desired Behaviors

1. Be in seat and ready to work when bell rings.
2. Listen during teacher presentations.
3. Participate in class discussions.
4. Attend to task during independent study time.
5. Complete homework.

Positive Home Consequences

Step I—Trip to ice cream store when 10 squares are filled
Step II—Extra hour of television when 20 squares are filled
Step III—Money for a movie when 40 squares are filled
Step IV—Extra hour before bedtime when 60 squares are filled
Step V—Supper at fast-food restaurant when 90 squares are filled

> Note. One square is filled for each desired behavior, each day. Five bonus squares are filled when all five desired behaviors are achieved for a given day. Start over after 90 squares. Change the positive consequences for each step.

Negative Home Consequences

Failure to demonstrate any of the desired behaviors during a given day:

1 violation—No phone calls
2 violations—No television viewing for the evening
3 violations—No outside-the-house activity after supper
4 violations—Confinement to house all day Saturday
5 violations—One week of confinement at home (no phone calls or television)

> Note. Begin with clean slate each day.

Contract is now to cover the period between _____ and _____.
  (date) (date)

Today's date _____

Signatures _____ _____
    (teacher) (student)

_____
    (parent[s])

Figure 4–1
Teacher–Parent–Student Behavioral Contract

Generally, the contract will include the following (regardless of the age or grade level of the student):

❏ A description of the desired behaviors
❏ A description of the home and school situations in which these behaviors are to occur
❏ The time span to be covered by the contract
❏ The positive consequences that will occur at home or school if the contract is honored
❏ The negative consequences that will occur at home or school if the contract is broken
❏ The date on which the contract was written
❏ A place for the signatures of the student, the parent(s), the teacher, and (if desired) the principal

Care should be exercised when you are making plans that cover long time periods and a large number of behavioral changes. An agreement can be reached about the need for future contracts and their content at the outset. Always keep the ultimate objective in mind and write a series of contracts that lead to the objective. Only the first contract needs to be completed with parents present, but all contracts must carry their signatures.

Generally, the cumulative effects of rewards are more profound when contracts specify small behavioral changes to be accomplished in short time periods. A single contract might include progressively more powerful inducements for desired behavior as the student fulfills the daily contract requirements. The parent(s) and the child can chart each day's achievements, on the basis of a report from the teacher, and use the charting activity as the basis for a conversation about events at school.

The behavioral contract generally includes at least three items: behavioral expectations, positive and negative consequences, and a specific time period. First, behavioral expectations should be explicitly stated. The behaviors that are direct opposites of the behaviors that are unacceptable should be specified first.

Second, negative consequences that will be applied for failure to exhibit the aforementioned behaviors should be stated. Likewise, it is imperative to include a corresponding list of positive consequences for demonstrating desired behaviors. Students may be invited to participate in making both lists of consequences. Sometimes a well-intentioned student will choose overly severe negative consequences for bad behavior and too little compensation for good behavior. Teachers are to be a moderating influence during the consequence-selection process and assist students in being supportive of their own efforts.

Finally, a time period for the contract should be specified. Remember that students who require more severe measures are generally unable to handle long-term commitments. Abiding by the terms of a contract for a single class period may be a big achievement for some students. Success should be the occasion for another contract. The same contract may be reinstated, or a new contract changing the positive and negative consequences might be written.

Lists of positive and negative consequences can be used to assist students in preparing their plans. Students can be helped to choose and administer their consequences. Students are ready to write contracts that cover longer periods of time after having successfully fulfilled the requirements of several short-term contracts. Keep in mind that students can also tire of negotiating contracts. There are various types of behavioral contracting, some less structured than others, that can prove useful.

Setting Limits Outside the Classroom

As Sprick et al. (1993) pointed out, large numbers of students move from one place in the school building to another many times a day. Halls are crowded and chaotic with running, shouting students and slammed locker doors. It is easy for students to carry their boisterousness into the classroom. It is hard for them to calm down and be ready to learn with all materials when the bell rings.

On the one hand, it is important that teachers remind themselves that this behavior is natural for students. Students are very interested in spending time with friends, and they must talk loudly to be heard above the hallway commotion. On the other hand, the fewer the consequences for hallway behavior, the faster and louder students become. Sprick (1985) offered the analogy of adults speeding on highways that are not frequently patrolled. Does this analogy get your attention? Great! Now you have a sense of what it is like for students to be enticed into speeding loudly through school hallways. Sprick offered some helpful tips on setting limits outside the classroom. We next look specifically at improving hallway and cafeteria behavior. These two examples should help you be creative in planning your management of other areas outside the classroom.

Supervising hallway behavior can accomplish the goal of getting the student body to take pride in adultlike functioning. Here's how it works. Seeing faculty in hallways prompts students to have appropriate behavior, just as seeing a police car prompts adults to drive at the speed limit. Students who break the rules are more likely to be noticed by hallway supervisors and to pay the consequences. The result is quieter hallways. Supervision time also prompts staff and student interaction. Supervisors should be relaxed and friendly and talk, greet, and joke with students.

First, staff must meet as a group and come to consensus on expectations and procedures. They will need to list unacceptable behaviors (e.g., running, shouting, slamming lockers, swearing, racial slurs) and agree on ways students can acceptably engage in frequently occurring borderline behaviors (e.g., affection in public, name-calling, disagreements).

Second, staff must list consequences for each misbehavior, keeping in mind that minor misbehaviors (e.g., running, slamming locker doors, shouting, swearing, and inappropriate intimacy) should have mild and easily implemented consequences with no paperwork. An example of a mild consequence for running would be to go to the end of the hallway and walk back. More serious misbehaviors, like talking back and noncompliance, should be referred to the office. (See chapter 7, which covers schoolwide discipline.)

Third, staff need to determine how they are going to provide ongoing hallway supervision. For about the first week of hallway supervision, it is recommended that every teacher be in the halls during passing times (Sprick et al., 1993). Massive supervision can change behavior rapidly and dramatically. If the first week goes well, you can switch to assigning each teacher to the halls during two or more passing periods per day. Structure this so that teachers have been assigned times in a way that every passing period is covered adequately. Be sure to cover darker hallways, corners, and out-of-the-way spots because it is those places in which students bully others and break more rules.

Include a positively stated rule in the schoolwide rules that can be applied to the expectations for hallway behavior. Remember to teach the rule by using examples and nonexamples. Also teach the negative consequences. Provide students with positive feedback when improvement is noted (e.g., an announcement over the intercom or at a pep assembly, an article in the school or community paper, announcements in parent newsletters).

Student conduct in the rest rooms, cafeteria, playground, and buses can be subject to the same procedures. For example, cafeteria behavior is not learned by osmosis—this behavior must be taught too. Teaching it in a chaotic 20-minute lunch period is seldom effective or efficient, but a planning session 5 to 10 minutes before lunchtime and a review session immediately following can prevent lunchroom problems from occurring. Once again, the teacher must describe and simulate the conditions, create episodes, ask students to role-play model behaviors, and use review sessions to augment them.

Similarly, other self-management skills can be taught through planning and review sessions. Investments early in the year will increase dividends at the end. Capital gains will be counted in teachers' own emotional well-being and that of their students. Achievement gains will also accompany this investment in good behavior.

Choosing and Using Consequences: Criteria

All of the consequences discussed in the preceding sections are merely illustrative. The teacher may have to alter consequences for some classes or some individuals. Some students might get a negative consequence for the first infraction. Although students start each day with a clean slate, some students may merit more consequences sooner. This decision can be communicated during planning and review sessions, during creation of individual behavioral contracts, or during individual conferences with students.

For example, neither a gentle oral reprimand nor taking away play objects reduced the incidence of Allisa's unacceptable behavior. The teacher knew that Allisa had all the necessary skills to complete assignments. Allisa was therefore informed that beginning tomorrow, she would owe time during recess (or after school) if she played with objects at her desk rather than completing her assignments. Allisa did not like to stay after school and was eager to go home and play. The same menu of consequences was used, but getting to the potent ones faster was viewed as the best solution in Allisa's case.

Some teachers decide to change the specific consequences after some experience with implementing them. A warning may result in a student's missing the next session on the computer, for example. Time owed could mean a student eats lunch in a designated "no talking" area or a student must remain in the classroom 5 minutes after other students leave for recess or home. Choosing effective consequences can be almost as important as consistently applying them when inappropriate behavior warrants their use. It is natural to gravitate toward the exclusive use of negative consequences for misbehavior. Be sure to balance their use with positive interactions, acknowledgment of responsible behavior, and positive consequences.

A teacher may want to use the practice of group consequences if more than one student in the group exhibits the unacceptable behaviors. Some teachers might be reluctant to impose the consequence because they fear reprisals from the innocent parties. However, group consequences may be the most effective way to teach the principle "We are all partially responsible for one another's behavior."

Finding consequences that students do not like but that are not physically or psychologically harmful is another test of appropriate negative consequences. Naturally, the teacher's power to manage conduct should be exercised in humane ways. Choosing negative consequences that are meaningful to students and, at the same time, humane is a rigorous test of a teacher's leadership role.

Negative consequences can be presented to students as a choice. For example, the elementary or middle school teacher could say, "Kendra, you can make a good choice or a bad choice. If you continue arguing, you will lose 5 minutes of center/free time. It is your choice." At the high school level, the teacher could say, "Wyatt, work quietly now or owe minutes after class. It is your choice." Teachers cannot insist that students behave, but students must know they will get a consequence if they choose to misbehave. Teachers should work earnestly to help students do their best.

Prolonged use of negative consequences, in the absence of positive behavior changes, can result in poor teacher–student relationships. It is recommended that educators typically pair negative consequences with positive interventions such as positive consequences, positive interactions, and interventions that teach desired behaviors.

Students find it easier to accept negative consequences and make adjustments in their behavior when violations of the rules are treated in a matter-of-fact manner. When painful consequences are used as a form of revenge, the student feels obliged to respond in kind. Hostility seems to provoke hostility. It is best not to add to the burden by telling students who they resemble or where they will end up. A succinct statement of the behavior that cannot be tolerated, followed by the consequence for noncompliance, is all that is required.

SEVERE BEHAVIOR COMPETENCIES

Most rule infractions involve minor offenses such as the following:

Students talk during seatwork or shout answers without being recognized.
They shove and push in the lunch line.

They make wisecracks or swear or chew gum.

Someone begins wandering around the room 10 seconds after a seatwork assignment has been given.

You have considered negative consequences that seem to fit these ordinary misbehaviors and have discussed the criteria for selecting and using these consequences. Now let us look at what is done when students are chronic troublemakers or engage in unacceptable behaviors that are more than ordinary offenses.

When a student willfully inflicts harm on another person or destroys property, overtly refuses to comply with a command, or stops an entire class, these are severe-clause behaviors that call for more complex actions. The criteria for selecting consequences are still good guidelines for dealing with these behaviors, but out-of-class consequences, reflecting a teacher's resolve to change a situation without delay, are needed. These behaviors result in office referrals, which are described in chapter 7. Some behaviors are resistant to intervention strategies presented in the text thus far. In these cases, teachers may need to seek help from colleagues at the building assistance team level. This team supports the teacher's problem solving, intervention planning, and implementation of strategies. Parents and the student should be invited to collaborate in the problem-solving process. Efficient teams convene once per week, and the teacher's wait time to be on the agenda is a few days. Quality teams provide at least one strategy for the teacher to try while the team conducts assessment that will lead to quality interventions. Sometimes a member on the team will become the teacher's partner and help carry out the strategy.

Teaching Desired Behaviors

The rest of this chapter is devoted to the how-tos of managing behaviors that do not respond to general management strategies. Many schools rely on punishment techniques such as detentions, suspensions, and expulsions to manage students with chronic and severe behaviors. This is not the time to rely on punishment alone to turn student behaviors around. This is a time for discussing and collaborating with students, their parents, and assistance team members in a problem-solving format. It is a time to determine what replacement behaviors students need and to teach them.

Teachers may ask guidance counselors, school psychologists, social workers, or others to develop lessons that teach students how to manage situations that cause difficulties. Lessons should include positive practice and feedback. Examples include (a) working with the class on conflict resolution strategies; (b) conducting lessons on life, job, or social skills; and (c) providing anger management skills. Common problems include the following five:

1. The student does not know how to handle poor peer relationships.
2. The student does not know how to be respectful to or accept corrective feedback from adults.
3. The student has bad habits such as making noise or masturbating in public.

4. The student is chronically off task because of daydreaming or a short attention span.
5. The student is orally or physically aggressive. Sprick et. al (1993) provided teaching procedures that teachers and support personnel can use with individuals or groups of students.

Using Reinforcement Systems

Both classroom and individual reinforcement systems are considered to be intrusive interventions and, therefore, must be used wisely. Structured reinforcement systems are based on the premise that external rewards can motivate students to improve their behavior, and there is an extensive body of research that supports this position. In contrast, educators who hold to humanistic theory, in particular, object to the use of external motivators (Kohn, 1997), and there is a substantial body of research in which the inappropriate use of rewards was found to actually decrease desirable behaviors. How do you make sense of these conflicting reports? If you can ensure that you are using reinforcement wisely, students will benefit. *Wise use* means that reinforcement systems are reserved for use with students who lack the interest and motivation to attempt to change. You must have a track record with the students that makes it clear the students did not respond to a series of other research-based interventions.

Those who subscribe to behavioral, cognitive-behavioral, social learning, and ecological theories support the appropriate use of structured reinforcement interventions. They define *appropriate use* as those short-term, structured reinforcement interventions that are applied to deeply ingrained, inappropriate behaviors resistant to other or simpler solutions (Sprick et al., 1993). Appropriate use targets students who are not motivated intrinsically to do their best in meeting expectations.

The rationale for the appropriate use of structured reinforcement is multifaceted. Targeted students should meet one or more of the following three facets: (1) Students need additional motivators because changing behaviors requires a lot of effort, (2) students are not motivated by success in school or do not value it, and (3) students' needs appear to be better met by inappropriate behavior than by doing what is expected or appropriate.

It is important to consider the concerns about reinforcement systems when you are developing a plan so that your interventions do not fall prey to certain weaknesses. First, a highly structured reinforcement system assists in getting the student's attention fixed right away on changing a behavior. Once the student has improved, the system must be faded gradually while you carry out a carefully designed component of teaching students to value success. Do not terminate reinforcement systems all at once as many teachers do, or students will probably stop working on the target behavior and rapidly revert to previous behaviors.

Second, you do not have to worry that students will always ask what they will get for doing something if you fade reinforcement systems and teach students to value their own success.

Third, do not consider reinforcement to be bribery. This is a common misunderstanding. Bribes occur when someone offers something, usually money, to someone else to influence them to do something wrong. For example, giving money to a presidential campaign in order to obtain protection of your business interests constitutes a bribe. In contrast, reinforcement is used to encourage someone to engage in behavior that is equated with success. An example of a reinforcer is awarding continuing education units (CEUs) toward maintaining professional licensure to teachers who attend a 1-day workshop. Likewise, awarding coupons toward a free lounge pass to students who set and attain work completion goals is an example of a reinforcer. Neither of the latter two situations has anything to do with bribery.

Fourth, other students will not object to some students' getting reinforcers if you follow at least one of three guidelines. These guidelines include keeping the reinforcement plan private, getting the nontargeted students to support the plan, and occasionally reinforcing the entire class for their support of a student's success.

Fifth, do not tell yourself that all students should be motivated and should behave without rewards. Remember that some students need to learn to value target behaviors (e.g., timely work completion), and without a structured reinforcement system they will continue to exhibit inappropriate behavior.

Sixth, remind yourself that reinforcing is no different from encouraging and facilitating. All students need different strokes. Teachers' encouraging words through positive interactions are more valued by some students than others. Teachers' reinforcements will work better for other students because that is what they currently value. Your job is to be sensitive to what students currently value and to use that to help them be immediately successful. Changing values takes time.

Educators who have little to no formal educational preparation in the implementation of structured reinforcement systems are urged to request help from their building assistance teams. The school counselor and the school psychologist are the two professionals in the building who are most likely to have the skills to help teachers implement a plan tailored to their needs. With these caveats in mind, an overview of the implementation of structured reinforcement systems follows.

Implementation of a Reinforcement System

As you get ready to implement a reinforcement plan, clearly define behaviors you want to change and establish boundaries between acceptable and unacceptable behaviors. Next, select your list of reinforcers. You can have a class brainstorming session to identify things that students might enjoy working for as a group. Give them 10 minutes to suggest as many things as possible. Tell students that no idea is stupid. Write all suggestions on the board. Keep ideas flowing and allow no discussion. At the end of 10 minutes, go through the list with students and eliminate unrealistic suggestions. Have students vote on the remainder, tally the votes, and arrange the list in order of preference. The first item on the list will be the first goal and so forth.

Specify what students must do to earn reinforcers and set up a reinforcement schedule. For example, a class problem of tardiness is resolved by giving one point every day when no one is late. When the class earns four points, they get 5 minutes of free time. Also develop a record-keeping system (e.g., keep information on a chart or a corner of the board where everyone can see).

Discuss and finalize the plan with students. Implement the plan and share students' progress each day. You might say, "You have just earned your first point. That gives you one point out of four. You are working very hard and will reach your goal by the end of the week at this rate." If there is an individual who keeps the whole group from earning points, take steps to change that person's behavior. Try any of the following plans. If the student is hooked on negative feedback, carefully explain this to the whole class and that they need to work on ignoring. The student may need a consequence of isolation. Reinforce him or her for cooperating in the group plan. You can also exclude the student from the class plan so that his or her behavior no longer affects classroom efforts. Set up an individual reinforcement system that will allow this student to earn the right to become part of the group again.

Example of a Reinforcement System

The following case example will acquaint you with the process of team problem solving that may be in place in your school building. Notice that the classroom teacher first tries to help the student by using in-class consequences and teaching desired behaviors. The teacher keeps records of the target behavior and the success of interventions. The teacher knows when her interventions and consequences are not producing the desired results and how to access more support.

You will also see the importance of ecological applications at the mesosystem level where home and school need to work together to help the student. You will see how structured reinforcement systems were implemented and paired with teaching desired behaviors. There also is an example of how to monitor the progress of a student by using simple graphing procedures. Teachers are expected to keep records of students' behavioral changes so that such changes can be graphed and monitored to gauge intervention success.

> Ms. Jackson is the kindergarten teacher of Shelby, who is aggressive at school. He hits, stomps, chokes, kicks, and pushes other children down. Ms. Jackson met with Shelby's mother and developed a plan to help Shelby improve his behavior. Ms. Jackson had already tried the following in-class consequences for aggressive behavior prior to talking to Shelby's mother: (a) orally sent Shelby to time-out and, more often, (b) physically carried him to time-out. Time-out was 5 minutes long. Shelby was then asked if he was ready to return to class. Five minutes was long enough for him to calm himself, and he returned to class each time. Ms. Jackson reported that the other students ignored him and continued with their work when he was being disruptive. She paired the time-out intervention with lessons on how to solve problems with peers. The guidance counselor had come to the class to help with the lessons and had scheduled Shelby in her play groups for additional instruction on conflict resolution.

Figure 4–2

Frequency of Aggressive Acts at
School per Day at Baseline

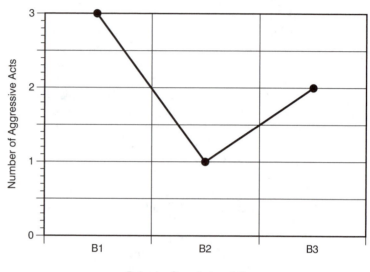

Behavior Sampled on 3 Days

Shelby's aggressive behaviors continued, and Ms. Jackson and the mother
decided to ask the building assistance team for support. Ms. Jackson and
the mother described the problem clearly and, in addition, provided records
of the aggressive behaviors. The team quickly graphed the frequency of
aggression (see Figure 4–2). You can see that the baseline of Shelby's target
behavior, aggression, averaged two aggressive acts per day. Success of
forthcoming interventions could be judged by continuing to count the frequency of aggressive behaviors and comparing it with the baseline.

On a scale from 0 to 10, in which a 0 indicated no problem and a 10 indicated
a severe problem, Ms. Jackson and the mother rated Shelby's physical
aggression as a 10. He attended morning kindergarten only and typically
had two angry outbursts each session. Aggressive behavior ranged from 3
to 5 minutes in duration. The teacher believed that Shelby's behavior was a
result of not getting his way. The behavior did not seem to be related to any
particular child in the classroom. Shelby's mother was not sure what the
behaviors were related to.

Team members determined that it was important to involve Shelby's mother in
all problem-solving attempts. They appointed the school psychologist to be
the case manager and work closely with the mother. The case manager
interviewed the mother to help determine antecedents and consequences of
the behavior and to see what strategies the mother had tried and their successes. She expressed great concern about Shelby's behavior and stated that
she would like assistance. She questioned whether fatigue, hunger, or other
physiological factors caused his angry reactions. At home, Shelby's aggressive behaviors occurred more often before mealtime and bedtime (i.e., must

turn off the television). He was not controlling his anger when faced with frustration or disappointment. He became physically and orally out of control. He would scratch, kick, hit, punch, and bite. He used objects to harm family members and the family dog. Home incidents occurred at the rate of two to three per day.

His mother described the antecedents to Shelby's behavior as follows: He does not receive something that he would like, something does not happen that he expected, there is a misunderstanding, or he is not in control of a situation. Transitions were a problem, particularly bedtime. For example, asking him to turn off the television and go to bed resulted in physically aggressive behavior. Ineffective interventions during these times had been: (a) making oral comments such as "Stop it, you're not going to get it" or "I know you're getting angry"; (b) trying to talk him out of it; (c) touching him; and (d) spanking him. Restraining him by holding him had worked somewhat. His mother would hold him until he agreed to stop the behavior. It would take about 10 minutes for him to become calm, but another outburst would usually occur when she let go of him. She had also tried having Shelby march around the house rather than become physically aggressive when he was upset. Sometimes he would march until he was calm. She did not use time-out because he refused to go. When she sent him to a time-out spot, she had to hold the door shut to keep him in the time-out space.

After reading about Shelby's behaviors at school and at home, you can clearly see that school interventions alone will not be sufficient to help him meet classroom expectations. It was wise of the teacher and the parent to ask the assistance team for help. On the basis of the information provided by the teacher and the parent during interviews, Shelby's target problem was identified as following adult directions the first time given. All of his angry outbursts occurred when a teacher or his mother asked him to do something that he did not want to do. Rather than focus on the aggression as the problem, the team determined that the focus should be upon helping him learn how to follow directions in a peaceable manner.

A reinforcement system was developed to provide rewards for following directions the first time given. Ms. Jackson and the mother agreed to meet with Shelby and discuss the new plan. His ideas about the plan were to be considered, but the adults were not to be talked out of using appropriate consequences. Specifically, they were to discuss and role-play how to demonstrate the target behavior of following directions the first time given, how Shelby would earn and record points, how to turn points in for a reinforcer, and how to go to and return from time-out.

Shelby's mother agreed to use the reinforcement program, time-out, and an instructional program to replace angry behaviors. The school psychologist provided instruction on how to use time-out appropriately. Specifically, Shelby's time would start when he was in the time-out space and quiet. That eliminated the mother's having to hold the door shut while he pulled from the other side in an attempt to get out. The teacher agreed to use the same interventions at school. She was instructed to start Shelby's time when he was in the time-out space and quiet. For every minute that he dawdled, another minute was added to his time-out, both at home and at school. These procedures eliminated having to physically take him to time-out.

Shelby completed a reinforcer survey and indicated he liked these things: fishing, swimming, movies, gold necklaces, candy, ice cream, stickers, computer time, playtime with toys, getting a pet, time with parent, and watching his favorite television programs. Point values for each of his reinforcers were determined by the teacher and the parent.

With reinforcement added to his school-based intervention, Shelby's aggressive behaviors at school began to decrease. When he had a week of one or no aggressive acts, the reinforcement system was to be faded. Fading in this situation would mean that he would be expected to have more good days in order to earn the same amount of points. Fading could also mean that the number of points that each reinforcer was worth increased. Fading is more successful when adults who give the rewards orally emphasize the importance of appropriate behavior rather than the value of the reward. For example, when fading, the teacher said, "Shelby, you made good choices all week and followed directions the first time given very well. Because you are showing me how good you are at following directions, I will not be marking every time you follow a direction. You won't know when I am marking so you will need to remember our rule about following directions and do it every time. Do you have any questions?" In summary, the structured reinforcement system is used to get Shelby's attention and quickly put a stop to harmful behaviors. At the same time, the teacher, the mother, and the guidance counselor continue to help Shelby develop conflict resolution skills.

Helping Students Learn Self-Management

Doyle (1986) reviewed interventions that teachers use to repair breakdowns in classroom order. He concluded that attention has shifted from having teachers implement behavior modification programs to helping students learn to self-monitor and self-control. Self-management in education consists of self-monitoring, self-reinforcing, self-evaluation, and self-instruction. Self-monitoring is described in this section. Considerable research evidence exists for the application of self-monitoring to school problems of students in regular education, with learning disabilities, with behavioral disorders, who are mentally retarded, who have multiple physical disabilities, and with attention deficit disorder.

Sprick et al. (1993) offered the following rationale for self-monitoring interventions. Some students are not aware of their actions that get labeled as behavioral problems. Because they are unaware of their actions, they end up seeing their problems as a reflection of who they are rather than the actions they take. For example, their actions may be impulsive, but they have learned to label themselves as irresponsible, obnoxious, or bad. Many students begin to feel hopeless; self-monitoring can help them regain hope through regaining control.

Additional rationales for the use of self-monitoring in educational settings include five major points (Lloyd, Landrum, & Hallahan, 1991). The first point is that instilling self-control in our youth is one of the primary goals of education. The second point is based on research that indicates self-monitoring may increase the effectiveness of interventions. Third, self-monitoring may decrease the demand for direct intervention by teachers, which saves them time. The final two points are that self-monitoring may improve the maintenance and transfer of intervention effects.

The purpose of self-monitoring is to increase a student's awareness of a particular area in which he or she lacks self-control. Students actually observe their own behavior. In turn, this helps them take responsibility for their behavior and control what they do. The hallmarks of successful self-monitoring include the following:

1. The student learns to pay close attention to what he or she is or is not doing.
2. The student counts and charts improvements, which enhances intrinsic motivation.
3. The student typically needs no further reinforcement than the sense of accomplishment.

Educators can use self-monitoring when a student has some motivation to change problems associated with mild behavioral problems: blurting out, complaining, all types of inappropriate comments, off-task behavior, careless work, and inappropriate interactions.

An example of a student who might benefit from self-monitoring is Sue, a gifted third grader who is very unhappy. She shows off her own accomplishments, subtly puts down peers' efforts, and uses her success to be the center of attention. Sue's peers do not want to be around her and form cliques that exclude her. Sue thinks that the other kids don't like her because she is smart. During problem solving, the teacher hypothesizes that the bragging, showing off, and criticizing of others are what peers don't like. She suggests to Sue that she is bright and can learn to be more sensitive. They decide to try a self-monitoring system to make Sue more aware of her comments.

The educator preplans by gathering relevant background information to help design the intervention. Unless you have practiced this intervention through course work or in-services, you should seek assistance (e.g., master teachers, school counselors, school psychologists) the first few times you use self-monitoring interventions.

After you develop the self-monitoring plan, it is best to complete a planned discussion with the student and the parent(s). Let's look at the example of Rita, a second grader who is pleasant and participates in class. Her work on in-class assignments is low-average to average. She needs directions repeated most of the time. Mrs. Brown, her teacher, has initiated planned discussions and a classwide structured reinforcement system that rewards all students for following directions.

They have yielded poor results for Rita. Mrs. Brown decides to seek consultative assistance. The consultant interviews the teacher and finds out this information:

1. *Schoolwork:* Rita was a low-average student in first grade. When teachers repeat directions, she is able to do the work. Rita wanders around the room, talks to others, and moves a great deal during group time on the carpet. She has difficulty following directions in multiple settings. She likes teacher attention. Mrs. Brown thinks that she has attention deficit hyperactivity disorder (ADHD) and needs medication to help her control her behavior.
2. *Social skills:* Rita has many friends. The teacher likes her and describes her as a pleasant student.

Before referring students for an evaluation for possible ADHD, teachers need to implement structured interventions with progress monitoring to see how successful the interventions can be. In this situation, Rita needs to self-monitor following directions the first time given. The teacher tallies the frequency with which Rita follows directions the first time given for 3 days. Days are divided into three time periods: morning, midday, and afternoon.

The consultant and the teacher set up a self-monitoring system that requires Rita to circle a smiley face or a sad face at the end of each class. A small paper with each class listed and faces are taped to her desk. Rita circles a smiley face if she follows about four of every five directions (or most of the time) the first time given.

The system should be fairly unobtrusive. The power of this intervention is decreased when a student is embarrassed. Older students, in particular, need to have the form inside a notebook. Younger students usually like the intervention and feel special. Other students may want to self-monitor, too, and you should let them. Any student can benefit from learning how to self-monitor. Sprick et al. (1993) provided self-monitoring recording forms that can be duplicated for use in classrooms. Consider these six examples of ways to record behaviors:

1. Tally on-task and off-task behavior during independent work.
2. Tally positive interactions with peers during specified times.
3. Give a plus (+) for responsible behavior or a minus (−) for irresponsible behavior.
4. Circle a number each time a task is completed successfully.
5. Rate effort.
6. Use a checklist for tasks that have to be completed.

Times when the student could record behavior include these five instances:

1. Monitor once a day at a specified time; choose the most problematic time. For example, if a student has the most difficulty paying attention during the afternoon, monitor only in the afternoon.

2. Monitor during certain activities. For example, if a student has difficulty keeping hands and feet to self when lining up or sitting together on the floor, monitor behavior during those activities.
3. Monitor at specified intervals. For example, if a student has difficulty with work completion, mark the number of problems completed in a 15-minute period.
4. Monitor at random intervals. For example, if a student has difficulty with on-task behavior, monitor behavior at random intervals.
5. Monitor all occurrences of the behavior. For example, use for hand raising, waiting to be called on, talking respectfully to the teacher, and engaging in positive self-talk.

It is important to design a cuing system to prompt the student to record. If he or she is counting specific behaviors, the behavior is the cue. If he or she is counting on-task behavior at random intervals, teachers can use a timer or a beep tape. A beep tape has prerecorded beeps that sound as cues to students who observe and record their own behavior.

Plan to have an adult occasionally monitor the student's behavior and compare results with the student's record. In early phases, an adult should monitor frequently as the student is self-monitoring. If the two agree on the rating, commend the student. If they do not agree, hold a discussion and make sure the student is clear on what to record. Fade adult monitoring when the student develops reliable self-monitoring skills.

You must identify ways to determine whether the intervention is helping the student reach his or her goal. It is recommended that you use at least two separate means of measuring effectiveness (e.g., records of student and adult, subjective impressions of student and adult, grades, attendance records, office referrals). Graph and discuss student progress. Figure 4–3 shows graphs of Rita's progress.

Figure 4–3

Frequency of Following Directions Prior to and After Self-Monitoring

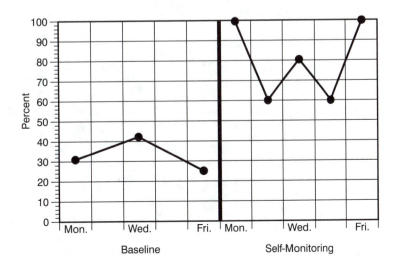

The first three data points represent her frequency of following directions prior to self-monitoring. This is referred to as her *baseline*. Note how the self-monitoring intervention increased her direction following within a week. Successful interventions such as this may decrease referrals for medical treatment of suspected ADHD.

It is important to encourage students in their efforts. Remember that learning new behaviors and discarding old ones are very difficult tasks for anyone. Students may need a lot of practice, the opportunity to make errors and adjustments, and a lot of encouragement along the way. Make periodic revisions and adjustments to the plan as necessary. When the student demonstrates consistent success, fade the intervention. Once the intervention has been faded, provide continued follow-up, support, and encouragement.

Obtaining Assistance from the Building-Level Problem-Solving Team

Many teachers struggle off and on during their professional careers to manage student behaviors successfully. Few teachers take to managing every possible student behavior as ducks take to water. Do not think that everyone besides you knows exactly what to do with problem behaviors. Most of us have to study and practice and study and practice some more in order to work successfully with students who do not respond to basic classroom management plans. School counselors, school

Specialists on the school's problem-solving team help teachers develop intervention plans.

psychologists, and school social workers earn advanced degrees in human services work, and they are available to assist teachers. Take advantage of their expertise to work together to help students grow socially, emotionally, and behaviorally.

Although support personnel are willing to assist teachers in developing intervention plans, teachers are the individuals in the classroom who have to carry out most plans. There are occasions when a support person will team with a teacher to implement behavior plans. Students develop prosocial behaviors best in their natural environment. That is why teachers are encouraged to implement behavior change plans in their own classrooms. For example, many teachers ask for specialists to take students out of their classrooms and provide social skills instruction. However, pullout programs in social skills training are generally not supported by research. Social skills development needs to be conducted with a group of peers in which esteemed peers are used as models, with follow-up in the natural environment of the school building, classrooms, and playground. In other words, social skills training is a systems-level intervention. The entire system needs to support the use of the targeted social skill across all students, not just the student who was selected as having social skills deficits. Asking the school psychologist or school counselor to pull a lone student in for counseling on social skills is rarely effective. A student may be able to demonstrate a skill in the counselor's office but will not generalize the skill to the classroom, hallways, or lunchroom. Individual sessions are mostly a waste of time.

COMPETENCIES IN LEGAL ASPECTS OF CONDUCT MANAGEMENT

The control that school authorities may exercise over the activities of students is circumscribed by the nature of the relationship between public schools and students. This relationship has been defined by common law according to the concept of *in loco parentis* (Reutter, 1975):

> This doctrine holds that school authorities stand in the place of the parent while the child is at school. As applied to discipline the inference is that school personnel may establish rules for the educational welfare of the child and the operation of the school and may use punishments for not following the rules. Obviously, however, a school employee legally cannot go as far as a parent can in enforcement of matters of taste, extent of punishment, or disregard of procedural due process. School rules that are contrary to expressed wishes of a parent generally will be subject to more careful judicial scrutiny than other rules. (p. 3)

The doctrine, as originally conceived, was intended to give teachers considerable discretion in disciplinary matters. It was presumed that teachers having this authority would act reasonably and with due regard to children's interests. The concept has undergone considerable change as a result of differences among adults about what constitutes appropriate discipline and also as a result of increased parental challenges to the reasonableness of disciplinary actions taken by school officials (Rossow & Hininger, 1991; Zirkel & Reichner, 1987).

The legal derivation of student rights has focused the court's attention on the First and Fourteenth Amendments of the U.S. Constitution. The First Amendment reads as follows:

> Congress shall make no law respecting an establishment of religion, or prohibiting the free exercise thereof; or abridging the freedom of speech, or of the press; or the right of the people peaceably to assemble and to petition the Government for a redress of grievances.

The Fourteenth Amendment (1868) states in part,

> No State shall make or enforce any law which shall abridge the privileges or immunities of citizens of the United States; nor shall any State deprive any person of life, liberty, or property, without due process of law; nor deny to any person within its jurisdiction the equal protection of the laws.

Because teachers are agents of the state, their actions are subject to constitutional scrutiny as provided by the Fourteenth Amendment. Thus, the freedoms granted in the First Amendment are made applicable to students through the Fourteenth Amendment.

The matter of due process, substantive and procedural, has been the basis for most litigation initiated by students and their parents. Thus, the remainder of this chapter is devoted to a discussion of due process and other school-related legal issues and the ramifications of court decisions for classroom teachers. Because the discussion focuses on the disciplinary situations and techniques typically associated with the instructional duties of teachers, the issues of freedom of expression—that is, guarantees of speech, symbolic expression, press, assembly, association, and matters of conscience—are not addressed.

Rules of Conduct and Due Process Considerations

Arguments about student rights generally occur on two levels: substantive and procedural. *Substantive due process* issues deal with whether an individual student's constitutional rights have been judiciously considered in the creation of regulations to manage and protect the school system and to protect the rights of other students to secure an education. The emphasis is on the fairness of the policy or the rule itself.

In determining the substantive rights of students, a person should ask,
1. Will the actions of the student cause substantial disruption to the educational process and/or the normal operation of the school?
2. Will the actions of the student be an invasion of the rights of others? (Furtwengler & Konnert, 1982, p. 201)

School officials who answer in the affirmative to either of these questions must still be prepared to defend the policy and their actions. The courts have taken a dim view of actions to circumvent student misconduct based on supposition and speculation.

Procedural due process provides students accused of misconduct or slated for punishment an opportunity to defend themselves. The students' rights are secured when they know what they are accused of doing, know the basis for the accusation, and are given an opportunity to present their side of the story. Thus, officials must proceed to take actions in a defensible and reasonable way, which ensures proper form and fairness for the accused.

Student claims for due process rights have been used to test the traditional management practices of U.S. school systems and to question the legal authority of school teachers and administrators. Many of these claims begin when students question the rules themselves and the reasons given for a denial of freedoms covered by the rules. A set of well-formulated, explicitly stated rules is the first step toward reducing disputes and reconciling conflicts without legal action. After having analyzed hundreds of cases decided in federal and appellate state courts, Reutter (1975) offered the following essentials for an enforceable rule:

1. The rule must be publicized to students. Whether it is issued orally or in writing, school authorities must take reasonable steps to bring the rule to the attention of students. A major exception is where the act for which a student is to be disciplined is obviously destructive of school property or disruptive of school operation.
2. The rule must have a legitimate educational purpose. The rule may affect an individual student's learning situation or the rights of other students in the education setting.
3. The rule must have a rational relationship to the achievement of the stated educational purpose.
4. The meaning of the rule must be reasonably clear. Although a rule of student conduct need not meet the strict requirements of a criminal statute, it must not be so vague as to be almost completely subject to the interpretation of the school authority invoking it.
5. The rule must be sufficiently narrow in scope so as not to encompass constitutionally protected activities along with those which constitutionally may be proscribed in the school setting.
6. If the rule infringes a fundamental constitutional right of students, a compelling interest of the school (state) in the enforcement of the rule must be shown. (p. 6)

In view of the aforementioned redefinition and enlargement of student civil liberties, prudence suggests student involvement in the formulation of the rules, periodic review of the rules with student input, and the designation of responsible authorities for the implementation of the rules.*

Corporal Punishment

The term *corporal punishment* refers to any type of punishment that inflicts physical pain to modify behavior. The term is usually used to refer to paddling within a school setting. There is much disagreement among educators regarding the necessity or the desirability of using corporal punishment as a disciplinary measure, and numerous local school boards and some states have banned its use. However, it is wise to know the legal implications (Henderson, 1986) because many educators continue to believe in and use this method of discipline.

* I wish to express my appreciation to Dr. E. Edmund Reutter for granting permission to reprint in this chapter large narrative sections of his publication, *The courts and Students Conduct* (1975), which was commissioned by ERIC Clearinghouse on Educational Management and published by the National Organization on Legal Problems of Education.

Supreme Court Decisions

Two U.S. Supreme Court decisions have established the boundaries within which teachers must operate, as discussed in the following subsections.

Ingraham v. Wright.   *Ingraham v. Wright* (1977) deals with issues of excessive punishment and whether or not such punishment violates the cruel and unusual punishment clause of the Eighth Amendment. The case originated in Dade County, Florida, where corporal punishment is specifically authorized but explicitly limited by school board policy. Two students were allegedly subjected to a severe paddling during the 1970–1971 school year. Ingraham was struck 20 times with a flat wooden paddle (15 times more than the school board policy permitted) because he was slow in responding to his teacher's instructions. The paddling resulted in hematoma, and the subject missed 11 days of school. The second student, Andrews, was paddled so severely on his arms that he lost full use of them for more than a week. A Florida law forbade punishment that was "degrading or unduly severe" or that took place prior to consultation with the principal or the teacher in charge of the school.

Thus, two issues were brought to the attention of the courts: (1) Was the use of corporal punishment in violation of the Eighth Amendment? and (2) Was some type of procedural due process required before a teacher or another disciplinarian could employ corporal punishment?

The Supreme Court ruled, as did the district court and the court of appeals, that the beatings, although excessive and unreasonable, did not violate the Eighth Amendment. The justices concluded, in a 5-to-4 decision, that the amendment was never intended to apply to schools but was created to control the punishment of criminals. In essence, corporal punishment is not cruel and unusual punishment.

With regard to the second question, the court stated, "We conclude that the Due Process Clause does not require notice and a hearing prior to the imposition of corporal punishment in the public schools, as that practice is authorized and limited by common law" (*Ingraham v. Wright,* 1977). The majority reasoned that the purpose of corporal punishment would be diluted if elaborate procedures had to be followed prior to its use.

Although these two rulings permit the use of corporal punishment without a formal due process hearing, educators are advised to investigate the facts before using this form of punishment. Students may still sue on the basis of violation of substantive due process rights, embodied in the Fourteenth Amendment, or seek remedies through an indictment for criminal assault and battery (Piele, 1978).

Baker v. Owen.   The second case that helps educators understand the issues and devise procedures for the use of corporal punishment was brought by a parent who wanted to restrict the use of corporal punishment on her child by school authorities. In this instance, the Supreme Court let stand a decision by a federal district court in North Carolina in *Baker v. Owen* (1975). Although the Court was sympathetic to the contention that parents have a fundamental right to select appropriate disciplinary methods for their children, it refused to support the argument that these rights extended into the school. In fact, the Court upheld the right of educators to administer corporal punishment over the objections of the parents because of the "legitimate and substantial interest" of the state "in maintaining order and discipline in the public schools." This court decision may have prompted some states (e.g., California) to pass laws that provide for prior written parental approval before a student may be spanked.

School personnel may have been given considerable latitude in the use of corporal punishment, but wisdom suggests using the minimal due process requirements that were an outgrowth of the *Baker v. Owen* decision. A simplified rendering of the *Baker v. Owen* case provides the following four procedural safeguards:

1. Generally, corporal punishment should not be used to correct first-offense behaviors.
2. Students should know what misbehaviors could lead to corporal punishment.
3. An adult witness should be present when the student is given reasons for the punishment and during the administration of the punishment.
4. On request, the disciplinarian should provide the student's parents with an explanation for the punishment.

Compliance with these guidelines will permit the educator to operate within the framework of the Eighth Amendment.

Civil Liability Considerations

What constitutes excessive use of corporal punishment? Although there is no exact way to ascertain the reasonableness of using corporal punishment or what constitutes moderation in its application, the disciplinarian would be well advised to consider

> the age, sex, and size of the pupil; his apparent physical strength and structure; that the type of instrument should be one suitable and proper for the purposes; and that punishment should be proportioned to the offense, the apparent motive and disposition of the offender, and the influence of his example and conduct on others. (Drury & Ray, 1967, p. 44)

Court opinions devoted to this issue have also provided some clues about what constitutes reasonable use of corporal punishment (O'Reilly & Green, 1983):

1. *It is consistent with the existing statutes.* Where corporal punishment is authorized by the statutes, and where boards of education have policies that are in compliance with the statute, or where corporal punishment is allowed by the statutes, the courts will—as a general rule—hold in favor of the board of education and its employees.
2. *It is a corrective remedy for undesirable behavior.* Occasionally, the teacher, like the parent, will need to resort to corporal punishment as the last means of correcting a child's errant behavior.
3. *It is neither cruel nor excessive.* The courts will weigh the evidence to determine if, in the face of the facts, the punishment was excessive—not reasonably believed at the time to be necessary for the child's discipline or training. If it is found to be excessive, the school authorities who inflicted it may be held liable in damages to the child and, if malice is shown, they may be subject to criminal penalties.
4. *There is no permanent or lasting injury.* The implication here is that there may be a temporary injury that is insufficient to bring a finding against the school official.

5. *Malice is not present.* It is a standard rule of thumb that no punishment should be administered in a fit of anger on the part of the teacher or principal. Revenge is not a valid reason for administering corporal punishment.
6. *The punishment is suitable for the age and sex of the child.* The standard to be applied here is one of reasonableness.
7. *An appropriate instrument is used.* The courts will consider the appropriateness of the instrument when given the evidence in the case. Among the various types of instruments that have been considered to be reasonable are a wooden paddle and a 12-inch ruler. The questionable factor is not the instrument used so much as the portion of the anatomy that is struck, the degree to which the instrument is used, and the end result of the corporal punishment. (pp. 144–145)*

These guidelines should not be regarded as unquestionable standards. Whether a punishment is unreasonable or excessive raises questions of fact that may have to be settled by a civil lawsuit.

Assault and Battery

When school personnel are charged with assault and battery, these charges usually arise from the administration of corporal punishment. The cases generally involve a person who is not authorized to administer corporal punishment or an authorized person who uses excessive punishment. In these instances, individuals may be required to defend themselves in criminal action against the charges of assault and battery.

Nolte (1980) defined *assault* as

an illegal attempt or offer (without actual contact) to beat or touch another person in such a way as to cause that person to apprehend immediate peril. Thus, the attempt must be coupled with the ability or what the person believes to be the ability to execute the threat. (p. 114)

Battery is described as

the willful touching of another person by the aggressor or by some substance put in motion by him; or as it is sometimes expressed, a battery is the consummation of the assault. (pp. 114–115)

Thus, assault is essentially a mental rather than a physical interference, whereas battery is physical damage to a person.

Assault and battery cases are generally decided by a jury with instructions from a judge. Because most civil suits do involve an alleged abuse of corporal punishment, the jury has to decide whether the teacher, acting *in loco parentis,* has behaved according to a standard of care that the average and normally prudent parent would have applied in the same or similar circumstances. Criteria used by the courts to identify excessive punishment, discussed earlier with regard to corporal punishment, are used to ascertain criminal wrongdoing.

---

* Reprinted by permission of Greenwood Publishing Group, Inc., Westport, CT, from *School Law for the Practitioner* (pp. 144–145) by Robert C. O'Reilly and Edward T. Green. Copyright by Roger C. O'Reilly and Edward T. Green and published in 1983 by Greenwood Press.

Generally, the reasoning in such cases involves the application of tort law, which is beyond the scope of this book. Suffice it to say that tort law provides a remedy for persons who believe a particular instance of corporal punishment exceeds the considerable latitude given educators and the forms of punishment that might be condoned by the Eighth Amendment.

Detention, Suspension, and Expulsion

In view of the serious nature and consequences of using corporal punishment to correct breaches of conduct in terms of both legal issues and the lack of evidence that punishment promotes child development, teachers frequently use detention or time owed. Students are detained during periods when they would usually be free, such as recess, lunchtime, and before and after school, as a form of punishment. The action is predicated on students' desire to avoid the loss of social contacts and fun-time activities that occur outside of the classroom. Teachers may impose detention for reasonable periods of time and for clearly punishable offenses with no legal question of authority. The practice has been tested in the courts, and school authorities' actions have been upheld (Peterson, Rossmiller, & Volz, 1978, p. 354).

Legal aspects of the use of suspension and expulsion are included in chapter 7, which covers schoolwide discipline. The law as it applies to both students in regular education and students in special education is explained.

Search and Seizure

A considerable amount of litigation associated with the public school setting has involved the "unreasonable search and seizure" phrase of the Fourth Amendment (Lincoln, 1986). Generally, lawsuits have been aimed at school personnel who have searched students or their school lockers. The courts have generally held that searches based on a "reasonable suspicion" that the student possessed some form of contraband in violation of the law could be conducted without the student's consent and without a valid warrant. Searches conducted when a student is believed to have stolen property that is sought as evidence in a non-school-related crime have also been sanctioned by the courts. Court decisions, for the most part, have supported these search practices by referring to the doctrine of *in loco parentis* or by finding that the search did not meet the standard of unreasonableness prohibited by the Fourteenth Amendment.

Teachers should be wary of using the *in loco parentis* doctrine to legitimize a search of a student's locker or desk or to justify asking a student to remove items from pockets, purses, or book bags. Although the school building is not a privileged sanctuary from the law, neither is it a place where students relinquish their due process rights. Teachers would do better to act as wise parents, intent on protecting the child's interests, rather than as state agents seeking evidence on which to convict the student.

The susceptibility of children and teenagers to the use of drugs has placed teachers in a special relationship to the problem. Parents who surrender their children to the school for large parts of each day expect school personnel to provide reasonable safeguards against young people's inexperience and lack of mature judgment. Thus, when judging the actions of school personnel, the courts weigh the constitutional safeguards of other individuals and the methods that school personnel use to maintain discipline. Random or arbitrary searches, even if announced in advance, are discouraged. McCarthy and Cambron (1981) have suggested that school personnel protect themselves from litigation by adhering to the following six guidelines:

1. If police officials are conducting a search in the school, either with or without the school's involvement, school authorities should ensure that a search warrant is obtained.
2. Students and parents should be informed at the beginning of the school term of the procedures for conducting locker searches and personal searches.
3. Before school personnel conduct a search, the student should be asked to turn over the contraband, as such voluntary submission of material can eliminate the necessity for a search.
4. The authorized person conducting a search should have another staff member present who can verify the procedures used in the search.
5. School personnel should refrain from using strip searches or mass searches of groups of students.
6. Any search should be based on at least "reasonable belief" or "suspicion" that the student is in possession of contraband that may be disruptive to the educational process. (pp. 307–308)

The courts have issued more stringent standards when the privacy of an individual's person is invaded. In this regard, compulsory drug testing for all students, specifically urinalysis, has been looked on with disfavor by the courts. This procedure, which has been compared to a strip search, involves students' Fourth Amendment rights (Rossow & Hininger, 1991).

The judgment in *Odenheim v. Carlstadt–East Rutherford Regional School District* (1985) was based on principles of search, wherein the school official must have reasonable grounds for suspecting that the search will reveal evidence that a rule or law has been violated. In this instance, it would be highly unlikely that every student in a school would give officials a "clear indication" that they were breaking a school rule concerning drug use. When standards of reasonableness cannot be met, it is improper for school officials to try to regulate the behavior of an entire student body.

Thus, "reasonable suspicion" may be sufficient for a locker search, but "probable cause," the standard used by law enforcement officials, is generally applied to body or strip searches. This means the school official must have evidence from highly reliable sources that a particular student is using or hiding illegal or dangerous materials. These more stringent standards are applied to protect the privacy of students and to prevent psychological damage to sensitive children.

OBSERVATION OF A TEACHER'S CONDUCT MANAGEMENT

There is no better way to learn about conduct management than to watch a teacher in action. Through a field-placement experience or some other means, ask a teacher for the opportunity to observe in the classroom. In Table 4–2 there is a list of conduct

Table 4–2
Conduct management indicators for classroom observation.

Statement of the Rules

1. Rules are stated as desired behaviors or actions.
2. Classroom rules are confined to five or six and are taught and modeled by the teacher.
3. Special activity procedures, as differentiated from rules, are clearly specified, demonstrated, and practiced.
4. Rules are publicly displayed for easy reference.
5. Rules are periodically reviewed, and appropriate behaviors are practiced.

Application of the Rules

6. Appropriate and inappropriate behavior can easily be detected and dealt with immediately.
7. Techniques for discilpline are applied consistently to all students.
8. Application of the stated rules minimizes distractions or disruptions that interfere with student academic progress.
9. Students do not disobey the rules simply to get attention.
10. The frequency and duration of disciplinary incidents are well within teacher expectations.
11. Classroom rules are consistent with or identical to the code of conduct for the building.
12. Disciplinary practices are clearly linked to the student's inappropriate behavior.

Consequences for Appropriate and Inappropriate Behavior

13. Appropriate student behavior is rewarded in a variety of ways and in ways that are appealing to students.
14. Occasional checks are made to be sure rewards continue to be attractive incentives.
15. Negative consequences are explicity stated and consistently applied.
16. Warnings and threats are not substituted for the administration of logical and/or negative consequences.
17. Occasional checks are made to ascertain the deterrent value of penalties.
18. Administration of the reward and penalty system does not take an inordinate amount of time.
19. A severe clause is used to deal with extreme and persistent disciplinary incidents.

Provisions for Cooperation

20. Students are developmentally equipped to meet the standards of conduct.
21. Students are knowledgeable about rewards for desired behavior and know what to do to get them.
22. Parents are provided a written copy of the rules and the consequences for lack of adherence to them.
23. Parents are periodically informed about their child's citizenship/character development.
24. The principal has been given an opportunity to review and suggest revisions of the classroom management plan.
25. The principal has agreed to participate in the use of predetermined positive and negative consequences.
26. Colleagues who are directly affected by the management plan have been apprised of the particulars and have been given an opportunity to suggest changes.
27. Colleagues who have been asked to participate in the administration of selected consequences approve of these procedures and their professional involvement.

management indicators that can be used to structure your classroom observation. Try to observe every criterion on the list. If any cannot be observed, ask the teacher for the opportunity to conduct a brief interview and ask about the remaining items.

On the basis of what you learned from your observation, the text, class discussions, and your own real-life experiences, construct your own conduct management plan. Appendix A offers a form that can be used for this purpose.

CONCLUSION

Conduct management creates another portion of the foundation for an orderly, task-oriented approach to teaching and learning. Conduct management serves to socialize students to the classroom and school building culture and deserves greater attention during the early months of the school year. Effectively handled conduct functions, although more controlling than may be appealing to many teachers, gradually prepare students for greater independence and autonomy.

At the microsystem level, teachers can develop competencies in the use of numerous strategies with all students in the group or individual students. At the mesosystem level, teachers can collaborate with parents and students to write behavioral contracts after microsystem strategies fail to produce successful behavioral change. There are legal considerations to the use of the various conduct management alternatives.

SUPPLEMENTARY QUESTIONS

Now that you have studied various interventions to use for classroom behavioral problems, you should be able to problem solve the following vignettes. See if you would manage them any differently after reading this chapter than you would have before reading this chapter. First, reflect and answer the question without looking at the options in parentheses. Second, compare your solutions with the options.

1. You walk into your first-hour class several minutes before the bell rings and see a group of students who have arrived early. Several of them are teasing a lone student who is crying. This student has never been a problem for you. How would you solve this problem?

   (*Options:* [a] Use a directive strategy focused on the classroom rule of respect for all people. [b] If the school has a bullying prevention or antiharassment/-teasing program, give all the students passes to go to the center, where they can spend 10 to 15 minutes resolving conflicts.)

2. You have a student who spends a great deal of class time either joking around or debating the inherent value of your lessons and assignments. Classmates laugh at his jokes and seem to like him. Today is no exception. During the first few minutes of the lesson, he first cracks a joke about it and then remarks that it is a waste of time and has no relevance to life outside of school. How would you solve this problem?

   (*Options:* [a] If you think the student is trying to obtain teacher and/or peer attention, follow the procedures described in the ignoring section of the text. [b] If you are sure that the behavior is not an attempt to get attention and that ignoring the student will not decrease the behavior, use a mild consequence. Have a conference with the student after class to discuss what the consequences will be. Support the student in making appropriate jokes outside of the classroom.)

3. You are leading the students in a review of some difficult course material. Two students seated toward the back of the room are quietly talking to each other. You have already asked them once to stop talking. Now they are talking again. How would you solve this problem?

(You have already given them a gentle oral reprimand. It is time to move on to another mild consequence—time owed.)

4. You are explaining the distribution of grades on the exam you just passed back to students. You describe how this one grade for the class fits into your grading system. One bright student begins to criticize your grading policies, saying that they are unfair. How would you solve this problem?

(Use a mild consequence of an oral cue, such as "I understand that you are feeling like the system is unfair. Please see me after class and we will discuss your concerns.")

5. Class is over and students are exiting the room. Two students begin to argue and one pushes the other with enough force that the student falls into nearby desks. How would you solve this problem?

(*Options:* [a] If you are certain that this behavior was typical "horseplay" between the peers, proximity control or an oral cue about keeping everyone safe is sufficient. [b] If you suspect bullying behavior, give passes to both students as in Question 1.)

REFERENCES

Baker v. Owen, 395 F. Supp. 294 (M.D.N.C. 1975), *aff'd,* 423 U.S. 907.

Doyle, W. (1986). Classroom organization and management. In M. C. Wittrock (Ed.), *Handbook of research on teaching* (pp. 392–431). New York: Macmillan.

Dreikurs, R., & Cassell, P. (1972). *Discipline without tears: What to do with children who misbehave.* New York: Hawthorn Books.

Drury, R. L., & Ray, K. C. (1967). *Essentials in school law.* New York: Appleton-Century-Crofts.

Furtwengler, W. J., & Konnert, W. (1982). *Improving school discipline: An administrator's guide.* Boston: Allyn & Bacon.

Henderson, D. H. (1986). Constitutional implications involving the use of corporal punishment in the public schools: A comprehensive review. *Journal of Law & Education, 15,* 255–269.

Hoy, W. K., & Woolfolk, A. E. (1990). Socialization of student teachers. *American Educational Research Journal, 27,* 279–290.

Ingraham v. Wright, 430 U.S. 651 (1977).

Kagan, D. M. (1992). Professional growth among preservice and beginning teachers. *Review of Educational Research, 62,* 129–169.

Kohn, A. (1997). How not to teach values: A critical look at character education. *Phi Delta Kappan, 78,* 429–439.

Lehman, J. D. (1982). *Three approaches to classroom management: Views from a psychological perspective.* Washington, DC: University Press of America.

Lincoln, E. A. (1986). Searches and seizures: The U.S. Supreme Court's decision on the Fourth Amendment. *Urban Education, 21,* 255–263.

Lloyd, J. W., Landrum, T. J., & Hallahan, D. P. (1991). Self-monitoring applications for classroom intervention. In G. Stoner, M. R. Shinn, & H. M. Walker (Eds.), *Interventions for achievement and behavior problems* (pp. 210–213). Silver Springs, MD: National Association of School Psychologists.

McCarthy, M. M., & Cambron, N. H. (1981). *Public school law: Teachers' and students' rights.* Boston: Allyn & Bacon.

McNeely, S. R., & Mertz, N. T. (1990, April). *Cognitive constructs of preservice teachers: Research on how student teachers think about teaching.* Paper presented at the annual meeting of the American Educational Research Association, Boston.

Nolte, M. C. (1980). *How to survive in teaching: The legal dimension.* Palm Desert, CA: Teach'em. *Odenheim v. Carlstadt–East Rutherford Regional School District,* 510A, 2d 709 (N.J. Saper. Ch. 1985).

O'Reilly, R. C., & Green, E. T. (1983). *School law for the practitioner.* Westport, CT: Greenwood Press.

Peterson, L. J., Rossmiller, R. A., & Volz, M. M. (1978). *The law and public school operation* (2nd ed.). New York: Harper & Row.

Piele, P. K. (1978). Neither corporal punishment cruel nor due process due: The United States Supreme Court's decision in *Ingraham v. Wright. Journal of Law & Education, 7,* 1–19.

Reutter, E. E. (1975). *The courts and student conduct.* Topeka, KS: National Organization on Legal Problems of Education.

Rich, J. M. (1988). Punishment and classroom control. *The Clearing House 61*(6), 261–264.

Rossow, L. F., & Hininger, J. A. (1991). *Students and the law.* Bloomington, IN: Phi Delta Kappa Educational Foundation.

Schloss, P. J. (1983). The prosocial response formation technique. *The Elementary School Journal 83*(3), 220–229.

Sprick, R. S. (1985). *Discipline in the secondary classroom: A problem-by-problem survival guide.* West Nyack, NY: Center for Applied Research in Education.

Sprick, R., Sprick, M., & Garrison, M. (1993). *Interventions: Collaborative planning for students at risk.* Longmont, CO: Sopris West.

Sugai, G., & Horner, R. (2001). School climate and discipline: Going to scale. *Communique, 30,* 16–17.

Swanson, H. L., O'Connor, J. E., & Cooney, J. B. (1990). An information processing analysis of expert and novice teachers' problem solving. *American Educational Research Journal, 27,* 533–556.

Welch, F. C., & Tisdale, P. C. (1986). *Between parent and teacher.* Springfield, IL: Thomas.

Zirkel, P. A., & Reichner, H. F. (1987). Is *in loco parentis* dead? *Phi Delta Kappan, 68*(6), 466–469.

CHAPTER 5

Competencies in Content Management: Instruction

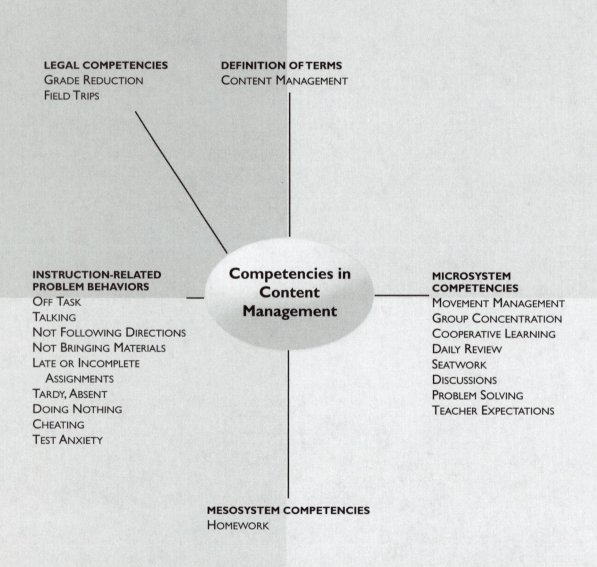

LEGAL COMPETENCIES
GRADE REDUCTION
FIELD TRIPS

DEFINITION OF TERMS
CONTENT MANAGEMENT

INSTRUCTION-RELATED PROBLEM BEHAVIORS
OFF TASK
TALKING
NOT FOLLOWING DIRECTIONS
NOT BRINGING MATERIALS
LATE OR INCOMPLETE
    ASSIGNMENTS
TARDY, ABSENT
DOING NOTHING
CHEATING
TEST ANXIETY

Competencies in Content Management

MICROSYSTEM COMPETENCIES
MOVEMENT MANAGEMENT
GROUP CONCENTRATION
COOPERATIVE LEARNING
DAILY REVIEW
SEATWORK
DISCUSSIONS
PROBLEM SOLVING
TEACHER EXPECTATIONS

MESOSYSTEM COMPETENCIES
HOMEWORK

An understanding of the material in this chapter will help you do the following:

❑ Identify teacher errors in the organization and delivery of instruction that can contribute to discipline problems, and cite ways to avoid these errors.
❑ Discuss the importance of teacher expectations on content management, and offer suggestions for equalizing opportunities for all students.
❑ Distinguish between expository and facilitative teaching methods and the content management responsibilities associated with each.
❑ Examine the characteristics of varied instructional activities, and identify the collateral content management requirements.
❑ Manage cooperative learning lessons successfully.
❑ Role-play ways to deal with instructionally related discipline problems.

Minnick (1983) conducted a study of excessive discipline problems at an inner-city junior high school in a large southwestern city. Classes of 21 target students who regularly misbehaved were monitored, as were classes of nondisruptive students. Teachers of classes with a high incidence of disciplinary problems failed to plan and design appropriate instructional tasks, rarely attempted to enhance a lesson with an overview or explanation of the topic's significance, neglected variety in lesson plans, seldom encouraged students to discuss or evaluate the material they were learning, did little to check student comprehension by carefully monitoring seatwork or through assignments and regularly graded papers, and never seemed able to establish enough order to begin to cover material effectively.

In contrast, those teachers maintaining strong and consistent instructional management and organizational skills had markedly fewer classroom disruptions. Minnick concluded that it may be more meaningful to speak of disruptive schools or disruptive classrooms rather than disruptive students. Other researchers whose work is examined in this chapter support these findings. This aspect of classroom management is labeled *content,* or *instructional, management.* How can teachers duplicate the success of the effective content managers described by Minnick?

Reflecting the position that student behavior in learning contexts is too complex to be addressed by any one theory or model, principles from several models of classroom management are offered. First, strategies from Kounin's (1977) research on movement management during instruction are described. Second, principles from Glasser's (1990, 1992, 1993) quality teaching model provide guidelines for instructional planning to minimize discipline problems. Last, interventions are described to be used with students whose behaviors present additional instructional challenges. These interventions tend to rely on shaping desired behavior (Sprick, 1985; Sprick, Sprick, & Garrison, 1993) and are developed in the context of discipline through dignity and hope (Curwin & Mendler, 1988). In this chapter, you learn a variety of theory-based procedures for effective content management.

MICROSYSTEM COMPETENCIES

Competencies in Content Management: Instructional Movement

Teachers are managing content when they manage space, materials, equipment, the movement of people, and lessons that make up a curriculum or program of studies. We have seen that the management of the setting in which this program takes place can affect the availability of time and the attention of students. When efficient setting management procedures reduce the occurrence of problems, students and teachers can concentrate their energies on learning and instruction.

Content, or *instructional, management* does not refer to skills peculiar to teaching a particular subject but rather to those skills that cut across subjects and activities. Such skills might be called *generic* because they are not subject or activity dependent.

Instructional management essentially involves gaining and maintaining the *cooperation* of students in learning *activities* (Doyle, 1986). Note the emphasis on cooperation and activities. Cooperation entails a willingness to adhere to the activity's requirements. Students who are willing participants are not likely to create disturbances that detract from learning (Glasser, 1990; Jones, 1989).

Meaningful student engagement can be increased if the teacher uses a variety of activities. The activities should be tied to student interests and have defensible educational aims (Glasser, 1992). Teachers also need to prepare students to make the most of the activity (Marshall, 1987). While activities serve as a way of achieving relevant instructional goals, they also make demands on the student that are independent of the material to be learned and impose unique management demands on the teacher (Doyle, 1986).

Lectures, classwide recitation, small-group instruction or discussion, seatwork, drill-and-practice sessions, role-playing, audiovisual presentations, simulation games, and independent and group projects are the common activities that fill the classroom day. Each activity is but a means for teaching a body of material and helping students acquire skills. The subject-matter competence of both teacher and student helps determine an activity's success. Equally important are the teacher's adeptness in organizing and presenting the activity and the students' receptiveness to the activity.

Kounin (1970) identified three clusters of instructional management skills:

1. *Movement management* refers to the teacher's effectiveness in pacing, maintaining momentum, and making transitions from one topic to another.
2. *Group focus* involves the ability to maintain group concentration.
3. *Avoidance of satiation* enables the teacher to minimize boredom and the feeling that "I have had enough already."

These skill clusters are independent of the subjects and contents customarily associated with instruction. Thus, they are considered management skills that influence the extent to which students participate in activity-related behaviors, maintain a high level of involvement, and display disciplinary problems.

Movement Management: Arranging and Directing Activity Flow

Kounin's research highlighted the mistakes that teachers make with respect to movement within and between lessons. By using videotapes of thousands of hours of classroom instruction, Kounin discovered two movement management mistakes: jerkiness and slowdowns. Each of these errors is an impediment to student concentration. When students have their concentration broken, they are more likely to engage in unacceptable behaviors.

Jerkiness

Thrusts. *Thrusts* occur when the teacher suddenly bursts into an ongoing activity without warning and gives directions for another activity. For example, imagine a group of students working at learning centers. The teacher, who has been circulating around the room, suddenly says, "Put the materials you are working with back in the boxes and folders and get ready for social studies."

The teacher did not inquire about progress, suggest the need to finish in the next 5 minutes, or in any way prepare students for a change in activity. Seemingly without regard for the students' involvement in one activity, the teacher instead tried to plunge them into another. The potential for disciplinary problems emerges as students scurry to fulfill the new set of directions, not quite sure what they are, and to culminate another activity at the same time. Experienced teachers report that this is frustrating for students and usually results in chaos.

Dangles. Jerky transitions can also be caused by what Kounin calls *dangles*. The teacher leaves one activity dangling in midair to go to another, only to return to the first. For example, the bell has just rung; students are seated and quiet. The teacher directs them to get out their math books and turn to the assignment on page 72. She is reminded of an announcement about a special assembly and says, "Before I forget, I have an announcement to read." After reading the announcement, she returns to the math assignment, but student attention has been momentarily diverted. Or perhaps the teacher decides to tell a short story. Students are left wondering what the connection of the story is and find it difficult to refocus on the original task.

How can students be expected to set aside the intrusion and get right back to the former task? Some will visit with their neighbors to discuss the assembly, and a few others will do so vicariously. The disruption has drawn student attention away from the first task and has made it more difficult to return to it. Is it any wonder teachers dislike those "May I have your attention for a moment please" announcements that are periodically broadcast from the school office each day?

Flip-Flop. The *flip-flop* is a variation of the dangle. The teacher seemingly terminates one activity, begins a second, and then surprises everyone with a flashback to the first. Students conclude a science activity with a short quiz, which is graded by exchanging papers. Scores are recorded by means of oral reporting. After the class begins a homework assignment, the teacher asks, "By the way, how many of you got all of the science quiz items right?"

Truncations.   Then there are the times when the teacher leaves one activity, goes to another, and never returns to the first. Kounin calls these movement errors *truncations.* In this instance, the teacher, after beginning an activity, is reminded of another activity that may have been neglected earlier and sets aside the present activity to resume work on the earlier one. For example, say students are doing seatwork; the teacher is grading papers and suddenly remembers parent conferences will be held a week from Friday. Since he or she wants students to write invitations to their parent(s), he or she instructs them to put their social studies assignment aside so that they can get the letters written today. The letter writing is followed by recess, math, and science. So what does the student do about the social studies? The clamor that the teacher likes to avoid at the end of the school day is likely to include some unsettling solutions to the original social studies assignment.

Slowdowns.   The pacing of a lesson is also a crucial factor in maintaining student attention. *Slowdowns,* the second major category of movement management problems, occur when instructional momentum is unnecessarily delayed by what Kounin calls *overdwelling* and *fragmentation.*

Overdwelling.   When students characterize teachers as being "a drag," they may well be referring to the overdwelling movement management problem. Rather than being too abrupt and jerky, the teacher is too ponderous. Kounin has identified several forms of overdwelling: task, behavior, actone, and prop.

   Task and *behavior overdwelling* involve spending too much time on directions and explanations. Sometimes the teacher wants to be sure the students follow instructions and gives more instructions than are necessary. At other times the teacher wants the student to stop misbehaving and offers a prolonged discourse expressing displeasure.

   In his book *Motivating Classroom Discipline,* Gnagey (1981) featured Mr. Harold in this illustration of task overdwelling:

> Mr. Harold had a little verbal routine that he went through every time he gave a spelling test. He repeated it so exactly that his students couldn't tell it from a Memorex tape. "Now clear your desks of everything except your pencil and spelling tablet. Remember that we slant our books a bit to the left, not to the right, unless of course you are left-handed. Your name should be printed, not written, in the upper left-hand corner on the top line. Please number your papers from 1 to 10 in two columns, 1 to 5 in the first column and 6 to 10 in the second. I will pronounce each spelling word twice, and you should write it as neatly as possible. If you want a word defined, please raise your hand after I have pronounced it for the second time. Ready? Here we go!"
>
>   After the third week of reruns, students began to show their impatience in many ways. One girl had become expert at lip-synching the act and amused everyone who saw her "speaking" in Harold's scholarly baritone. (p. 66)

Ms. Eckrich is the central character in Gnagey's example of what is meant by behavior overdwelling:

> "You should know better than that, Ronald," glared Ms. Eckrich. "We always put our books away before we take a test. I have told you over and over again that your desk must be clear during a test. You should have learned that in the fourth grade and yet here you are at the end of fifth and you still haven't caught on." Ms. E's voice had now risen half an octave and the last sentence was delivered at a volume just below a shriek. "If you insist on breaking the rules again and again, I don't see much hope for you. You will probably end up in reform school with all the other dummies who wouldn't listen to their teachers!" By this time some of the other students were rolling their eyes and not taking the teacher seriously: "Here she goes again." Many shifted uncomfortably in their seats. Few if any were ready for the test that was supposed to be the central activity for the day. (p. 65)

Actone overdwelling occurs when the teacher gets so enthralled with details that everyone loses sight of the main idea. Recall the history teacher who talks so incessantly about names, dates, and places that he loses sight of the significant event, or the math teacher so captivated by an elegant solution to a problem that she neglects the principle that can be used to solve a class of similar problems. A teacher's enthusiasm and expertise can be an invitation to student participation, or they can be a deadly weapon, killing interest and annihilating anticipation.

Finally, *prop overdwelling* happens when a teacher becomes so enamored with the physical prop that the lesson goes awry. Mr. Byte was introducing students to a new computer. He wanted to give them a chance to work some math problems and have the benefit of immediate feedback. However, Mr. Byte got so carried away talking about the various features of the computer that the students were able to spend only a few minutes working problems.

Fragmentation. The final form of slowdown, fragmentation, is in a class by itself. *Fragmentation* consists of breaking down, into what seems like an infinite number of parts, an activity that does not require such discrete units. It begs student indulgence. Some teachers think that every activity must be done a row at a time, in 5-minute blocks or according to directions given one step at a time. Students are left waiting. They must find diversions of some kind, a task at which they are ingenious, or they will go stark raving mad.

Aggravation and annoyance are the by-products of slowdowns due to overdwelling and fragmentation. Students get fed up and either tune out or cut up. In either case, the student's contribution often provokes a response from the teacher similar to that which originally prompted the student's misbehavior. Now the entire group is out of sorts, hardly an optimal condition for learning.

Competencies in Maintaining Group Concentration

The second cluster of instructional management skills involves group focus, the ability to maintain group alertness and effort. Kounin (1970) contended that teachers can be catalysts for a productive group by managing the (1) group format, (2) degree of accountability, and (3) attention.

Group Format.   Managing a group format requires organizational skills and techniques that promote a sense of cohesiveness and cooperation. The job to be done becomes a joint enterprise, with everyone sharing their knowledge and skills. Several researchers have offered some interesting insights into how to effectively manage the group format.

Kerman and Martin (1980) completed a 3-year study of the relationship between 15 specific forms of motivational and supportive interactions and the academic performance of low achievers. They found that all of the teachers from more than 30 school districts in Los Angeles County practiced the 15 interactions more frequently with high achievers. This research culminated in the model presented in Table 5-1.

Table 5–1
Equal opportunities in the classroom interaction model.

Strand A: Response opportunities	
1. Equitable distribution	"I am going to be called on to perform in this class."
2. Individual help	"My teacher is concerned about me and wants me to succeed."
3. Latency	"I have time to think."
4. Delving	"My teacher is making a special effort in helping me to answer."
5. Higher level questioning	"My teacher really expects me to think."
Strand B: Feedback	
1. Affirmation or correction	"I am going to be told promptly that my classwork is acceptable or not."
2. Praise	"My teacher is especially pleased with my classwork."
3. Reasons for praise	"My teacher is going to tell me why he or she likes what I accomplish in this class."
4. Listening	"My teacher is really interested in what I have to say."
5. Accepting feelings	"My teacher understands how I feel, and that's okay."
Stand C: Personal regard	
1. Proximity	"My teacher is close by, and it doesn't bother me."
2. Courtesy	"My teacher respects me."
3. Personal interest/ compliments	"I am more than just a student to my teacher; my teacher compliments me."
4. Touching	"My teacher likes me."
5. Desisting	"The teacher is upset with what I'm doing, but not with me as a person."

Source: From *Teacher Expectations and Student Achievement: Teacher Handbook* (formerly *Equal Opportunity in the Classroom*) by Sam Kerman and Mary Martin, 1980, Bloomington, IN: Phi Delta Kappa. Copyright 1980 by Los Angeles County Office of Education. Reprinted by permission.

Promoting the interactions in Strand A and Strand B of Table 5–1 appears to be an effective way to facilitate group focus. Examine the first five interactions in the table and ask yourself why these techniques would not be practiced as frequently with low achievers as with high achievers. Do you begin to see the role of teacher expectations? Can you think of reasons for a teacher to call on "highs" more frequently than "lows"? To prompt or cue a high who does not respond, but call on another student when a low appears not to know? Allow a high time to think when he or she is unable to respond immediately, but quickly get the low "off the hook"? Help a high formulate an answer, but ignore an incomplete or inaccurate response from a low? Ask a high questions that call for understanding and judgment, but ask a low to recall simple facts?

Communication of expectations for student performance is related to achievement (Kagan, 1992). Brophy and Good (1970) presented the earliest findings of differences in the expectations teachers held for high- versus low-achieving students. The frequency of teacher contact was the same, but look at the differences in the content of interactions:

❑ Criticized high achievers much less and praised them more
❑ Cued and questioned high achievers when they struggled with accuracy
❑ Increased opportunities for high achievers to respond (three to four times as often)

This initial investigation of teacher expectations was based on observation data (e.g., when the student is doing this, the teacher is doing that). Observation data are correlational and do not establish a cause-and-effect relationship. All that could be said on the basis of Brophy and Good's observation data was that teachers praised and called on students who were doing well academically. One could not say that teacher praise and calling on students caused them to perform well academically.

Kerman (1982) conducted a large experimental, or cause-and-effect, study that is referred to as *TESA (Teacher Expectations and Student Achievement)*. Teachers from 30 California school districts volunteered to participate in the study. Experimental group teachers received in-service training on the 15 strategies from Table 5–1 for interacting with all students equitably. All students in the experimental classrooms made significant academic gains compared with all students in control classrooms. Specifically, the 2,000 low achievers whose teachers learned interaction strategies significantly outperformed the low achievers in the control classes whose teachers did not learn interaction strategies. In addition, such students had significantly reduced absences and discipline referrals.

Other researchers found that lows were given fewer chances to respond and less time to answer, were provided more negative feedback and less classroom freedom/opportunities, were seated away from the teacher, and received less eye contact (Good & Brophy, 1984; Weinstein, Marshall, Brattesani, & Middlestadt, 1982; Weinstein & Middlestadt, 1979).

Because the question and recitation/discussion are primary instructional tools, it is incumbent on teachers to use them on behalf of all learners. A group format that excludes or only marginally involves a large portion of the pupil population results in

A master teacher uses a group format that includes all students, regardless of race, class, gender, or disability.

apathy and, worse, a loss of self-esteem. Some students may choose to withdraw completely. They drop out but stay in; they have for all practical purposes chosen not to be a part of the group. Others will engage in various forms of attention getting. They want desperately to be a part of the group. If they cannot do so constructively, they will do so destructively. Unfortunately, their behavior does not always seem destructive to other students; the class clown often has a winning way with peers.

Degree of Accountability.   Accountability is the second form of group focus. The instructional leader has to create a feeling that everyone is responsible for what happens in the group and for learning the material that is the subject of the group's focus. Note the five interactions under Strand B in Table 5–1. Feedback provides the teacher an opportunity to reward correct answers, help students untangle confusing ideas, and set students straight when they do not understand. Recall that teachers are less likely to give feedback to low achievers; if the number of response opportunities is negligible in the first place, there will be few opportunities to give feedback. When the teacher increases response interactions and the amount of feedback for all students, they experience a sense of fulfillment and accountability. These complementary functions also bolster positive personal regard (see Table 5–1).

Attention.   Students are more likely to be attentive if they believe that they will derive some benefits, and personal regard is certainly a payoff that matters. When students feel that they matter, they are also more receptive to the ideas and activities the teacher believes to be important. When their welfare and well-being are bound up in the aims and aspirations of others, they are more likely to give their allegiance to the group. Securing and sustaining student attention is not just a matter of being a subject-matter expert; it is a matter of knowing how to use management techniques to optimize pupil involvement (Slade & Callaghan, 1988). When all students are involved and all efforts are pointed in the same direction, teachers find it easier to achieve their goals. Students can cause obstructions or they can cooperate; leadership determines their choice and the way they exercise it.

Averting Boredom: Avoidance of Satiation

Kounin's final category of instructional management skills concerns the teacher's ability to forestall boredom. Progress, variety, and challenge are the hedges against satiation. Let us look briefly at each of these ways to counteract conditions that are potential causes of discipline problems.

Progress. Progress is the feeling a person gets when he or she is steadily moving toward some significant objective. Certainly the skills associated with movement management and group focus contribute to this sense of accomplishment. However, even with the effective use of these group management techniques, obstacles and setbacks can still arise. How might the teacher act to minimize impediments to progress? Several techniques proposed by Redl and Wattenberg (1959) can be very helpful.

Restructuring the program might be necessary when progress is halted, either by student resistance to the subject matter or by extenuating circumstances that siphon students' energy. Admittedly, some educational goals do not elicit enthusiasm or determination. Under these circumstances teachers might ask whether they control the program or whether the program controls them. When encountering resistance to selected educational aims, the teacher might ask whether these aims are worth fighting for. Can a compelling case be made for what the teacher believes are significant educational aims? Teachers need not capitulate to win student approval and cooperation. Nor should they be staunch advocates for programs and practices because students should be taught to "tough it out." There are times when restructuring the program is the most reasonable way to promote progress.

The extracurricular program, seasonal changes, and holiday periods are extenuating circumstances that might suggest a restructuring of the classroom program. Sometimes it just does not pay to compete with a basketball tournament game on Friday night, the first snowfall of the year, or the winter holiday. This is not to say teachers should relinquish responsibility for teaching during these periods. Rather, they should try to capitalize on the interest in these circumstances and make the program the beneficiary.

Sometimes progress is stymied by intellectual roadblocks. Students are unable to move ahead because they lack the information or skill to fulfill the requirements of a particular task. For this situation, Redl and Wattenberg (1959) propose hurdle help. There is no point in letting frustration grow until students seek a nonacademic outlet. Discipline problems can be averted by knowing how much frustration students can tolerate. Some teachers let students decide; they have a prearranged signal system that enables students to request help when they have exhausted personal resources. Other teachers prefer to use knowledge of and previous experience with a student, along with nonspoken cues, as a basis for making personal assistance decisions. Whatever the detection system, it is wise to help students make steady progress by removing hurdles they cannot jump over and too often try to run around.

Variety.   In addition to being the spice of life, variety is also an effective way to avoid satiation. Interest boosting and support from routine are classroom management techniques that Redl and Wattenberg (1959) advocate to help revive a program that might be undermined by insufficient variety.

Restlessness is probably the most reliable sign that interest is waning. Helping a child or class mobilize interest to sustain constructive activity becomes the most immediate problem. Teachers commonly tap an area of interest that has previously produced positive results. A good grasp of age and stage characteristics of students and recalling their individual tastes can be used to pull back anyone teetering on the brink of disinterest.

Routine is the archenemy of variety. Whenever routine has the upper edge, there is a greater likelihood satiation will set in. Students tire easily of repetition, yet practice is essential to some forms of learning. When confronted by daily routines, students go aimlessly through the motions. Yet routines are necessary to preserve order and organization. Teachers must learn to sense when enough is enough. Enterprising activities that invite inquisitiveness and excitement help minimize the diversions from routines that students create for themselves.

Providing structure, without imposing a litany of particulars, can also be liberating rather than constraining. Students need guideposts so that they can monitor their own progress and experience the joy of increasing competence. Although teachers do prescribe and moderate the circumstances of life in a classroom, they can also relieve the monotony and tediousness of the routines they create. Achieving accord between the repetitions that serve and those that do not calls for a deft balancing act. Respites from routines may be the only solution in some instances; in others, teachers should periodically examine the purposes served and look for less dreadful alternatives.

Challenge.   When the challenge is sufficient to court the best efforts of students, satiation is seldom a problem. Students look on learning as a test of their intellectual powers. They want to succeed because success is evidence of their ability to take on a challenge and come out a winner. Some students will create challenges for themselves. Others may prefer the alternatives teachers propose. In either case, students do not tire of success if the success is a genuine test of their abilities and culminates in personally relevant accomplishments.

Discipline problems are often the by-products of a challenge unaccepted or unrealized. Fear of failure may discourage some students from accepting the challenge. Others may be distressed when they accept the challenge and do not succeed. It is better to moderate these conditions through management techniques that foster competence.

Planning an Instructional Program

Deciding on the Appropriate Teaching Structure

Lessons and the activities designed to achieve lesson objectives can be organized around two teaching structures: one that favors expository teaching and receptive learning (Gersten, Carnine, & Woodward, 1987; Rosenshine, 1983, 1986) and one that favors facilitative, inductive teaching and discovery learning (Charles, 1983). Teachers find that some lesson objectives are better attained by using direct and deductive-based teaching methods, whereas other objectives may be better suited to indirect and inductive-based methods. The management requirements depend on the teacher's decision to use one of these primary instructional delivery systems.

Direct, or *expository, teaching* is generally characterized as highly structured, efficient, and formal. Advocates of the method generally view the teacher as a scholar and a purveyor of information. The teacher's management responsibilities are aimed at controlling all aspects of the lesson: objectives, activities, materials, assignments, and evaluation.

Charles (1983) identified 11 widely used methods of teaching. These methods can be arranged on a continuum from most to least structured to illustrate the difference between direct and indirect methods. The first 5 methods are typically used as the basis for direct teaching activities:

1. Diagnostic prescriptive teaching
2. Expository teaching
3. Modeling
4. Read/review/recite
5. Competency-based education

The other 6 methods, however, are commonly associated with more indirect methods of teaching:

6. Simulations
7. Projects
8. Group process
9. Inquiry/discovery
10. Facilitation
11. Open experience

All of the direct methods of instruction emphasize teacher control. Teachers have few management-of-materials problems. The focus is on the teacher and the textbook as the primary instruments of instruction. Direct instructional methods used with groups of students are subject to weak instructional matches, however. For example, some students do not have the prior knowledge to benefit from the lecture. Behavioral problems tend to increase under these conditions. Students become frustrated, disinterested, bored, and inattentive. Management success needs to be based on altering instruction to achieve a better match with learner characteristics.

Indirect, or *inductive-based, teaching* methods emphasize process over product. These methods are aimed at eliciting student participation and contribute to divergent rather than convergent production. That is, a lesson does not always have to be aimed at achieving specific objectives but can entertain myriad possibilities. Proponents of this position trust the learner to be a responsible participant in the selection of objectives, methods, materials, and evaluation procedures (Pinnell & Galloway, 1987). This approach is in direct contrast to that of direct instruction. Rogers (1977) asserts that teaching that ignores the learners' desire to achieve personal meanings will produce only inconsequential learnings. According to this view, the teacher should become a facilitator rather than a director of learning. Facilitators do not attempt to impart or impose their knowledge. According to Rogers, facilitating the learning process involves the following:

1. Asking questions that tap student interests, concerns, fears, and aspirations
2. Helping students identify what really counts in their lives and then assisting them in their search for human and material resources that discern these matters
3. Establishing a climate that fosters curiosity, allows mistakes, and encourages students to experience all aspects of their environment
4. Using activities that stimulate students to raise questions, search for information, and make decisions
5. Helping students organize and share the results of inquiry with others

This process opens students up to the experiences of themselves and others. Advocates claim this process produces both enduring ideas and ideals.

The facilitative process is distinguished by its emphasis on learner-oriented and directed methods. It makes use of simulation games, creative problem solving, group and individual projects, and open-ended enrichment exercises to put learners in control of their own learning. Such activities are believed to be sufficiently engaging to sustain the interest and involvement of the learner. The act of discovery (Bruner, 1961) inherent in all of these activities leads to the construction of knowledge that is viable for other types of learning. The student participates in a process of knowledge getting (Bruner, 1966).

Critics of discovery/inquiry and individual/group project methods claim that these approaches are inefficient and unpredictable. The subject-matter expertise of the teacher, they say, is largely discounted or compromised to permit more learner latitude. Thus, the teacher's management role is largely confined to the following seven activities:

1. Helping students identify acceptable topics for inquiry
2. Scheduling convenient times for students to meet
3. Assisting students during the planning stages of their investigations
4. Providing students access to resources needed for their work

5. Responding to students' requests for space and help
6. Scheduling time periodically for students to report their findings
7. Designing accountability measures that fulfill schoolwide reporting requirements while allowing students personal appraisals of their accomplishments

The eclectic teacher–leader will use both expository (direct) and discovery (indirect) methods of instruction. Curriculum and lesson objectives will determine methods of instruction. Regardless of the methods selected, the teacher must possess a wide variety of management skills.

Analyzing Instructional Activities for Management Requirements

Doyle (1986) acknowledged that cooperative learning activities, in particular, are some of the most complex in terms of classroom arrangement and demands on attention. Cooperative learning activities require well-developed classroom management skills. Let's pause and take an in-depth look at the management and control implications of cooperative learning activities.

Analyzing the Management Requirements of Cooperative Learning Activities.
Many educators know what cooperative learning is and how it is different from competitive and individualistic learning. They may also know that research suggests that cooperative learning results in (a) a greater effort to achieve, (b) more positive interpersonal relationships, and (c) greater psychological health (Johnson, Johnson, & Holubec, 1990). Educators can often cite that the essence of cooperative learning is positive interdependence or the student mentality that "we are in this together." Educators also know that there are additional components of cooperative learning that are essential: (a) individual accountability, (b) face-to-face interaction, (c) social skills, and (d) processing group effectiveness.

Management of the procedures, steps, and how-tos of the cooperative learning process is often less well known. Expert teachers, with little or no experience in group learning processes, pale at the thought of managing a cooperative learning activity. It is no wonder then that many preservice and first-year teachers prefer to stand behind the podium with a direct instruction plan based on large-group lecture and the use of the overhead projector. That is not to say that novices are unable to manage the procedures of cooperative learning methods. Many beginning teachers are able to manage them quite well because they analyzed the activity in terms of its management requirements and planned their management strategies accordingly. Successful management of cooperative learning simply requires thinking of and planning for all the components of the cooperative learning lesson and the concomitant procedures that students need to know how to follow in order to have a successful cooperative learning experience.

For example, a preservice teacher at a field experience in a language arts classroom wanted to teach a lesson using cooperative learning methods. She received input from her peers and professors regarding how to plan thoroughly and teach her students each procedure of the cooperative learning lesson. Although she did some planning, she decided that she could also rely on informally addressing concerns that came up in the process. She regretted that decision later; there were too many procedural aspects for which she was unprepared. Although she maintained control of the class during the cooperative learning lesson, students did not benefit from the lesson as much as she had anticipated because of management shortcomings. Her lesson is described following a discussion of procedural planning.

In planning a cooperative learning lesson, first list all the procedures that students will need to learn in order to complete an activity. Do some brainstorming of the procedural steps that a cooperative learning lesson would entail. Then look at Figure 5–1, which provides examples that can be used as a master list. What did you consider and what did you forget? Take the list in Figure 5–1 and order the procedures to reflect the approximate place in which they would occur in a lesson.

On the basis of these exercises, you should begin to see the need for preplanning the management of cooperative learning lessons. Once you learn the basic management

Figure 5–1
Brainstormed List of Procedures to Teach in a Cooperative Learning Lesson

goal of lesson

end product, expectations

which students assigned to which groups

roles of group members

how and when to assign roles

directions for moving from large group to cooperative groups

directions for material use in group

directions to complete lesson (model task, guided practice, follow-up questions)

when to move to small groups

when to give directions

time limits

accountability

social skill

how to evaluate social skill

how to evaluate group process

what to do when group is finished

how to return to large group

dispersal of materials

how to seek assistance

rules for group work

managing the student who is not an effective group member

process, there will be few occasions to vary it. After some opportunities to manage cooperative learning lessons, you will carry out procedures automatically. That will free your thinking for planning the cognitive aspects of learning and instruction.

Students who have not participated in structured cooperative learning or social skills activities may not be able to learn all the procedures the first time you want to use cooperative learning structures. You may need to divide the procedures of the cooperative learning process into units and teach the units during a period of days.

Following is a case study of a preservice teacher's management of cooperative learning. The presentation is explicit; novices should be able to use it as a model for facilitating their own successful management. This preservice teacher's cooperative learning lesson was presented in a gamelike format, but it is important to point out that all cooperative lessons are not gamelike. It is not the intent to comprehensively educate readers about the methods of cooperative learning but rather to familiarize them with the management considerations. There are 17 relatively separate features of cooperative learning lessons to attend to in preplanning. The features (Johnson et al., 1990) are represented in the following bulleted list as a brief review for those who have little background in cooperative learning:

❏ Instructional objectives and the academic task
❏ Task assistance
❏ Size of the groups
❏ Assignment to groups
❏ Lesson closure
❏ Evaluation of learning
❏ Room arrangement
❏ Instructional materials that promote interdependence
❏ Roles that promote interdependence
❏ Positive goal interdependence
❏ Individual accountability
❏ Intergroup cooperation
❏ Criteria for success
❏ Desired behaviors
❏ Monitoring behaviors
❏ Collaborative skills interventions
❏ Evaluation of group functioning

You now have the opportunity to study the preservice teacher's management procedures during her cooperative learning lesson. Management and instructional processes are intertwined in many lessons, and particularly in cooperative lessons. Therefore, many instructional aspects of the lesson are presented and critiqued for their contributions to management outcomes.

The teacher we are studying, Ms. Hammer, was a preservice, language arts teacher completing a course in schoolwide discipline and classroom management. A requirement of the management course was to participate in a classroom-based field experience. After spending 4 weeks in a seventh-grade classroom observing aspects of the expert teacher's classroom management, Ms. Hammer was ready to teach her first lesson to the class while also practicing her newly acquired management skills. She decided to go for the gusto and attempted to teach and manage a cooperative learning lesson.

The students were completing a unit on six folk tales and were to take a test on them the following week. Ms. Hammer decided to conduct a review of the main characters by grouping students cooperatively and having them play a game she created: Folk Tale Taboo. Ms. Hammer planned the lesson and management procedures in advance. She now stands in front of the 22 students, ready to begin the lesson and feeling somewhat confident because of her preplanning and advanced preparation. Following is a description of her instructional management. After you study it carefully, note what she planned and managed well. Make a list of problems that you foresee her having because of inadequate management planning. Reflect on how you would manage the cooperative learning lesson if you were in front of the class of seventh graders.

LESSON: FOLK TALE TABOO

Ms. Hammer is in front of the class; students are in rows and columns. Ms. Hammer has her materials for the lesson on a nearby table, and materials for the cooperative learning activity are already on the tables where the groups will gather. There are two sheets of butcher paper taped to the blackboard with directions on them. Directions are also placed on each of the cooperative learning tables. Ms. Hammer begins:

"Good morning. Have you ever wanted to describe something to someone else so they would know exactly what you meant, but you just couldn't find the words? For example, let's say that I want to tell you about a character in a folk tale and I cannot remember the character's name! I could start describing the character to you and then you might figure out who I was talking about. Let's try that. I am thinking of a folk tale character but I cannot say the name. I want you to help me out. Listen to my description and anyone call out at any time who I am talking about.

"It's this little boy. He can fly all over. There's a bad guy with a hook on his arm that the flying boy is afraid of. . . ."

(Students call out "Peter Pan.")

"That's right. That's who I was thinking of. Good job. Today you will have an opportunity to develop communication skills as you describe folk tale characters to one another. This is also an opportunity for you to review characters from your six folk tales. Toward the end of the class, you will be writing descriptively about how well you worked with others to communicate about the characters.

"Now I want you to think of the name of a character in one of the six folk tales we have been studying. After you have the name in mind, think of four good descriptive words or phrases for that character. I am going to

> pass out cards and you will write down the name of your character and the four descriptive words or phrases under the name. Place the character's name at the top of the card. Below the name, number down the side of the card with one, two, three, and four. Then write a descriptor next to each number. J.D., would you retell the directions for everyone. (Pause.) Before I pass out the cards, are there any questions? (Pause.) While I pass out the notecards, you can be thinking of a character and four descriptive words or phrases."

Note that the teacher obtains student attention and interest in her opening. In stating directions before she passes out writing materials, she maintains their attention to the directions. She makes sure that everyone understands the directions prior to her passing out cards. While students write on cards, she circulates and helps those who are having difficulty.

> "Everyone has completed their cards. Pass them to the person in front of you and I'll pick them up from the first person in each row."

Ms. Hammer picks up cards quickly and moves to the front of the room to conduct a large-group discussion.

Ms. Hammer asks, "Who has played the game Taboo before?" A student responds and is asked to explain the rules of the game. Ms. Hammer asks another student to restate the rules to check for comprehension. She moves to the blackboard by the butcher paper with the directions for the cooperative learning lesson. Students have heard the rules presented orally. They will now see the rules presented visually. Repeated presentations of the directions for a lesson decrease behavioral problems during the completion of tasks.

> "For 15 minutes you will be playing Folk Tale Taboo, a wonderfully fun game that you and I created just for you. I made some game cards before class and I am adding the ones that you just now completed."
> (Ms. Hammer reads through the rules written on the butcher paper.)
> "Rules: (1) You will be assigned to your regular base group and each group serves as a team. (2) Two teams compete with each other to see who can earn the most points. (3) Each time a card is played, you will set a timer for 1 minute. Describe as many cards as the other team can name in a 1-minute period. When 1 minute is up, the timer is reset and a member of the opposite team draws a card to describe. It is important that the describer work quickly so the other team has a chance to guess the name. Remember, you get only 1 minute. (4) The name at the top of the card and the four words or phrases listed below the name are Taboo words and cannot be used when you are giving a description. If the describer says a Taboo word, the timer is reset and the describer draws another card and begins again. (5) Teams record each others' points.

> "Just for practice, let's run through how to play a card. Here's the first card. Jess, Shamu, and Eric are on a team together and will be guessing the name of a character that I am describing."

Ms. Hammer turns to the group to model how to play the first round with a card. She holds up a large version of a card that all students except the three can read from their seats. A student holds up his hand and Ms. Hammer calls on him. He indicates that he would like to try describing the character instead of Ms. Hammer's providing the description. She agrees. The students play the card. Ms. Hammer asks if there are any questions about this aspect of the game.

Ms. Hammer steps to the second piece of butcher paper taped to the blackboard and goes over the learning goals and the social skill of the lesson. The learning goals are to practice (a) thinking skills, (b) speaking skills, and (c) character recall. The social skill is to practice teamwork, which she describes as working together to solve problems and showing respect for the person trying to describe.

Ms. Hammer tells each student what group he or she is in and assigns one person per group as reporter. The reporter is told to draw the first card and begin describing. She then tells them what area of the room to go to and what materials they will find there: timer, cards, paper, pencil. There are four people per group, which places eight people around each table.

Ms. Hammer tells the students to go to their area. While they are seating themselves, Ms. Hammer interrupts to tell them that the first group to obtain 15 points will be the winner. The teams begin the competition. There is some jostling and debating about who will run the timer, who will record the points, and who the players will be each time a new card is drawn. Some team members are engrossed in the game, some stare off, and some talk with one another. Ms. Hammer interrupts several of the groups during the competition to teach them how to use the timers.

(Pause here and brainstorm what poorly managed procedures caused problems during the Taboo game. Use the 17 features of cooperative learning lessons listed earlier to help you decide what could be problematic. Indicate the strengths of the teacher's management procedures. A critique is provided at the end of the narrative about the cooperative activity.)

When 14 minutes have passed, Ms. Hammer reminds the groups that they have one more round before time is up. She waits for the final round to be completed and asks the students to go back to their seats. As they are returning to their regularly assigned seats, she speaks over the noise and commotion and asks them to get out paper and pencil for the writing assignment. When all are seated and ready with materials, she asks them to pick one of the three learning goals or the social skill for a writing topic. Students are directed to write for 5 minutes about how the experience helped them practice attaining a goal or the social skill. Papers are turned in after 5 minutes and class is dismissed.

(Pause here and add the strengths of Ms. Hammer's instructional management to the list you started earlier. Brainstorm and record any components of her cooperative learning lesson that led to management problems. When you have your lists, continue reading the following critique of management strengths and areas for improvement.)

Critique of the Management of the Cooperative Lesson.   The teacher's first planning requirement is to determine the academic and collaborative or social skills objectives. It is a common error to indicate academic objectives and ignore collaborative skills objectives. Omissions lead to management problems because students need to be taught how to work cooperatively with one another. Cooperative interactions do not happen naturally.

In the preceding example, the instructional objectives and the academic tasks were clear. Both were orally and visually presented by the teacher. She asked students to repeat directions for the task and gave them opportunities to ask questions. She also placed directions for the task on the competition tables. The teacher modeled the task once and provided guided practice once. The use of all of these instructional strategies decreased the likelihood of management problems later during group work.

In contrast, students did not know how to use timers, and this caused groups to be off task and disruptive as they argued with one another. Ms. Hammer interrupted some groups in the middle of the game to demonstrate how to use the timer accurately. She should have assigned the task of timekeeper to someone in each group and taught the timekeepers the use of the equipment. The role of recorder of points also needed to be assigned. Because it was not, students were off task, arguing with one another about who should perform this task. Ms. Hammer had a collaborative skill of the day that she briefly described. More time modeling and discussing the skill, with thorough checks for understanding, would have prevented problems in the group later.

Clear objectives help teachers decide the best size for learning groups, which tend to range from two to six students per group. Johnson et al. (1990) advise beginning teachers to start with pairs. The larger the group, the more social skills students need to be successful and the more behavior management problems surface. Regardless of teachers' skills in facilitating cooperative learning groups, they should not have students working in groups of more than three until students have the skills to do it competently. Finally, the less time there is for group work, the smaller the group should be. Everyone needs the opportunity to contribute. Given the advice of Johnson and his colleagues, Ms. Hammer would have been a more successful manager if she had made her groups smaller. Two people per group would be advisable for this activity. That would place four people around the competition table. When one person would be describing, there would be only the one partner who could be sitting there uninvolved. Out of every describing team of two, only one would have the potential to be uninvolved. Thus, there would be more opportunities for each student to be actively involved in the lesson the majority of the time. Ms. Hammer's teams of four meant that when one was describing, as many as three teammates might be sitting idly by. Three idle students potentially increase the occurrence of management problems. Smaller teams also mean that fewer people in a group have to practice the social skill at any one time.

Figure 5–2

Sociometric Exercise for Forming
Cooperative Learning Groups

Circle the names of three students with whom you would most like to do group work in the classroom.		
Adrianna	Del	Omar
Andy	Grant	Patisha
Azim	Jerome	Schwanda
Bathsheba	Lil	Weldon
Carlos	Miguel	Zach

Teacher-made groups typically are more task oriented than are student-selected groups because teachers place non-task-oriented students with task-oriented students. Students prefer to be in groups with peers that they like. Some teachers allow students to complete a peer nomination form (see Figure 5–2) on which each student indicates three peers with whom they most like to work. Then, teachers sometimes can place students in groups with one of their choices and one or two others that the teacher selected. Groups should stay intact until they can successfully work together. Then it is appropriate to interchange group membership.

Ms. Hammer had a management problem with lesson closure that could be labeled a *truncation* (Kounin, 1970). She terminated the cooperative learning activity and never asked groups to share the number of points they earned. She told them previously that the team with the most points would win. The criterion for success was presented but was not addressed at the end of the lesson. The groups were not required to evaluate their group functioning either.

There was no large-group sharing time in which to talk about cards that were difficult to describe, to process how difficult it is to describe things, or to share tips with one another about how to describe. The evaluation of learning and individual accountability factors were addressed by requiring students to descriptively write about their attainment of a goal area or the social skill. The final writing activity provided some lesson closure, but it was not sufficient.

If Ms. Hammer had interrupted their writing and said, "Oh, by the way, which team obtained the highest number of points for Folk Tale Taboo?" she would have executed another management faux pas, Kounin's undesirable *flip-flop*. However, following the writing activity, she could have acknowledged teams' efforts. This management strategy would have helped students cooperate in future lessons.

Ms. Hammer's setting management was adequate: She planned ahead, had the room arranged for cooperative learning, and had materials ready. Circles are usually the best management of the physical environment. The key is to place students so they can see all their materials, see one another, talk without raising their voices, and make exchanges comfortably. In other words, the closer, the better. Ms. Hammer used circles and students were close to one another. She gave no instructions about using quiet voices. Fortunately, she had no major difficulties with noise level.

She could have potentially had management difficulties in moving students from large to small groups because she did not provide students with instructions about how to proceed to their tables. Perhaps she was relying on their knowing that they had only 15 minutes for the tournament. The time limit could have influenced them to go quickly to their tables and begin the game, but she forgot to tell them about the time limit. It was not until they were moving to their work areas that she committed a *dangle* (Kounin, 1970) by reminding them of something she forgot to tell them earlier.

Instructional materials, planned to promote interdependence, also prevent management problems. New groups with few collaborative skills can be given one copy of the materials. This increases the likelihood that students will work together. In Ms. Hammer's classroom, the nature of the task promoted interdependence for the team that was trying to guess the name on the card. They could share ideas and work together to obtain the correct answer.

If the describers had been given 1 minute to work as a team to come up with descriptors, then interdependence would have been present for them also. Interdependence can also be achieved by structuring intergroup competition. In intergroup competition, groups usually prepare their members to compete in a tournament with other groups. Students of the same ability level across teams compete against one another. Ultimately, the group whose members' combined score is best wins. Positive goal interdependence was present because Ms. Hammer used outside enemy interdependence (Johnson et al., 1990). In order to promote interdependence without using outside enemies, Ms. Hammer might have required that every member of the listening team record the name of the character being described. Disagreements would have been discussed and resolved by the team members. Another option would have been to have each listener record the name and for every correct answer, a point would have been added to the group score.

Interdependence is also ensured by assigning interconnected roles to each member of the group. Roles include the following:

❑ *Summarizer,* who restates the group's major conclusions or answers
❑ *Checker,* who makes sure that all members can explicitly describe how to arrive at an answer
❑ *Accuracy coach,* who corrects mistakes in another's explanations
❑ *Elaboration seeker,* who asks others to relate current information to prior studies
❑ *Researcher,* who gets materials for the group and communicates with the teacher and other groups
❑ *Recorder,* who writes down group decisions and edits group reports
❑ *Observer,* who notes how well the group is collaborating

Roles were not clearly assigned or described; therefore, roles did not promote interdependence. Subsequently, some students not directly involved in the game were noisy and off task. A lack of role assignment in cooperative learning tasks generally results in management problems for the teacher to solve.

In summary, Ms. Hammer's management of the cooperative learning activity was generally successful. Her management strengths included clear lesson presentation, obtainment of group interest, checks for understanding, and organization of materials. Although she did not prepare students thoroughly for every procedure they needed, students remained on task and cooperative for the most part.

Ms. Hammer needs to improve her management of cooperative learning in the following ways. First, she needs to become more skillful at managing group work that promotes interdependence and individual accountability at the same time. Specifically, she needs to assign roles and ensure that students are taught how to fulfill their roles.

Second, she needs to consider the developmental level of her students in her management of time limits. Her criterion was that the team who obtained 15 points first would win. She provided a 15-minute time period. That meant that a team would need to get one card right every minute. Many seventh-grade students struggled to provide even one descriptor in the 60-second period. That did not give the listening team an opportunity to make a single guess. Perhaps the following instruction would have been more appropriate: The describing team has 60 seconds to pool their ideas about descriptive words and another 60 seconds for the describer to communicate the descriptions. Finally, Ms. Hammer needed to manage closure activities to ensure that students would continue to participate and take the learning activities seriously.

This cooperative learning lesson demonstrates how novice teachers can successfully manage complex instruction. Careful management planning ensures that students will stay on task, cooperate with one another, learn a great deal, and have fun.

Sequencing and Integrating Additional Instructional Activities

Teachers who can entice students to become active participants in the educational process will have fewer discipline problems. This educational process is largely a matter of selecting and sequencing appealing activities and helping students make the most of their participation in them. Removing restlessness, passivity, and boredom from the classroom also removes potential discipline problems (Glasser, 1992).

Envisioning activities that will spark interest and sustain student involvement is an important instructional function and an equally significant management function (Parker & Gehrke, 1986). Students who are meaningfully involved are less likely to seek other outlets for their energy and imagination. Sequencing and coalescing several activities builds momentum and a commitment to learning. Units of instruction and daily lesson plans serve this integrating function. They contribute to the critical mass that students bring to each new learning event.

Good and Grouws (1979) conducted a number of teacher-effectiveness studies and used their findings to formulate a sequence for teaching basic mathematics skills. Outlined in Table 5–2, the sequence provides a series of activities in lesson plan format that can easily be adapted to other subject areas. The categories and specifications within the table can be used to visualize the preventive disciplinary characteristics associated with this format for content management.

Table 5–2
Activity sequence outline.

Daily Review: (First 8 minutes except Mondays)

Review the concepts and skills associated with the homework.

Collect and deal with homework assignments.

Ask students to do several mental computational exercises.

Development: (About 20 minutes)

Briefly focus on prerequisite skills and concepts.

Focus on meaning and prompting student understanding by using lively explanations, demonstrations, process explanations, illustrations, and so on.

Assess student comprehension by using process/product questions (active interaction) and controlled practice.

Repeat and elaborate on the meaning portion as necessary.

Seatwork: (About 15 minutes)

Provide uninterrupted successful practice.

Build momentum—keep the ball rolling—get everyone involved, then sustain involvement.

Alert students; let them know their work will be checked at the end of the period.

Promote accountability—check students' work.

Homework Assignment:

Assign, on a regular basis at the end of each math class except Fridays, about 15 minutes of work to be done at home, including one or two review problems.

Special Reviews:

Conduct weekly review/maintenance during the first 20 minutes each Monday.

Focus on skills and concepts covered during the previous week.

Conduct monthly review/maintenance every fourth Monday.

Focus on skills and concepts covered since the last monthly review.

Managing Daily Review Sessions.   Students need opportunities to practice and apply what they learn. Homework affords students that opportunity, as do review sessions at the beginning of the class. Generally, each lesson begins with a review of seatwork and/or homework, and the review sets the stage for new learning. It may be tempting to forgo the time devoted to review in favor of the new lesson, especially when students performed well during the guided practice session the previous day. However, the review session should not be omitted. Not only are regular homework assignments, even if in modest amounts, followed by a daily review session a good accountability measure, but they also provide a predictable academic environment.

Plan for management of the review so that it is not boring, repetitive, or a cursory treatment of the topic. If a gamelike format is used, ensure that all students are accountable and participatory throughout the lesson. Following is an example of a gamelike unit review that took an entire class period. This review was poorly constructed; note what not to do in a review.

> The social studies teacher prepared eighth-grade students for a unit exam by conducting a social studies "bee". The students began the class period by standing beside their desks. The 24 students waited their turn to answer questions posed by the teacher. When a student responded incorrectly, the student sat down for the rest of the period. The last person standing was the winner. Can you imagine what seated students were doing during the remainder of the bee? Of course you can! They visited, laughed, passed notes, scuffled over pencils, grew frustrated with one another, and even began name-calling.

The form of the daily review session is often dictated by the type of material to be learned. Skills might be demonstrated by sending several students to the chalkboard and using their work to review the steps in a process. Recitation of factual information can be made more lively by creating gamelike conditions—an element of competition adds excitement. Checking for understanding might involve dividing the class into groups to share their ideas and the basis for arriving at their conclusions. Brief reports from each group can be used to summarize key points.

Managing Lectures and Presentation Sessions.   Because teaching is often equated with talking, it is not surprising that the lecture is often chosen to deliver material. Lectures can be an efficient way to dispense information if well conceived and delivered in an interesting fashion. Students also need to be equipped with skills in note taking. The following seven suggestions should enhance the effective use of this technique:

1.   All teaching techniques require collateral learning skills. Teachers who lecture must help students learn how to listen and take notes. The first step in developing both skills may be to supply students with the key points in outline form. Students can later compare the points they have recorded under each section with those given by the instructor.

2.   Ausubel (1963) coined the term *advanced organizers* to refer to concepts and methods that a teacher uses to connect a new lesson to previous learnings. When the advanced organizer is a part of a written outline or is displayed on a transparency, students can readily see the connection between a previous lesson and a new lesson. Beginning a new lesson always involves a risk, but the teacher can reduce initial anxiety by showing students how this lesson is built on things they have previously learned.

3.   The lecturer must be attentive to nonspoken cues from students and must likewise give nonspoken cues to help students stay on track. Pace, voice gesticulation, gestures, and eye contact can maintain attention. Well-placed questions and brief discussions can provide an occasional respite from teacher talk.

4. The use of audiovisual media and a variety of written supplements can also embellish the delivery of a lecture. Illustrations and applications of the lecture can be presented through audio- and videotape, films and slides, or CDs or DVDs. Portions of the lecture might be delivered by other speakers.

5. Some teachers vary the distance between themselves and students by moving about the room. If students must shift focus as the teacher changes positions, they are more likely to be attentive. A voice emanating from nearby is also likely to command greater attention.

6. Nothing commands our attention more than hearing our name interjected into a conversation. Teachers can capitalize on this tendency by interspersing names of students within the lecture. This can be done in a speculative way—"Suppose Mary was convinced . . . ," —or in a retrospective way—"Recall the other day when Jim . . ."

7. Periodic checks on student understanding and comprehension can help maintain attentiveness. If students are confused because the teacher refers to something they were supposed to have learned earlier, are perplexed by the terminology, or are frustrated because they cannot keep up with the pace of delivery, they are likely to throw in the towel. Teachers can lace the lecture with open-ended queries and pointed questions to check for presentation clarity and coherence.

Managing Seatwork. Students spend considerable instructional time engaged in independent seatwork assignments. Teachers may work with a subset of students during these times. Learning to manage seatwork is an important feature of the teacher's day. There are essentially four instructional and managerial tasks associated with seatwork (Anderson, Brubaker, Alleman-Brooks, & Duffy, 1983), each of which is accomplished through the use of routines: selecting, presenting, monitoring, and evaluating.

Selecting Assignments. Typically, teachers give whole-class seatwork assignments and use small groups for more individualized instruction. The selection of seatwork assignments can create problems for low achievers. Students who encounter difficulties in completing the seatwork become discouraged and look for outlets for their frustration. Teachers can overcome this problem by conducting remedial instruction with a small group. The rest of the class can be completing independent seatwork.

Presenting Assignments. Some of the problems that students encounter while they are doing seatwork originate in the way that assignments are presented. Anderson et al. (1983) analyzed teacher explanations for seatwork assignments to ascertain the types of information given to students. They found that the majority of explanations (79%) included procedural directions and/or isolated hints to help students focus their efforts. Teachers gave fewer explicit explanations about the purposes of the work (5%), specifically what benefits would accrue to the student, and even fewer explicit descriptions of the cognitive strategy to be used to do the assignments (1.5%). Iverson and Stack's (1996) review of the literature also showed that teachers rarely provided instruction in

Students engage in independent seatwork when they use comupters. Teachers manage the selection of computer lessons.

the cognitive strategies needed to complete learning tasks. Although information about purposes and strategies might not be essential for all assignments, these are precisely the motivational and task cues needed by students who exhibit discipline problems.

Monitoring Performance.   Seatwork is often performed while the teacher is working with another group. Monitoring the performance of students completing individual seatwork must also occur. What can teachers do to maintain the benefits of working with one group while the remainder of the class is engaged in seatwork? Anderson et al. (1983) recommended the following five pointers:

1.   Do not begin work with a small group focused on content, skill, or a project immediately after the seatwork assignment is given. Instead, allow 5 minutes during which you circulate among students, making a special point to pass by students who revealed some signs of difficulty while the assignment material was being presented and/or who typically have problems with this type of instruction. Only after everyone has gotten started should a small group be convened.

2.   Circulate among students after dismissal of one small group and before engaging in an activity with another. Again, concentrate on students who may have problems. If it appears that several students are having a similar problem, a short lesson may be called for. Take a few minutes between the groups. Sometimes the assignment may have to be changed or the student may need to be given other work until the teacher can provide more extended assistance.

3.   Troubleshooting rounds can be more productive if the teacher provides help in the form of questions. Students learn to be more reflective and less dependent on the teacher for answers. They also learn that the process of problem resolution can be just as important as the end result, the answer.

4. The teacher need not be the only source of help. Peers can be taught how to provide assistance without giving answers. Or a student can use a "help card" (Paine, Radicchi, Rosellini, Deutchman, & Darch, 1983) to indicate that assistance is required the next time the teacher is free. The reverse side of the help card that faces the student might be labeled "keep working." Another method is a folder of "surefire" work, often drill-and-practice sheets for elementary students, or "waiting work," incomplete assignments or supplementary reading assignments for high school students. Finally, the teacher may devise a set of signals for letting students know when it is acceptable to interrupt small-group instruction.

5. As the year progresses, students should begin to value themselves as independent learners and seek help only after exhausting self-help strategies that they have been taught throughout the year. Thus, early in the school year the teacher should systematically integrate self-help activities into regular lessons. The strategies that students lack can often be discovered by paying close attention to the questions they ask and those needed to lead them toward greater understanding of a task. Devoting time to building self-help attitudes and skills early in the school year can save time and reduce competition for a teacher's attention throughout the year.

Evaluating Assignments. Routines for evaluating seatwork should emphasize getting information about student thinking processes and comprehension. Some teachers may be more interested in the completeness and accuracy of work. Thus, their feedback to students is often confined to reporting the number right or wrong and some brief indication of their satisfaction with the work. In such cases, little may be done to help students understand why an answer is incorrect and what needs to be done so that the error is not repeated. Without such encouragement and help, students tend to think that the most important thing is to have an answer, any answer. Because seatwork occupies so much classroom time and is an instrument that teachers rely on to deepen understanding and develop or refine skills, teachers should design defensible ways to select, explain, monitor, and evaluate this type of work.

Managing Discussion Sessions. Students need opportunities to process ideas from teacher presentations, reading assignments, and other activities. Discussion sessions help students attach personal meaning to ideas, validate understanding, and find out how others perceive a point. These sessions also help make ideas more memorable by connecting them to the personal experience of the participants. Many human relations and communication skills are practiced as students exchange ideas. Discussion sessions can be more productive if planning takes into consideration the following six suggestions:

1. Maintaining the attention and involvement of all students during whole-class discussions can be facilitated by seating arrangements that permit everyone to see everyone else. The small amount of time required to move furniture can be more than offset by favorable speaking and listening conditions. Early in the year the teacher might have students practice moving furniture into several types of grouping arrangements.

2.   The teacher should not assume at the beginning of the year that students know how to participate in discussions. Procedures for this activity need to be devised and taught. As the school year progresses, directions may need to be reviewed periodically. Because certain skills increase and distribute participation, early discussion sessions might emphasize one of these skills. Prior to the discussion, a small amount of time might be devoted to presenting and demonstrating the skill so that students become aware of it and practice using it.

3.   The focus of the discussion can be sharpened if the teacher lets students know its purpose. It is easy to stray from the topic when there is ambiguity about the end product. When several questions are to be answered, the group might begin with those that are to elicit factual responses. This procedure permits early success, promotes a sense of progress, and creates a positive expectation for subsequent questions. As the group entertains more open-ended questions, the facts collected may be the springboard for answering subsequent items.

4.   Teachers should orchestrate whole-class sessions by determining who speaks, the length of time allotted to an individual, the order of turns, the type and amount of assistance provided reticent or struggling participants, and the termination points within the topic. The study by Kerman and Martin (1980), discussed earlier in this chapter, addressed several aspects of this situation. Note the variety of ways teachers influence the participation of students and the effects of their decisions on pupil expectations (see Table 5–1). The amount and quality of student participation can be adversely affected by how teachers perceive the potential contributions of students and how teachers act out these expectations. Even nonoral cues can encourage or discourage a student.

5.   Discussions are an effective way to promote retention and transfer, the twin problems of teaching. Some discussion sessions should involve the integration of material presented earlier. It is imperative that students be given directions that structure the discussion and provide progress checks along the way.

6.   Listening is just as crucial during discussions as during teacher presentations, but students may not think so because of the belief that when it comes down to tests and grades, what counts is teacher talk. Teachers can enhance respect for student contributions by being respectful listeners and using student contributions as the preface to some of their own. Or students may be asked to summarize a peer's remarks before offering their own. And, of course, teachers can do more to ensure that evaluation instruments are designed to elicit information and skills acquired during group discussions.

Managing Projects and Problem-Solving Sessions.   Teachers generally use what have come to be called *higher order questions* to promote problem solving. The "cognitive taxonomy" of Bloom, Engelhart, Frost, Hill, and Krathwohl (1956) might be used to frame questions that require application, analysis, synthesis, and evaluation processes. These processes are more intellectually demanding and require conditions unlike those appropriate for recitation sessions. Five guidelines for helping students stretch their intellect and imagination follow:

1.   Students must be given periods of silence to think. To reduce their initial feelings of uneasiness during these periods, the teacher might provide for very short periods of silence and less involved questions at the beginning of the year. During the school year, the length of silent periods and intellectual demands can gradually be increased.

2.   Students might be encouraged to record, in abbreviated fashion, their thoughts during these periods of silence. Rather than writing paragraphs, students might jot down key words and phrases, use arrows to show a progression of ideas, or develop a diagram of key parts. This practice increases the likelihood that students will participate in the public forum and will be able to make a more straightforward presentation. A teacher who circulates while students are at work can check the responses of students for what should be included in the discussion, look for particularly meritorious points, and begin to chart the direction of the discussion. If students are going to be placed in small groups, the written responses can be used to make grouping decisions.

3.   When silence and written responses are a prelude to a whole-group discussion, the teacher might want to make some preliminary remarks about the steps in the problem-solving process. Students may be directed to submit their ideas without any expectation of group reactions. Only after the teacher has recorded the products of everyone's thinking on the chalkboard should the group engage in a critical examination of the output. When the group works with a summary, the focus is on achieving greater clarity, looking for relationships, and forming generalizations. There is a concerted effort to evaluate the data rather than the person who offered it. Students begin to value the diverse ways of looking at problems, and the prospect of more than one successful solution.

4.   As students discuss the material on the chalkboard, the teacher should underscore the significance of some points by offering speculative remarks and raising questions. The teacher's "I wonder if . . . ," "Did you consider . . . ?" "Does this mean . . . ?" and "How about . . . ?" queries are aimed at getting students to mine their initial thoughts for new possibilities. The teacher's attitude should be one of helping students make the best use of their ideas rather than supplementing the material with ideas of his or her own.

5.   Teachers need to be aware that students like some form of closure at the end of a problem-solving session. Sometimes the teacher may have to reassure students by promising to reopen the discussion at a specific time or during the study of a related topic. However, closure can generally be accomplished by scaling down the problem. For example, students can work on selected aspects of much larger problems. Or problems may be selected to illustrate a curriculum theme that connects a collection of units of instruction. For example, "Managing Our Environment" might be the theme, with units and problem-solving activities devoted to various aspects of

our environment. In this way, closure achieved by solving one problem serves as groundwork for dealing with the next problem. Students are much more motivated to engage in problem-solving activities when they can experience the satisfaction of growing competence.

Communicating Teacher Expectations.   *The Instructional Environment System–II* (Ysseldyke & Christenson, 1993–1994) provides a list of specific teacher behaviors to cultivate as you develop instructional management skills. They are adapted here for your use:

❏ Determine each student's current level of performance and expect ambitious growth. Communicate this by helping students set high but realistic goals. Develop ways to graph progress and require students to do the graphing. Keep portfolios of work products that include the baseline level of performance and subsequent products. Intermittently, request the students to look back and evaluate their progress.

❏ Clearly communicate objectives of each lesson and make sure that every student knows what is to be learned. Objectives can be written on the blackboard, overhead transparencies, or butcher paper on the wall. Students can write them in their notebooks, and objectives can be referred to at various times throughout the lesson.

❏ Consistently model using class time well by starting on time, being prepared with all materials, and managing smooth and short transitions. Explicitly communicate to students that they are to be on time with all necessary materials and be ready to learn. Some teachers record on the blackboard the materials needed for the lesson beside the objectives of the lesson. Then they set a timer and ask students to be ready when the timer rings. Explicitly teach students how to transition smoothly and efficiently. Also explicitly communicate your expectations for the use of in-class study time.

❏ Clearly communicate your standards for performance. Provide models of expected performance and teach students how to use them to guide their own performance. Clearly communicate the consequences of not achieving the expected standards of performance. For example, students can be told that products that meet the expected standard will be considered final pieces of work. Those not meeting the standard will be considered drafts and students will redo work until it meets the standard.

❏ Call on students equally and expect them to answer. Use a class roster to check who has been called on. Another method is to put each student's name on a stick. All sticks are placed in a cup and sticks are drawn randomly; no student knows who will be called on until a stick is drawn. It is very important to ask low achievers questions that are most likely to provide success experiences. Therefore, when names are drawn, teachers may need to modify the question that they were going to ask next. After low achievers have experienced some initial success, ask them moderately difficult questions and be prepared to prompt and cue them just as much as you would prompt and cue a high-achieving student answering a moderately to very difficult question.

❏ Explicitly communicate that you expect all students to be actively involved in learning. Purposefully structure learning activities to provide low achievers opportunities to respond actively. For example, the boy with a learning disability has difficulty reading the text and recording group members' responses during cooperative learning in language arts. However, he is one of the best artists in the school. Structure the cooperative learning activity in a way that can lead to either oral or visual responses. Another example is telling a struggling reader ahead of time what passage he will be reading before the class. With time to prepare, he is able to succeed.

Implementing these guidelines for communicating teacher expectations is important to effective instructional management. If you implement them, as found in the Kerman (1982) experimental study, you can expect a reduced number of disciplinary referrals.

MESOSYSTEM COMPETENCIES

Managing Homework

Homework is a distinctive learning activity because it takes place largely outside the teacher's purview and provides students an opportunity for solitary study. Although the beginning stages of a homework assignment might be done in class, this step is generally to ensure that directions are understood and that initial efforts are error free. The majority of homework is completed in the student's home. Some parents are unable or unwilling to assist their children with homework completion because of the following factors:

An actual or a perceived lack of time

A lack of content knowledge to be able to help

A lack of interest in their children's studies

Teachers and support personnel must make a specific effort to reach out and collaborate with parents on completion of schoolwork at home if all students are to benefit and learn from homework assignments.

Standards for assigned homework should be discussed and reasons given for them. Students should record the standards in their notebooks, and the standards should be periodically reviewed during the early weeks of school. A projector can be used to show examples of well-done homework from previous classes, or exemplary work can be displayed on a bulletin board. Standards might address the type of writing instrument to be used, the kind of paper, the type of notebook, the required heading, and allowances for erasing. Such standards help students develop good work habits and become more proficient in the subject covered by the homework. They learn how to learn and how to manage themselves in the classroom.

The amount of homework will vary with grade level and lesson objectives. Homework composed of drill-and-practice exercises, in which boredom and fatigue can undermine performance, should be limited to 20 to 30 minutes. Assignments that challenge the critical and creative abilities of students will require longer time periods. The amount of work given should be tempered by the frequency of assignments. Regular assignments, requiring modest amounts of time, are preferable to huge assignments followed by long periods without homework. When planning lessons, teachers should look for ways to capture and sustain student attention. This is also an important consideration for homework assignments. The following 10 positive steps are commonly used by teachers to minimize the use of punitive controls (e.g., marking the student down or giving a zero or a demerit as a procedure for handling incomplete work) (Cangelosi, 1988; Chernow & Chernow, 1981):

1. After you are confident students understand what has been taught, demonstrate the connection between the day's lesson and the homework assignment.
2. Find imaginative ways to introduce homework assignments, to make worksheets attractive, and to make the homework itself challenging but doable.
3. Teach students procedures for budgeting time and routines for completing work.
4. Design charts and graphs to provide a graphic record of achievement and progress.
5. Motivate by example; share your homework experience with students.
6. Appeal to the current interests and activities of students when you are designing assignments.
7. Motivate by the way you respond to completed homework. Develop an extravagant vocabulary for expressing your satisfaction. Written comments on papers and occasional notes home will elevate student persistence and performance.
8. Check most work. Students will be less lax and are less likely to gamble that work will not be collected or read if work is regularly checked for completeness and accuracy. Diligence should be rewarded.
9. Because students are test conscious, homework that consistently contributes to test success will be taken more seriously.
10. Develop intermediate steps for long-range assignments and set short-term deadlines and dates to check progress. Completed homework promotes class control and self-control.

The time required to check homework may discourage the use of this practice, particularly when the teacher must correct every piece of assigned work. Thus, the following five techniques may prove to be helpful:

1. At the beginning of the class period or day, students may be sent to checking centers to mark their own papers or those of their classmates. Meanwhile, the teacher can do some spot checking at the centers. Special marking pens will help the teacher quickly go over all the papers to check the success rate of students.

2.   With some subjects and some assignments, correct responses can be placed on the chalkboard or on an overhead transparency. Students can check their work at their seats during the review session preceding the daily lesson. After the day's lesson, the teacher can look at these prechecked papers while circulating and assisting students with their homework for the next day.

3.   Correction may be limited to selected items each day. While students are working on a seatwork assignment, the teacher can check all or some student homework assignments, perhaps concentrating on those of students who generally have problems or who are negligent about completing work. Conscientious students may be given reinforcement during the discussion. Some of the work that the teacher sees while he or she is circulating can be collected and displayed to reinforce responsible homework behavior.

4.   A perfect paper can be rewarded with helper status. A student is told that the reward for a perfect paper tomorrow will be the student's being able to assist someone who has not completed their work. This procedure can be an incentive to those who frequently submit incomplete work. A surprise selection each day might keep everyone on his or her toes.

5.   The teacher can provide each student with a folder or notebook for homework and assign everyone a number between one and five. On a given day, all number-three students would submit their folders or notebooks for correction. The teacher could read this subsample during seatwork.

Some homework assignments serve as a synthesis experience in which the ideas and skills taught during an earlier unit of instruction must be applied. Generally this kind of assignment is best accomplished in parts, with each part corresponding to a section of the unit. Thus, periodic progress checks can be made by collecting student work and checking specified parts of the assignments. Each section might be graded separately, or the student might have to demonstrate a predetermined level of sufficiency or mastery before proceeding. In either instance, the teacher would have to give only cursory attention to the previously evaluated work when checking the final product. Homework can play an important role in the amount and quality of student learning, but it can also be a hassle for both students and teachers. Some of the procedures suggested should help both parties deal more effectively with this instructional tool.

When teachers and support personnel collaborate with parents, they are better able to understand the context in which students must complete assignments. Accordingly, teachers can modify assignments and alter their classroom environments to better meet the needs of families. The barriers to completing assignments at home fall into five main categories:

1. A lack of a consistent, quiet place to study
2. A lack of a regular schedule or time to complete homework
3. Difficulties in organization of materials and assignments

4. A high level of dependency on others for assistance
5. Motivational difficulties

A minimum of five brief training sessions for parents can be used to prepare them to better assist their children with homework. Sessions can be conducted by support personnel or teachers.

DEALING WITH INSTRUCTION-RELATED DISCIPLINE PROBLEMS

When students exhibit behavioral problems during the learning and instruction process, teachers need to problem solve on behalf of those individuals. The teacher's first step in problem solving is to check his or her own classroom management plan. The teacher should ask him- or herself: "How is my plan working? Have I sufficiently taught the rules and how to follow them? Do I need to reteach any of the rules? Does every student know the rules and how to follow them? Have I been consistent in following through with the appropriate use of both positive and negative consequences?" If teachers can answer these questions satisfactorily and a particular student is still having problems in the instructional setting, teachers need to analyze the contributions of the instructional environment to the problem. The environment includes setting, movement management, group focus, instructional presentations, and activities.

Sometimes teachers can analyze the instructional environment to isolate the cause(s) and then select effective solutions on their own. Sometimes they will be more successful in developing appropriate intervention strategies if they participate in group problem solving with the designated team in the building. These teams are referred to by such names as *child assistance teams, student assistance teams, or building assistance teams* (*BATs*). Building principals, school counselors, and veteran teachers can tell you how to gain access to problem-solving teams.

As a way to assist educators in problem solving, guidelines from Sprick (1985) are discussed next for the following problem areas:

❏ Off-task behavior
❏ Talking without permission (during lectures, during class, failing to raise hand)
❏ Poor listening and not following directions
❏ Not bringing materials to class
❏ Late or incomplete assignments
❏ Tardiness or absenteeism
❏ Failure to be motivated or doing nothing
❏ Cheating
❏ Test anxiety

These problems are listed in a somewhat hierarchical order. It is hierarchical in the sense that the problems first in the list tend to occur more frequently and are usually, but not always, easier for the teacher to solve without team assistance.

Off-Task Behavior

This discussion of off-task behavior is based on the work of Sprick (1985). The greatest proportion of off-task behavior occurs during independent seatwork. For example, the science teacher, Mrs. Suce, provides 20 minutes of class time for studying assignments and writing lab reports. Most students are off task, talking, doing nothing, resting their heads on desks, reading for pleasure, and so forth. Mrs. Suce reminds the students periodically to get to work, and most do for a few minutes following the reminder. Mrs. Suce wants to problem solve and she asks herself why students behave this way in her science class. She knows that the same students use their study time well in Mrs. Vander's math class. Several times she stood outside the math classroom and observed all students on task during their study time. Mrs. Vander rarely says a word to the students.

There are several reasons students are off task during study time: (a) It is normal to relax versus work, (b) students have difficulty with time management, and (c) students may be unable to do the work independently. The first two points are discussed as a pair. The third point is addressed separately.

It is natural and normal for students to want to socialize or relax rather than work. It is also typical of students not to be adept at managing their time and not to understand that effort in the classroom leads to success. Pair these two and it should become apparent that teachers must learn how to set up structures that help students take responsibility for using time productively.

Mrs. Suce's structure to get students on task was to remind, remind, remind. In other words, Mrs. Suce actually took the responsibility for getting students to use time productively. In her class, students learned to relax, have a good time, and wait for the next signal from Mrs. Suce to get to work. Additionally, some students like any kind of attention, whether positive or negative. Mrs. Suce's criticism or nagging to get back to work may serve as a reward for off-task behavior. What should she do in setting up a new management structure? The emphasis should be on devising strategies that are not punitive and can be integrated into learning activities. When the management structure is determined, she should present the problem of off-task behavior and the plan to the entire class before implementing it.

Such a plan might be as follows: First, give one reminder to the whole class. Most will get to work. Look directly at any students remaining off task until all are back at work. Intermittently provide acknowledgments to all students who are on task: "Elana, at the rate you're going, you should not have homework tonight." Be quiet. Be brief. Be matter of fact. Be adultlike. Be sure to orally acknowledge students who have a history of poor work habits. With these students, strive hard to meet the recommended ratio of three positive comments to every negative comment.

Second, do not become engrossed with other activities. Establish the practice of visually scanning the room, especially when you first implement a plan to increase on-task behavior. Scan using an unpredictable order.

Third, teach students how to continue working while they are waiting for teacher assistance. Students need instruction about how to proceed with other parts of the assignment. They also need a way to cue the teacher without holding their hands up for prolonged periods. An example of a cue is standing a partially opened book on their desk in a vertical position. Elementary teachers have successfully used the help card described earlier in this chapter. Whatever signal is used, inform students that they are to use the signal and work quietly in order to obtain help. Make sure to do room scans frequently or students will give up on the system. They will begin calling out for help or being off task. Students may also serve as assistants. Train them how to assist, let them know when you want them to assist, and rotate assistants so they can get their work done also.

Fourth, use a class roster to mark off-task behaviors with an *O* beside student names when you do class scans. A logical consequence for not using class time wisely would be time owed. Time owed means that the student would stay after class or spend time with you at another time during the day to complete the assigned work. For example, a student who earned three *O*s during class would owe you 3 minutes at another time during the day. Such a short amount of owed time may seem a bit ridiculous to you, but it can be very effective in helping students take responsibility for managing their class time well. It is not convenient to have to return to a teacher's class for 3 minutes when a student wants to be with friends.

Students who actually seek one-on-one time with adults may enjoy time owed. Their on-task behavior in class will not increase and their off-task behavior will stay the same or increase. If this happens, you should hold a planned discussion (see chapter 8) with the student that emphasizes obtaining the goal of using class time well. Time with an adult can be earned by increasing time on task, and off-task behavior will be ignored. Be creative in providing time with an adult. The student may have favorite adults in the building, and those people may have tasks to do during the day that would benefit from student assistance.

On the basis of the tips just outlined, develop your management plan for dealing with off-task behavior. Be sure to present it to the students before implementing it. Let them know that you will be aware of their efforts to be on task and will acknowledge them. Remember to acknowledge students' efforts to take responsibility for using time well. For example, when you first implement the plan, let the whole class know that you are pleased with their efforts. After a 10-minute period of whole-class on-task behavior, say, "Each of you has worked hard for 10 minutes. Everyone is showing how good his or her concentration is." Give 5 minutes of free time after several days of all on-task behavior.

The second major reason that students are off task during study time is that they may be unable to complete assignments independently because of insufficient instruction. Insufficient instruction takes various forms. It may be that students did not listen to or did not remember instructions. It may be that the instructional presentation did not match student skill levels. Thus, the students did not profit from instruction.

Let's return to Mrs. Suce's science class during the lab sessions that occur twice a week. Half a dozen students have questions at one time as they work on lab exercises. Mrs. Suce is busily trying to help each student, but some have to wait several minutes for her to have time for them. Students grow weary of waiting and holding their hands up. They begin to visit and wander around. Lab feels chaotic to the teacher and to observers. Mrs. Suce describes the students as immature and unable to work independently. In actuality, Mrs. Suce's conclusion should be this: "Many students are asking for assistance. That must mean that we need to work on clarity of instructions or that there was not a match between my instruction and their skill level. Uh-oh. It's time to check out where the problem is. Then I can provide more and different instruction prior to expecting them to work independently."

Note the difference in the attributional statements the teacher made for the same group of students. The negative attribution was that the students were immature. The positive attribution, although unspoken, was that students were capable of working independently when the teacher provided an instructional match.

Let's return to the teacher's self-talk statement: "Many students are asking for assistance. . . ." In order for Mrs. Suce to check out where the problem is, she should take inventory of the kinds of questions students asked as she circulated around the room. Questions will generally fall into one of several categories. The categories guide the teacher to adapt instruction in certain ways in order to achieve a match. Consider the following three categories and how the teacher uses the category information to change instruction.

In the first category, basic questions about the assignment are asked, such as which pages to read and which questions to answer. Explicitly inform students that you will give the assignment once and will ignore questions regarding information that you already addressed. You would be right to ask if this is fair to students who have language-processing problems. One good solution is to write assignments on the board, read them to students, and require students to copy them across the top of their papers. Tell students that assignments must be written across the top before you will accept papers. Anticipate the typical student questions that accompany assignments and include the information in the assignment as you give it. For example, students may ask if they can answer the question with one or a few words rather than a complete sentence.

When students can complete this copying strategy accurately for a week, try giving assignments orally and requiring students to write them across the top of papers. Be careful to monitor student success with oral presentations of assignments minus the visual presentation. Many classrooms have at least one student who profits most from visual presentations of assignments.

In the second category, basic questions are asked about procedures or use of equipment. This may be a good time to teach not only equipment use but also note-taking skills. Be explicit as you teach equipment use or procedures. This means that you will have to analyze the task and break it down into as many steps as possible. Proceed slowly through the steps. Provide comprehensive and explicit instruction at each step, paraphrase the instruction, and write the paraphrase on the board. Require students to copy the paraphrase for each step. After you have modeled paraphrasing several procedures across several days, begin to call on students to paraphrase and write their versions of the procedures on the board. Remember to call on lower performing students; ask them to paraphrase the easiest steps and write their paraphrases on the board. As students become comfortable and successful with paraphrasing, discontinue writing on the board and require that they write paraphrases on their papers after listening but not seeing. Periodically, check their work to see who is having difficulty. Consider assigning points for note taking. Before students begin their independent work, ask hypothetical questions. Allow students to answer from their notes and cite the step that would answer the question.

In the third category, basic questions are asked about meaning (e.g., important concepts or vocabulary). Make sure that you go over assignments during instructional planning and try to anticipate areas in which problems will arise. Specifically plan to emphasize these areas through methods like drill and practice prior to independent work. A few students may still not be ready, and you will need to work with them further in a small group while others are working independently.

Talking Without Permission

Iverson (1990) found that teachers reported talking as one of the top three problems demonstrated by students in classrooms. Achenbach (1991) also reported that teachers rated talking as one of the most frequent behavioral problems in their classrooms. Accordingly, educators need a way to think about this prevalent behavior and a way to intervene when talking is disruptive.

It is helpful to observe and think about talking behaviors in learning contexts of humans across the life span. It is particularly enlightening to begin with adults. The author has presented, and attended, numerous workshops and in-services for adult learners who engaged in high rates of talking to one another during the lectures and transitions. At one national conference on religion with more than 300 attendees, guidelines and instructions for conference participation were mailed to registrants 2 to 3 weeks in advance. Attendees were specifically asked to refrain from talking during presentations. This request did not stop most adult learners from talking to one another whenever they wanted. That was one noisy conference. The author has also taught young adult learners in college classrooms where talking occurs frequently during transitions.

Do these descriptions of adult talking behaviors sound like those teachers provide of child and adolescent learners in our schools? Actually, there are a few differences. Talking appears to be a high-frequency behavior in learning environments for all age groups. It is critical that people learn the social skill of listening when another person is speaking and to take turns speaking. In chapter 2 you read that some classrooms make this a rule. Positive and negative consequences were provided for following the rule and breaking the rule, respectively.

Transitions appear to pull people into talking behavior. If educators do not want students talking to one another during the change from one activity to another, they need to provide explicit instructions about not talking during transitions. If these transition rules are learned by students, off-task behavior and talking will occur infrequently and instructional time will be increased.

Well-taught rules and procedures for transitions are usually sufficient for decreasing the frequency of talking. However, some students continue to have difficulty successfully managing their talking. The question becomes how to better manage instructional settings in order for students to take responsibility for talking at appropriate times only. Management of talking is next examined in terms of students' talking during lectures, one or two students' talking during class, more than just a few students' talking during class, and students' failing to raise hands.

Talking During Lectures

Let's look at Mrs. Suce's science class again. The students continually talk during her lectures. It is not just a few students; all students talk at one time or another. Mrs. Suce teaches the same class three times a day and the other two sections do not talk during lectures. Therefore, she does not think that the explanation is that she is presenting boring lectures. The other two sections responded to the basic classroom management plan that included the rule of no talking when others are speaking. She has tried the usual negative consequences: issuing a whole-class directive, using eye contact, using proximity control, giving gentle oral reprimands, giving time owed, and telling students to listen. All of these strategies helped, but only for a few minutes each time. The talking is now a pattern for most students, having occurred for a period of several weeks.

Mrs. Suce needs to emphasize accountability for talking with applications of both positive and negative consequences as appropriate. The teacher may want to devise a plan during a class meeting (see chapter 3) in which students help make decisions. It will be important for the class to clearly and explicitly state the guidelines for student behavior during lectures. One way to do this is by eliminating confusion about who can talk. The rule can become "No talking without raising your hand and being granted permission." All other talking is unacceptable and results in negative consequences.

The class can determine the negative consequences together. It is recommended that the mild consequence of oral reprimands be used the first day the plan begins. After that, consequences should be moderate in nature but never severe. Excessive talking, although frustrating, is a relatively minor misbehavior. Severe consequences would be inappropriately matched to the misbehavior, and they are usually more difficult to implement consistently. Teachers need consequences that are reasonable and moderately aversive. More than likely, classes like Mrs. Suce's are made up of students who like to socialize. They like to talk to one another. Natural positive consequences would be giving them permission to socialize at appropriate times after they have demonstrated an increase in following the rule. Natural negative consequences would be removing them from the social environment for short periods of time for breaking the rule.

How would negative consequences work? There are two basic choices: in-class time-out and time owed. Remember that students may have ideas of their own that will serve even better. One group of students decided that talkers would lose the privilege of sitting in their chairs for 7 minutes after the first warning. In other words, the student who talked had to stand up beside his or her desk for 7 minutes. Any student who reacted (e.g., laughed, pointed) also had to stand up for 7 minutes. In less than a week, students were assuming responsibility for listening while others were speaking. It is important to note that the students agreed among themselves to try this consequence. The teacher had them role-play it a few times to help them decide how they would feel about standing up for 7 minutes. All students participated in role-plays and determined that they wanted the teacher to use the consequence. Without student participation in such decisions, students may interpret consequences as unfair, humiliating, or punitive. The end result is large-scale rebellion against the teacher.

The choices of in-class time-outs and time owed can be described for students during a class meeting and discussed as options. An in-class time-out is isolation of a student in the classroom setting for a period of time. Time-out usually consists of 1 minute per year of age and not more than 5 minutes total. In other words, a 3-year-old would have a time-out of 3 minutes and a 5-year-old would have a time-out of 5 minutes. A 6-year-old and a 16-year-old would also have a time-out of 5 minutes. The exception to the 5-minute maximum rule is giving longer time-outs to students who are not able to calm themselves by the end of 5 minutes. When students return to the group after 5 minutes and are upset and likely to misbehave immediately, the length of time-out should be extended. This is not done to punish students more severely but to provide them with ample time to calm themselves and be successful in class upon their return.

An example of how a time-out works follows. A teacher taught in a classroom that had a refrigerator in it. The students agreed that an in-class time-out was a negative consequence that would be appropriate to use for talking without permission. They helped the teacher move the refrigerator away from the wall and placed a chair behind it and away from the class. (Of course, the teacher checked the wiring and so forth for safety.) The students made a big sign for the front of the refrigerator that said "Siberia" on it. When an in-class time-out was the consequence, the teacher would say, "Five minutes in Siberia." Whole-class planning and participation in developing the consequence created camaraderie, and students were good natured about going to Siberia. Classmates were supportive of one another's efforts to decrease talking.

Again, this may seem a strange occurrence to some, but it illustrates how creative students can be in deciding how best to help themselves assume responsibility. Negative consequences like those just described have been constructed by students and therefore seem to be less threatening and more palatable than those constructed by a teacher. They are mutually agreed-on cues that say, "Pay attention to your behavior. Monitor your behavior."

An in-class time-out for talking may be difficult to manage because talking often involves two students, and there may be only one time-out setting. In that case, teachers may need to rely on time owed. A logical consequence for wasting time by talking is to pay back time out of minutes that students value. One episode of talking during a lecture could result in 1 minute of time owed. Such a brief time owed could be done immediately after class. This may seem such a minor conse-quence that it would have no impact. However, brief time owed after class may be very effective with students who like to socialize. They just gave up the few precious minutes between class when they can always socialize without negative conse-quences. All other students are allowed to leave while the student remains seated for an extra minute. The student is to sit quietly without talking or studying. Time starts when the student is quiet. Time owed in larger blocks (e.g., 5 minutes) can be con-ducted before school, after school, during a break, and so forth.

Talking Incessantly During Class: One or Two Students

Sylvia has always been a talker at school and has been reprimanded repeatedly in the past. This year she has been talking more than ever. She has so many things that she wants to say to her girlfriends about boys and going to the movies and so forth. During independent seatwork, she constantly talks, even if no one is listening.

Every teacher is having the same problem with Sylvia: getting her quiet and on task. They have tried many things, including sending her to the office. She is not fazed and laughs cheerfully about the negative consequences. This may be an exam-ple of a chronic talker, one who talks out of habit. Talking is reinforcing in and of itself, regardless of the reactions of people around her. Sylvia may know that she is in control, too, because her behavior has adults so upset.

It will not be easy to change Sylvia's behavior. It will take concerted effort and patience. The following plan to help Sylvia decrease her talking may seem severe, but it can be successful with chronic talkers. Before all of her teachers implement the plan, one or two teachers need to hold a planned discussion with Sylvia to col-laborate on the development of the plan and gain her cooperation in carrying out the plan. Sylvia needs to know that her excessive talking is a habit and that her peers and others will listen better to her if they know that when she speaks, she is saying something important. As one of her teachers, you must tell her of the sequence of consequences you will be using.

You tell her that she will spend time in an isolated area of the classroom where she is not to talk even during class discussions. Decide together what you will call it. For instance, it could be called "quiet time."

Assign her a desk among her classmates but close to the teacher's desk for moni-toring purposes. None of the peers around her should be her close friends with whom she most likes to talk. Consistently give her positive feedback when she is quiet but do not comment on her lack of talking. Instead, focus on her effort and participation in learning. Arrange an isolation area in the classroom that is as far away from peers as possible. The students who are nearest the isolation area must be able to ignore anyone in isolation. Determine the sequence of consequences for talking.

One example of a sequence that could be used is as follows: (1) Give one oral reprimand and warning per period. "Sylvia, you are breaking the rule of talking without permission. Next time you talk without permission, you will go to quiet time for this period and our next class period." (2) At the second occurrence of talking without permission, say, "Sylvia, you need to go to quiet time for the rest of the period and all of our next class. You may return to your desk after one entire period of no talking." Be calm, do not argue or negotiate, and ignore student comments. (3) For each incident of talking during quiet time, the student owes an additional 15 minutes, but this time is owed before or after school or during lunch. "Sylvia, for talking you owe another 15 minutes during your lunchtime today." (4) After she successfully remains quiet during an entire class period, say, "Sylvia, you may return to your regular seat tomorrow. I am pleased that you were able to follow the rules for quiet time." (5) Reward the student's efforts: Write a note to the parents, have leaders that Sylvia looks up to congratulate her on her growth, or give her a responsibility in your class.

Talking Incessantly During Class: Several Students

The major difference between the situation in which several students talk incessantly during class and the previous situation is that these students are all enjoying talking and listening to one another so much that the usual negative consequences have not deterred any of them. They do not have a history of being chronic talkers to the point of talking when no one is listening. It is important to meet with these students together and explain the plan. Again, be neutral, be calm, and ignore student complaints. Students in the company of one another during a discussion may be more prone to complain about being treated like babies when you explain the consequences. Tell the complaining student that you will impose consequences only if he or she does not act maturely.

During the discussion, make a list of appropriate talking during class time and another one of inappropriate talking. Examples and nonexamples should come from the students' past behaviors. Consequences for inappropriate talking could be changing seat assignments to separate the students for a week. Talking in the new seat could result in time owed. As always, catch the students being good and give positive feedback. If there is no improvement with this plan after 2 weeks of implementation, develop a reinforcement system (see chapter 4). Ask the parents to participate in this plan.

Failing to Raise Hands

Many teachers attempt to conduct class informally and allow students to participate freely and with spontaneity. This can become a problem when a few assertive students dominate class discussions or call out for help during seatwork while less assertive students remain silent and unassisted. Under these circumstances, teachers will need to designate periods in which students are expected to raise their hands and periods in which it is not necessary to raise hands. Even with designation tactics, developmentally younger children will tend to have a difficult time remembering that during such and such a time period, they are to raise their hands. When reminded, they will initially follow the procedure but will forget as the time period progresses. Be careful in your applications of differential times to raise hands. You do not want to give negative consequences to students who are excited about participating and cannot remember that this is the time to raise hands versus calling out.

Even with older students, when calling out is a habit, students may have difficulty remembering to raise their hands. Structured teaching procedures will need to be implemented to correct this. Begin by clearly communicating teacher expectations at the beginning of a class period. Following is an example of what you might say:

> "During certain activities in our class, it is important that everyone has an equal opportunity to talk or ask questions. Therefore, we will be using a new procedure in our class but one that you are familiar with from previous classes—raising hands for the opportunity to participate. I will let you know when the activity of the day requires raising hands and when you can participate without raising your hands. Generally, in small-group work I will not require you to raise your hand. With fewer students, there is time for everyone to participate and we need to be able to freely share. However, in most large-group discussions, I will require that you raise your hand and wait to be called on so that everyone has an equal chance to contribute."

Teachers who are used to responding to students who call out will have some difficulty ignoring call-outs at first. Teachers may also momentarily forget that this is a time period in which hands are to be raised and call-outs ignored. However, ignore they must as they strive to be consistent. They are not to use a student's call-out, even if it is polite and at a convenient time, as a teachable moment in which they remind the student of the rule and then allow him or her to share. Students will not learn to follow the rule 100% of the time if teachers do not consistently ignore call-outs. Instead, teachers need to quickly call on students whose hands are raised. Students who have more difficulty remembering to raise their hands should be called on quickly also. Teachers' responses to them should be prefaced with statements like the following: "Mark, your hand is raised. What would you do if you were Horton the elephant hatching the egg?" The first 2 weeks will be the most difficult, but teachers who are consistent for that length of time will have most students raising hands appropriately.

Poor Listening and Not Following Oral Directions

It is important to have a classroom rule about listening such as "Listen when other people are speaking." When you are ready to make an important announcement such as oral directions and you do not want to have to repeat them, it is critical to begin with an oral prompt such as "Everyone please listen." Then give the oral directions. Later in the period, students who were not listening will ask teachers questions about what they said. Now comes the consequence, and it must be used consistently with every student. Ignore the questions and tell students that you cannot answer because you already gave that information. As students improve in listening, let them know you appreciate their efforts.

Not Bringing Materials to Class

Materials for class include paper, writing utensils, textbooks, homework, and any other supplies. The reasons why students do not bring needed materials to class range from forgetting to bring them to attempting to avoid consequences for not being prepared. Interventions for not bringing materials vary considerably. Some interventionists advise a structured plan in which students lose points toward their final grade and owe time for forgetting textbooks. Others use a barter system. Students who need to borrow supplies (e.g., paper, pencil, textbook) from the teacher do so before class begins and give the teacher a valued personal possession (e.g., watch, ring, wallet, shoe, jacket) as barter. At the end of class, students can get their possessions back if they return the supplies they borrowed. The author prefers the latter intervention because it does not penalize students who have legitimate and significant difficulties with organization and memory for details. Students who consistently use the barter system can be targeted for individualized interventions to improve organizational skills. Interventions for students who come to class without their homework are addressed in the next section.

Late or Incomplete Assignments

Problems with receiving completed homework from students vary from their turning work in late to their turning in incomplete work to their not turning in work at all. The number of students in a classroom that have the problem can range from one or two individuals to many. Just as the nature of the problems vary, so do the reasons for late or incomplete assignments vary. Sprick's (1985) interventions are described in this section.

Contributing factors to late or incomplete assignments fall into three general categories: (1) Students grow lax in timely productivity because teachers are inconsistent in collecting, recording, and returning work; (2) consequences for late work are negligible; and (3) students lack skills to do the work. The first two categories are addressed together. The third category, skill deficiency, is presented at the end of the discussion.

Before the school year begins, teachers need to plan how to deal with homework. In addition to tips on managing homework presented earlier in this chapter, the following suggestions can be considered as teachers develop their homework plans. Students need a well-designed grading system in order to know exactly what they need to do to pass the class. Parents need information about the homework routine in order to support their children. Accordingly, teachers need to develop consistent routines for assigning, collecting, recording, and returning homework.

From week to week, students and parents should be able to count on about the same amount of homework that is due on a regular schedule. Students who have not learned to pace themselves on long assignments need explicit instruction in how to complete portions of an assignment across a number of days.

Always collect homework at the beginning of the period. Doing so will prevent students from putting off homework and trying to finish it during class time. Collecting homework in person as students enter the door also encourages timely homework completion. Give students feedback and send notes to parents when students hand their work to you on time. Have a policy for late work and explicitly communicate it to your students. Define *late*. For example, "Late work means the work was turned in after the teacher began the class." Obviously, teachers will need to start classes on time if they are using that definition. Define the consequence. For example, "The consequence for late work is a loss of 10% of the points for each day the assignment is late."

Students need some in-class time to begin new or difficult assignments. This provides time to ask questions and seek teacher assistance. Students with academic skill deficiencies also may not know how to manage homework: may not write assignments down, may not keep track of what they have completed, may not know due dates, may not pace themselves on long assignments, may not understand grading practices, and may not have time management skills. Determine whether the student has the academic and management skills to complete assignments. If not, ask all the other teachers to work with you. Make arrangements for the student to get help with any areas of deficiency. Develop a homework routine and obtain parental support.

Tardiness or Absenteeism

According to Sprick (1985), several factors may contribute to chronic tardiness. First, there may be insufficient consequences for tardiness. Second, many teachers do not begin instruction immediately, often tarrying even 10 or 12 minutes before beginning the lesson. Students do not believe that they are missing out on anything important and they either slip in a bit later or tarry in the hallways to socialize. Some schools develop schoolwide discipline policies that include a hierarchy of consequences designed to deal with chronic tardiness. In addition to following school policies, teachers should have their own classroom policies in place (which, of course, should not contradict school policy). Teachers may be successful in decreasing tardiness at the classroom level by incorporating the following strategies.

One thing that teachers can do is construct grading systems that award points for participation and effort. Opening activities that begin as soon as the class begins earn participation points for students who are present. These activities and their points cannot be made up by tardy students. A second thing that teachers can do is stand at the door and greet students as they come in, even taking attendance. Students will learn that such teachers are prepared and ready to go when the bell rings.

Failure to Be Motivated or Doing Nothing

Nylan is a student who fails to turn any work in to his teachers. Since first grade, he has had a history of doing little or nothing, but it seems worse this year. Teachers say that he sits in class doing and saying nothing. In language arts, the teacher tried extra hard recently to develop a unit that would motivate Nylan. It involved World Wide Web searches on the computer and, indeed, Nylan showed an interest in the project and immediately went to work in the library. However, when the teacher came by his computer station to monitor his progress, he was cruising the Web in an area that had nothing to do with the project. He was unable to demonstrate any progress on the actual project.

Passive resistance and poor motivation in the area of academic achievement are some of the most difficult problems to solve. Sprick (1985) stated that students with this profile definitely need intensive help and offered the guidelines described next. Typically, it will be necessary to involve support services: school counselors, school psychologists, and social workers. There are potentially many causes for the problems, and it is difficult to even speculate on the causes of Nylan's behavior without more information. It is most likely true that Nylan, and students like him, are discouraged and have given up. Sometimes a factor in the problem is that students either do not have or think that they do not have the skills to complete assignments. Problem solving will be based on identifying the student's skills and helping the student develop and obtain realistic goals.

Although Nylan has exhibited passive behavior since first grade, some students' withdrawn behaviors represent a recent change. It is important for teachers to approach students with recent behavior changes differently. Recent changes suggest that students are going through something difficult. Such changes may be indicators of suicidal ideation. When teachers suspect that students are experiencing significant feelings of hopelessness or suicidal thoughts, it is time to seek the assistance of the building assistance team or counselors or psychologists.

After establishing the history of withdrawal, the teacher must obtain accurate information about the student's skill levels. The best way to do this is to work with Nylan individually. If he can complete the majority of the work without assistance, the teacher can proceed with a plan to increase motivation. If he cannot complete the work accurately, he will need remediation of basic skills. In this case, Nylan has the basic skills that he needs to accomplish the tasks. In fact, his skills are better than those of many of his peers. Incidentally, Nylan's parents wondered if their son was gifted and, therefore, bored with the curriculum. Psychological assessment did not support their hypothesis of giftedness.

The teacher can record Nylan's specific behaviors during the last few weeks that have been of concern. The teacher needs to be as detailed and specific as possible. First, the teacher should record all concerns. In Nylan's case, concerns might include these: Does not participate in discussions, does not speak to anyone, does not bring materials to class, does not turn to the page in the book, does not take notes or work on problems displayed on the overhead projector, does not use time in class to work on new assignments, rarely uses class time to start homework, does not turn in assignments, sits passively, stares ahead or at hands, acts bored or apathetic.

Second, the teacher should select a target behavior from the listing. The target behavior should be the one that is most critical to success. For example, the teacher

Student_____ Teacher_____ Date_____

Goal 1 _____

Student Objective a _____

Student Objective b _____

Student Objective c _____

Teacher Support a _____

Teacher Support b _____

Teacher Support c _____

Evaluation Process _____

Date of Goal Evaluation _____

_____

Student Signature

_____

Teacher Signature

Figure 5–3
Goals and Objectives

might select "does not complete assignments" as the target behavior. Now the teacher must clarify exactly what he or she expects Nylan to do, write a goal, and assign responsibilities to obtain the goal. Educators will be most successful when they hold planned discussions with students and write goals collaboratively (see chapter 8). Figure 5–3 shows a sample form that could be used for goal setting and attainment.

The teacher is now ready to hold a planned discussion with Nylan. Nylan will probably make few contributions to the discussion; the teacher should not be discouraged. It is a beginning to engage him in the process of solving his own problems. Now the hard work begins. The busy teacher must clear time in his or her schedule to make frequent contact with Nylan. If he shows any improvement, it must be noted by giving him positive feedback. If he makes no effort to meet goals, another brief planned discussion should be held at the end of the first week. The teacher should be calm, be supportive, and restate his or her expectations that Nylan will make the effort to reach the goal. If Nylan has not made any efforts after 2 or 3 weeks, the teacher probably needs to develop a highly structured reinforcement system. In the meantime, support services personnel assigned to the building should be conducting problem-solving assessment that will direct additional intervention development.

Cheating

Cheating is a common problem with several underlying causes (Sprick, 1985). The most basic explanation for why students cheat is that students want to succeed. Adults come back with the comment, "Then work hard and you will succeed." It is necessary to look beyond that simple belief to student beliefs about why they cannot succeed without cheating. First, many truly do not have the academic skills to succeed. Second, some are under tremendous pressure to excel and, thus, succumb to cheating. The third group better fits the adult adage of "Work hard and you will succeed." The students in this group either did not take enough time to prepare or have learned that cheating is a quicker, easier route to success than studying. Regardless of the reason, there are three supportive strategies for teachers to use that reduce incidents of cheating.

First, teachers should monitor the environment to prevent cheating. Test security, seating arrangements, cleared desks and floors around desks, teachers' visual scanning and moving about the room, and removal of baseball caps are good starting points for reducing cheating. Baseball caps? Yes, the underside of the bill offers a nice place to anchor critical points of information. Try one on and you will see how handy a cap can be during an exam.

Second, just as important as cheat-proofing the environment is the academic preparation of students that will help them be successful. Determine why the student thought he or she needed to cheat. On the basis of your determination, provide one or more of the following: basic skills training (e.g., note taking, highlighting, distributed practice, test-taking skills), peer tutoring, and time management training.

Third, the first time a student is caught cheating, discuss it privately and not publicly with him or her. Give the student an opportunity to earn alternative credit, determine the reason, and match your intervention to the reason. Tell the student that, although you do not expect him or her to have another episode of cheating, a further incident will automatically result in a failing mark.

Test Anxiety

Various factors can contribute to the debilitating feeling of panic called *test anxiety* that students experience when they are taking exams (Sprick, 1985). Pressure from parents and self may be a factor leading to test anxiety. Students who experienced early difficulty in their test-taking histories may think they cannot take tests, and test anxiety develops. Tests may actually be difficult to take because students have never learned test-taking strategies and approaches.

To problem solve how to best help students reduce their test anxiety, consider the following guidelines. Teachers should unobtrusively observe the strategies test-anxious students use and record them. Teachers need to meet with parents and seek their support in the problem-solving process. Parents can support their children by reducing any pressure to excel. They can give permission for their children to receive support help (e.g., relaxation training). Teachers should then begin an instructional program that prepares all students to use strategies of completing easy items first while marking difficult items to return to later, using answers from easier items to help answer more difficult items, using the process of elimination strategy, taking a brief break to relax, and guessing on blank items at the end of the session. Teachers may take it for granted that students already know how to use the described strategies to take tests, but many do not know them. Students need explicit instruction in test-taking strategies. Giving frequent, short tests also reduces the stress of completing infrequent, comprehensive exams.

COMPETENCIES IN LEGAL ASPECTS OF CONTENT MANAGEMENT

Grade Reduction as an Academic Sanction

The courts have consistently held that school authorities have the right to impose academic sanctions for poor academic performance. There has been less agreement regarding the use of grade reductions as punishment for student misconduct or absences. The use of academic penalties for nonacademic reasons raises complex legal issues. The practice also raises serious educational issues.

> Grades are very specialized criteria in education. They are supposed to denote a student's accomplishment in a particular subject. They are an indication of student understanding of concepts, facts, and skills. They are not indicators of attendance, although grades may reflect low accomplishment due to poor attendance. They are not indicators of deportment. They are not indicators of whether or not the teacher's personality meshes well with the student's personality. Grades, then, are purely objective, *measurable* indicators of a student's mastery of the material in a given subject area. It is when a grade attempts to become more than this that the issue becomes a legal one. (Connors, 1979, pp. 49–50)

Thus, both the legal and the educational issues remain open to challenges. In the case of the legal issues, challenges may proceed through the Family Educational Rights and Privacy Act (FERPA, 1974), which affords parents the right to challenge inaccurate or misleading information in student records (McCarthy & Cambron, 1981, p. 298).

The practice of lowering grades as an automatic penalty, such as "each day missed is a zero," is suspect. The courts would be sympathetic to extenuating circumstances, which the student is entitled to tell the teacher. "Blanket" policies for lowering grades, regardless of the reasons, are also open to court challenge (Nolte, 1980, p. 71).

Generally, the courts have held that teachers have considerable discretion when they are evaluating student work. The courts will intervene in this process only if a student can show that a grade was lowered for nonacademic reasons or can verify that the teacher acted maliciously or arbitrarily. The burden of proof for such claims resides with the student. Such contentions are difficult to prove. I have been unable to find any court-reported challenges to grades received by students in elementary and secondary schools.

The use of grade reductions as a disciplinary measure is quite prevalent among teachers. Although the courts are reluctant to enter such disputes and generally refuse to substitute their judgment for that of the teacher, educators who use this penalty should be sure that it is reasonable and related to legitimate educational objectives. A separate evaluation for conduct or citizenship would be a better practice. Official notification through a student handbook, when the practice is used schoolwide, or through a course syllabus is also a prudent legal protection.

Away-From-School Injuries: Field Trips

Field trips represent one category of away-from-school situations in which disciplinary problems may culminate in injuries. Similarly, pupil conduct problems may result in a student's being injured en route to and from school. Injuries may also occur on, near, or because of school buses. Schools have used the *in loco parentis* doctrine to claim disciplinary control over children in all of these situations. This claim has been challenged by parents to justify bringing civil suits for children's injuries sustained in these activities. The review in this section is confined to field trips because they represent a more direct supervision responsibility for classroom teachers.

Field trips are high-liability events because of the high probability of someone's sustaining an injury. Parents should be asked to sign a "liability release" form, even though these forms do not relieve the teacher from claims of negligence.

Educators can lessen the likelihood of an injury through judicious planning and responsible supervision. Consideration should be given to the type of facility or program to be visited, the number and age of the pupils, and the general composition of the student body. A teacher can better foresee the potential dangers by inspecting the sites to be visited. Problems can also be reduced by instructing students about these hazards and by providing sufficient supervision to secure adherence to precautionary measures. Finally, the teacher should be sure that the transportation is adequate—that is, that it is fully insured and that a safe driver is provided. Prudence in these matters provides reasonable protection for students and a controlling factor in the recovery of damages in a civil suit.

OBSERVATION OF A TEACHER'S CONTENT MANAGEMENT

There is no better way to learn about content management than to watch a teacher in action. Through a field-placement experience or some other means, ask a teacher for the opportunity to observe in the classroom. In Figure 5–4 there is a check-list of

Observation of Content Management

_____   _____
(Observer)   (Time)

_____   _____
(Class)   (Date)

_____   _____
(Teacher)   (Grade Level)

_____
(Schoolwide discipline plan)

_____
(Rules taught, posted, consequences)

_____
(Description of lesson: Activities and size of group, transitions)

Seating arrangement appropriate
____Yes   ____No   Circle(s), semi-circles, rows and columns, rectangles

Movement Management

___Yes ___No   1. Thrusts (bursts into activity without warning and gives directions for another activity)
                  If yes, describe any management problems that arose _____

___Yes ___No   2. Dangles (leaves one activity dangling in midair, begins another, returns to the first)
                  If yes, describe any management problems that arose _____

___Yes ___No   3. Truncations (leaves one activity, goes to another, never returns to the first)
                  If yes, describe any management problems that arose _____

___Yes ___No   4. Flip flop (terminates an activity, begins a second, surprises with a flashback to the first)
                  If yes, describe any management problems that arose _____

___Yes ___No   5. Overdwelling (spending too much time on directions, explanations, details to the exclusion of the main idea, prolonged discourse expressing displeasure)
                  If yes, describe any management problems that arose _____

___Yes ___No   6. Fragmentation (breaking down into an infinite number of parts an activity that does not require such discrete units)
                  If yes, describe any management problems that arose _____

Group focus

___Yes ___No   7. Group format (everyone shares knowledge and skills/teacher expectations)
                  If yes, describe any management problems that arose _____

___Yes ___No   8. Degree of accountability (creates a sense that everyone is responsible for what happens in the group)
                  If yes, describe any management problems that arose _____

Figure 5–4
Content Management Observation Protocol

Avoidance of Satiation

___Yes ___No 9. Progress (restructure the program to promote movement forward)
If yes, describe any management problems that arose _____

___Yes ___No 10. Variety (when interest is waning)
If yes, describe any management problems that arose _____

___Yes ___No 11. Challenge (appropriate to each student)
If yes, describe any management problems that arose _____

___Yes ___No 12. Communicating expectations
___lesson objectives
___be on time and have materials ready
___standards for performance
___equal opportunity to participate

Teacher Expectations*

___Yes ___No 1. Goal of lesson was clear to all students and all were told what was to be learned (not what was to be done).
Evidence _____

___Yes ___No 2. Teacher provided opportunities for all students to respond actively.
Evidence _____

___Yes ___No 3. Teacher provided equal opportunities for all students to respond.
Evidence _____

___Yes ___No 4. Teacher provided prompts and cues for all students to respond successfully.
Evidence _____

___Yes ___No 5. Student knows she/he is held accountable for work.
Evidence _____

___Yes ___No 6. Amount of work to be done is clearly communicated to all students.
Evidence_____

___Yes ___No 7. Accuracy of work to be done is clearly communicated to all students.
Evidence _____

___Yes ___No 8. Expectations are realistic and high for amount and accuracy of work (evidence that expectations are based on students' current level of performance)
Evidence _____

___Yes ___No 9. Teacher checked students' understanding of expectations for work to be completed.
Evidence _____

___Yes ___No 10. Teacher checked students' understanding of how mastery will be demonstrated.
Evidence _____

*Based on Ysseldyke, J., & Christenson, S. (1993–1994). *The instructional environment system—II: A system to identify a student's instructional needs.* Longmont, CO: Sopris West.

Figure 5–4
Continued

___Yes ___No 11. Students know the consequences of not achieving expected standards of performance.

Evidence _____

___Yes ___No 12. Expectations for use of time in the classroom are clear.

Evidence _____

Teaching Structure

___Yes ___No 1. Daily Review

If yes, describe any management problems that arose _____

___Yes ___No 2. Presentation

If yes, describe any management problems that arose _____

___Yes ___No 3. Seatwork

If yes, describe any management problems that arose _____

___Yes ___No 4. Homework

If yes, describe any management problems that arose _____

___Yes ___No 5. Special Review

If yes, describe any management problems that arose _____

___Yes ___No 6. Discussion

If yes, describe any management problems that arose _____

___Yes ___No 7. Projects

If yes, describe any management problems that arose _____

Problem Solving

___Yes ___No 1. Off task

If yes, describe any management problems that arose _____

___Yes ___No 2. Talking without permission (during lectures, during class, failing to raise hand)

If yes, describe any management problems that arose _____

___Yes ___No 3. Poor listening and not following directions

If yes, describe any management problems that arose _____

___Yes ___No 4. Not bringing materials to class

If yes, describe any management problems that arose _____

___Yes ___No 5. Late or incomplete assignments

If yes, describe any management problems that arose _____

___Yes ___No 6. Tardiness

If yes, describe any management problems that arose _____

___Yes ___No 7. Failure to be motivated

If yes, describe any management problems that arose _____

___Yes ___No 8. Cheating

If yes, describe any management problems that arose _____

___Yes ___No 9. Test anxiety

If yes, describe any management problems that arose _____

content management indicators that can be used to structure your classroom observation. Try to observe every criterion on the list. If any cannot be observed, ask the teacher for the opportunity to conduct a brief interview and ask about the remaining items.

You may find there are too many things to observe during one class period. Ask to return and continue your observations. On the basis of what you learned from your observations, the text, class discussions, and your own real-life experiences, construct your own content management plan. Appendix A offers a form that can be used for this purpose.

CONCLUSION

Instructional management takes you a step closer to the teacher's primary function, the actual teaching of the curriculum. *Instructional management* refers to a set of generic skills that cuts across subjects and activities. The observation checklist in Figure 5–4 summarizes the critical instructional management behaviors presented in this chapter. Use the list to assist you in observing various aspects of content management in classrooms. The list can also be used as a self-rating form as you prepare to teach a lesson or to critique your lesson presentation after you have completed it. Begin working on your own content management by completing the form in Appendix A.

SUPPLEMENTARY QUESTIONS

1. Some teachers hesitate to use debates, role-playing, panel discussions, group projects, field trips, and a host of other procedures that add variety to the question-and-answer recitation pattern. Their reluctance may be due to fears about a loss of control. Speculate about the loss-of-control factors that might be inherent in these activities and the ways to counter the anxieties associated with using each of these activities.

2. Workbooks and worksheets may be used as control measures because they keep students occupied. However, because students often regard these assignments as busywork, they often race through them, giving cursory attention to the material, or seek relief from the boredom by engaging in unacceptable off-task behavior. How can a teacher capitalize on the educational and management benefits of workbooks and worksheets without incurring the adverse effects of negative student attitudes?

3. Anticipating what could go wrong can be an effective way to evaluate a prospective lesson

activity. Select a lesson delivery activity, and identify potential management considerations for its use. What can be done to minimize the likelihood that there will be management difficulties?

4. Consider this technique: After placing all students' names in a tin can, the teacher asks a question and pulls a name out of the tin can. If the student answers correctly, the student's name is left out of the can. If the student answers incorrectly, the name is put back in the can. What are the advantages and disadvantages of this technique? What are some ways it can be used (e.g., every fifth name drawn is eligible for an individual or a group reward)?

5. "Goofing off" is a common way teachers characterize pupil misbehavior. These behaviors often occur during seatwork. What explanations can be given for these behaviors? What preventive and supportive measures might be used to minimize the incidence of these behaviors?

SUPPLEMENTARY PROJECTS

1. Elementary teachers often deliver lessons using a teacher's manual. Secondary teachers often lecture while using the textbook as a content outline. Interview students to secure their reactions to these two lesson development practices. You might camouflage your intentions by including these practices within a discussion of several other practices.

2. Make a list of common methods of instruction, for example, teacher presentations, class discussions, debates, and so on. Prepare an instrument to discover student perceptions about why each method succeeds or fails. Students could respond to a series of open-ended statements, such as the following: "Teacher presentations are an effective teaching tool because . . ." or "Teacher presentations often fail because . . ."

3. Teachers sometimes believe they have taught something well, only to find out later that many students did not learn. Interview several teachers about their explanations for the occasional discrepancy between their perceptions of student attainment and actual results. Which explanations are grounded in the management aspects of the lesson?

4. Teachers may be the cause of disciplinary problems: Flaws in the planning, organization, and delivery of instruction can be the impetus for disciplinary incidents. Ask a teacher to identify two or three students who present chronic behavioral problems. Observe their behavior for several days, paying particular attention to the instructional antecedents of on- and off-task behaviors. Do your observations suggest some connections between student behavioral problems and the teacher's management of instructional functions?

5. In many cases, students can help one another with particular educational tasks. One student may teach a subject to another for designated periods of time. A teacher gains a more individualized program of instruction without adversely affecting the learning of the tutor or the tutored. Work with a classroom teacher to organize a short-term peer-tutoring program, possibly with a subset of students in a particular classroom. Keep a record of student achievement during the period of the program. Compare student performance with that obtained prior to instituting the peer-tutoring program.

REFERENCES

Achenbach, T. M. (1991). *Manual for the teacher's report form and 1991 profile.* Burlington: University of Vermont Department of Psychiatry.

Anderson, L., Brubaker, N., Alleman-Brooks, J., & Duffy, G. (1983). *Student responses to classroom instruction: Final report* (NIE-G-80-0073). East Lansing: Institute for Research on Teaching, Michigan State University.

Ausubel, D. (1963). *The psychology of meaningful verbal learning.* New York: Grune & Stratton.

Bloom, B. S., Engelhart, M. D., Frost, E. J., Hill, W. H., & Krathwohl, D. R. (1956). *Taxonomy of educational objectives. Handbook I: Cognitive domain.* New York: David McKay Company.

Brophy, J. E., & Good, T. L. (1970). Teachers' communication of differential expectations for children's classroom performance. *Journal of Educational Psychology, 61,* 365–374.

Bruner, J. (1961). The act of discovery. *Harvard Educational Review, 31,* 21–32.

Bruner, J. (1966). *Toward a theory of instruction.* Cambridge, MA: Belknap Press of Harvard University Press.

Cangelosi, J. S. (1988). *Classroom management strategies: Gaining and maintaining students' cooperation.* New York: Longman.

Charles, C. (1983). *Elementary classroom management: A handbook of excellence in teaching.* New York: Longman.

Chernow, F. B., & Chernow, C. (1981). *Classroom discipline and control: 101 practical techniques.* West Nyack, NY: Parker.

Connors, E. T. (1979). *Student discipline and the law.* Bloomington, IN: Phi Delta Kappa Educational Foundation.

Curwin, R., & Mendler, A. (1988). *Discipline with dignity.* Alexandria, VA: Association for Supervision and Curriculum Development.

Doyle, W. (1986). Classroom organization and management. In M. C. Wittrock (Ed.), *Handbook of research on teaching* (pp. 392–431). New York: Macmillan.

Gersten, R., Carnine, D., & Woodward, J. (1987). Direct instruction research: The third decade. *Remedial and Special Education, 8*(6), 48–56.

Glasser, W. (1990). *The quality school: Managing students without coercion.* New York: Harper & Row.

Glasser, W. (1992). The quality school curriculum. *Phi Delta Kappan, 73,* 690–694.

Glasser, W. (1993). *The quality school teacher.* New York: Harper Perennial.

Gnagey, W. J. (1981). *Motivating classroom discipline.* New York: Macmillan.

Good, T., & Brophy, J. (1984). *Looking in classrooms* (3rd ed.). New York: Harper & Row.

Good, T. L., & Grouws, D. A. (1979). Teaching and mathematics learning. *Educational Leadership, 37,* 39–45.

Iverson, A. M., & Stack, D. (1996). *Preservice teachers' use of learning strategy instruction.* Unpublished manuscript, University of Northern Iowa, Cedar Falls.

Iverson, S. J. (1990). *Cognitive behavioral interventions for students in the regular classroom setting: Grades four through eight.* Unpublished manuscript, Heartland Area Education Agency, Johnston, IA.

Johnson, D. W., Johnson, R. T., & Holubec, E. J. (1990). *Circles of learning: Cooperation in the classroom* (3rd ed.). Edina, MN: Interaction Books.

Jones, V. F. (1989). Classroom management: Clarifying theory and improving practice. *Education, 109*(3), 330–339.

Kagan, D. M. (1992). Implications of research on teacher beliefs. *Educational Psychologist, 27,* 65–90.

Kerman, S. (1982). *Teacher expectations and student achievement* [Workshop handout]. TESA Training.

Kerman, S., & Martin, M. (1980). *Teacher expectations and student achievement: Teacher handbook.* Bloomington, IN: Phi Delta Kappa Educational Foundation.

Kounin, J. S. (1970). *Discipline and group management in classrooms.* New York: Holt, Rinehart & Winston.

Kounin, J. S. (1977). *Discipline and group management in classrooms* (Rev. ed.). New York: Holt, Rinehart & Winston.

Marshall, H. H. (1987). Building a learning orientation. *Theory Into Practice 26,* 8–14.

McCarthy, M. M., & Cambron, N. H. (1981). *Public school law: Teachers' and students' rights.* Boston: Allyn & Bacon.

Minnick, B. (Ed.). (1983). Student disruption: Classroom chaos linked to teacher practices. *R&DCTE Review, The Newsletter of the Research and Development Center for Teacher Education, 1,* 2–3.

Nolte, M. C. (1980). *How to survive in teaching: The legal dimension.* Palm Desert, CA: Teach'em.

Paine, S. C., Radicchi, J., Rosellini, L. C., Deutchman, L., & Darch, C. B. (1983). *Structuring your classroom for academic success.* Champaign, IL: Research Press.

Parker, W. C., & Gehrke, N. J. (1986). Learning activities and teacher decision making: Some grounded hypotheses. *American Educational Research Journal, 23,* 227–242.

Pinnell, G. S., & Galloway, C. M. (1987). Human development, language, and communication: Then and now [Special issue]. *Theory Into Practice, 26,* 353–357.

Redl, F., & Wattenberg, W. (1959). *Mental hygiene in teaching.* New York: Harcourt, Brace, & World.

Rogers, C. (1977). Forget you are a teacher. *Instructor, 81,* 65–66.

Rosenshine, B. (1983). Direct instruction. In T. Husen & T. N. Postlethwaite (Eds.), *International Encyclopedia of Education* (Vol. 3, pp. 1395–1400). Oxford, England: Pergamon.

Rosenshine, B. (1986). Synthesis of research on explicit teaching. *Educational Leadership, 43*(7), 60–69.

Slade, D., & Callaghan, T. (1988). Preventing management problems. *Academic Therapy, 23*(3), 229–235.

Sprick, R. S. (1985). *Discipline in the secondary classroom: A problem-by-problem survival guide.* West Nyack, NY: Center for Applied Research in Education.

Sprick, R., Sprick, M., & Garrison, M. (1993). *Interventions: Collaborative planning for students at risk.* Longmont, CO: Sopris West.

Weinstein, R. S., Marshall, H. H., Brattesani, K. A., & Middlestadt, S. E. (1982). Student perceptions of differential treatment in open and traditional classrooms. *Journal of Educational Psychology, 74,* 678–692.

Weinstein, R. S., & Middlestadt, S. E. (1979). Student perceptions of teacher interactions with male high and low achievers. *Journal of Educational Psychology, 71,* 421–431.

Ysseldyke, J., & Christenson, S. (1993–1994). *The instructional environment system—II: A system to identify a student's instructional needs.* Longmont, CO: Sopris West.

PART III

Ecological Competencies in Classroom Management and Discipline

CHAPTER 6

Competencies in Home–School Collaboration

DEFINITION OF TERMS
COLLABORATION
What it is
What it is not

Competencies in Home–School Collaboration

HISTORY OF HOME–SCHOOL COLLABORATION
EDUCATION AND REFORM
RESEARCH
Collaboration Effectiveness
Collaboration Barriers
Collaboration Principles
Family Competencies

HOME–SCHOOL COLLABORATION COMPETENCIES
EPSTEIN'S MODEL
Types I–VI

An understanding of the material in this chapter will help you do the following:

❏ Be collaborative partners with parents in classroom management and discipline.
❏ Discuss reasons for collaborating with parents, based on research and theory.
❏ Identify reasons why parents might resist a teacher's efforts to collaborate with them.
❏ Identify ways to increase parents' receptivity to invitations to become involved in their child's education.
❏ Discuss ways to use parent volunteers.

> Families and teachers might wish that the school could do the job alone. But today's school needs families, and today's families need the school. In many ways, this mutual need may be the greatest hope for change.
>
> —Rich, 1987, p. 62

At the end of a psychologically demanding and physically exhausting day in the classroom, a teacher feels reluctant to meet and discuss a behavioral problem with Ty's parents. Most parental contacts occur at the end of a school day, and they are often scheduled to deal with problems. A teacher's enthusiasm is further dimmed by thoughts of losing time needed to grade papers and make plans for the next day. Given this context of working with parents, it is not surprising that some teachers lack enthusiasm for collaboration.

Tired feet, headaches, and paperwork aside, teachers face genuine apprehensions about working with parents. Teachers are not sure that parents will understand their point of view or appreciate the circumstances that often restrict their options when they are dealing with problem behaviors. Teachers often feel that parents sit in judgment of them because they are employed by the community. This feeling is intensified when the parents' education and experience is equal to or exceeds that of the teacher.

Given the impediments to school–home relations, a teacher might ask, "Why should I try to work with parents? How will the time spent working with parents benefit me and my students?" Answers to these questions can be found in the literature, a knowledge base that increased 10-fold from the late 1980s to the early 1990s (Christenson, 1995). Summary information from the literature is included in this chapter.

DEFINITION: COLLABORATION

Home–school collaboration is not an activity but an attitude (Christenson, 1995). You can tell when the attitude is present because parents and teachers share common goals, treat one another with respect, and participate in meaningful ways to improve educational outcomes for children. Home and school have a history of working together that has typically not been collaborative. As a way to clarify what is meant by *collaborative,* it may be helpful to look at what it is not (Collins, Moles, & Cross, 1982):

Contacts with parents only when students are failing

Parents in schools only as volunteers

Parent–teacher conferences in which teachers do most of the information sharing

Parents serving on advisory boards but not being listened to

Parent resource centers on school grounds with no collaboration

Parent education programs without parental input

HISTORY OF HOME–SCHOOL COLLABORATION

Education and Reform

Recent waves of school reform have focused on the coordination of schools, families, and communities to help students be successful academically, socially, emotionally, and behaviorally. Reform efforts have been driven by research, theory, and social and political forces described in chapter 1.

A chronological unfolding of events has led us to this important time in history in which schools and parents are expected to collaborate together. A time line depicting these events is shown in Figure 6–1. Most of these events were discussed in chapter 1. Since the late 1980s, federal grant moneys have flowed to states and from states to local school districts to fund collaboration initiatives. Projects have a common theme of developing collaborative partnerships between home and school to improve students' academic achievement and social–emotional–behavioral development. Chicago's public school projects serve as an excellent example.

Chicago Public School Reform

In 1989, the Chicago public schools began a radical experiment in school district decentralization (Smylie, Crowson, Chou, & Levin, 1996). Each of the nearly 600 schools acquired its own governing board, with 6 of the 11 members being parents and community representatives. Another project entitled "The Nation of Tomorrow" espoused an ecological view of children's learning and development and contained three major components. The first component, "Family Ties," focused on parental education and involvement of parents in the education of their children at school. Chicago's collaboration projects have become so successful that other school districts have used them as models in developing their own initiatives.

Research

Collaboration Effectiveness

Researchers have demonstrated that effective schools emphasize the desire to connect with all families to increase student success (Swap, 1992). Five factors found

mid-1700s	Education reformers said social stability and individual welfare require universal access to schools; responsibility appeared to be totally on schools
1960s	Political decentralization of urban schools Coleman Report brought attention to equity issues and earl effective-schools research
1979	Edmonds' five correlates of effective schools: emphasis on city schools, attempt to get schools themselves to change, no mention of parental and community involvement, too simplistic and ineffective Bronfenbrenner's ecological theory, which addressed the whole ecology in which children learn and develop
1983	*A Nation At Risk:* decreased SAT scores
1984	Walberg's synthesis of thousands of studies found decreased home fostering of learning
mid-1980s	New school-effectiveness programs for all schools with an emphasis on the following: 1. Instruction 2. Parental involvement 3. Parent education about parents' role in supporting the work of schools Business influence on statutes of many states: 1. Raise teacher quality 2. Make students work harder and longer 3. Demand greater accountability Business and university partnerships with schools: 1. Some stimulated systemic change. 2. Most focused on teachers and students (e.g., teacher initiatives, student mentoring programs, jobs for graduates).
Late 1980s	Site-based management composed of teachers, parents, and community representatives Emphasis on the professionalization of teaching
1990s	Coordination of schools, families, communities Emphasis on "It takes a village to raise a child"

Figure 6–1
Time Line of School Reform

in successful parental-involvement programs are climate, relevance, convenience, publicity, and commitment (Ross, 1988). In particular, successful educators welcome all parents, develop programs that parents say are needed, help remove transportation and day-care barriers so parents can be involved, communicate in multiple ways with parents, and are committed to the priority of working with parents.

Collaboration Barriers

In spite of the emphasis on home–school collaboration, it has been a difficult-change process, and many schools can demonstrate little success. Liontos (1992) identified barriers to collaboration for both parents and educators.

Barriers for Parents.   Liontos said that for parents, barriers included feelings of inadequacy, prior bad experiences with schools, suspiciousness of institutions, limited knowledge of schooling processes, and economic and emotional constraints. Barriers to parental involvement are described in more detail in the following subsections.

Although most parents are congenial and cooperative, some will resist involvement or appear unwilling to cooperate. Knowing some of the reasons for such behavior can help the teacher approach the parents and gradually engage them in a participatory role. Silberman and Wheelan (1980) described parents' feelings and beliefs in the following six ways.

Guilt About Lack of Parenting Skills.   Trouble at school can be taken as a personal indictment. Just as teachers often regard disciplinary problems as a sign of their own

---

Management Challenge 6–1

Dealing with a Parent's Complaint

Mr. and Mrs. Samuelsen are irate because you have been using cooperative learning strategies that appear to be detrimental to their child. Alexa has complained about having to spend so much of her time helping the less able members of the class. Her parents are upset because she is being deprived of enrichment activities provided in other classes when she finishes her work. They insist that you excuse her from the cooperative group activities in the interests of her education.

1. What do you see as the problem? What do you think accounts for the problem?
2. What do you know about Alexa that might help you deal with this situation?
3. What do you know about the benefits of cooperative learning that might be pertinent in this situation?
4. How would you like this problem to be resolved? On what do you think this solution might depend?

incompetence, parents feel that their child's unacceptable or ineffective behavior reflects negatively on them as parents. They have tried to be better parents, but it does not seem to have made any difference.

Belief That They Would Not Know How to Participate. Some parents may not be convinced that the teacher is doing everything possible for their child, but they do not believe that they know how to improve the situation either. Others may have some ideas about how to make things better but lack the confidence to take their case to school. In both instances, the parents may be intimidated by an ingrained submissive role as student, a lack of education, or the bureaucratic attitude that contends that, when it comes right down to it, the teacher is generally right.

Belief That the Teacher Is Trying to Shift Responsibility. Some parents believe that the child is the school's responsibility during school hours. School personnel should take care of the students' problems at school. Some parents may feel that the teacher and the school created the problems in the first place. Their attitude is "Jerad never acted like that at home."

Some parents feel that they already have all they can do to cope with life. If they are not careful, their life will be further complicated by demands made on them by school personnel. It is thus best, they think, to keep a safe distance from school and the chances of getting asked to do yet one more thing.

Reluctance to Interfere in the Teacher's Work. There are parents who believe that they can best express their confidence in teachers by staying out of the way. They may have heard teachers complain about parents who look over their shoulders or have

---

Management Challenge 6–2

Appropriateness of Seeking Parental Assistance

Educators differ about the appropriateness of asking parents to help settle disciplinary problems. Some believe that if the problem originates at school, school personnel should be responsible for solving it. Others think that the school is frequently a convenient outlet for venting problems originating at home and that joint action is called for.

1. On which side of this issue do you find yourself? What is the basis for your position?
2. What circumstances might make you more favorably inclined toward the other side of this issue?
3. Do you think that parents share your convictions about this matter? Why or why not?
4. Do you think students favor your stance? Why or why not?

heard accounts of teachers who felt that their hands were tied by a disgruntled or an influential parent. Rather than being accused of being pests or know-it-alls, such parents adopt a hands-off policy. When they do not see eye to eye with the teacher, they dismiss the differences as a matter of philosophy or as half-truths perpetuated by malcontents, or they view the teacher's course of action as suitable and reasonable if all the facts were known. Thus, they can keep their distance, hope for the best, and take some pride in their attitude of noninterference.

Panic Over the Child's Possible Failure.   Parents' hopes and aspirations for their children often include success in school. Parents sometimes have grave forebodings that their children will not succeed. Any hint that things are not going well, and they imagine that their worst fears are coming true.

People consumed with fear want to protect themselves from anything that will make things worse. The teacher is often perceived as a person who will make things worse. Rather than face the situation, some parents try to deny the situation exists and thereby reduce the threat. These parents may not attend problem-solving meetings because of their denial that there is a problem.

Fear of Divulging Conflicts at Home.   Many people are quite private about their personal problems. The intent is to protect the individual's reputation and to be well regarded. Even when problems at home are unbearable, many parents shoulder the entire burden all by themselves. They do not talk to relatives, friends, clergy, or professional counselors. Why, then, would they want to disclose problems to educators?

Some parents, as a matter of principle, do not want teachers to intrude on their private lives. They believe that home and school are separate aspects of living and that it is best to keep it that way. Parents may also fear revealing how conflicts are resolved at home. Some parents may be abusive to their children and have been abused as children themselves. Formerly abused adults may lack the skills to deal with difficult children or to cope with stressful events in their lives.

Parental views of teachers and schools are not without foundation. The ways in which teachers conduct themselves and in which schools deal with the community can build and sustain parental suspicion, fear, guilt, and hopelessness. Parents, like teachers, mean well. Yet, well-intentioned people are sometimes reluctant to get involved, particularly if they have doubts about themselves. Knowing possible reasons for parents' reluctance will help educators remove barriers to involvement. Educators who are sensitive to the full range of parental viewpoints and uncertainties can more effectively promote home–school collaboration.

Barriers for Educators.   Liontos's (1992) list of barriers for educators included being inadequately committed to parental involvement, believing that parents have too many problems already, having negative communication patterns with parents, believing parents to be dysfunctional, expecting parents to come to the school, and having a lack of partnership skills.

Collaboration Principles

Ooms and Hara (1991) developed nine family–school partnership principles. In examining them, you can see how necessary educator commitment is to the success of collaboration. The nine principles are as follows:

1. The school building and climate are completely open, helpful, and friendly to parents.
2. Communication with parents is frequent, is clear, and goes both ways.
3. Parents' expertise is valued, and parents are treated by teachers as collaborators.
4. The school takes responsibility to partner with all families, not just those that are easily accessible.
5. School administrators are partners with families, both in words and in actions.
6. The school supports all parents in volunteer work by providing options at home and at school.
7. The school helps parents get their needs met.
8. The school seeks parents' expertise in solving schoolwide problems and developing policies.
9. The school facilitates families' access to support services in order for children to better learn.

The preceding principles operate within a no-fault model; blame for students' problems is not placed on the home or on the school. Families are believed to have strengths and parents are believed to care about their children and to be able to learn new ways of helping them. Families are respected as competent and able to engage in collaborative efforts.

Family Competencies

Research shows that families are characterized by diversity and not homogeneity as popularized by television. Some family constellations that have become more prevalent are construed by many educators as problem families. Single-parent, stepparent, and newly relocated families are often targeted unfairly as dysfunctional. Knowledge of the special circumstances of these families can facilitate sensitive and supportive collaboration efforts. The work of Carlson (1995) illustrates how to recognize family competencies in order to collaborate for the benefit of the children.

Single-Parent Families.   *Single-parent households* are those in which an adult raises children alone without the presence of a second adult. As many as 34% have a second adult dwelling in the home but are still termed *single-parent. Binuclear* single-parent systems occur when children visit two linked households.

Some educators assume that children from single-parent homes will have educational problems. This is an unfair and inaccurate assumption. In fact, when income level is controlled, children from single-parent homes perform as well as children from two-parent families. Poverty, then, is a better predictor of lower academic achievement. Whether children are from single-parent homes or two-parent families, if they are poor they will have more problems in school. In terms of academic achievement, it has been shown that girls living with single fathers have better science and history test scores and greater access to home computers and newspapers.

The one difference for children from single-parent homes is that they are 3 times more likely to drop out of school than are children from intact families. This dropout rate occurs despite comparable academic achievement. Specifically, there is an increased dropout risk for boys in mother-headed homes and for girls in father-headed homes. Dropout rates for these children appear to be more a function of social deviance than cognitive deficiency.

Adjustment problems and social deviance of children from single-parent homes is statistically more likely than for children from two-parent families, but the differences are very small. This finding can be interpreted that children from single-parent homes are at slightly more risk as follows:

❏ More risk of alcohol and tobacco use, depression, suicide, antisocial behavior, and sexual activity
❏ More risk for Caucasian youth than for youth of color
❏ More risk of adolescent depression when the adolescent perceives her or his family to be lower in cohesion and parent–child communication to be unsatisfactory
❏ At particularly high risk for depression if preceding family conditions coexist with low perceived friendship support

Parenting quality is a stronger predictor of child social competence than any other variable is. Parenting that puts children at risk includes the following:

❏ More risk associated with *permissive parenting*—characteristic of both mother- and father-headed homes—defined as few or inconsistent rules, low monitoring, and low involvement in school
❏ Higher risk when there is physical abuse of children
❏ Higher rates of very severe violence in poor, mother-headed homes
❏ Higher rates of very severe violence in mother-headed homes with another caretaker present
❏ Highest rates of very severe violence in father-headed homes and incomes less than $10,000
❏ More risk when there is interparental conflict, hostile and noncooperative relationships between divorced spouses that produces custodial single-parent rejection or withdrawal from children
❏ More risk with maternal depression and low quality of intimate relationship

In contrast, there are family processes that create resiliency in children, regardless of the family constellation. Thrivers report living in homes with family support (e.g., school and social) and parental control (e.g., discipline for broken rules, monitoring of whereabouts, fewer than three nights out per week for fun). Thrivers also have families with support systems around them.

The preceding findings regarding children from single-parent homes underscore the importance of collaborative partnerships as a necessary support system to single-parent families.

Stepfamilies.   *Stepfamily systems* are households in which at least one adult is a stepparent. Researchers have found that, on the average, the stepparent situation is beneficial for boys and detrimental for girls. The second major finding is that risk associated with remarriage is heightened during early adolescence. Educational problems were reported to be lower grades, lower achievement test scores, lower class rank, and twice the likelihood of repeating a grade. The dropout risk increases for girls whose mothers remarry and for boys whose fathers remarry. In terms of adjustment problems and social deviance, stepchildren may be at higher risk than children from two-parent or single-parent homes.

The course of adaptation to remarriage is difficult and shows little improvement during a 2-year period. Sibling and parent–child relationship problems usually persist in spite of good marital adjustment and authoritative parenting of both parents. In other words, do not assume that problems in the home are indicative of poor parenting and poor marital adjustment. Within father–stepmother families, a high parental education level predicts greater stepchild problems (i.e., active parenting on a stepmother's part creates conflict and resentment in the child). Typically, young children adjust to remarriage within 2 to 2.5 years. Adolescents adjust in 6 to 9 years at about the same time that family cohesion occurs.

Research-based indicators for children from stepparent families can be used to help educators and stepparent families effectively collaborate on behalf of the children. For example, teachers and parents in collaboration could encourage stepchildren to participate in support groups with other stepchildren. Likewise, stepparent education seminars could be conducted for stepparents and their spouses.

Relocated Families.   There also are research findings for families who move, as reported in a summary by Medway (1995). Statistics indicate the following:

Seventeen percent of all families move per year.

Thirty percent of families with preschoolers move per year.

Military families relocate as often as every 2 years.

Five and a half percent of high schoolers have moved at least seven times.

Common reactions of students are

Anxiety

Loneliness

Sense of loss

Uncertainty

Worries about losing friends and making new ones

These emotional reactions send up warning flags for parents and teachers, who can take comfort in research findings that suggest that there is very little cause for concern for the vast majority of children. Research has revealed the following indicators:

Children who are well adjusted prior to the move will be well adjusted after. Emotional reactions are normal and short term. Moving does not have long-term negative effects on average children.

Children with academic or adjustment deficits prior to the move tend to be at risk for similar or greater problems after a move. They require structure, consistency, and special attention.

The most vulnerable ages for children to move are preschool and early adolescence. These children need the most emotional support. Young adolescents report 3 times as much difficulty forming friendships as do elementary children.

Males may react more negatively than females to relocation.

Schools are advised to facilitate family moving and children's relocation to different schools in the following two ways:

1. Do not hold back children simply because they moved.
2. Provide school-based transition services that facilitate the adjustment of relocating students.

Why do erroneous beliefs about significant negative effects on relocated students persist? It is because poorly designed ways of gathering data do not control for bias. The following methods, when poorly designed, have yielded results that have contributed to erroneous beliefs:

Case study reports

Clinical impressions

Methodologically flawed studies

Validations of personal experiences

The best of what is known about the effect of relocation on families is as follows:

Relocation is a normal life transition and adjustment process.

Relocation can have either positive or negative effects on the family. Parents can influence the outcome by what they do and say.

Relocation effects can be short term or long term. Parents can influence the outcome by what they do and say.

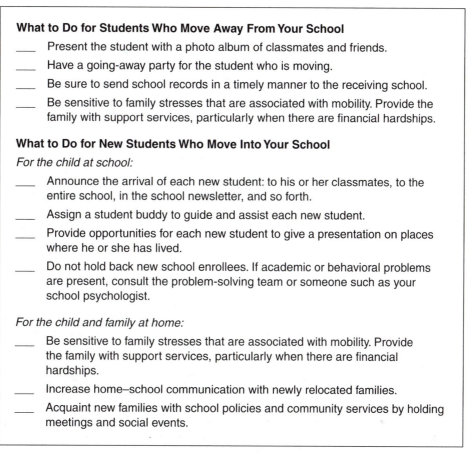

What to Do for Students Who Move Away From Your School

____ Present the student with a photo album of classmates and friends.

____ Have a going-away party for the student who is moving.

____ Be sure to send school records in a timely manner to the receiving school.

____ Be sensitive to family stresses that are associated with mobility. Provide the family with support services, particularly when there are financial hardships.

What to Do for New Students Who Move Into Your School

For the child at school:

____ Announce the arrival of each new student: to his or her classmates, to the entire school, in the school newsletter, and so forth.

____ Assign a student buddy to guide and assist each new student.

____ Provide opportunities for each new student to give a presentation on places where he or she has lived.

____ Do not hold back new school enrollees. If academic or behavioral problems are present, consult the problem-solving team or someone such as your school psychologist.

For the child and family at home:

____ Be sensitive to family stresses that are associated with mobility. Provide the family with support services, particularly when there are financial hardships.

____ Increase home–school communication with newly relocated families.

____ Acquaint new families with school policies and community services by holding meetings and social events.

Figure 6–2
Assisting Students Who Move: A Checklist for School Systems

Initial adjustment can last about 6 months, and adjustment difficulties are normal and to be expected.

Following the first 6 months of relocation, it is time to appraise the long-term impact of the move. Home and school should collaborate on developing supports for children who are having academic and behavioral problems. To assist students who move, school personnel can consult the checklist provided in Figure 6–2. An example of a helpful news release to assist parents in thinking about the effects of moving on their children is shown in Figure 6–3. It can be published in the local newspaper or the school newsletter at any time; the best time is typically toward the end of the school year when families are thinking about relocating during the summer months.

What Should Parents Know About Moving Their Children?

Is your family part of the 17% of all families who will move this year? If so, there are a number of things you can do and say to help your children make a successful transition. Each family member will have strong and mixed emotions. Adults may feel excitement about the new possibilities that come with a new job and a new residence. At the same time, they may worry about how they will get everything packed on time, how they will pay for the expenses of moving, and whether their children will be harmed academically or emotionally.

Parental concerns about the effects of moving on their children stem from two sources. First, children commonly react to the news of moving with anxiety, unhappiness, and even tears. Second, the media commonly portrays moving as one of the most stressful life events, likely to have negative effects on your children. Is this correct? What can research tell us about the long-term effects of moving on children?

Although children express unhappiness about moving both before and after the move, almost all make a satisfactory adjustment within 6 months of the relocation. The following list provides some of the important research findings:

❏ Moving does not have long-term negative effects on average, well-adjusted children.
❏ Children with academic or adjustment concerns prior to the move tend to be at risk for similar or greater problems after a move. To make a satisfactory adjustment, they require extra structure, consistency, and attention.
❏ The most difficult ages for children to move are preschool and early adolescence.
❏ Children should not be held back at a new school simply because they moved.
❏ Provision of supports at school helps children adjust.

A complete checklist of the supports that parents and schools can provide to help children move successfully is attached. Contact your local school psychologist for additional information on the how tos of successful relocation.

Figure 6–3
News Release Appropriate for Local Newspapers and School Newsletters

HOME–SCHOOL COLLABORATION COMPETENCIES

Many schools do not have trusting relationships with parents, which renders collaboration less possible. When there are barriers between parents and educators, trust-building activities should be conducted. Such activities promote everyone's ability to find friendly faces at school. Examples of trust-building, or climate-building, activities are listed in Figure 6–4. The goal of trust-building activities is to develop information-sharing, non-problem-oriented relationships. When friendly relationships and school climates are established, parents and educators can come together around a problem-solving table to collaboratively construct and implement preventive programs and solutions for diverse problems that impact students.

Trust-Building Events

Grade-level bagel breakfasts

Multicultural potluck dinners

Family's evening out (e.g., movies, skating, gym night)

Saturday sports relays for the family

Adult male's lunch day with child

Figure 6–4
Building Trust and a Positive School Climate

Prior to the 1980s, parental involvement began with the open house that often inaugurates the school year, continued through occasional notes and telephone conversations as the year progressed, and concluded with a conference that summarized a student's accomplishments. This level of parental involvement was considered adequate at the time, but that is no longer true. Parental involvement today must be collaborative in nature with multiple options available.

Epstein's Model

Joyce Epstein is a well-known, long-time researcher in the field of home–school collaboration. In 1992, she published a model of collaboration characterized by six types of activities in which effective schools need to engage. Each type is described next and in a separate figure with examples of collaborative actions.

Type I deals with families' own basic responsibilities for their children's health and safety and positive home conditions for learning. Schools are to collaborate with families and communities to obtain the support families need to meet their responsibilities. See Figure 6–5.

Type II involves school responsibilities to communicate with parents. The activities are listed in Figure 6–6.

Type III encompasses activities for all volunteer efforts in the school; relevant activities are listed in Figure 6–7. Figure 6–8 provides numerous examples of ways volunteers can assist teachers. Another adult in the classroom can be a powerful inducement to good behavior. When this adult is an additional source of recognition and approval, students are likely to be on their best behavior. Without some very specific guidelines and duties, however, parent volunteers can also be a distraction. A teacher should be prepared to redirect volunteer activities that are not helpful, to schedule help and accept it only during appointed time blocks, and to ask that help be provided on the teacher's terms. Although volunteer input is to be valued, teachers must initially provide both the substance and the structure for their work.

Arrangements for using parent volunteers proceed best when the class day is visualized as a series of activities. Teachers can consider possible uses of parent volunteers

---

Type I: Basic Obligations of Families

This category refers to the responsibilities of families for their children's health and safety, parenting and child-rearing skills at each age level, and positive home conditions for learning at each grade level.

Schools should provide information on the following:

Parenting skills
Child development
Grade-level expectations
Homework policies

Schools should help provide ways to build positive home-learning conditions through the following:

Printed materials
Videotapes
Workshops
Parental support programs
Lending libraries

Schools should create a parent/family center.

Teachers should consult with parents about specific ways to support student learning and behavior in school.

Teachers should make home visits to reinforce home-based learning programs.

Schools should conduct workshops on ways to maintain healthy child development and school success across grade levels.

Figure 6–5
Home–School Collaboration Competencies: Type I

when they look at the requirements for each activity—organization, content, duration, space, type and number of students, props and resources, expected behavior from students. Assuming that the desired activity is a lecture, the teacher might have the parent arrange for an outside speaker, type assignment materials, prepare transparencies, set up the demonstration portion of the presentation, keep a record of student responses to questions during the lecture, chart the incidence of selected teacher behaviors, or assist with student independent practice exercises following the lecture.

If parent volunteers are used effectively, teachers can acquire additional time to perform instructional functions. Students will also benefit from additional adult help because teachers cannot possibly do all the things associated with planning and delivering quality instruction, much less find time to treat individual differences the way they would like. Parental involvement activities that help all children can be balanced by activities that serve the interests of a single child. Additional suggestions

Type II: Communications from the School

This category refers to the responsibilities of schools not only for communications from school to home about school programs and children's progress in forms and words all families can understand, but also for options for home-to-school communications.

Schools should do the following:

Help develop frequent, efficient, and varied forms of all communication that are understood by all parents, such as

Memos
Good news telephone calls
Report cards
Conferences

Develop structures for

Effective parent–teacher conferences
Routine phone calling/contact system
Contacting parents at the first sign of a problem

Have personnel meet with parents to explain school programs and children's progress

Develop unique communication strategies for nonliterate parents and communicate in parents' first language

Facilitate conferences and family–school meetings to develop interventions to improve the child's school success and grades

Create cooperative relationships between parents and educators

Help educators emphasize the positive:

Put up an inviting welcome sign

Emphasize goals to teach rather than deficits

Invite parents to help solve problems

Guide and show parents what to do

Communicate at the first sign of a concern

Invite parents to the classroom

Provide four positive contacts in curriculum/deeds/progress/strengths

Implement an ongoing contact system for all families

Provide ways to learn about school policies and teacher expectations

Reach out to the most distressed

Figure 6–6
Home–School Collaboration Competencies: Type II

Type III: Volunteers

This category refers to the persons who assist teachers, administrators, and children in classrooms, parent rooms, or other areas of the school; to those who assist at home; and to those who come to school to support student performance and events.

Schools should do the following:

> Organize a parent volunteer program to assist teachers
>
> Ensure that schedules are varied so all families can participate either as volunteers or the audience
>
> Train volunteers to increase their effectiveness
>
> Ensure that transportation and day care are provided for families
>
> Encourage parents to attend school performances or other events
>
> Have personnel contact parents who do not attend scheduled conferences or need follow-up contacts
>
> Develop a buddy system to remove the barriers of transportation or alienation for some parents

---

Figure 6–7
Home–School Collaboration Competencies: Type III

Management Challenge 6–3

Training a Parent Volunteer

Mrs. Luiz has volunteered to help you work with children who are falling behind in their work. She is very conscientious and is well received by students in your classroom. However, she views helping as giving answers. Students soon learn that they can rely on her when they want to get an assignment done with the least amount of time and effort.

1. How might you work with Mrs. Luiz to help her understand the basis for and the long-term consequences of her actions?
2. How might your approach to solving this problem serve as a model of what it means to help?
3. What kinds of skills will she need to learn in order to be a suitable helper? How might you help her to acquire these skills?
4. What might you do to ease the change by alerting students to her new helping role?

Make a presentation on:
1. Interests and hobbies
2. Trip(s)
3. Occupation(s)
4. Memorable experience(s)
5. Goals and aspirations
6. A favorite book
7. Fascinating person(s)
8. Controversial issue
9. Public service project
10. Family holiday observances

Provide clerical and auxiliary services:
1. Grade papers
2. Chart pupil progress
3. Prepare bulletin boards
4. Make telephone calls
5. Arrange special activity
6. Write notes to children
7. Observe and record student behaviors
8. Type handout materials
9. Prepare art materials
10. Prepare classroom events calendar
11. Record material on audiotape
12. Set up science lab
13. Write as child dictates
14. Prepare graphic materials
15. Check out reference materials
16. Develop parent and nonparent resource file
17. Organize and maintain class library
18. Take attendance and prepare proper forms
19. Collect money and keep records
20. Beautify classroom

Provide supervision:
1. Serve as a field trip escort
2. Chaperon parties
3. Be a playground attendant
4. Serve as a library aide
5. Assist with extracurricular event
6. Assist students with money-raising project
7. Help with learning games/simulation exercises
8. Assist at school assemblies
9. Serve as club coordinator
10. Help student volunteers

Engage in home-based support activities:
1. Assist with contingency management program for school behavioral problems
2. Assist with homework
3. Guide use of television watching
4. Assist with creative ideas/suggestions
5. Prepare child for special school project
6. Build inexpensive home library
7. Take child to museum
8. Converse with child about school activities
9. Provide teacher feedback on home-based activities
10. Talk to other parents about home-based support activities

Provide remedial and enrichment experiences:
1. Locate materials
2. Listen to students read
3. Tutor a student
4. Teach a skill
5. Conduct small-group discussions
6. Discuss homework assignments
7. Develop learning packages
8. Present drill work
9. Construct a learning center
10. Conduct outdoor, on-school-site activities

Figure 6–8
Forms of Parental Involvement

Type IV: Learning Activities at Home and Connections to Curriculum

This category refers to parent-initiated, child-initiated, or teacher-initiated ideas to monitor, discuss, or assist children at home with learning activities that are coordinated with children's classwork.

Schools should do the following:

Provide in-service training to teachers on home-learning activities and other ways to involve parents with children's class work

Provide information on how to monitor homework, on grade-level expectations, and on practice and enrichment activities

Encourage teachers to make use of TIPS (Teachers Involve Parents in Schoolwork) as a resource

Have personnel meet with groups or individual parents to share strategies to increase student success in school

Plan, coordinate, and monitor interventions implemented by parents and teachers

---

Figure 6–9
Home–School Collaboration Competencies: Type IV

and references for building home–school enterprises can be found in Haley and Berry's (1988) *Home and School as Partners: Helping Parents Help Their Children.*

The demands that parental involvement activities make on the teacher's time and abilities should be carefully considered. By listing these demands next to each activity, teachers can initially make selections that play to their professional strengths. Parents will also normally choose from the original list according to their strengths. As the list is enlarged, more parents will find a place where they feel comfortable and confident.

Type IV of Epstein's model is about facilitating children's learning by means of homework. See Figure 6–9 for possible activities. Type V, described in Figure 6–10, consists of ways parents can participate in decision making. Type VI addresses collaboration with communities; activities are listed in Figure 6–11.

Most parents believe that school will help their child make the most of life, but many do not know how to support their child's efforts in school. Some parents had limited success in school themselves and may feel incapable of doing anything more than telling their child to behave and mind the teacher. Some parents, although they mean well, can be perceived by busy teachers as demanding, tiresome, and exasperating. A teacher who gives them the benefit of the doubt can generally convert parents' good intentions into appropriate volunteer support.

Type V: Decision-Making, Committee, Advocacy, and Other Leadership Roles

This category refers to parent participation in decisions in PTA/PTO, advisory councils, other committees or groups at school, or independent advocacy groups.

Schools should do the following:

> Create participatory roles for parents and community members in PTA/PTO, advisory councils, Chapter I programs (remedial programs; e.g., for reading), and committees
>
> Train parent representatives in decision-making skills, collaboration, and ways to communicate with other parents about school-improvement activities
>
> Facilitate development of basic policies on curriculum, homework, and assessment
>
> Implement PATHS (Parents and Teachers Heading to Success)

Figure 6–10
Home–School Collaboration Competencies: Type V

Type VI: Collaboration and Exchange with Community Organizations

This category refers to school actions and programs that provide or coordinate student and family access to community and support services. Also included is collaboration with businesses, cultural organizations, and other groups to improve school programs for children and services for families to support their child rearing and guidance of children as students, and to improve the effectiveness of the other types of involvement.

Schools should do the following:

> Consult with teachers and administrators about forming business partnerships and community linkages to promote student success in school
>
> Consult about forming family resource centers of school-linked services to meet children's needs through health and social service agencies
>
> Develop resources and a referral network
>
> Develop and coordinate a family resource center to provide family education, counseling, tutoring, food and clothing, or routine medical care

---

Figure 6–11
Home–School Collaboration Competencies: Type VI

The parental participation program should be aimed at helping children succeed in school (Brandt, 1989; Comer & Haynes, 1991; D'Angelo & Adler, 1991; Epstein, 1990; Kennedy, 1991; Warner, 1991). Teachers should be sure that the things parents are asked to do are not merely to serve the teacher. When the teacher can demonstrate direct connections between parents' activities and the well-being of their children, parents are more likely to participate and do so without feeling used (Parents—Your First Partners, 1986).

Cultivating home–school contacts is likely to be confined to school-required conferences, open houses, and chronic disciplinary problems unless the teacher develops a plan and conducts periodic progress checks. The plan, which can simply be a list of activities and a time frame for implementing them, can easily be converted into a checklist (see Figure 6–12). This can be reviewed each month and the variety and extent of contacts noted. From such an analysis, the amount and emphasis of a teacher's activities can be modulated.

	Sep	Oct	Nov	Dec	Jan	Feb	Mar	Apr	May	Jun
1. Sent an information newsletter to parents										
2. Called parents to report on positive achievement of child										
3. Invited parent to spend portion of a school day in classroom										
4. Invited parent to serve as resource speaker										
5. Conversed with a parent at school event										
6. Conversed with parent in non-school setting										
7. Reported to class/colleague on conversation with parent										
8. Sent congratulatory note to parent on student's achievement										
9. Sent questionnaire to parents to solicit opinions										
10. Called parent to seek assistance and/or express concern about student										

Figure 6–12
Parental Involvement Checklist

CONCLUSION

Home–school collaboration to enhance student outcomes is very much desired by a host of stakeholders. Multiple efforts, including legislative actions and federal funding of initiatives, have been made to increase the quantity and quality of collaboration, yet it is still not the norm. Researchers suggest that there are barriers to overcome and competencies to build in learning to work with parents and communities. Furthermore, they assert that all the efforts are worth the profound differences collaboration can make in the quality of life of students.

Parents can be a particularly valuable resource in teachers' classroom management and disciplinary programs. Parents are a primary influence in their child's motivation to learn, and the formative effects of their input last through the high school years and beyond (Jaynes & Wlodkowski, 1990). When students realize that parents and teachers are partners of one mind, they will be more likely to make their own commitments to learn and grow.

SUPPLEMENTARY QUESTIONS

1. Both teachers and parents describe meetings with each other as an anxiety-provoking experience. Why are such situations stressful? Is this a desirable or an undesirable state of affairs? Explain. If you regard it as undesirable, what measures might be taken to ease the emotional stress associated with such meetings?
2. Some educators claim that there has been a steady rise in disciplinary problems in schools and a corresponding increase in similar problems in the home. Assuming that this statement is an accurate assessment, what do you think are the common denominators in the school and home that might account for this situation?
3. When children are persistent troublemakers in school, some teachers are prone to place the blame on parents. What do you think accounts for this disposition?
4. Teachers are often distressed because the parents who really need to be partners rarely are. Speculate about why these parents are not available. On the basis of your speculations, what could be done to increase these parents' participation in the education of their children? Refer to the reasons these parents do not now participate as you defend your suggestions.

SUPPLEMENTARY PROJECTS

1. Interview several parents who have children in the age group that you plan to teach. Select questions that will reveal their conceptions of schooling and of the teacher's role and functions. Prepare a paper wherein you discuss the similarities and differences between their views and your own. Assuming that their children hold views similar to those of their parents, discuss the implications for your work with their children.
2. Ask permission to attend a conference in which a consultative team is dealing with a chronically disruptive student. Keep a record of the words the teacher uses to describe this student, the ways in which the teacher has tried to deal with these behaviors, and why the teacher believes these interventions have failed. Place a check mark next to each of these items whenever someone on the team refers to these remarks of the teacher. What do you conclude from this analysis?

3. Volunteer to begin a parental resource file for a teacher. Create an instrument for collecting data from parents regarding their availability for assisting with classroom activities and their willingness to make a presentation about their job, hobbies, or travel. Develop a handy resource card for compiling the data. Secure permission from the principal to administer your instrument to a small sample of parents. Assemble the results.

4. Observe one student during a large block of the school day, both inside and outside of the classroom, and read all of the student's work submitted for teacher evaluation. Then prepare a hypothetical progress report that you could send to parents. Discuss your report with the student's teacher. How similar or dissimilar are your views?

5. Interview several parents to find out what kinds of persistent behavioral problems they think would justify the teacher's seeking their assistance. As you listen to the parents describe the incidents, note what they believe precipitates such problems, the corrective measures that they would advocate, and how they view their role in dealing with chronic behavioral problems.

REFERENCES

Brandt, R. (1989). On parents and schools: A conversation with Joyce Epstein. *Educational Leadership, 47*(2), 24–27.

Carlson, C. (1995). Working with single-parent and stepfamily systems. In A. Thomas & J. Grimes (Eds.), *Best Practices in School Psychology, III* (pp. 1097–1110). Washington, DC: National Association of School Psychologists.

Christenson, S. L. (1995). Best practices in supporting home–school collaboration. In A. Thomas & J. Grimes (Eds.), *Best Practices in School Psychology, III* (pp. 253–267). Washington DC: National Association of School Psychologists.

Collins, C. H., Moles, O., & Cross, M. (1982). *The home–school connection: Selected partnership programs in large cities.* Boston: Institute for Responsive Education.

Comer, J. P., & Haynes, N. M. (1991). Parent involvement in schools: An ecological approach. *The Elementary School Journal, 91*(3), 271–277.

D'Angelo, D. A., & Adler, C. R. (1991). Chapter 1: A catalyst for improving parental involvement. *Phi Delta Kappan, 72*(5), 350–354.

Epstein, J. L. (1990). *School programs and teacher practices of parental involvement in inner-city elementary and middle schools.* Baltimore: Johns Hopkins University Center for Research on University and Middle Schools.

Epstein, J. L. (1992). School and family partnerships: Leadership roles for school psychologists. In S. L. Christenson & J. C. Conoley (Eds.), *Home–school collaboration: Enhancing children's academic and social competence* (pp. 499–515). Silver Spring, MD: National Association of School Psychologists.

Haley, P., & Berry, K. (1988). *Home and school as partners: Helping parents help their children.* Andover, MA: Regional Laboratory for Educational Improvement of the Northeast and Islands.

Jaynes, J. H., & Wlodkowski, R. J. (1990). *Eager to learn: Helping children become motivated and love learning.* San Francisco: Jossey-Bass.

Kennedy, C. (1991). Parent involvement: It takes P.E.P. *Principal, 70*(4), 25, 27–28.

Liontos, L. B. (1992). *At-risk families and schools: Becoming partners.* Eugene: ERIC Clearinghouse on Educational Management, College of Education, University of Oregon.

Medway, F. J. (1995). Best practices in assisting families who move and relocate. In A. Thomas & J. Grimes (Eds.), *Best Practices in School Psychology, III* (pp. 977–986). Washington, DC: National Association of School Psychologists.

Ooms, T., & Hara, S. (1991). *The family-school partnership: A critical component of school reform*. Washington, DC: The Family Impact Seminar.

Parents—Your first partners [Special issue]. (1986). *Instructor and Teacher,* Winter, 12–16.

Rich, D. (1987). *Schools and families: Issues and actions*. Washington, DC: National Education Association.

Ross, V. M. (1988). *Helping parents help their kids*. Arlington, VA: National School Public Relations Association.

Silberman, M., & Wheelan, S. (1980). *How to discipline without feeling guilty: Assertive relationships with children*. Champaign, IL: Research Press.

Smylie, M. A., Crowson, R. L., Chou, V., & Levin, R. A. (1996). The principal and community–school connections in Chicago's radical reform. In J. G. Cibulka & W. J. Kritek (Eds.), *Coordination among schools, families, and communities: Prospects for educational reform*. Albany: State University of New York Press.

Swap, S. M. (1992). Parent involvement and success for all children: What we know now. In S. L. Christenson & J. C. Conoley (Eds.), *Home–school collaboration: Enhancing children's academic and social competence* (pp. 499–515). Silver Spring, MD: National Association of School Psychologists.

Warner, I. (1991). Parents in touch: District leadership for parent involvement. *Phi Delta Kappan, 72*(5), 372–375.

CHAPTER 7

Competencies in Schoolwide Discipline

SYSTEM-LEVEL PREPLANNING
POSITIVE EXPECTATIONS
SCHOOL DISCIPLINE PLAN
CLASSROOM RULES
CONSEQUENCES
   In-Class

Schoolwide Discipline Competencies

LEGAL COMPETENCIES
DUE PROCESS
SUSPENSION
   Short-Term
   Students With Disabilities
   Long-Term
   Extracurricular Activities
EXPULSION

OUT-OF-CLASS
ADMINISTRATIVE REFERRALS
   Discussions
   Detention
   In-School Suspension
   Saturday School
   Instructional
      Interventions
   Record Keeping
   Repeated Referrals

CRISIS MANAGEMENT

An understanding of the material in this chapter will help you do the following:

❑ Appreciate the contribution of ecological theory to the management of student behavior.
❑ Develop a visible schoolwide prevention agenda for problem behavior.
❑ Participate in planning and implementing schoolwide discipline policies and procedures.
❑ Administer out-of-class consequences appropriately.
❑ Seek assistance from specialists to help problem solve on behalf of students who are repeatedly given out-of-class consequences.
❑ Adhere to legal aspects of disciplining students.

The final bell rang to signal the beginning of the first period of the day. Ms. Doe noticed Tony, who was obviously late for his class but walking very slowly down the hall. The teacher shook her head slightly as she thought about Tony's future. "After all," she thought to herself, "How could anyone with such badly groomed hair, unbrushed teeth, and raggedy shoes and pants be successful in school or in life? To add insult to injury, here he is late and not making much of an attempt to get to class. He probably slept in or was hanging out on the corner with that bad crowd of boys who smoke every morning. He has one bad attitude for me to manage."

Ms. Doe walked quickly down the hall to stop Tony and ask him why he was still in the hallway. She used her best tone of voice to communicate scathing sarcasm and suspicion of his motives. He responded with profanity and turned around and left the building. Ms. Doe proceeded to the office and reported Tony's insubordination and truancy. In her oral report to the principal, she added that Tony's behavior was just as she had predicted, "He will never be successful here."

Hyman (1997) applied an ecological, or systems, management approach to a case similar to that just described. How would thinking ecologically contribute to the outcome of Ms. Doe's and Tony's interaction? An ecological, systems-level approach to schoolwide and classroom management and discipline would be based on the belief that student misbehavior is a function of the interactions among people and every aspect of the environment. An ecological theorist would determine what influences in the school contributed to Ms. Doe's beliefs about students who look like Tony: Did administrators or other staff previously model subtle comments or bold statements about some students? Has school been disrupted by students who dress like Tony? Have parents of students like Tony caused problems for the school?

In keeping with a renewed emphasis on ecological approaches to discipline in the schools, centers for schoolwide positive behavior supports (PBSs) have developed throughout the country. Systems that support PBSs must be proactive, inclusive, flexible, and respectful of diversity.

This chapter prepares educators to think and function at a systems level in matters of discipline. Preplanning of schoolwide discipline policies and procedures is the focus. Such preplanning should be done in an informed manner, with careful reflection and preplanning of positive systems-level management practices.

PREPLANNING AT THE SYSTEMS LEVEL

Professional educators who think about management at a systems level match their classroom management plans with the schoolwide discipline policy, the culture of the school, and the culture of the community. Accordingly, educators need to study the school district or school building discipline plan. If educators disagree with the building discipline plan, they can precipitate change. Teachers will experience difficulty when attempting to carry out classroom management plans that do not fit with building discipline plans. Consider a teacher who wants to allow food and drink in the classroom at any time even though the building discipline plan states that food and drink can be consumed only at designated holiday observances with administrator consent. When teachers are knowledgeable about building discipline plans, they can write better tentative classroom management plans. Teachers should give copies of their tentative plans to building principals and obtain support for the plans.

Recall that schoolwide discipline policies from the early 1900s were based on punitive and exclusionary practices. At that time, success in school was not a prerequisite to getting a job. Schools did not have the goal of educating everyone and graduated only 6% of the population. Accordingly, schools were oriented toward children and adolescents who were academically inclined and had socially acceptable behaviors. Discipline policies were based on punishment for breaking the rules and included suspension and expulsion. Such policies were a major way to exclude less able, less motivated, or poorly behaved students.

Some educators believe that punitive and exclusionary discipline policies served us well and should continue to be acceptable practices, and suspension and expulsion procedures continue to be used widely. However, many educators now assert that school discipline policies based on suspension and expulsion are no longer appropriate in today's world. Young people today need a high school education for life success. Since the 1960s, nearly 100% of all children attend school, and 75% of them complete school. Schools can no longer function with discipline policies that, in effect, cause them to be exclusive systems. These educators assert that traditional approaches will fail today because they are based on assumptions that were more true for the 6% of children in school in the early 1900s than for the 100% of children in school in the 21st century.

The first faulty assumption of an exclusionary mentality is that children attending school today know the right way to behave and are making a choice to be defiant. On the basis of the assumption of defiance, educators think that punishment will stop inappropriate behaviors and increase appropriate behaviors. Unfortunately, some students come from homes where education is not valued, parental guidance is limited, interactions are disrespectful and hostile, and fighting is encouraged as a way to solve problems. Thus, educators are not making a good choice if they implement discipline policies that discriminate against students from homes where guardians do not know how to or do not care to prepare their children with the socially acceptable behaviors needed to follow school rules. The issue becomes this: Do educators punish disrespect and irresponsibility or teach respect and responsibility?

The second faulty assumption is that all students have a strong desire to be in school. Therefore, discipline policies of suspension or expulsion will serve as deterrents for all students. This is not a reasonable assumption for many students who are suspended or expelled. They actually may not have a strong desire to be in school. The threat of punishment by suspension or expulsion is no threat at all.

This assumption and its ensuing disciplinary practices of suspension and expulsion are also tied to legal concerns. Provisions of IDEA '97 (Individuals With Disabilities Education Act Amendments of 1997) protect students with disabilities. Exclusionary discipline practices may violate the following four provisions of these laws: (1) the right to a free and appropriate education, (2) the right to prescribed procedures prior to a change of placement, (3) the right to an education in the least restrictive environment, and (4) the right to stay in the current placement while due process is pending.

Educators who take a revised view of discipline can develop effective, nonexclusionary schoolwide discipline policies for all students experiencing social, emotional, and behavioral problems, including those identified as behaviorally disordered. One step toward a revised view is a change in attitude. Ask educators to define *discipline*. The most common response will be that discipline is punishment of those who do not obey or follow the rules. In other words, discipline is concerned with punishing misconduct. Educators further talk about lists of prohibitive rules and hierarchies of increasingly severe punishments.

Contrast the common response with an additional definition of discipline of which many people are not aware: preventing misconduct through "training to act in accordance with rules" and "instruction and exercise designed to train to proper conduct or action" (Barnhart & Stein, 1962). The attitude change is that the primary focus of discipline is training, instruction, and teaching. In learning basic reading and math skills, students are carefully instructed, given plenty of opportunities to practice, and provided corrective feedback and encouragement. Teachers respond to academic errors with corrective teaching. What about the social errors that students make every day? Should educators automatically respond with punishment, or should they use the same instructional concepts that facilitate academic learning: direct instruction, practice, encouragement, and corrective feedback?

The revised view of discipline is instructional, with an emphasis on teaching students to behave responsibly in school. Educators must be able to view misbehavior as a teaching opportunity. This viewpoint helps educators remain objective and not react defensively or punitively. Contemporary schoolwide discipline plans provide paired procedures for negative consequences (punishment) and instruction for teaching replacement behaviors.

Sprick (1985) developed a prototype of a schoolwide discipline plan. His recommended policies and procedures set forth common expectations for student behavior and consistent guidelines for dealing with misbehavior. Implementation of the

The schoolwide discipline plan's creed is a positive greeting to everyone who enters the school building.

comprehensive plan helps students learn that staff share basic expectations for student behavior whether the students are in the classroom, halls, cafeteria, or restrooms.

This phase of planning may be difficult for educators with either a psychodynamic or a humanistic set of assumptions. Educators who hold psychodynamic assumptions may approach schoolwide discipline planning with an exclusionary attitude. Essentially, these educators may expect students to come to school with the necessary prerequisite social skills instilled by guardians. Students who do not follow school rules successfully may be punished, suspended, expelled, or sent to alternative resources for their education and other assistance. The biggest attitude shift for these educators is the willingness to offer school-based, prosocial education while keeping students in regular education.

Educators with humanistic assumptions may believe that developing a positive school climate characterized by an abundance of adult acceptance and support of all students would be the necessary and sufficient condition to meet in schoolwide policy planning. It is believed that given optimally supportive school climates, students will make good choices for themselves. Rules, guidelines, and expectations will not need to be explicitly stated by the adults in the environment. It is preferred that students generate these on their own. This approach to schoolwide discipline planning, however, is flawed. First, the probability of efficient systems-level management of hundreds of culturally diverse students without a uniform set of expectations is low indeed. If systems wait on hundreds of students to generate their own common guidelines, a long period of confusion will result. Following are two examples of expectations that might need clarification: (1) Some students carry weapons in their neighborhood to be safe. Weapons on school grounds are considered unsafe. (2) In the home, some students know that it is acceptable to be loud and noisy, talk back to their guardians, and refuse to follow directions. In schools, learning environments are disrupted when students exhibit these same behaviors.

Second, students are accustomed to following numerous rules that they had no part in developing in the community external to schools. There is an understanding that community rules are developed to keep the environment and people safe. Most people follow the rules and are not irritated by them. Students read on the restaurant entrance "No shoes, no shirt, no service" and know that they cannot enter without shoes and a shirt. Consider the notice posted in the U.S. Post Office lobby: "No loitering." You will not see students or adults hanging out there. At the swimming pool, people read, "No running. No glass containers. No street clothes. No talking to lifeguards while on duty." Those who break the rules lose their privilege of using the swimming pool.

School environments need be no different from communities in terms of communicating rules clearly. Systems-level management plans that keep environments and people safe must be developed, implemented, and upheld for culturally diverse student bodies. Keys to success are to teach the rules explicitly and to teach the prosocial behaviors that students need to follow the rules successfully.

School personnel interested in developing or revising building discipline policies may wish to use Sprick's (1985) model as an exemplar. Administrators, teachers, parents, and students need to work together closely to establish policies and procedures that will work for their school. Broad-based student representation should be included in the democratic process of policy planning. *Broad-based* representation means that students of various backgrounds and interests should participate: the athlete, the musician, the actor, the mechanic, the scholar, the potential dropout. This increases understanding and acceptance of the rules by diverse student leaders who can communicate with their peers accordingly.

The basics of Sprick's schoolwide plan include the following: a school building statement of positive expectations for student behavior that is discussed with students, teachers' classroom rules, lists of consequences and procedures for implementing them, guidelines for office referrals, action guidelines for student lawbreakers, record-keeping procedures, and follow-up procedures for repeated problems. These important components of any schoolwide discipline plan are described next.

State Positive Expectations for Student Behavior

Rosell (1986) found that most schools do not have simple, general statements of expectations. It is critical that school discipline plans clearly articulate the behaviors necessary to ensure a positive learning environment. An example follows of an overall statement of expectations for behavior. Illustrations of how to teach the responsibilities to students are provided in chapter 2.

> Your parents and community provide you with buildings, equipment, and staff to prepare you for success. We will give you the best education we can. We know that you will proudly keep our school "Blue Ribbon" by assuming the following four responsibilities:
>
> 1. Attend class regularly and on time.
> 2. Give every assignment your best effort.
> 3. Treat all students, teachers, and property with respect.
> 4. Follow the specific rules in each class.

Educators can be guilty of assumptive teaching, that is, assuming that students know the expectations or appropriate behavior as a function of age: "He's 12 years old; he should know how to behave at school." Regardless of age, troublesome youth may not have learned acceptable social behaviors. Therefore, educators should explicitly teach behavioral expectations through direct instruction, modeling, use of rationales, role-playing, rehearsal or practice, and reinforcement.

The culture of school buildings is determined by the staff. Positive cultures can be created and maintained by informed, educated staff. Administrators should facilitate staff development to ensure that all school personnel—from bus drivers, custodians, and cooks to associates, teachers, and principals—are giving students positive feedback for following school expectations. Research shows that the rate of three positive feedback statements to one negative feedback statement from adults to students relieves 20% of the behavioral problems occurring in the building (Batsche, 1996).

Write the School Discipline Plan

School discipline plans are more effective when a collaborative committee writes them. Administrator, teacher, school employee (e.g., custodians, cooks, secretaries), parent, and student representatives all make important contributions to the plan.

Teachers should discuss the school discipline plan with students and include their input. A description of positive expectations such as those described earlier should be included, as well as a list of misbehaviors that will lead to immediate referral to the office and predetermined consequences. Both of these latter points are comprehensively described later in this chapter. The building plan should be distributed and discussed during homeroom or all first-period classes on the first day of school or prior to implementation. It should not be assumed that students or personnel will remember all the policies after hearing them once. Periodic reviews are typically necessary every quarter or semester.

Teach and Uphold Classroom Rules

Sprick (1985) reported that students tend to have no difficulty working within a variety of rules as long as each teacher has outlined clear expectations for behavior. Batsche (1996), whose research was conducted in schools with culturally diverse populations and high incidences of behavioral problems, recommended that teachers collaborate to write mutual rules common to all classrooms. Batsche's recommendation is sensitive to demands placed on students' memories when different teachers or areas of the school building have different rules and expectations. Examples of common classroom rules and how to teach them explicitly are presented in chapter 2. Teachers can add rules specific to their particular classrooms as necessary.

Determine In-Class or Out-of-Class Consequences

Teachers may rely heavily on the consequence of sending students to the office for administrators to handle. This tactic is frustrating for building principals, who have only a slim menu of consequences (e.g., "lecturing," suspension) from which to choose. Their choices of consequences are limited to those that are relatively punitive, and such consequences are not appropriate for minor misbehaviors. Schoolwide discipline policies must emphasize that the majority of inappropriate behaviors will be handled in the classroom.

Teachers need to document their attempts to resolve minor misbehaviors within the classroom. Attempts to resolve minor misbehaviors include reteaching rules and procedures, holding class meetings, implementing student-centered problem solving, giving time owed, making parental contact, and isolating the student within the classroom. These consequences are described in this and other chapters. Office referrals are reserved for major misbehaviors, as cited in the next section.

Make Referrals to the Administration

Referrals should be made to the office only when the misbehavior cannot be handled in the classroom. If severe misbehaviors are identified as part of the school policy, then there will be no question as to whether a behavior should be referred or not. The following examples and nonexamples can be used to guide your own discussion of what misbehaviors should result in office referrals.

- ❏ *General examples:* Behaviors that completely disrupt the learning environment, threaten the safety of others, demonstrate direct and persistent defiance, or break the law
- ❏ *Actual examples:* Using drugs, fighting, throwing furniture, possessing a dangerous weapon, or refusing to comply with a direct teacher command that was given when the student was disrupting the learning environment completely
- ❏ *Nonexamples:* Talking back in class, being loud and disruptive in class but stopping when requested to do so, orally arguing with other students in class, or swearing in class

Office Referral Forms

Office referrals should be accompanied by a completed referral form and a guardian contact. The following points should be entered on the referral form:

1. Specify what the problem is and describe what happened.
2. Describe your response to the problem and what has been done previously to try to solve the problem.

Consequences for Office Referrals

Sprick (1985) offered a partial menu of consequences from which to select at the office referral level. These consequences are familiar to most people; however, Sprick innovatively revised some of them. Referring parties need to respect the judgment of building principals in selecting the most appropriate consequences. If referring parties tend to disagree with the pattern of consequences selected by the principal across several referrals, they should resolve conflicts with the administrator by using the same respectful, peaceable strategies students are expected to use when they disagree or have conflicts with others.

Discussions.   Procedures should be in place that will eliminate students' waiting in the office to see the person in charge of discipline. For instance, someone should always be "on call" to handle discipline problems, or the waiting area should be nonstimulating (i.e., student cannot talk to or watch others).

Discussions should be used for the first minor offense only. If a discussion can help a student change his or her behavior, the student will not be back in the office again. A discussion should include the following four steps:

1. Identify the problem.
2. Determine whether the misbehavior is partially caused by an inability to handle the classroom work (if so, provide appropriate academic follow-through).
3. Explore alternative ways for the student to handle a similar problem in the future.
4. Assist the student in recognizing that he or she has the ability to choose personal responses.

After-School Detention.   Most people are familiar with the consequence of after-school detention (ASD). ASD is often selected as a consequence even though there are problems with its implementation. If ASD is used, one recommendation is that schools run an ASD room every day, with teachers rotating duty for 1 week at a time. Transportation problems can be resolved by having the student report to detention the day after the student has been referred. This allows ample time for the student to make transportation arrangements.

Guardian approval and support is needed for this plan to work. Letters home the first day of school can garner guardian support (see Figure 7–1). Guardians need to provide phone numbers where they can be reached or where messages can be left in order to inform them of ASDs.

When individual teachers supervise their own ASD, this classroom consequence is sometimes referred to as *time owed.* Time owed is considered to be a more natural consequence than ASD served with some third party. Consequences are considered natural if they are reasonable and likely outcomes of behaviors. When students are not following classroom rules, they are usually wasting class time. Teachers who use time owed require students to spend additional time in their classrooms as a natural payback. This consequence is the most effective form of ASD and should not require the use of the formal referral procedure (Sprick, 1985).

In-School Suspension.   In-school suspension (ISS) is another popular and often-used consequence. Its use should be restricted to instances of severe misbehaviors that merit an office referral. When school records show that students are receiving ISS for mild problems, it is an indication that systems-level problems are present and need to be solved. For example, teachers may need in-service training in classroom management.

ISS has potential for great misuse, but when applied to severe misbehaviors it offers a number of benefits. Sprick (1985) cited the seven benefits of ISS as follows:

Dear Parents/Guardians,

I am pleased to have your child in my room. We are going to have a challenging and interesting year. You as parents or guardians are important to your child's progress in my class and it is important for us to communicate. The best time to reach me is between 3:00 and 3:45 p.m. at 555-5555 or you can call the central office for an appointment. I will return your call as soon as possible.

To have the best learning environment, the students and I selected four rules that students are expected to follow at school and in my classroom:

1. Act with respect in our actions toward all people and property.
2. Be on time, prepared with all materials, and ready to learn.
3. Promptly follow directions.
4. Follow all school rules.

The students and I have talked about the rules and practiced them in class. It would be very helpful to me if you would also discuss the rules to make sure your child understands them.

Special problems may call for consequences such as keeping your child after school or requiring your child to phone you to discuss a problem. Check the box to indicate your permission to use these rules and consequences with your child. If you have concerns, please write them in the space provided and I will work with you to decide on acceptable consequences.

I am pleased to have your child in my room this year. I look forward to a year of growth.

Sincerely,

_____

____ Agree with rules and consequences   ____ Do not agree

_____(Name)

Concerns: _____

_____

Figure 7–1
Example of a Letter to Parents or Guardians Explaining School and Classroom Rules and Procedures

(1) It removes students' problems from the classroom, (2) it keeps students within the school, (3) it reduces the likelihood that suspension is a student holiday, (4) it demonstrates to students and guardians that the school will deal with misbehavior, (5) it usually meets with guardian support, (6) students are not turned onto the

street, and (7) ineffective guardians are not asked to handle problems that schools cannot handle.

To implement ISS effectively, educators need to preplan the parameters. The weaknesses of typical applications, as well as innovative adaptations, of ISS are enumerated subsequently. Following are Sprick's (1985) recommended parameters for implementing ISS:

1. Select a completely isolated area at least 8 feet square with walls from floor to ceiling.
2. Determine how long students will spend in ISS and how the time will be spent.

Four weaknesses of the typical 3-day ISS are as follows: (1) Out-of-school suspension (OSS) is usually recommended on the third offense (following two ISSs). Students with significant problems could quickly accumulate a third offense and quickly receive an OSS. School discipline plans should avoid the use of OSS as much as possible. (2) Difficulties in only one class cause students to be removed from all classes for 3 days. (3) Subsequently, all teachers are required to design independent assignments for the student. (4) Under these conditions, the following questions tend to arise: Who determines whether assignments have been completed satisfactorily? What happens if the student fails to complete work during the 3-day ISS? What happens if the student lacks the academic ability to do the work independently?

Alternative ISS programs have graduated schedules of consequences. An example follows:

1. *First referral:* Fifteen minutes in ISS with student doing nothing
2. *Second referral:* One hour in ISS with student doing nothing
3. *Third referral from same class:* Three days in ISS during the class period in which problems occurred, with class assignments from the teacher who has referred the student
4. *Fourth referral:* Three full days in ISS with assignments from all classes
5. Option of using automatic 3-day ISS for certain severe problems such as use of drugs or violence

The strengths of an alternative ISS program are multiple. First, the mild consequences of the first and second referrals are aversive to students because they are not allowed to do anything. The mild consequences also serve as a buffer zone against the possibility that a particular teacher was having a difficult day and overreacted to a possible misunderstanding.

Second, the graduated schedule of consequences provides extra steps prior to the use of OSS. This extra time gives staff additional opportunities to assist the student in learning prosocial behaviors. Third, students do not miss out on large amounts of class time. Compare two referrals on the alternative plan (1 hour and 15 minutes of missing the class in which the behavior occurred) with two referrals on the 3-day plan (6 full days of missing all classes).

ISS supervisors should reflect on the following criteria when determining guidelines for behavior and how to handle misbehavior in ISS:

1. Clearly state to students and guardians that any abuse of ISS results in OSS.
2. Clearly communicate rules to students. Sprick's examples include these:
   - Stay quiet.
   - Stay seated.
   - Raise your hand quietly if you need to use the restroom. Restroom breaks can be taken only during times listed on the board.
   - If you are completing assignments, the supervisor can give you assistance two times each hour.
3. Decide who will supervise ISS. Train them and give them written guidelines to follow. Sprick's examples include the following:
   - Remain neutral.
   - Do not try to counsel the students.
   - Interact as little as possible with students.
   - Tell the student the rules when the student checks into ISS.
   - Ask for questions and assign a seat.
   - If the student talks or makes noise, the time owed in ISS starts over.
   - Contact administration if the student becomes violent or defies a direct instruction.
   - With more than one student, do not allow interactions. Place desks so that students cannot look at one another. Start the time over if students turn to one another or interact in any way.
4. Evaluate the effectiveness of the ISS program on the basis of repeated referrals.

Educators should note that the ISS program may be an inherently weak deterrent for some students who want to get out of class. ISS becomes a positive consequence for students who find classrooms aversive places. Alternative consequences (e.g., time owed, Saturday school) should be selected for these students.

Saturday School. Some schools dedicate Saturday mornings, rather than Monday through Friday, to ISS or time owed, for the following reasons. Some students do not find missing classes during the week to be enough of an abrasive event that they would change their behavior rather than serve an ISS. The purpose of negative consequences is to decrease the occurrence of inappropriate behaviors. Saturdays are considered precious time by most students, who might monitor their behaviors in school better if they knew adverse behavior would result in spending time at school on a Saturday. Additionally, schools may not have a room available for ISS during the school week.

Schools may pay teachers extra salary in order to have staff to cover Saturday school. Sometimes teachers take turns supervising Saturday school without extra pay rather than take their time to supervise students in or after school Monday through Friday.

Saturday school should not be considered an intervention that will dramatically change the behavior of most habitual offenders in ISS. It is simply one more option of natural, negative consequences that can be used to gain students' attention and communicate that their behaviors are not acceptable. To that end, the negative consequence of Saturday school should not be used for minor offenses (e.g., being tardy, not following instructions, talking out of turn in class). Educators should not make the mistake of following up a few detentions for the same minor offense with ISS or Saturday school. Teachers who are unable to find a successful intervention for repetitive, minor misbehaviors should seek assistance from colleagues, child or building assistance teams, or others who can brainstorm alternative interventions with them. Students should not be sent to the office for minor offenses, even if they are repeated offenses. Minor offenses should be managed in the classroom.

Some people may question why such a large portion of preplanning is devoted to managing a small minority of students whose inappropriate behaviors merit referral to the office. The answer is that school personnel who are prepared for management at every level of the system will be prepared to deal most effectively with various misbehaviors. Recall the case of Jerad at the opening of chapter 1. Effective management practices at the following levels could have prevented the melee and subsequent bad press in the local newspaper: letter home at the beginning of the year, guardian agreement with negative consequences, teacher's explicitly taught classroom rules and consequences, appropriate referrals to the office, and appropriate consequences at the office level.

Instructional Interventions

Batsche (1996) criticized school management for attempting to decrease negative behaviors without getting at the source of the misbehaviors. Often the source of negative behaviors is that students do not know how to display the positive behaviors that are required. He urged managers to overcome this critical flaw by teaching replacement behaviors. Sprick, Sprick, and Garrison (1993) developed a user-friendly set of materials for educators who have little or no background in teaching replacement behaviors. School counselors and school psychologists tend to have more extensive training in interventions for various behavioral problems and can assist building principals and teachers with the following: using structured reinforcement systems, increasing positive interactions, training students in self-control, teaching self-monitoring, teaching desired behaviors, assessing and teaching social skills, restructuring students' and educators' self-talk, and mentoring. These are described more fully in other chapters.

Students who have already been referred to the office or are at risk for office referrals need to receive instruction in prosocial behavior. School policies may address the need to provide instruction to such students versus merely meting out negative consequences.

Implementing Consequences for Office Referrals

It is of paramount importance that personnel immediately process behavioral referrals and consistently implement consequences. Educators must be creative with resources in order to accomplish this. Schools get ineffective results from office referrals when students wait in the office because their misbehavior is reinforced: They get to spend time out of class, interact with people passing through the office, and enjoy being on display as troublemakers.

Record-Keeping Procedures

The Family Educational Rights and Privacy Act (1974), also referred to as the *Buckley Amendment,* addresses who may access students' school records and how to protect student and family privacy. Only the school personnel who have a *need to know* may access student records. "Need to know" is present if the person accessing the records uses the information to facilitate positive student outcomes (e.g., socially, academically).

Batsche (1996) reported building plans in which school psychologists were responsible for entering data from office referral records and graphing results. Graphs helped the staff determine whether current policies were working for individual students and teachers. For example, with graphs, personnel could determine answers to the following eight questions:

1. How many referrals were made by an individual teacher?
2. What grade level had the most referrals?
3. What period of the day had the most referrals?
4. What time period of the year had the most referrals?
5. What percentage of referrals was for problems outside the classroom?
6. What category of misbehavior led to the most referrals?
7. How many students had more than five referrals? Two referrals?
8. Given an individual student who had several referrals:
   a. Who referred the student?
   b. What consequences were implemented?
   c. What procedures were implemented to get the student more motivated or to teach the student prosocial behaviors?
   d. What was done to get parents involved?

Analyzing these kinds of data can lead to more effective systems-level interventions. For example, if the month of October yielded the most office referrals for 2 or more years, school personnel might want to emphasize citizenship during the month of October. They may wish to focus on teaching school rules and how to follow them, recognize student attempts to follow the rules, or participate in developing school spirit through a variety of activities.

If a Student Breaks a Law

The portion of the schoolwide policy regarding student lawbreakers should be completed in conjunction with local officials. Police, juvenile authorities, and a judge can give recommendations on when to involve authorities in offenses of vandalism, use of alcohol or other controlled substances, truancy, possession of weapons, and physical violence. Police can state at what point behaviors in school should be turned over to civil authorities.

Repeated Referrals

Record keeping assists administrators in identifying students who need an additional support system. Four or more office referrals indicate obvious trouble adjusting to the school rules and expectations. Students who are repeatedly referred require the ongoing intervention support of various professionals (e.g., school guidance counselors, school psychologists, adult mentors). As mentioned earlier, intervention support could take the following forms: using structured reinforcement systems, increasing positive interactions, training students in self-control, teaching self-monitoring, teaching desired behaviors, assessing and teaching social skills, restructuring students' and educators' self-talk, and mentoring. These interventions are described in other chapters.

Teachers who refer large numbers of students from their classrooms may need help with classroom management. If many office referrals come from a particular place such as the cafeteria, staff can design procedures to decrease misbehaviors for that area.

CRISIS MANAGEMENT PLANNING

In addition to a schoolwide discipline plan, schools need an explicit and comprehensive crisis management plan. Comprehensive crisis management plans include policies and procedures for managing (a) natural disasters (e.g., floods, hurricanes, earthquakes, fires); (b) deaths of students or school personnel, including suicide and suicide attempts

Teachers and principals on this school's problem-solving team collaboratively write the building's crisis management plan.

of students or school personnel; and (c) aggressive behaviors in the classroom and on school property (e.g., physical fights or threats with weapons by students, school personnel, or outsiders entering the building).

Policy and procedural planning for crisis management at the building level is not presented in this text. However, in the section on conduct management in chapter 2, teachers learn to manage aggressive behaviors in their classrooms. Each classroom teacher needs to develop a crisis management plan for aggression that matches the building crisis management plan, obtain the principal's approval for the crisis management plan, and file it in the principal's office.

COMPETENCIES IN LEGAL ASPECTS OF SCHOOLWIDE DISCIPLINE

The control that school authorities may exercise over the activities of students is circumscribed by the nature of the relationship between public schools and students. This relationship has been defined by common law according to the concept of *in loco parentis* (Reutter, 1975):

> This doctrine holds that school authorities stand in the place of the parent while the child is at school. As applied to discipline the inference is that school personnel may establish rules for the educational welfare of the child and the operation of the school and may use punishments for not following the rules. Obviously, however, a school employee legally cannot go as far as a parent can in enforcement of matters of taste, extent of punishment, or disregard of procedural due process. School rules that are contrary to expressed wishes of a parent generally will be subject to more careful judicial scrutiny than other rules. (p. 3)

The doctrine, as originally conceived, was intended to give teachers considerable discretion in disciplinary matters. It was presumed that teachers having this authority would act reasonably and with due regard to children's interests. The concept has undergone considerable change as a result of differences among adults about what constitutes appropriate discipline and also as a result of increased parental challenges to the reasonableness of disciplinary actions taken by school officials (Rossow & Hininger, 1991; Zirkel & Reichner, 1987).

The legal derivation of student rights has focused the court's attention on the First and Fourteenth Amendments of the U.S. Constitution. The First Amendment reads as follows:

> Congress shall make no law respecting an establishment of religion, or prohibiting the free exercise thereof; or abridging the freedom of speech, or of the press; or the right of the people peaceably to assemble and to petition the Government for a redress of grievances.

The Fourteenth Amendment (1868) states in part,

> No State shall make or enforce any law which shall abridge the privileges or immunities of citizens of the United States; nor shall any State deprive any person of life, liberty, or property, without due process of law; nor deny to any person within its jurisdiction the equal protection of the laws.

Because teachers are agents of the state, their actions are subject to constitutional scrutiny as provided by the Fourteenth Amendment. Thus, the freedoms granted in the First Amendment are made applicable to students through the Fourteenth Amendment.

The matter of due process, substantive and procedural, has been the basis for most litigation initiated by students and their parents. Thus, the remainder of this chapter is devoted to a discussion of due process and other school-related legal issues and the ramifications of court decisions for classroom teachers. Because the discussion focuses on the disciplinary situations and techniques typically associated with the instructional duties of teachers, the issues of freedom of expression—that is, guarantees of speech, symbolic expression, press, assembly, association, and matters of conscience—are not addressed.

Rules of Conduct and Due Process Considerations

Arguments about student rights generally occur on two levels: substantive and procedural. *Substantive due process* issues deal with whether an individual student's constitutional rights have been judiciously considered in the creation of regulations to manage and protect the school system and to protect the rights of other students to secure an education. The emphasis is on the fairness of the policy or the rule itself.

In determining the substantive rights of students, a person should ask,
1. Will the actions of the student cause substantial disruption to the educational process and/or the normal operation of the school?
2. Will the actions of the student be an invasion of the rights of others? (Furtwengler & Konnert, 1982, p. 201)

School officials who answer in the affirmative to either of these questions must still be prepared to defend the policy and their actions. The courts have taken a dim view of actions to circumvent student misconduct based on supposition and speculation.

Procedural due process provides students accused of misconduct or slated for punishment an opportunity to defend themselves. The students' rights are secured when they know what they are accused of doing, know the basis for the accusation, and are given an opportunity to present their side of the story. Thus, officials must proceed to take actions in a defensible and reasonable way, which ensures proper form and fairness for the accused.

Student claims for due process rights have been used to test the traditional management practices of U.S. school systems and to question the legal authority of school teachers and administrators. Many of these claims begin when students question the rules themselves and the reasons given for a denial of freedoms covered by the rules. A set of well-formulated, explicitly stated rules is the first step toward reducing disputes and reconciling conflicts without legal action. After having analyzed hundreds of cases decided in federal and appellate state courts, Reutter (1975) offered the following essentials for an enforceable rule:

1. The rule must be publicized to students. Whether it is issued orally or in writing, school authorities must take reasonable steps to bring the rule to the attention of

students. A major exception is where the act for which a student is to be disciplined is obviously destructive of school property or disruptive of school operation.

2. The rule must have a legitimate educational purpose. The rule may affect an individual student's learning situation or the rights of other students in the education setting.

3. The rule must have a rational relationship to the achievement of the stated educational purpose.

4. The meaning of the rule must be reasonably clear. Although a rule of student conduct need not meet the strict requirements of a criminal statute, it must not be so vague as to be almost completely subject to the interpretation of the school authority invoking it.

5. The rule must be sufficiently narrow in scope so as not to encompass constitutionally protected activities along with those which constitutionally may be proscribed in the school setting.

6. If the rule infringes a fundamental constitutional right of students, a compelling interest of the school (state) in the enforcement of the rule must be shown. (p. 6)

In view of the aforementioned redefinition and enlargement of student civil liberties, prudence suggests student involvement in the formulation of the rules, periodic review of the rules with student input, and the designation of responsible authorities for the implementation of the rules.*

Suspension

Although teachers have a legal right to suspend a student, pending board action, most teachers are reluctant to use suspension to secure compliance with classroom rules or to preserve the rights of other class members. Teachers do not like to deny students access to the educational benefits of schooling, nor do they want to deprive them of the social interaction that is such an integral part of classroom living. Yet despite a concerted effort to secure students' cooperation, some students do not obey the rules. Suspension is an effort to convey the serious nature of their actions and to muster a greater resolve on the part of all parties to the dispute.

Educators who propose to include suspension in their schoolwide management plan should understand the distinctions between short- and long-term suspensions. The opinion issued by the U.S. Supreme Court in *Goss v. Lopez* (1975) established distinctions between these two types of suspensions and set guidelines for their proper administration.

Short-Term Suspension

A *short-term suspension* is an involuntary absence on the part of the student from school for a period of 10 days or less. Prior to *Goss v. Lopez,* there was considerable uncertainty

*I wish to express my appreciation to Dr. E. Edmund Reutter for granting permission to reprint in this chapter large narrative sections of his publication *The Courts and Student Conduct* (1975), which was commissioned by ERIC Clearinghouse on Educational Management and published by the National Organization on Legal Problems of Education.

about the length of time a student could be suspended without a hearing. Lopez brought the issue to a head by claiming that he was an innocent bystander in a school lunchroom disturbance, that he was never told what he was accused of doing, and that no evidence was presented against him. Thus, he was suspended without ever having a chance to tell his side of the story. Similar allegations were made by other students who were also suspended for up to 10 days for allegedly disruptive or disobedient conduct.

The Supreme Court examined the complaint as a procedural due process issue; that is, the Court viewed the educational process as a property right and a right not to be taken lightly. Thus, the due process provisions of the Fourteenth Amendment were applicable. The Court ruled in a 5-to-4 decision that at the very minimum, therefore, students facing suspension and the consequent interference with a protected property interest must be given *some* kind of notice and afforded *some* kind of hearing [Court's italics] (Connors, 1979, p. 15).

The Court proceeded to describe the type of minimal due process hearing procedure that should be followed, even when a suspension is for a single day:

> Students facing temporary suspension have interest qualifying for protection of the due process clause, and due process requires, in connection with a suspension of 10 days or less, that the student be given oral or written notice of the charges against him [or her] and, if he [or she] denies them, an explanation of the evidence the authorities have and an opportunity to present his [or her] side of the story. The clause requires at least these rudimentary precautions against unfair or mistaken findings of misconduct and arbitrary exclusion from school. (Connors, 1979, pp. 15–16)

These procedures were viewed by the Court as "rudimentary precautions against unfair or mistaken findings of misconduct and arbitrary expulsion from school" (*Goss v. Lopez,* 1975). The justices saw no need for a delay between the time that notice is given and the time of the hearing. In emergencies, when lives and property are endangered, prior notice and a hearing can occur "as soon as practicable." Thus, the hearing may be informal and conducted with dispatch. The fulfillment of due process standards was not intended to jeopardize the school's disciplinary authority.

Schools can adhere to the spirit and the substance of this ruling by following simple guidelines. Rules governing the hearings should be formulated by the faculty and student government representatives and should be published. The procedures should adhere to the following due process considerations (Connors, 1979):

1. The disciplinarian should inform the student as to what rule he or she broke.
2. The disciplinarian should tell the student how he or she became aware of the fact that the student broke the rule.
3. The disciplinarian should give the student an opportunity to tell his or her side of the story.
4. If there are contradicting facts, the disciplinarian should at least make a rudimentary check on the facts before imposing a suspension.
5. A student should not be suspended for more than 10 days. (p. 16)

These procedures are so simple and require so little time that they should not deter a teacher or an administrator from using short-term suspension as a disciplinary measure. Educators should know that this is a lawfully constituted method.

Suspension of Students with Disabilities

The Individuals With Disabilities Education Act (IDEA) does not specifically address the suspension or expulsion of students with disabilities (Maloney, 1994b). In matters of school discipline, these students were initially treated no differently than students without disabilities. However, the late 1970 and early 1980 federal court decisions in cases involving students with disabilities shaped new directions for school discipline policies.

In addition to *Goss v. Lopez* (1975), described earlier, a second landmark Supreme Court case had significant effects on current discipline procedures and practices for students with disabilities. In *Honig v. Doe* (1988), school officials were prevented from unilaterally removing students with disabilities from classrooms when their dangerous behavior was related to their disability. The district court ruled that indefinite suspensions deprived students of their right to a free and appropriate public education under the then Education of the Handicapped Act. The court ruled that (a) the school district may use only 2- and 5-day suspensions against any student whose behavior arises from his or her disability, (b) the district may not make any change in educational placement without parental consent during due process proceedings, (c) the state may not authorize districts to make unilateral placement changes, (d) the state must develop a compliance-monitoring system for districts, and (e) the state must provide educational services directly to students when a school district does not.

It now appears clear that a 10-day rule exists under IDEA; it is less clear under Section 504 of the Americans With Disabilities Act. Recent Office of Civil Rights (OCR) rulings on cumulative suspensions in excess of 10 days have found those suspensions to illegally constitute a significant change in placement (Bay County, FL, School District, 1993; Cobb County, GA, School District, 1993; San Juan, CA, School District, 1993) and have ordered schools to cease such suspensions (Ponca City, OK, School District, 1993). Other recent cases of suspension beyond 10 days have been faulted for not invoking a reevaluation of the student (Montebello, CA, Unified School District, 1993; San Juan, CA, School District, 1993). When counting suspension days, districts should not forget to count ISSs or extended time-outs. ISSs can deprive a student of a free and appropriate education as much as an OSS can (Lincoln, 1994). When students have been denied a free and appropriate education, courts have awarded compensatory education and reasonable attorneys' fees to parents. An exception to a prohibition on a school district's unilateral removal of a student with a disability from its official program occurs when that student brings a gun or a bomb to school. This is described later in the section on expulsion.

Long-Term Suspension

A *long-term suspension* is an involuntary absence from school for a specified period of time, generally for periods in excess of 10 days. Drury and Ray (1967) wrote this:

> It has been judicially held that a child may be suspended or expelled for disrespect toward school authorities; for immorality; for drinking; for smoking; the use of

cosmetics contrary to school regulations; irregular or tardy attendance at school; refusal to write a composition; refusal to follow proper orders; refusal to obey when told to read from a school-book; refusal to submit to the examination of the school physician on the grounds of conscientious objections; refusal to give the name of a pupil who has been guilty of a breach of rules when he [or she] knows the name of the pupil; making a speech in a school meeting criticizing the board of education; being drunk on Christmas Day; publishing in a newspaper a satirical poem reflecting on school policy; failure to maintain a required scholastic standing, although there is substantial authority to the contrary; failure to pay for school property willfully or maliciously destroyed; and for general failure to obey the school rules or orders reasonably issued by any teacher or administrator. (p. 46)

The authors later pointed this out:

It has been held that a child cannot be suspended or expelled merely because of marriage, unless the married person's conduct is detrimental to the good order and discipline of the school; or the pupil is difficult to teach; or he [or she] refuses by direction of his [or her] parents to follow a particular branch of study; or he [or she] is involved in the loss of school property because of mere negligence. (p. 47)

The courts are less clear about the appropriate length and administration of long-term suspensions. However, because the student is deprived of a property interest for an extended period, the courts have generally enforced more stringent hearing requirements.

Some civil liberty lawyers contend that suspensions that last longer than a few days should be treated as disciplinary reprisals by school authorities and preceded by notice and hearings. Thus, serious breaches of discipline or an accumulation of minor offenses must be handled with due process to ensure that charges are true and actions appropriate.

When the school disciplinarian deems a long-term suspension to be an appropriate remedy for a problem, the following procedure should be followed (Connors, 1979):

1. The student and parents should be given written notice of the charges against him [or her].
2. A hearing date should be scheduled giving the student enough time to prepare a defense—but not too far in advance to damage his [or her] property interest.
   It is suggested that this hearing be scheduled within 2 weeks of the date of the infraction (unless the student requests otherwise).
3. At the hearing, the student has the right to be represented by legal counsel.
4. At the hearing, the student has the right to face his [or her] accusers.
5. At the hearing, the student has the right to cross-examine witnesses.
6. At the hearing, the student has the right to present a defense. This includes calling witnesses and presenting evidence.
7. The student has the right to an impartial tribunal at the hearing. This requirement has been the subject of much litigation in the last 10 years. While some courts hold that the school principal is an "impartial" judge, it is recommended that some adult(s) totally unfamiliar with the incident be used for the tribunal. Citizen advisory groups are especially valuable for this purpose.

8. The decision of the tribunal must be based solely on the facts presented at the hearing. A student cannot be suspended for something that is unrelated to the infraction that instigated the hearing. (pp. 17–18)

School personnel are well advised to be represented by legal counsel if the student is so represented. Attorneys should review both procedural and substantive issues before the hearing. The courts do not look on school personnel kindly if due process rights have been violated or if the actions appear to be predicated on malice or to serve as a defense for earlier unreasonable actions.

Extracurricular Activity Suspensions

Depriving students of extracurricular activities has become a popular disciplinary measure. In the past, this practice was only infrequently challenged because such participation was regarded as a privilege. However, recent court decisions have upheld participation in extracurricular activities as a property right and have applied suspension standards to these activities.

> A student may not be prohibited from participation because of his [or her] dress or appearance unless it impairs his [or her] ability to perform or constitutes a danger to his [or her] health or safety or that of others. Marriage, pregnancy, or parenthood may not be used (in and of themselves) as a reason for exclusion from extracurricular activities or from regular classroom activities. (Furtwengler & Konnert, 1982, p. 203)

These provisions in law are consistent with educator claims that such activities are actually cocurricular and an integral part of the educational program. Thus, to suspend a student from such activity requires the same procedural due process rights. The informal and formal hearing procedures prescribed for short- and long-term suspensions should be applied to corresponding periods of involuntary absence from an extracurricular activity. Teachers who want to enforce a conduct rule or an academic requirement by suspending a student from an extracurricular activity need not fear legal reprisal if they follow the aforementioned suspension procedures.

Expulsion

Two federal court decisions, *Doe v. Koger* (1979) and *Stuart v. Nappi* (1985), held that students with disabilities could not be expelled for reasons that were related to their disabilities. Two other decisions prohibited schools from discontinuing educational services to students with disabilities when they were expelled for reasons not related to their disability (*Kaeline v. Grubbs*, 1982; *S-1 v. Turlington*, 1981).

A significant change took place in 1994 when the Elementary and Secondary Education Act of 1965 (ESEA) was amended to include the Gun-Free Schools Act. The act states that in order to continue to receive federal funds under ESEA, a school district must have a policy in effect that requires the expulsion from school for a period of not less than 1 year any student who brings a weapon to school. *Weapons* has been carefully defined as the instruments described in Section 921 of Title 18 in the U.S. Code. They can basically be any firearm that can expel a projectile by the action of an explosive or any other destructive device (e.g., bombs, grenades, rockets, missiles, mines, or any similar device). Even after the Gun-Free Schools Act was enacted, students in special education were required, in most circumstances, to be returned to their original placement (e.g., "stay put") after 10 days of suspension.

Under the 1994 Jeffords Amendment to the IDEA, students with disabilities who bring weapons to school may be placed in an "interim alternative educational setting" for not more than 45 days. After 45 days or less, the multidisciplinary team must have a more permanent educational placement determined for the student. If a qualified multidisciplinary team determines that the incident was unrelated to the student's disability, the student may be expelled to an alternative educational placement (Maloney, 1994a). Conversely, if the incident was related to the student's disability, the student may not be expelled from school for bringing the weapon.

CONCLUSION

Understanding misbehavior as a symptom of the system suggests that schoolwide discipline practices are critical. In this chapter, the importance of preplanning schoolwide and classroom management from a systems-level perspective was discussed. The perspective is eclectic; it uses what works best in the ecological context. Educators must be completely familiar with the school building discipline plan and be able to implement it with integrity. Teachers who are sensitive to the impact of the entire system on students will want to file their crisis management plan and tentative classroom management plan in the office after approval by the principal. Positive schoolwide management practices are foundational to effective classroom management, as presented in previous chapters.

SUPPLEMENTARY QUESTIONS

1. What questions about schoolwide discipline practices in a school district should a recent undergraduate ask when he or she is interviewing for a teaching position?

2. If you were employed as a teacher in a school district that had ineffective schoolwide discipline policies, what could you do to make improvements?

SUPPLEMENTARY PROJECTS

1. Obtain the written schoolwide discipline plan of a school, perhaps where you are completing a field experience, and critique it using Sprick's recommendations in this chapter.

2. Interview some middle school and high school students to find out what they know and their opinions about their school's discipline policies and practices.

REFERENCES

Barnhart, C. L., & Stein, J. (Eds.). (1962). *American college dictionary*. New York: Random House.

Batsche, G. M. (1996, October). *Implementing a comprehensive program for students with difficulties with anger control and aggression: Building on classroom strategies*. Paper presented at the Iowa Behavioral Initiative Conference, Des Moines.

Bay County, FL, School District, 20 IDELR 920 (1993).

Cobb County, GA, School District, 20 KDELR 1171 (1993).

Connors, E. T. (1979). *Student discipline and the law*. Bloomington, IN: Phi Delta Kappa Educational Foundation.

Doe v. Koger, 480 F. Supp. 225 (N.D. Ind. 1979).

Drury, R. L., & Ray, K. C. (1967). *Essentials in school law*. New York: Appleton-Century-Crofts.

Family Educational Rights and Privacy Act, 20 U.S.C. 1232g (1974).

Furtwengler, W. J., & Konnert, W. (1982). *Improving school discipline: An administrator's guide*. Boston: Allyn & Bacon.

Goss v. Lopez, 419 U.S. 565, 729 (1975).

Honig v. Doe, 108 S. Ct. 592 (1988).

Hyman, I. A. (1997). *School discipline and school violence: The teacher variance approach*. Boston: Allyn & Bacon.

Kaeline v. Grubbs, 682 F.2d 595 (6th Cir. 1982).

Lincoln, E. A. (1994, May). *In-school suspension: Is the child deprived of FAPE?* Seminar presented at the 15th National Institute on Legal Issues of Educating Individuals With Disabilities, San Francisco, CA.

Maloney, M. (1994a). A flowchart for disciplining gun-toting students with disabilities. *Individuals With Disabilities Education Law Report, 21,* 75–76.

Maloney, M. (1994b). Introduction. In *Disciplining violent or disruptive students with disabilities*. Danvers, MA: LRP Publications.

Montebello, CA, Unified School District, 20 IDELR 388 (1994).

Ponca City, OK, School District, 20 IDELR 549 (1993).

Reutter, E. E. (1975). *The courts and student conduct*. Topeka, KS: National Organization on Legal Problems of Education.

Rosell, J. (1986). *An analysis of school district policies for disciplinary action with handicapped students*. Unpublished manuscript.

Rossow, L. F., & Hininger, J. A. (1991). *Students and the law*. Bloomington, IN: Phi Delta Kappa Educational Foundation.

S-1 v. Turlington, 635 F.2d 342 (5th Cir. 1981).

San Juan, CA, School District, 20 IDELR 549 (1993).

Sprick, R. S. (1985). *Discipline in the secondary classroom: A problem-by-problem survival guide*. West Nyack, NY: Center for Applied Research in Education.

Sprick, R., Sprick, M., & Garrison, M. (1993). *Interventions: Collaborative planning for students at risk*. Longmont, CO: Sopris West.

Stuart v. Nappi, EHLR 557:101 (D. Conn. 1985).

Zirkel, P. A., & Reichner, H. F. (1987). Is *in loco parentis* dead? *Phi Delta Kappan, 68*(6), 466–469.

CHAPTER 8

Competencies in Communication

DEFINITION OF TERMS
COMMUNICATION

Communication
Competencies

COMPETENCIES
POSITIVE SELF-TALK
    Attribution Retraining
BODY LANGUAGE
LISTENING
SENDING VERBAL MESSAGES
PROBLEM-CENTERED
    DISCUSSIONS
DIRECT CONFRONTATION
ANGER MANAGEMENT

**ETHICAL AND LEGAL
COMPETENCIES**
CODE OF ETHICS
DEFAMATION AND RIGHTS
    TO PRIVACY

An understanding of the material in this chapter will help you do the following:

❑ Recognize the strengths and weaknesses in your own communication skills.
❑ Develop body language, listening, and message-sending skills of communication.
❑ Implement restructuring self-talk in positive ways.
❑ Adhere to ethical and legal guidelines for communication.
❑ De-escalate conflict by using communication skills.

> A word aptly spoken is like apples of gold in settings of silver.
>
> —*Proverbs 25:11 (Barker, 1985, p. 1248)*

What people say and how they say it powerfully affects themselves and those to whom they speak. The old adage "Sticks and stones may break my bones but words will never hurt me" is true only if the hearer has learned to ignore hurtful words. Most young people typically have not learned how to cope effectively with the hurtful words that are heard in school buildings. When adult messages to students have been hurtful for years, by middle school or junior high age those same students will appear to no longer be listening. They are turned off and tuned out. Undoing the harm will take repeated, consistent, and persistent use of effective communication skills.

This chapter presents numerous communication skills that can be implemented by educators to help themselves and their students. The skills are not only helpful but also necessary at the prevention, intervention, and remediation levels. Although the nonverbal and verbal interventions described are necessary in all situations, they are not sufficient to resolve all problems. The skills introduced in a single chapter cannot satisfy all needs or fulfill all expectations. Educators should seek additional professional assistance for themselves or students when their communication behaviors significantly and chronically impede success.

OVERVIEW OF COMMUNICATION

Definition of Communication

Communication is defined as the transmission of information through listening and speaking. Communication has various forms: body language and spoken and written messages. In this chapter, skills in positive self-talk (e.g., positive attributions), listening, and talking to others through oral or written form are emphasized.

Effective communication in schools prevents problems from occurring. An example of communication at the *prevention* level is giving students school handbooks that contain the schoolwide discipline policies and procedures and teaching them periodically throughout the school year. This prepares students to meet expectations.

Intervention that requires communication skills might be the use of peer mediation programming. *Rehabilitation* efforts that rely on the foundation of communication skills include knowing how to use communication to de-escalate a crisis situation with an angry, acting-out adolescent and forge a partnership to learn new ways of managing anger.

Importance of Communication

Ginott was one of the first people to draw attention to the importance of educators' communication skills (Charles, 1996). In fact, Ginott (1971) wrote the following often-quoted words, which appear widely in teachers' portfolios and on bulletin boards, often without attribution to him:

> I am the decisive element in the classroom. It is my personal approach that creates the climate. It is my daily mood that makes the weather. As a teacher I possess tremendous power to make a child's life miserable or joyous. I can be a tool of torture or an instrument of inspiration. I can humiliate or humor, hurt or heal. In all situations it is my response that decides whether a crisis will be escalated or de-escalated, and a child humanized or dehumanized. (p. 13)

Ginott offered a model of communication with a simple underlying principle: When speaking to a student, an adult must always address the situation, not the student's character or personality. Ginott asserted that communication interventions had to be used repeatedly with time for their power to take effect. This is an important concept that bears repeating: Many individual communication efforts are necessary for a long period of time before a teacher may reap success, but it is worth it. Educators should not give up but instead keep rehearsing effective communication skills until they are finely honed.

In class discussions and role-plays of management scenarios, one of the problems that both undergraduate students and graduate students face is using effective communication skills. They have a tendency to display Ginott's communication no-no's, which drive wedges between speakers and listeners (Charles, 1996):

- ❏ Label students negatively (e.g., "Some students are being pretty lazy this morning." "Are you hard of hearing?").
- ❏ Ask students "why" questions (e.g., "Why did you trip her?" "Why is your assignment always late?").
- ❏ Lecture (e.g., "What's the problem back there? This is math class, not the bus ride to the game tonight. If you expect to play in the game, I would suggest that you do your own work and stop bothering others who are trying to learn something. I want quiet. If you have a question, ask me.").
- ❏ Make sarcastic remarks (e.g., "Good move, Juan." "Oh, so you remembered something for once.").
- ❏ Demand cooperation (e.g., "Class, this morning I will not put up with any nonsense. All eyes on the guest lecturer now.").

❏ Lose self-control (e.g., "I have had it with you! I have asked you repeatedly to get to work. Go to the office now!").
❏ Manipulate students with nonspecific praise (e.g., "You are super!").

Readers who have used any of these negative communication behaviors will find the skills in this chapter critical to master. Good communication skills are the foundation of effective management in schools. They are a necessary condition for successful management, but in themselves they are not entirely sufficient. Rather, educators who seek to improve their communication skills must also cultivate an overall attitude of respect for themselves and children and adolescents. Such educators must adhere to the following guidelines described by Grossman (1995) and Jones and Jones (1995):

❏ Educators must never prejudge or hold grudges, both of which color communication and cause it to sound negative. Respectful educators must hold positive attributions for students and believe that students want to be and are responsible most of the time.
❏ Educators at their best must communicate dignity. Educators at their worst belittle students.
❏ Educators must describe situations and what needs to be done instead of bossing. Educators must not perceive the goal of an adult–student confrontation to be "adult wins and student loses." Rather, they must allow students to share responsibility for resolving problems.
❏ In recognition of cultural differences, educators must adjust communication patterns to students' needs and clearly explain and teach the various communication skills that will be used in the classroom.

Novice educators often lack confidence and feel insecure and timid about communicating with students. Novices have special needs for praise and recognition. They are often preoccupied with themselves. "How am I doing? How am I being regarded?" dominates much of their thinking. Like everyone else, they want their own needs for recognition and approval met. Because of these needs at this particular time in their professional careers, novices find it more difficult than experts do to communicate successfully. Developing effective communication skills takes lots and lots of practice for most people but does wonders for building confidence. Paradoxically, when novices use communication skills that meet the needs of others, their own needs for self-validation are also better served.

After completing a communication skills unit during a classroom management course, preservice teachers wrote brief descriptions of their own communication profiles, including strengths and weaknesses (Iverson, 1996). Most of the preservice teachers in the sample demonstrated accurate awareness of their own communication strengths and weaknesses. They also selected appropriate strategies that could be used to improve their weaknesses. Most of these individuals indicated that, prior to the instructional unit on communication skills, they could not remember receiving

procedural training in how to communicate effectively during uncomfortable interpersonal situations in schools. Six examples are included next to demonstrate how
varied people's communication styles are. The examples also indicate that most educators have a need to equip themselves with new and better communication skills.

EXAMPLE 1

"I can talk to parents calmly. I talk a lot, but I will become passive if someone is
upset. I will be quiet and let the person be in total control. I will lose control of
the situation if someone is very irrational. I would like to improve professional
talk, such as saying 'yes' instead of 'yup.' I need to avoid arguments with
children and not say so much. I most need to work on principles to follow if
someone gets upset or irrational or argumentative."

EXAMPLE 2

"I become too empathetic or sympathetic and dwell on how horrible something is
for a parent or child. I need to engage in emotional separation and still be
pleasing and respectful. I most need to develop the skill of reframing."

EXAMPLE 3

"Trying to be calm and confident is difficult. I overcompensate by being authoritarian. However, being authoritarian is very uncomfortable for me. I need to
be better prepared for the different scenarios that could come up and to not
get defensive. I need to practice the skill of positive self-talk in order to
maintain objectivity versus subjectivity. I need to practice reinforcing what
others say versus getting defensive."

EXAMPLE 4

"I tend to be passive. It takes a while for me to determine an appropriate
response, be professional, and know where to go next in my response. I
think that there is probably a list of generic responses that can be adjusted
to fit about any situation."
"Knowing how to begin to respond seems very important; after that the
follow-through comes more naturally. I think I am good at telling things
straight but still padding it."
"I need to remember that it is okay to take my time to construct a response. I
could generate a list of generic responses and practice using them as ways
to begin responding."

EXAMPLE 5

"When others are belligerent, my natural reaction is to arch my back, and my
neck hair stands up. I should think ahead about how to handle difficult situations and the need to create a calm atmosphere for me and the other person."

"Role-playing and having steps written down would help. The more you practice, the more natural it will feel."

Example 6

"I sometimes have difficulty getting the right ideas across. I like to be blunt and shoot straight. Good communication processes are unnatural for me and don't sound real. I need to work on listening to the other person and practice skills of clarifying and summarizing. They need the most work."

Rogerian theory, with roots in humanism, has shaped some of the basic communication skills presented in this chapter. Rogerian theory is based on assumptions that people are able to solve their own problems by talking about them with an accepting, supportive, and nondirective other. According to the theory, nondirective listeners exhibit unconditional positive regard and reflect the speaker's thoughts back. This process assists the speaker in reaching his or her own problem resolution. Communication skills from this theoretical position include body language basics and listening.

Behavioral theory has also yielded a number of communication skills. Recall that behavioral theory yields strategies that are environmentally based and directive. The listener directs the strategies and problem solving rather than allowing them to originate from the speaker. Ethical behavior demands that the speaker agree with the strategies and that they not be applied to the speaker without informed consent. These strategies include body language and verbal message–sending skills.

In addition to the skills already mentioned, cognitive-behaviorists would include the strategy of positive self-talk. The three skill areas of self-talk, body language, and listening receive a great deal of attention in this chapter. They are important categories of communication skills and are different from the category that we tend to think of first—sending verbal messages. Educators need to cultivate skills in all four areas to convey effective verbal messages.

COMPETENCIES IN COMMUNICATION

Positive Self-Talk

All of us use self-talk every day. Self-talk influences how we think and feel about ourselves, and it influences our behavior. Consider the following example. Several ninth-grade students are ignoring teacher directions and laughing and talking among themselves. The teacher may engage in positive or negative self-talk about the students' actions. The affective direction in which the teacher's self-talk takes him or her will affect his or her thoughts, feelings, and outward behavior. When the affective direction is positive, teachers' self-talk could take on many forms but might sound like this:

"They are sure enjoying themselves but I need to use a strategy to obtain everyone's attention. I will call on one of them (Berry) to repeat the directions for the class. Berry may not have heard me but it will gain everyone's attention. If she cannot repeat the directions, I will remain neutral and simply ask for a volunteer from the class to repeat them. That will probably be a successful strategy for now. If the same students continue to have the same kinds of behaviors in the future, I may need to try a different strategy."

It may seem a little ridiculous to take the time to go through that much self-talk. Some people may say that it makes no sense and is not practical for teachers who need to make split-second decisions to rehearse all of the preceding self-talk prior to halting the off-task behavior of talking and laughing. However, this is precisely the kind of talk that occurs following an incident or during the reflective times before and after school. Without self-talk, people tend to jump into solutions immediately, solutions that tend to be high control and punitive. Novices actually do need to take the time to run through that much self-talk. Experts in positive self-talk will actually say an abbreviated version that resembles the following: ". . . having fun . . . need attention . . . Berry repeat . . . volunteer . . . pattern, different strategy."

Contrast the preceding example with the following negative self-talk of a teacher:

"I know those kids are laughing and fooling around because they think that I am stupid and the assignment is stupid. I'll show them who's stupid. I'll call on each one of them by name and ask them to repeat the directions. The entire class will sit here until they can come up with them."

People process statements like these when engaging in negative self-talk. Take a moment and think about your own personal experiences and recall instances of negative self-talk. Did it ultimately affect your thoughts, feelings, and outward behavior? When self-talk is chronically negative, restructuring self-talk and attribution retraining may be effective strategies to try.

Restructuring Self-Talk

Changing the way people talk to themselves is helpful when they experience excessive self-criticism, negative attitudes about themselves, putting themselves down, and self-control problems. Negative self-talk is associated with feelings of frustration, powerlessness, and anger. When negative self-talk occurs across situations and time, it creates barriers to success.

Educators who recognize these behaviors in themselves or in students may want to use a restructuring self-talk strategy in order to resolve problems successfully. When an educator is implementing self-talk interventions with students, it is usually a good idea for him or her to seek assistance from school counselors and school psychologists. They will often take the lead in developing the intervention but, obviously, need the assistance of the teacher for prompting students and monitoring improvements in the regular classroom.

Support services staff can help teachers by conducting assessments to detect the patterns of students' faulty assumptions underlying negative self-statements. Nine types of cognitive errors or faulty assumptions that students make follow:

1. *Overgeneralizing:* "If I am not good at geometry, I am not a good student at all."
2. *Selective abstraction/self-criticism:* "I am a good student only if I don't make any mistakes."
3. *Excessive responsibility:* "I am responsible for all failure or bad things that occur."
4. *Assuming temporal causality:* "If I did it poorly in the past, I will always do it poorly."
5. *Self-references:* "I am the cause of all bad things that happen to me" or "Everybody should like me."
6. *Awfulizing:* "All bad things happen to me and nothing will ever change."
7. *Dichotomous thinking:* "Everything is perfect." The next day, "Everything is ruined."
8. *Demanding:* "People should always listen to me."
9. *Low frustration tolerance:* "Things should always come easily to me."

Restructuring self-talk may need to be paired with other interventions that address problems in a comprehensive manner. Support services staff can also assist with determining the nature of paired interventions.

Sprick, Sprick, and Garrison (1993) offered step-by-step procedures, scripts, and props for conducting self-talk interventions. Their intervention procedures typically follow the same three-step format. It is briefly summarized next to illustrate all aspects of the intervention: (1) preplanning so that educators can think more clearly about the problem before they discuss it with the student, (2) working with the student to define the problem and determine a plan, and (3) implementing the plan. An example follows of a teacher and a school psychologist's working together to develop a self-talk strategy or intervention for a student. Any educator who has the skills can carry out this intervention. It does not necessarily require a support person to conduct the three phases. Note the importance of the preplanning phase of the restructuring self-talk intervention.

Preplanning.   The teacher describes for the school psychologist all the conditions surrounding the problem.

The teacher lists typical negative statements. (Negative comments have an all-or-none quality and tend to make unrealistic demands. They have key words like *can't ever, should, always, never, nobody, everybody.*)

The teacher and the school psychologist collaboratively analyze the list of negative statements, identify the cognitive errors of the statements, and look for a trend or pattern. (See previous list of nine types of cognitive errors.)

The school psychologist and/or the teacher writes a positive statement to replace each negative. For example, the student says, "I'm never going to be good at math." A positive replacement statement could be "I might do better if I would ask questions when I don't understand."

The school psychologist and/or the teacher identifies prompts to signal the student when he or she is engaging in negative self-talk. Examples include teacher touching the student's desk, teacher touching the student's ear, and student carrying a stop sign as a physical reminder.

The school psychologist and the teacher collaboratively develop a self-monitoring procedure. They identify who will be the adult case manager and develop procedures to monitor the student's improvement in replacing negative self-talk with positive self-talk.

Collaborating with the Student.   The student should collaborate on the final plan. Either the school psychologist or the teacher should introduce the tentative plan. The educator's script follows:

> "We are meeting today because I am concerned that sometimes you say things to yourself that affect how well you do on an assignment. For example, I think you tell yourself that you are never going to be good at math. Can you think of some other things that you say to yourself that are put-downs? (Pause.) These thoughts fill up your brain with yuk. That makes it hard for you to do well. How do you think I would feel and act if I told myself that I have to get everything right all of the time?"

After a brief discussion, the student has the opportunity to write positive self-talk alternatives independently or collaboratively with the teacher. The teacher and the student role-play the self-talk alternatives. Together they select a signal and role-play sending the signal. The student learns how to use the self-monitoring procedure and sets a consistent schedule for practicing positive self-talk.

Implementing the Plan.   The student begins using the plan immediately. It is not necessary to wait to start on a Monday. The adults should evaluate progress at the end of 5 to 10 school days and revise the plan if there are any glitches. The plan needs to be faded gradually after the student demonstrates consistent success with time. Most school counselors and school psychologists know how to fade plans, and other educators can ask them for assistance with this. The student's continued success should be followed up intermittently.

Attribution Retraining.   Attribution retraining is a special subtype of restructuring self-talk. Attribution retraining focuses on changing how students talk to themselves about the causes of academic success and failure. A typical goal of attribution retraining is to encourage students to explain failure in terms of lack of effort rather than lack of ability. In real life, students who do not succeed at an academic task tend to have negative attributions. That is, they tend to explain their failure by stating that the task was

This teacher encourages students to try their best on a task and to say, "I did a good job because I used the right strategy."

too hard or that they were not smart enough. Both statements mean the same thing—that students believe they lack the ability.

Heider's (1958) naive psychology is recognized as the birthplace of attribution theory. His theory led to the development of strategies for attribution retraining. Heider stated that a person's behavior is meaningless until we attribute a cause to it. We are constantly trying to navigate the world by understanding cause-and-effect relationships. We like a world that is predictable; we can make better choices when the world is dependable.

Consider the following example of Mr. Wilson, a fictitious teacher. When Mr. Wilson wins the Teacher of the Year award, it is a relatively momentary event. What does it even mean to be Teacher of the Year? The award makes sense when it is referred (i.e., attributed) to a relatively permanent property such as his portfolio containing 20 years of evidence of excellent teaching. Most people then feel assured that such an award predicts a successful teaching career. Conversely, if Mr. Wilson's award is referred (i.e., attributed) to easy judges or easy criteria or no other applicants, most people would not feel assured that the award does indeed predict successful teaching.

The importance of this discussion is that people will behave differently toward the awardee on the basis of their understanding of the Teacher of the Year award. This in turn could influence Mr. Wilson's future teaching performance. In fact, the way Mr. Wilson himself understands his award could influence his future teaching performance.

Attributions can then be defined as a person's beliefs about why he or she or someone else succeeded or failed at a task. Attributions or beliefs can influence people's self-talk and resulting behaviors. Attribution concepts are introduced in this section to make educators not only aware of attributional influences on their own behavior and the behavior of students but also able to implement strategies to retrain attributions.

Students can attribute success on assignments either to ability, effort, knowledge, and other internal attributes or to luck, help from others, task difficulty, and other external attributes. Students with learned helplessness attribute failure to lack of ability. Ability is viewed as an internal, stable, and global cause. They are inclined to say to themselves, "I would have passed the test if I were smart" or "I'm just not smart enough to ever get this." Dweck (1975) showed that when students who generally attribute failure to a lack of ability were instructed instead to attribute failure to a lack of effort, they showed more resilience to academic setbacks and disappointments. Multon, Brown, and Lent (1991) reviewed 39 studies of the relationship between students' beliefs in their ability to be successful and their academic outcomes. These researchers concluded that the relationship was positive and causal. In other words, as students' beliefs in their ability to be successful increased, their academic success also increased. This meta-analytic investigation provided compelling support for the potential value of intervening in low-achieving students' attributions. Restructuring self-talk, what a person says about success or a lack of it, has a profound influence on future performance.

Attribution theories have been reformulated since the mid-1940s, and research has supported the use of attribution-retraining strategies. In spite of attribution theory's lengthy history, Reeder (1996) found that educators had little knowledge of and experience in understanding the importance of people's attributions and how to conduct attribution retraining. When presented with the procedures for attribution retraining, regular educators, special educators, and school psychologists expressed a high degree of interest in learning how to implement them.

Educators who teach and encourage effort attributions must be sure that targeted students have *not* been making the necessary efforts. Attribution retraining should be coupled with learning-strategy instruction when students lack learning strategies necessary for them to be successful on a task. In other words, simply teaching students to tell themselves "I tried hard and that's why I succeeded" will not make them more successful academically. They must also use the learning strategies that lead to successful task completion.

Long-term benefits are more likely when teachers incorporate attribution retraining into everyday instructional repertoires. Some teaching procedures follow for paired learning-strategy instruction and attribution retraining. The procedures can be used with a large or small group of students or with an individual student.

Step 1:   Model the use of the learning strategy to students (e.g., developing a story web prior to completing the language arts assignment of writing a creative story).

Step 2:   Model correct and incorrect examples of learning-strategy use by working through actual examples. Teach learning-strategy use until students can execute the strategy.

Step 3:   Teach the use of positive attributions ("I finished the story because I used our study time to work really hard.")

Step 4:   Teach students to pair positive attribution statements with learning-strategy use (e.g., "I used my story web and I worked really hard. That really helped me a lot in successfully writing the story.").

Step 5:   Allow students to practice making a positive attribution statement after they successfully use a learning strategy, and give feedback.

Step 6:   On a daily basis, remind the students to continue monitoring their use of positive attributions paired with learning strategies (e.g., reinforce them for making appropriate attributions and challenge students when they offer explanations likely to induce helplessness).

Attribution retraining paired with learning-strategy instruction is a long-term intervention that will need to be implemented for at least several weeks, if not a year or longer. For the most effective implementation of these interventions, it is important to involve many people who have direct contact with the student (e.g., teacher, parent, principal, school counselor). This will expose the student to as much modeling and practice of the intervention as possible. The ultimate outcome is student attributions that emphasize effort rather than ability as the primary cause for success and achievement.

Influence of Race, Socioeconomic Status, and Gender on Teachers' Attributions.   Little research has been done on the effects of race, class, and gender on teachers' attributions for students. Some evidence shows that teachers hold Caucasian, middle-class children more responsible than minority students for academic outcomes. Teachers may also expect African American and lower-class Caucasian students to fail more than middle-class Caucasian students (Baron, Tom, & Cooper, 1985; Cooper, Baron, & Lowe, 1975; Wiley & Eskilson, 1978). Conversely, Asian Americans may benefit from beliefs held by teachers. Research shows that elementary teachers attributed the academic success of Caucasian, middle-class, and Asian students to internal factors and academic failure to external factors (Tom & Cooper, 1986). The same teachers did not hold the same attributions for lower-class Caucasian students. Compared with Caucasian students, Asian American students have also been rated as more academically competent (Wong, 1980), and their academic performance has been evaluated more favorably (Tom, Cooper, & McGraw, 1984).

No research evidence suggests that teachers attribute different causes to male and female students' academic behaviors (Heller & Parsons, 1981; Wiley & Eskilson, 1978). What is known is that teachers label some subjects as more gender appropriate for males than for females (e.g., math is gender appropriate for males and gender inappropriate for females) and vice versa (e.g., English is gender appropriate for females and gender inappropriate for males). Bernard (1979) found that teachers evaluated male students more highly in English than they did females when males performed well in the gender-inappropriate domain.

In summary, the importance of teachers' attributions is that teachers must put the emphasis on students' effort and acquired skills in explaining academic success. In turn, students will learn to attribute their failures to lack of effort or to needing assistance to acquire the necessary skills for the task.

Body Language

Body language is a visual form of communication and includes body posture, body tension, and facial expressions. When an educator leans forward with hands on hips and has a serious demeanor on his or her face, no spoken message is needed to communicate to most students that this person means business. That is the power of body language.

People use body language intentionally, but it can also be used unintentionally. For example, many people, without conscious, purposeful intent, cross their arms and move their body away from a speaker when the speaker's message is not accepted or the speaker is disliked, distrusted, or perceived in some other negative fashion. Speakers understand these body movements as negative messages (e.g., "She does not like me" or "She does not like what I am saying"). Educators need to become aware of their own body language and monitor its effects.

There are cultural differences in body language, or nonverbal communication. The differences, as described by Grossman (1995), are enumerated next as general guidelines, with specific examples included for each of the body language goals. Emotion, eye contact, and muscle tension are some of the body language variables to manage. Emotion is expressed differently across cultures. Some Asian Pacific people laugh or giggle when they are embarrassed. Some Hispanic Americans display more physical affection (e.g., touching, kissing, males hugging and patting each other on the back) than do some European Americans. Cultures vary in how they typically express anger and defiance: some African Americans roll their eyes, some Asian Pacific Americans force smiles, and some European Americans give silent stares. It is important to remember that these are general guidelines that apply on the average. They do not apply to every person in a specific cultural group.

Cultural backgrounds also influence how people show submission. Some African Americans and Asians avoid direct eye contact. Some Asians also nod their heads repeatedly and do not make critical comments. Cooperman (1975) suggested that some African American students may be more sensitive to nonverbal communications. Gay and Abrahams (1973) indicated that some African American children are taught to be suspicious of Caucasians. Some African American students may initially be suspicious of Caucasian teachers' positive behavior. This may lessen with time as positive behavior remains consistent.

Seven body language goals for educators are as follows:

1. Relax muscles and posture when sitting or standing (e.g., arms and hands held loosely at the sides, hands resting lightly over each other

in front of the body, standing erect without leaning forward or backward).

2. Relax facial muscles (e.g., relaxed versus clenched jaw muscles).
3. Make eye contact (e.g., focus on speaker's mouth rather than steady eye gaze). Some African American students may show respect by avoiding eye contact with those in authority (Gilliam & Van Den Berg, 1980). Some Hispanic Americans may be brought up to look away when they are being reprimanded (Grossman, 1995).
4. Stay outside another's personal space (e.g., when another individual is moving away, he or she may be indicating that his or her personal space has been invaded). Aiello and Jones (1971) reported that some African American students maintained less physical distance between themselves and others. Some Hispanic American and Latino students may also stand closer. Some Oriental students need more space than that required by some European Americans (Grossman, 1984).
5. Nod head and smile to communicate acceptance.
6. When shaking hands, use a firm grip, no matter how you are feeling.
7. Breathe at a moderate rate (i.e., slowly and deeply versus rapidly and shallowly).

There are enough cultural differences in the use of body language that educators need to observe, listen, and ask questions about the use of body language in their school culture and subcultures. Teachers should not take anything for granted or make sweeping generalizations about issues of body language.

Body language goals are more difficult to demonstrate when the social situation is uncomfortable, but these are the times when it is most important to use them. Uncomfortable social situations occur when there are angry, sad, embarrassed, and guilty feelings involved. For example, a father attends a school meeting to help develop a plan to improve the academic achievement of his 10th-grade son. The father and son, four teachers, the special services director, and the school psychologist are at the meeting. Early in the meeting, the father loudly declares to the science teacher that, if she knew how to teach, his son would not be skipping her class and shirking the assignments.

The science teacher can react in a number of ways. At one extreme, she could cross her arms tightly across her chest, lean forward, tighten her facial muscles and clench her jaw, and just as loudly say something such as "How would either of you know whether I can teach? Your son has rarely been in my class and you, sir, have never been in it." At the other extreme, she could shrink back and try to look small, look down at the floor with a red face, with quivering lip shed a tear or two, and mumble something incoherent or leave the room.

It is time to apply body language basics in the most professional manner. This teacher will be most successful if she practices all of the following five behaviors: (1) breathe slowly and deeply, (2) maintain a relaxed posture with arms resting at her sides or on the table, (3) sit in a relaxed but erect position and neither lean forward nor lean backward, (4) maintain relaxed facial muscles, and (5) establish eye contact with the father (depending on cultural norms). People who are orally attacked are often caught off guard. Unless they are highly skilled in effective communication, their quick responses are typically unproductive. Momentary silence is a good strategy, and other professionals around the table should all be comfortable with it. The teacher is now ready to respond in any number of acceptable ways that will promote problem solving and conflict resolution. For example, she could say, "I did not realize that my teaching style was Darrell's reason for not attending my class or completing assignments. When he was in class, he did the work, and the quality of his work indicated that he understood the lesson. If my class is the only one of your classes where you feel this way, Darrell, we should discuss this after the meeting is over or at another time. That way we won't take up everyone else's time. Let's talk further after the meeting."

With practice, educators can learn to use effective body language and effective communication (e.g., listening and speaking) skills. They will experience greater success in most, if not all, interpersonal interactions.

Signal Interference Cuing

Signal interference cuing is a form of body language used to assist students who seem to be unaware that they are engaging in inappropriate behavior. Often, the behaviors that students engage in, without being aware, appear disrespectful to adults. These behaviors include swearing, blurting out, complaining, being sarcastic, criticizing, bragging, being noncompliant, shouting out comments or rude remarks, being noisy, arguing, talking back, being rude, and having the "last word." The cuing intervention is also helpful with misdirected attention and lack of attention to task.

Signal interference cuing is used to help students become aware of and control their own impulsive, excessive, habitual, or off-task behavior. The strategy operates on the premise that students become aware of their behavior and learn self-management. Adults provide students with predetermined cues whenever they begin to exhibit behavior that has previously been identified as inappropriate. Cuing is especially effective with students who have the ability to behave appropriately but tend to act inappropriately without thinking first.

Simply teaching students to respond to a cue will be enough to change the inappropriate behavior for some students, but not all. Educators should remember that they can always seek a support person's help in implementing signal interference cuing (e.g., educational consultant, guidance counselor, school psychologist). Some reasons to seek help are for assistance in measuring the student's progress in improving behavior and implementing concurrent interventions.

Signal interference cuing should be viewed as a temporary measure until students can learn to monitor their own behavior. When students require intensive training to learn new behaviors, a teacher can couple signal interference cuing with interventions like teaching desired behaviors, restructuring self-talk, mentoring, using structured reinforcement systems, and increasing positive interactions (see chapter 4). Teachers can run one or two individual signal interference cuing plans at a time. More than that will probably be too demanding on a teacher's time.

Before implementing signal interference cuing, the teacher should complete a planned discussion with the student (see discussion later in this chapter). It is always important to contact students' parents to discuss problems and keep them informed of all aspects of their child's educational plan. Sprick et al. (1993) provided a set of detailed procedures for implementing signal interference cuing. Procedures follow Sprick et al.'s typical format of preplanning, final planning in collaboration with the student, and implementing the plan. The following steps indicate how to implement a detailed plan for using signal interference cuing with Rory, who has low rates of eye contact with the teacher and does not pay attention in class.

Rory's behaviors result in not following directions the first time given. The teacher checked Rory's health records and knows that there is not a hearing problem. The teacher also checked Rory's skill levels, and she thinks that her instruction matches what Rory is capable of doing. She hypothesizes that Rory's difficulties are chronic inattention or off-task behavior and that he is unaware of how his behavior is causing difficulties in following directions the first time given.

Preplanning

During the preplanning phase, the teacher first identifies when Rory is likely to have problems. It is determined that direction following decreases in the afternoon, no activity is any more likely to result in inattention, and being grouped with a best friend decreases attention and following directions.

Second, the teacher identifies possible signals that might be used to cue Rory to pay attention to directions the first time given. Following are some ideas for signals:

❏ Say the student's name quietly.
❏ Hold up a hand like a stop sign.
❏ Hold up a finger to the lips.
❏ Touch your earlobe.
❏ Give a quick oral cue such as "Think."
❏ Stand by the student's desk or touch the student's desk.

Third, Rory helps choose the cue. It needs to be oral and not visual because Rory does not look at the teacher very often. A visual cue can be used if Rory responds to cue cards placed on his desk. The teacher decides that when Rory responds to the signal and follows directions, she could give him a mark on a tally card that she carries with her. The marks could be graphed to provide feedback to Rory about his improvement. She knows that Rory may have some additional ideas of consequences when they meet together.

Fourth, the teacher tentatively decides on two ways to determine whether the intervention is helping Rory reach his goal of following directions the first time given. The teacher generates the following list of ideas for monitoring Rory's progress:

❏ Check with each person in the plan to get his or her impressions of whether the plan is helping.

❏ Use a student self-monitoring system.
❏ Use a tally of appropriate and inappropriate behavior kept by the teacher.
❏ Use an anecdotal log.
❏ Conduct periodic observations.
❏ Use a daily rating system.

Fifth, the teacher schedules quick debriefings with Rory's parents every 2 weeks and a quick check with Rory to discuss progress a few times each week. The teacher also determines who will meet with Rory to discuss and finalize the plan.

SCRIPT

"Rory, I am pleased to have you in class with me this year. One of the things I do for some students is periodically set up special goals to help them be successful. A special goal that I'd like to plan with you is learning to follow directions the first time given. When we follow directions the first time they are stated, we are more successful inside and outside of school. I have arranged to meet with you and your mom during math tomorrow. Another teacher will take the class. It's hard to find time to talk with students individually so this is a special opportunity. I'm pleased that we'll have a chance to work on this. Is this okay with you?

"We'll talk more tomorrow. In the meantime, do a little thinking about ways that you might follow directions the first time given. Tomorrow, we will figure out how we can all help you with that goal."

Collaborating With the Student and the Parent

The teacher meets with the student and the parent to collaboratively develop the plan. The teacher begins the meeting by sharing her view of Rory's strengths. Rory and his parent then have the opportunity to talk about Rory's strengths. The teacher next involves Rory in reviewing the problem and setting goals. She shares how she thinks Rory has responded to directions during the past few weeks and asks Rory to share his view. The parent is asked to comment on how Rory does at following directions.

SCRIPT

"Rory, I'd like to help you reach your goal of following directions the first time given. Here is one idea that has been very successful with other students. I'll give you a signal when you need to think about what you are doing. For example, if I see you looking away from me, I could say to you quietly 'Rory, look and listen' or 'Rory, first' or 'Think.' We can choose one of those or something else. When you hear me say the cue, you will know that you need to listen for directions and follow them the first time given."

(The teacher then helps the student select a signal to use and practice following the signal.)

After role-playing, the teacher describes what will happen when the student responds appropriately or fails to respond to the signal. Together they review everyone's roles and responsibilities. Finally, they set up regular meeting times to debrief. The teacher always concludes meetings with words of encouragement.

SCRIPT

"Rory, you learn very fast and I'm looking forward to working with you on this. It will be fun for you to see your own improvements."

Implementing the Plan

The key to implementing the plan is to get started. Once a plan is developed, the teacher should not put it off. She should watch for opportunities to reinforce Rory for responding to the signal and for not needing the signal.

SCRIPT

"Rory, there were several times today that I didn't provide you with the signal. On your own, you were very thoughtful about following directions. You have been respectful toward others and me. Everyone gets through the activity so much faster when I do not have to repeat the directions. I enjoy watching you make good choices."

The teacher continues to monitor progress and makes periodic revisions to the plan as necessary. When Rory shows consistency in following directions the first time given, the frequency of providing the signal can be decreased and finally stopped. The teacher continues to make sure that Rory consistently follows directions without a signal and provides continued support and encouragement.

COMPETENCIES IN ETHICAL AND LEGAL ASPECTS OF COMMUNICATION

Self-talk, body language, and signal interference cuing procedures have been presented. As skills in listening and sending verbal messages are discussed, it is important to enumerate ethical and legal considerations in communicating. Different professional bodies each have their own code of ethics. Administrators, guidance counselors, school psychologists, and teachers all have ethical codes. Many similarities are seen across professional groups. Teachers' ethical standards are presented next as an example.

Code of Ethics

The *Code of Ethics of the Education Profession,* adopted by the 1975 National Education Association (NEA) Committee on Professional Ethics, provides standards by which educators should monitor and judge their conduct. The first ethical principle focuses on commitment to the student. Three of the criteria under the first principle shed considerable light on the ethics of communication. Specifically, educators are to make reasonable efforts to protect students from conditions harmful to learning, not to intentionally expose students to embarrassment or disparagement, and not to disclose information about students obtained in the course of professional service without a compelling professional or legal purpose. For example, it is unethical for a teacher to take a red ink pen and mark a large *F* across the front page of a test. When a student in the class questions, "Why didn't you mark this one wrong? I had it wrong," it is unethical for the teacher to respond in front of the entire class, "You had so many wrong that I got tired of marking them."

It is unethical for educators to embarrass students by telling them that if they are going to act like first graders they can spend the day in first grade. It is also unethical for educators to talk about students' problems in the lounge, where few or none of the listeners has a compelling professional reason to be involved.

It is an ethical responsibility for educators to maintain the privacy and confidentiality of all information that students reveal about themselves, with two exceptions. First, students may give educators permission to share information. Second, the law requires that educators provide authorities with information when students reveal that they or someone else is in danger (e.g., suspected child abuse, suicidal or homicidal ideation).

The NEA's second ethical principle focuses on educators' commitment to the profession. This principle directs educators not to disclose information about colleagues without a compelling professional purpose and not to make false or malicious statements about colleagues. Not only are certain behaviors unethical, but they are also subject to legal sanction.

Defamation and Rights to Privacy

Defamation is a derogatory communication to a third person. Derogatory words and insults directed at an individual do not constitute defamation of character. Basically, defamation involves libel or slander. If the untrue statement is written, it is called *libel;* if spread by word of mouth, it is called *slander.* Legislation and recent shifts in the court's approach to defamation suits make teachers vulnerable to both types of suits.

Teachers can be sued for defamatory statements published in students' permanent records. A teacher can avoid culpability in this area by confining record entries to pertinent, factual, and objective observations and by excluding subjective observations and conclusions that may be difficult to prove. The truthfulness of the information should be unquestionable. Objective statements can easily be verified.

Teachers frequently express their discontent with misbehaving students, often mentioning the particularly disagreeable characteristics during informal conversations with colleagues. The conversations often conclude with both parties' feeling a little less favorably inclined toward the offensive students. The teachers' remarks could be construed as slanderous to the extent that they subject the student to the scorn and hatred or to the sorrow and pity of a third party.

At one time, a true statement was considered to be the ultimate and absolute defense against slander, regardless of how damaging the statement might be. However, court decisions indicate that if the intent of the statement is to cause harm, irrespective of the truth of the communication, an individual can be held accountable for defamation (Connors, 1981, p. 130). Teachers can be found guilty of slander if they knowingly spread gossip that harms a student's reputation. On the contrary, the courts have given teacher communications a conditionally privileged status if they are made as part of a disciplinary process or administrative responsibilities.

COMMUNICATION: LISTENING AND SPEAKING

Educators need listening and speaking skills for dealing with community members, parents, students, and fellow educators. Most people do not naturally develop effective communication skills but must prepare and rehearse how to listen and how to deliver messages across different situations. In fact, many people have developed some bad habits because they do not know about effective communication strategies. Educators are better managers when they are prepared to deliver difficult messages, to mediate and de-escalate misunderstandings of messages, and to know when to obtain the assistance of consultants with expertise in effective communication.

Listening Before Speaking

Students learn more and behave better when they like their teachers. More important, students like teachers who listen to them and communicate understanding (Anderson, Evertson, & Emmer, 1979; Kounin, 1970).

Listening is a critical communication skill. Many times conflicts or problems can be prevented or defused simply by using good listening skills. Although it is difficult for many readers to imagine that the use of simple listening skills can have a significant management impact, those who cultivate and use listening skills become believers.

Listening means hearing precisely and helping the speaker feel understood. Gordon (1974) refers to this kind of listening as *active listening.* Specific oral skills are used to help the speaker feel that he or she was understood: acknowledging, reflecting, paraphrasing, summarizing, and clarifying (Conoley & Conoley, 1992).

Grossman (1995) reported that some students from diverse ethnic backgrounds (i.e., Asian Pacific Americans, Hispanic Americans, Native Americans) may not be comfortable discussing their thoughts, feelings, and problems with their teachers. Educators need to use active listening skills but not force others to engage in the process. Wei (1980) found that some Vietnamese students may be shy and withdrawn around the openness of American teachers. Nguyen (1987) reported that some Cambodian, Laotian, and Vietnamese students may find teachers' direct ways to be rude, even attacking. Therefore, culturally sensitive use of the following listening skills is recommended.

Acknowledging

Acknowledging is a listening or communication skill that many people use every day. As a communication skill, acknowledging helps build initial relationships. When people make the following types of statements, they are using the skill of acknowledging: "yes," "really," "wow," "right," "good."

Acknowledging is used to (a) encourage others to speak and (b) communicate some awareness of the emotional content of the other person's message. The use of acknowledging statements is especially helpful with persons who are hesitant to talk. Educators may wish to use various acknowledging statements with persons who feel insecure about their ability to be successful in a given situation. Students experiencing learned helplessness and parents who speak infrequently are two examples. Acknowledging statements are good to use when it is important to let the speaker know he or she is heard, yet the listener needs to hear more before responding further. Acknowledging statements can serve to "buy" time.

Reflecting

Reflecting means repeating the words that someone spoke. A person's words may contain two types of message content: cognitive and affective. The listener can selectively reflect part of the message to underscore the importance of some information or to move the conversation in a particular direction (e.g., begin the process of analyzing the problem, direct the conversation toward the speaker's emotional responses to the situation). Teachers and administrators typically need to focus on the cognitive portion of the message. Guidance counselors, school psychologists, and school social workers are prepared by education and training to reflect both cognition and emotion, on the basis of what seems most appropriate at the time.

Later in the chapter, examples are provided of teachers' using reflection to communicate with students. The following illustration of reflection is used when a teacher is communicating with a parent. A parent says to a teacher, "I am really frustrated that Sally is not turning in her assignments. I have tried everything." The teacher as the listener has to decide whether to respond to the parent's cognition, or thinking (e.g., "I have tried everything to assist Sally in turning in her assignments") or the parent's affect, or emotion (e.g., "I am really frustrated that Sally is not turning in her assignments after all of my efforts").

1.   If the teacher reflects by stating "I hear you saying that you are really frustrated that Sally is not turning in her assignments," the focus is on the affective, or emotional, portion of the message. This reflection emphasizes the importance of the feeling of frustration and could lead potentially to two opposite emotional reactions: the parent's crying and feeling hopeless about solving the problem or becoming angry and punitive toward Sally. When this happens, it may reduce the ability of both parent and teacher to problem solve constructively.

2.   If the teacher reflects the following, he or she is focusing on the cognitive portion of the message with the intent of analyzing the problem. "Yes, you have tried many things to help Sally turn in her assignments during the past 2 weeks. Let's investigate whether there was anything that happened about 2 weeks ago that caused Sally to quit turning in assignments."

3.   The teacher could also focus on doing or intervening by reflecting the parent's cognitive message. "You tried a number of things to help Sally turn in her assignments. Let's talk about what both of us tried in chronological order and how each attempt worked."

Either Choice 2 or Choice 3 is probably a better choice for the teacher than Choice 1 is. The focus is on the cognitive message and leads to constructive problem solving. That is not to say that educators are to ignore emotionally distraught parents or students by reflecting exclusively cognitive messages. This would be inappropriate. The parent cannot problem solve without a calm atmosphere and that means emotions must be calm. Educators can reflect the speakers' emotions in the following ways: "I can see that this is upsetting to you" or "I know that things like this can be frustrating" or "It's okay to cry. Take your time." After reflection, the educator needs to be quiet and comfortable with silence. When parents or students cry or are struggling to control an emotion, educators can offer tissues and then wait patiently. The educator should not stare at the person but instead quietly look away or down or through materials. This gives the person time to regain his or her composure. The teacher can proceed when the parent either speaks or seems to be quieting. The teacher should not dwell on the parent's emotional reactions. A brief statement that first acknowledges feelings and then engages the parent in cognition and problem solving is recommended. For example, a teacher might say, "It can be discouraging to work so hard to help Sally with her homework, only to find out later that she is still failing her subjects. She is probably frustrated, too. Let's analyze what has worked the best for her. If we determine the areas in which she is the most successful, we can use the same strategies to help her in problem areas." By now, the person is ready to proceed with the purpose of the meeting.

Ethical codes require that the proceedings of such a meeting be kept confidential. In other words, it is not okay for the teacher to report in the faculty lounge the next day that Sally's mom cried during the parent–teacher conference.

Paraphrasing

A third skill that communicates listening is *paraphrasing*. Paraphrasing is more complex than reflective listening, is used to cue the speaker to slight variations in his or her message, is offered tentatively, and may be used to indirectly challenge but without disagreeing. It involves substituting synonyms that heighten or reduce the power of what is said or slightly change the meaning or make no change. This listening skill resembles therapeutic techniques of counselors and psychologists and is not recommended for use by the untrained. It is explained in this section to help build awareness of how various listening techniques impact the direction of interpersonal communication.

An example of paraphrasing follows. Many teachers bypass this kind of listening and request special assistance from support personnel who are trained in advanced listening techniques. For this example, a school guidance counselor is talking to Sally's parent about incomplete assignments.

> *Parent:* I have tried and tried to help Sally get her assignments done, in her book bag, and back to school to turn in. I remind her every morning as she leaves the house to turn them in to you. She just does not pay attention to what I say.
> *Counselor:* You seem to be angry with Sally because you think she is not paying attention to you.

Parent: I'm not angry with her. I don't get angry with my children. That's not my job. My job is to help them and my help isn't working.

Counselor: I may have misunderstood. I know some behaviors do make me angry when I've tried to correct them. I find that my anger is a good barometer of how frustrating a situation is for me.

Parent: Well, that's certainly true. I've been frustrated with Sally.

Counselor: And I find that the more angry I become, the less creative I am at finding solutions. That's when it's good to get somebody else's ideas.

Parent: That's probably where I am right this minute with Sally.

Summarizing

Summarizing is a listening or communication skill that pleases and surprises the speaker. The speaker is probably saying to him- or herself, "Someone listened carefully enough to be able to list back most of the important points that I made." Summarizing also seems to help in making decisions, preserving information, and ending meetings.

Teacher: So far, you've told me about Sally's problems with assignments, her behavior problems at home, and some family problems. You think that all these things are probably contributing to her assignment incompletion.

Parent: You have a great memory. I have told you a lot.

Teacher: Do you think this might be a good time to choose a high-priority problem to work on? If you do, we could set up a meeting with the student assistance team during which team members can help us brainstorm and develop a plan.

Clarifying

Clarifying is asking questions that invite elaboration on previously made points. This is done in order to get such a clear depiction of an event that the listener can see and hear it as if he or she were right there when something happened. Clarifying questions seek descriptions rather than explanations. Thus, they begin with "what" and not "why." People have difficulty answering "why" questions and often feel defensive when asked why they did something. Clarifying questions ask the person to define terms and ask about what happened before (antecedent conditions) and what happened after (consequences). They are used to gain information. Clarifying questions do not occur rapid fire but are sensitive to the speaker's leads. They are used to give speakers the opportunity to put their information together in helpful, problem-solving ways.

Consider the fruitlessness of the teacher's asking "why" questions in the following scenario. The problem is not clarified at all, and, in fact, the student is less able to problem solve because he becomes more agitated while he is answering "why" questions.

Student: I was having a good day and then math class came along and spoiled it. I just want out of here.

Teacher: Why is that?
Student: Because this place sucks, especially the pencil-headed teacher! He
really makes me mad. It's not fair!

Let's look at an instant replay, but with a "what" question rather than a "why" question. Note that more information is obtained when a "what" clarifier is used.

Student: I was having a good day and then math class came along and spoiled
it all. I just want out of here.
Teacher: What happened in math class?
Student: Mr. Numero wouldn't let me turn in my assignment. And I had it all
done. It's not fair.
Teacher: What happened that you could not turn in your assignment? (versus
"Why did he do that?")
Student: I left it in the wrong notebook in my locker and when I asked to go
get it, he said I couldn't.

Through these examples you should see more clearly just how important clarifying questions can be to the communication process, especially if they begin with "what." As previously stated, "why" questions press the speaker to explain rather than describe. When most of us are immediately asked to explain, we are going to blame the other guy. That is just what the student did, in a less-than-respectful manner. In contrast, when "what" questions were used, the student was invited to describe what happened. The series of well-stated "what" questions led to the student's admitting his contribution to the problem.

Elaborating

Elaborating is a skill that results in building on what has already been introduced. Elaboration allows for more complex and comprehensive plans to be formulated. It makes people feel invested in the process because their ideas have been heard, valued, and used. There are times when elaboration can be used to link listener suggestions to speaker verbalizations. Then the final plan is more clearly a collaborative, joint effort.

Parent: I think the only way to handle this problem is to get Sally to grow up
and take responsibility for getting her own assignments in. I don't have time
for this anymore and it's not right that I should keep babying her.
Teacher: The idea of Sally's independence appeals to you. We could work
together to teach her how to self-monitor. Your schedule would have time
for helping her be more independent, wouldn't it?

Compare the following communication skills of teachers speaking to students. The communication skill the teacher uses is in parentheses following the response, unless no skill was used from the list given earlier. Note how the first teacher uses responses that quickly draw the conversation to a close without her gaining insight into the student's real problem. The second teacher uses effective communication skills to increase his insight into the student's problem and his ability to assist in problem solving.

In the first example, the teacher does not use basic listening or communication skills:

> *Student:* I don't have the assignment done.
> *Teacher:* You don't?
> *Student:* No, I don't! It took way too much time and was a stupid assignment.
> *Teacher:* What was so stupid? (clarifying, but focused on the inappropriate affect of the message)
> *Student:* Reading and then writing.
> *Teacher:* Really?
> *Student:* Yeah.
> *Teacher:* Are you serious? (clarifying, but focused on the inappropriate affect of the message)
> *Student:* Yep.

This student has now dug herself into a hole by insisting that the assignment was stupid. This reflects negative attributions for success, and the teacher's responses helped entrench this student in her way of thinking. The teacher did not remain objective but became defensive and controlling.

In the next example, the teacher reserves judgment, listens, and responds neutrally; in other words, he does use basic listening or communication skills. This creates an atmosphere of safety, and the student provides more information that will assist the teacher and student in collaborative problem solving.

> *Student:* I don't have the assignment done.
> *Teacher:* Really? (acknowledging)
> *Student:* No, I don't! It took way too much time and was a stupid assignment. (negative attribution statement, external cause beyond student's control)
> *Teacher:* It seemed time consuming to you. (reflecting cognition, not affect "stupid assignment")
> *Student:* It took all my study time to finish the reading and then there wasn't any time left to write.
> *Teacher:* Show me what you read and tell me how much time you spent on it. (clarifying)
> *Student:* I read this story just like you told us to. I started about 9:00 last night and read until 9:30. By then it was too late to start answering the questions that you assigned and I went to bed.

The teacher is now prepared to ask more clarifying questions to determine why the student left the English assignment until 9:00 p.m. The teacher would not say: "Why did you wait until 9:00 p.m. to start your homework?" This question communicates a feeling of disrespect or judgment. Educators need to avoid "why" questions. Instead, an effective clarifying question might follow a summarization, as in the following example: "You told me that you started the assignment at 9:00. A half hour later you had finished the reading but you had to go to bed. What were you doing before 9:00?"

After complete information is gathered, both the teacher and the student can discuss study skills that may prevent problems like this from occurring in the future. The student needs to articulate positive attributions for failure. For example, it may have been more accurate for the student to state, "I understood what to do but I miscalculated how long it would take me and I ran out of time." This statement reflects an effort attribution and has been linked to higher student achievement. Educators are to assist students in making these kinds of positive attributions in which the student links success to effort.

Reframing

Reframing is the process of (a) casting a problem in a new light, (b) emphasizing the positive aspects of the problem over its negative consequences, and (c) highlighting what adaptive purposes the problem serves. In the next example, a student's constant talking to the teacher is cast in a new light that emphasizes the positive aspects of talking to the teacher.

EXAMPLE

A student's constant talking to the teacher is seen by the teacher and others as an annoying habit. It can be reframed by casting the problem in a new light. For example, the student's behaviors are viewed as evidence that the student likes the teacher and is positively attached to her. This suggests that the teacher can have a positive influence on the student's learning. Reframing shifts the emphasis from an earlier focus on the negative consequences (i.e., teacher is annoyed and irritated because the student is constantly demanding attention) to the teacher's seeing how influential she can be in the student's life. Teachers can also focus on additional values to students of positive attachments (e.g., feelings of security, trust, and so on necessary to students' normal development).

Communication skills to this point have emphasized self-talk, body language, signal interference cuing, and active listening. The final form of communication described is sending verbal messages to others. Included are all the verbal messages educators initiate with others.

Sending Verbal Messages

Effective skills in sending verbal messages facilitate (a) relationships with students, (b) appropriate confrontation of students' disruptive behavior, and (c) specific feedback to students about their academic achievement (Jones & Jones, 1995). Facilitating quality student relationships by using verbal messages and appropriate confrontation skills is described in this chapter. Communication skills for giving specific feedback about academic performance were presented in chapter 5.

Schools can facilitate quality relationships by emphasizing positive verbal messages at the schoolhouse door.

In order to promote quality relationships, educators need to have positive interactions with students across time and situations. Interactions are those times that adults pay attention to students. Positive interactions include everything from saying hello to students to asking students how they are doing to complimenting students who are responsible and make good choices. See Figure 8–1 for examples of positive interactions.

Positive interactions have nothing to do with the tone or substance of actions. They occur when adults pay attention to students who display appropriate behavior. Increasing positive interactions is best implemented at the systems level. It is desirable that schools include it as a goal in their buildings' strategic plans. All staff in the building should be trained in how to conduct positive interactions. Many educators engage in numerous positive interactions, and this helps to define the culture of the building. Staff and students have quality relationships and a sense of community. Behavioral problems are less frequent when students believe they have the goodwill of adults. When students do not have the goodwill of adults, the intervention of increasing positive interactions is required.

Figure 8–1
Examples of Positive Interactions

Greet student as soon as he or she enters classroom.

Give student a job to do in the class.

Seat student near the source of instruction.

Make friendly eye contact.

Ask student a question when you know he or she can be successful.

Go by student's seat and check to see how things are going.

Give student a class responsibility when he or she finishes his or her work.

Walk with student in the hall on the way to another destination.

Ask student how he or she is, about his or her weekend, etc.

Wish student a great weekend, a happy vacation, and so on.

Tell student that you look forward to seeing him or her tomorrow.

Visit with student about his or her interests.

Write a positive note to student.

Write a positive note to student's guardian(s).

Ask additional staff in building to do preceding activities.

Positive interactions with students are lacking in some school contexts for a number of reasons. First, staff get busy, focus on tasks, and decrease the frequency of interpersonal interactions with students. Second, staff do not recognize the importance of having frequent positive interactions with students. Third, students exhibit behaviors that staff react to negatively. It is the third circumstance that can necessitate the implementation of a specific intervention.

Negative, avoidant reactions lead to reduced positive interactions. For example, staff who view students as sassy and disrespectful often begin to avoid them or to interact negatively with them. Some staff respond negatively and decrease their positive interactions with students who have poor self-concepts and seem to cling to adults or act helpless. Staff find it particularly difficult to sustain positive interactions with students who exhibit chronic attention-getting behaviors of arguing, negotiating, teasing, tattling, making excuses, being off task, and disrupting.

When staff members find themselves using the following self-talk or sending the following oral messages to others about a particular student, it is probably necessary to focus on intense applications of positive interactions: "I can see nothing positive about this student" or "This student is always off task." Teachers do not typically have the time to commit to the first phase of this intervention (preplanning) and need assistance. Educators should choose partners to work with them. Partners may include teachers, educational consultants, school counselors, school psychologists, and principals.

Prior to implementing the intervention, partners gather baseline data by observing the educators who want to increase the frequency of positive interactions. Partners also observe intermittently after implementation to see if the frequency of positive interactions is increasing. Ideal ratios of positive to negative interactions have been cited in the range of 3 positives to 1 negative all the way to 10 positives to 1 negative. It is important to achieve the ratio that best assists students in overcoming inappropriate behaviors.

An adaptation of Sprick et al.'s (1993) procedures for increasing positive interactions follows. Note that the procedures follow Sprick et al.'s typical outline: develop a plan, meet with the student to collaborate on and finalize the plan, and implement the plan.

Preplanning

First, the partner observes and counts the current level of the educator's positive to negative interactions. The educator and the partner define the problem and set goal(s). The two list all of the student's negative behaviors, determine the best consequences to use for each type of negative behavior, and rehearse how to use the consequences.

Next, they make a list of noncontingent positive interactions. *Noncontingent* means that the interactions will occur regardless of the student's negative or positive behaviors.

It is also necessary to make a list of contingent positive feedback. This feedback will be given to recognize the student's positive behaviors. It is important to ask other adults to increase their positive interactions also. One reason is that students who are targeted for positive interactions often are hungry for positive regard and attention. If the teacher is the only person engaging in positive interactions with the target student, the student may begin to hover around the teacher in a way that the teacher finds stressful. The student has several adults to relate to when positive interactions are coming from a variety of sources. Last, the partners develop an evaluation plan by which they will judge goal attainment.

Collaborating with the Student

The educator and the student collaboratively review the student's problem and set goal(s). The educator then assists the student in practicing actions to take in attaining the goal(s). The educator and the student discuss possible consequences for misbehaviors. They then review the positive interactions menu, and the student knows that the two of them will be having positive interactions also. They schedule regular discussions to check progress toward the goals. They review the plan, and the educator concludes with words of encouragement.

Implementing the Plan

The educator follows the plan to increase the ratio of positive to negative interactions. The partner evaluates how the teacher is doing by making regular checks, and the educator makes adjustments as necessary.

The partner helps the educator fade the intervention following consistent student progress. The partner follows up and encourages the educator intermittently. Although this intervention can be faded, it is always important to promote positive interactions.

Educators' Friendliness Toward Students

Preservice teachers often comment that they want students to know they are the students' friends, and these teachers ask questions about how best to do that. Teachers are advised to be *friendly* rather than to be *friends*. To be friendly requires (a) being open and approachable, (b) being willing to listen to things not directly related to students' classes, and (c) sharing their own feelings and opinions. The teacher who is friendly must also be the person in charge and provide the leadership that students need. This represents the demarcation between being friendly and being friends. For example, a teacher can demonstrate friendliness in his or her willingness to listen to a group of juniors planning an event at the local pizza place on Friday night. The teacher might express his or her own feelings by sharing how much he or she liked to do those things in high school. However, if the group asks the teacher to join them, the line of demarcation pops up and social distance needs to be established. The teacher needs to say something like the following, "Thank you for thinking of me, but I had my time with my friends in high school. It is your turn to have a good time with one another."

Grossman (1995) noted that not all students prefer teachers to be friendly. Some Asian Pacific American students are used to formal relationships with teachers.

Some students with emotional problems feel threatened by any close relationship. Educators need to be sensitive and not push friendliness in these situations.

Problem-Centered Discussions Between Educators and Students

Probably every building administrator, teacher, teacher associate, guidance counselor, and other educator has had talks with students who were experiencing problems in school (e.g., tattling, being disorganized, listening poorly, exhibiting disruptive behavior, fighting, cheating). Many of those talks occurred after the problem was chronic or severe and went something like the following:

> "Sherida, we have talked about this many times before. What do you have to say for yourself? (Pause.) What are we going to do? You are constantly coming to class without your materials. I have tried everything and nothing is working. I am tired of talking to you about knowing where your assignments are and getting them in on time. You are starting 10th grade next year, and I think it is time for you to take some responsibility. From now on, starting today, you are responsible for bringing your materials to class—no more passes to go get them. I won't remind you anymore about your assignments. If they are late or never get in, you will have to suffer the consequences of low grades. Do you understand?"

Educators often feel that the litany of complaints and threats, like that in the preceding illustration, constitutes an adequate presentation of the problem. However, active participation by the student is woefully lacking. Interactions that are lecture-like do not usually result in significant behavioral change.

Sprick et al. (1993) developed semistructured procedures that facilitate a collaborative and positive discussion between an educator and a student to resolve a particular problem. These researchers called the procedures *planned discussions*. The purpose of planned discussions is to let students know that there is a problem, to get students actively involved in problem solving, and to let them know that the educator is there to help them learn and grow.

Many teachers do have "chats" with students about problem behaviors. Planned discussions ensure that the time teachers spend talking to students about their problem behaviors is collaborative and problem solving in nature. Sprick et al. (1993) suggested that planned discussions should be the first step in any plan intended to assist students in behavioral change. Such discussions are often sufficient interventions for problems addressed in the early stages. More intensive interventions may never be needed when educators use a series of planned discussions in early intervention work. Minor problems that benefit from planned discussions include annoying behaviors like tattling and producing sloppy work. Solving moderate problems like off-task behavior, disruptive behavior, tardiness, and poor listening should start with a planned discussion and may need additional interventions. Planned discussions are also used for chronic and severe problems, but only as part of a broader intervention plan.

Teachers' immediate thoughts may be "When will I ever have time to complete a series of planned discussions?" It is important to realize that approximately one half of classroom time is taken up with noninstructional activities. Discipline problems are responsible for a significant portion of this lost instructional time (Cotton, 1990). Well-planned discussions could potentially alleviate future discipline problems, which would thereby free up time. Figure 8–2 provides a list of alternative times that teachers may consider using for conducting planned discussions.

For minor problems, and to prevent future problems, teachers may want to schedule several planned discussions per week during independent seat time. This allows teachers to have contact with all students in the class. Teachers can use the time to provide positive feedback and encouragement. If the teacher schedules individual discussions with all students, no particular student will feel alienated or singled out. Another benefit of this approach is early resolution or prevention of a problem, which saves time, energy, and frustration. Busy teachers can also ask a support person to partner with them in carrying out planned discussions. School counselors and school psychologists are usually pleased to team with teachers and take responsibility for assisting with planned discussions. Student discussions with teachers may be more beneficial than discussions with someone outside of the classroom. Teams can determine together who would be the better choice to carry out the planned discussion.

Cultural contexts must be considered prior to conduction of planned discussions. Some Southeast Asians may find this intervention to be too open and direct. Some Hispanic students may further label the discussion as hostile and disrespectful when teachers seek to ascertain both sides of the situation and facilitate dialogue.

Procedures or phases of Sprick et al.'s (1993) planned discussion include (a) a preplanning phase for the educator to define the problem before he or she discusses it with the student, (b) working with the student to define the problem and

Figure 8–2
Alternative Times That Could Be Used to Conduct Planned Discussions

Before school
After school
During recess
During music, physical education, and other special classes (with prior teacher approval)
During independent seatwork (if the problem is minor)
During study hall
During library time
During free reading time
During a class meeting (if the problem involves several students)
Arrange for someone else to cover the teacher's class (two teachers may form a collaborative partnership to assist each other at times like this)

determine a final plan, and (c) implementing the plan. Two required elements of a successful planned discussion are (1) follow the procedures and (2) use effective communication skills. Following is an example of the planned discussion intervention that could be used, for instance, at the earliest signs that a student has weak organizational skills (e.g., arriving in class without materials and assignments).

Preplanning

The form in Figure 8–3 can be used to prepare for discussions. The planned discussion should be scheduled at a neutral time with the student and the parties chosen to

Describe the problem before discussing it with the student:

_____

_____

Who is involved? _____

Severity of the problem on a scale of 0 (no problem) to 10 (severe): _____

Where does the problem occur?

_____

How often does the problem occur?

_____

Situational factors:

Is the problem academic, social/behavioral, or both?   (Circle one.)

Establish a focus. (When the student has interrelated difficulties, introducing too may concerns can overwhelm the student and increase a student's sense of inadequacy.) The specific area that is of most concern is:

_____

Who will participate in the planned discussion? _____

Is this problem minor or severe?   (Circle one.)

Does the educator feel a need for assistance?   Yes or No   (Circle one.)

Check all of those who will participate:

____ Principal (alone when the student is sent to the office from the class for discipline)

____ Teacher (alone when the problem is minor)

____ Parents or guardians (when the problem is more severe or the teacher thinks they should be included in developing and implementing the plan)

____ Support service personnel (when the educator feels the need for specialized assistance)

Figure 8–3
Form Used to Prepare for Planned Discussions with Students

participate. A script that can be used with the parents and the student when the educator is making the initial scheduling contact follows.

EDUCATOR'S SCRIPT

"[Name], I need your help with a problem. What I am concerned about is [describe problem]. Let's get together to talk about this soon. Could you meet on [date]? Before we meet, it would be helpful if you would think about ways that we can work on this problem. I will think about solutions, too. [Name of participant] is invited to come to the meeting. I am sure she will have some good ideas about how to help. I am looking forward to working with both of you. I am sure that we can come up with some creative ideas."

Collaborating with the Student

The educator should conduct a collaborative meeting with the student and complete a discussion record. First, the educator and the student collaboratively define the problem.

EDUCATOR'S SCRIPT

"Thank you for meeting with me today to help solve [describe problem]. Solutions usually turn out better if we work on this together. [Name], what do you think is causing the [name type of problem]?"

If the student responds with "I don't know," the teacher should give the student something concrete to do to help cue him or her, or ask the student, "What makes [name the problem] difficult?" If the student still has difficulty answering and a third party is involved in the discussion, the teacher may request assistance from the third party in helping define the problem. Next, everyone generates action ideas to solve the problem.

EDUCATOR'S SCRIPT

"We're at the best part now—deciding our plan. Let's list all the things that you and I and [name other participants] can do to help you with [name type of problem]. Let's share as many ideas as we can. Every idea is a good one. After we write them down, we'll pick what we want to try."
(Select an idea or ideas that will be relatively easy to implement.)
"[Name], thank you for your great ideas about things that would help with [type of problem]. Out of all the ideas, let's decide on a few that seem best and we'll talk about how each of the best ideas could be carried out."

The teacher next assigns responsibilities and sets times to carry them out. Then he or she schedules a follow-up meeting and sends the student off with encouragement.

Implementing the Plan

Privately, and on a daily basis, the teacher must encourage student efforts. He or she should continue periodic discussions of progress with the student and adjust the plan as necessary. The educator must keep that momentum going and should conduct a planned discussion any time it is important to see if more structured interventions are required.

Interventions involving providing academic assistance, restructuring self-talk, using signal interference cuing, setting goals and using behavioral contracting, teaching self-monitoring, and using structured reinforcement systems may be included for intervention plans that need greater depth. (See chapter 4 for interventions not discussed in this chapter.) The educator needs to provide continued follow-up and encouragement.

Sprick et al. (1993) provided discussion records for educators to use in note taking and comprehensive procedures for the intervention. Most educators need only a brief time to master the steps of this intervention. Although students do participate, they typically do not talk at length. Thus, a planned discussion can take as little as 4 or 5 minutes. Educators who role-play procedures of the planned discussion react quite favorably to the intervention and report benefits of the approach.

Direct Confrontation

Additional oral skills that may be needed include those used in direct confrontation situations. Confrontation is an intermediate to advanced skill that must be used with professional objectivity to be effective. This is a skill that counselors, psychologists, and social workers may feel more comfortable using than teachers or principals may. With this communication skill, the listener may be identifying the speaker as the target of the feedback. Using the earlier case of Sally, who did not turn in assignments, the educator might say to the parent: "I see that you did not try the techniques we discussed to increase Sally's turning in assignments. I'm wondering if you are feeling unable to help her and are hoping that someone else will."

Indirect confrontation is conceptualizing the problem as the issue it represents and placing the problem on the issue. "I didn't notice you trying the techniques we discussed to help Sally turn her assignments in. This suggests to me that the ideas we developed don't seem to fit as well as I'd hoped. What have you experienced?"

Educators who want to confront effectively those students who exhibit inappropriate or disruptive behavior must adhere to the practices of (a) confronting only present behavior, (b) talking to the student rather than around the student to someone else, and (c) using "I" messages. It is necessary to look at these students as if they have a clean slate. This does not mean that educators forget the past or that they do not use the pattern of behavioral problems to help them problem solve. It does mean that educators "bag" past incidents and concentrate on the present problems in order to avoid prejudging or holding grudges against students. Contrast the following two approaches to talking to a student about a late assignment.

EXAMPLE 1

"Jerad, we have been through this before. Is it going to start again—not getting assignments in on time? I am getting pretty tired of policing you. You are in ninth grade now and need to act like it. Teachers aren't going to babysit you. Figure out how you are going to turn this around and let me know."

EXAMPLE 2

"Jerad, thank you for meeting with me. The reason that we are meeting is to work together to solve a problem of getting assignments in on time. One of my jobs is to help students learn to be steady workers. For 2 weeks you have been a steady worker, and now you have a late assignment. I am not sure how I can help you, so I thought we could work on this together. Jerad, what is going on that you had trouble getting this assignment in on time?"

"I" messages consist of two types. The first type focuses on educators' expressing demands by beginning the message with "I." Examples are "I need you to put the pencil down" and "I expect you to follow rule one in our class: Be respectful to all people at all times." The second type of "I" message requires educators to begin the oral message with "I," continue by stating their feelings, and end with the effect the students' behaviors are having on the educators. Examples are "I am frustrated because I cannot teach the lesson if you are interrupting" and "I feel angry and uncomfortable with your debates about the value of the assignments I give."

"I" messages require educators to take full responsibility and ownership of their feelings and the effect of student behaviors on them as educators. This intervention moves squarely away from attacking the student and requires educators to be more vulnerable by focusing on only their own feelings. What is responsible for the success of "I" messages? It seems to be the lack of attack on the student paired with the concomitant vulnerability of educators who share their own feelings.

Ultimately, it is important for educators to recognize that some unpleasant interactions are a part of working with people and to know that they cannot attend to every one of them. Some educators find this difficult to do because of their own angry responses.

Educators' Management of Their Own Anger

Most educators know, without any discussion, that freely expressing their own anger on the job is not an acceptable practice. There are two opposite and extreme methods for managing anger, and many people engage in one or the other. First, people let it all hang out and say and act exactly how they are feeling. An example would be the principal who becomes red in the face, shouts at the noncompliant student, and strikes the metal trash can by his desk with a yardstick for emphasis.

At the opposite extreme for managing personal anger is to smile and withdraw and act like no one is angry, especially you. An example would be the teacher who is repeatedly engaged by a student in a debate about the value of the lesson and assignments. The student skillfully debates, and the teacher is unable to proffer an accepted justification. The teacher smiles after several minutes and walks away but feels angry inside after a few weeks of not only this daily sparring but also no completed student work. Neither of these two methods for managing anger is effective; they are simply not good choices.

Educators' angry, hurt, frustrated, or guilty feelings are natural. Everybody experiences such reactions when interacting with others. The previous discussions of communication skills provided the means for educators to begin to change their attitudes about communication and conflict, which should reduce the frequency of having angry feelings. Well-developed positive self-talk and attributional thinking skills can be instrumental in reducing anger responses to others' actions. Body language basics of open postures, relaxed muscles, and deep breathing are the exact opposite of the physiological responses of anger. Therefore, when they are practiced, they reduce the likelihood of heightened anger responses.

Effective listening skills focus educators' attention on hearing and understanding the intent of a speaker's message, whether the intent is affective or cognitive. Using effective listening skills puts educators in the role of helping speakers solve their own problems rather than educators' being responsible for the problems that speakers are sharing. This change in attitude can reduce educators' angry responses to speakers' messages. The skill domain of sending verbal messages is the appropriate domain for educators to express, in effective ways, their personal anger.

Paramount importance is placed on telling the other party how you feel without attacking that person. Consider the situation in which the building principal, Ms. Neat, sent a written memo to the curriculum committee members. In it, Ms. Neat named the members who had completed their assignments by the deadline and the one member who had not. That one member is Ms. Act. Ms. Act is angry that Ms. Neat made this information public without first contacting her to obtain her work, especially because the deadline had never been communicated. Ms. Act feels as though her reputation was impacted negatively by Ms. Neat's thoughtless and insensitive memo. How should Ms. Act respond? (1) She can let Ms. Neat have it— orally. (2) She can smile sweetly and withdraw but feel angry and vengeful inside. (3) Or she can respond somewhere in between by letting Ms. Neat know how she feels without attacking her personally. Listen to the following response that Ms. Act delivers in a quiet tone to Ms. Neat.

> "Ms. Neat, I did not know when the deadline was. It was never communicated to any of us. You publicly broadcast to the committee that I was the only one who did not make the deadline. That is so like you."

What is wrong with this message? Rather than communicate explicitly how she felt, Ms. Act merely inferred how she felt and orally attacked Ms. Neat by saying, "That is so like you." An attack generally provokes a defensive posture and creates obstacles to communication. Even though this oral message was delivered quietly, it was not the most effective way to resolve the problem.

Consider a new version of the message that better fits the criteria of stating how you feel without attacking Ms. Neat personally. Remember to focus on Ms. Neat's behavior rather than on her as a person.

> "Ms. Neat, I am angry that you announced in a memo to the committee that I was the only one who did not make the deadline. I did not know when the deadline was; I have no record that it was ever communicated to me. I think this type of public announcement hurts my reputation. I would like to discuss with you how to resolve this problem and prevent it from happening in the future. When could we schedule a time to do that?"

Consider another example of angry feelings, but this time the interaction is between a teacher and a student. Rudy likes to debate the value of lessons and assignments and will serve as an excellent example because many adults have angry reactions to "Rudy-like" behavior. Recall that adults who experience angry feelings either vent their anger on the student (who then feels as if he or she has successfully accomplished the goal of getting an adult to sputter out of control) or smile sweetly and withdraw, feeling angry and vengeful inside. Reflect for a minute on what you would communicate to Rudy if you were angry, and compose your response. Then read ahead. It should sound something like this:

> "Rudy, I get angry when you persist in asking questions about the value of lessons and assignments. It is good that you think critically about what you study. However, repeated questions disrupt the class for me and other students. This has become a serious problem. We need to schedule a time to meet and collaborate together on a resolution. I see from your schedule that we could both meet during sixth hour. What day would be good for you this week?"

The strengths of this response are several. The teacher communicated his true feelings without attacking the student. In fact, the teacher used the skill of reframing to cast Rudy's annoying debate behaviors in a positive light of thinking critically. The teacher also communicated that problem solving would be collaborative rather than authoritarian. Finally, the teacher structured the time of the meeting but gave the student choices of what day of the week they would meet.

In the preceding situation, imagine that Rudy is a Hispanic American male and the teacher is female. How would communication change? Some male Hispanic

American students will listen better to an adult male (Grossman, 1995). When students have difficulty accepting female teachers' authority, teachers may want to try stating requests versus issuing orders. A male administrator may be needed in more severe situations.

Students' Management of Their Own Anger with Educator Assistance

Students' angry, hurt, frustrated, or guilty feelings are also natural. Everybody has them as natural reactions to conflicted interpersonal interactions. Educators are to assist students in learning how to express their anger appropriately. As stated previously, active listening skills can be very effective in helping others regain their self-control. A special focus in active listening requires educators to acknowledge and validate students' feelings. An example might be, "David, I know that it makes you angry when the guys accuse you of cheating. Swearing at them and threatening them are not okay to do at school. Take a few minutes to think about what you could do instead. After that we will talk about your ideas."

Educators can also provide appropriate ways for students to "let off steam." Physical activities are especially helpful: (a) cleaning areas in classrooms, (b) running errands for teachers, and (c) running laps, doing jumping jacks, or doing push-ups. Nonphysical activities that serve as relaxants are helpful to some students: (a) eating or drinking, (b) listening to music, and (c) talking calmly. Educators must ensure, however, that when they use these activities to help students calm down, students do not respond as if they had been rewarded for getting angry. One way to overcome any possible negative effects of relaxation techniques is to be sure to require students to make up work time that they missed during relaxation activities.

Educators may wish to provide a way for students to escape from the environment in which they are experiencing strong feelings. There may be a place in the building where students can go to calm themselves. Many teachers use signal interference cuing with students who may need to escape. The idea is to let students be alone where it is easier to become calm. We all need to have a calm atmosphere before we can problem solve effectively. How do you think this intervention would have worked with Jerad, the boy in chapter 1 who tried to leave the room and was grabbed around the neck by the teacher?

Natural consequences for the inappropriate expression of strong feelings may include making apologies. Grossman (1995) reported that some students from diverse ethnic backgrounds (e.g., Hispanic Americans) may be more likely to apologize in subtle ways as opposed to overt, direct ways.

Finally, more specific interventions for students with severe anger control deficits were described in chapter 4. Figure 8–4 provides a list of some common school situations that educators can use as the context for practicing body language and communication skills.

Administrators

1. Employee is frustrated with administrator for the way a student's behavior problem was disciplined.

2. Female student is suspended for being tardy to class and her parents are in the administrator's office and are emotionally upset but are not showing anger.

3. Female student is suspended for being tardy to class and her parents are in the administrator's office and are angry and loudly threatening to sue.

4. Administrator calls parent(s) to communicate bad news about their child (e.g., student was in a fight or brought a weapon to school or was in possession of drugs).

5. Student was consistently disruptive to classroom learning environment and sent out of class to principal's office. Student is angry, swears at principal, and paces around the office.

6. Student was consistently disruptive to classroom learning environment and was sent out of class to principal's office. Student is argumentative but not angry with principal.

Teachers

1. Student made a low grade for the quarter. It is parent conference time and the parent is feeling discouraged and becomes teary-eyed during the conference.

2. Parent unexpectedly comes by at the end of the school day to talk to the teacher. The parent is angry about an assignment that requires students to write about a historic figure that the parent believes was racist. Parent accuses teacher of being racist.

3. Teacher makes a telephone call to the home and requests a meeting with the parent(s) to discuss student's lack of progress.

4. Student is quietly noncompliant with teacher requests.

5. Student is loud and noncompliant with teacher requests.

6. Student argues with teacher decisions.

7. Student constantly exhibits behaviors that are borderline unacceptable.

8. Student responds to new or difficult tasks with frustration and says something like one of the following: (a) This task is stupid. (b) I can't do this. (c) This is too hard.

Figure 8–4
Practice Scenarios of Common School Situations

Assessment of Professional Communication Skills

Figures 8–5 and 8–6 are examples of rating scales that educators may want to use to routinely assess their communication skills after a difficult interpersonal encounter at school. Figure 8–5 focuses on listening, and Figure 8–6 focuses on how well the educator did at receiving critical feedback from the speaker.

(Name)	1 = Poor
	2 = Fair
	3 = Average
(Grade) (Date)	4 = Superior
	5 = Excellent

Assessment of Listening Skills

1 2 3 4 5   1. I heard precisely.

1 2 3 4 5   2. I helped the speaker feel understood.

1 2 3 4 5   3. I effectively used acknowledging (yes, really, wow, right).
　　　　　　　____used to encourage person to speak
　　　　　　　____used to communicate awareness of emotional content

1 2 3 4 5   4. I effectively used reflecting (repeating back).
　　　　　　　____selected to underline emotional responses
　　　　　　　____selected to begin behavior analysis

1 2 3 4 5   5. I effectively used paraphrasing (offered tentatively).
　　　　　　　___used to cue speaker to slight variations in message

1 2 3 4 5   6. I effectively used summarizing.
　　　　　　　___seemed to help make decisions
　　　　　　　___preserved information
　　　　　　　___used to end a meeting

1 2 3 4 5   7. I effectively used clarifying (asked questions for elaboration).
　　　　　　　___used to get a complete picture, snapshot, or movie
　　　　　　　___used to help speaker put information together
　　　　　　　___used "what," not "why," questions

1 2 3 4 5   8. I effectively used elaboration (building on information introduced).
　　　　　　　___used to link speaker's talk to my suggestions

Yes   No   9. I appropriately gave the speaker credit for having all the best ideas.

Figure 8–5
Assessment of Listening Skills

CONCLUSION

Effective communication skills in the domains of self-talk, body language basics, listening, and sending verbal messages are not developed overnight or during the course of a college semester of study and practice. This chapter provided basic knowledge and procedural skills as a foundation on which educators can continue to build.

Consider the following 10 situations and practice the communication skills necessary to best manage them. When you can select the appropriate communication procedures and role-play the situations adequately, you can be assured that you have the foundational communication skills that will help you develop into an expert

Yes No	1.	I used a relaxation response when I became aware that feedback was imminent.
Yes No	2.	I listened closely to everything the speaker was saying and did not begin to formulate a response until I heard the entire message.
Yes No	3.	I tried to catch the essence of the speaker's feelings.
Yes No	4.	Before I spoke, I studied my own feelings and was able to label them.
Yes No	5.	I repeated back what I heard. I asked for clarification. If I was in a group, I checked to see if others saw me the same way.
Yes No	6.	I reminded myself that I have no way to control the way others see me and that I am completely responsible only for my own behavior.
Yes No	7.	I decided to change the behavior, realizing that the person's feelings may not change about me.
Yes No	8.	There is a content misunderstanding between me and speaker. I gave reasons why I behaved the way I did.
Yes No	9.	The misunderstanding is not one of content. I did not get defensive and give reasons why I behaved the way I did.

Figure 8–6
Assessment of Feedback Skills (Feedback Received by Educator)

communicator or manager. Your competence will grow, and your appreciation of what you have accomplished will be reassuring.

1. You find yourself making the following comments about a highly distractible student who is often off task: "Rudy never pays attention. I am so tired of his always disrupting the class. I am on him every minute of the day."
2. A student is unable to work cooperatively with peers in small-group math lessons but can work better in cooperative groups focused on reading or science. He has a pattern of making negative statements about math assignments: "This is stupid" and "This is too difficult; I can't do it."
3. You are angry with a student who is disrespectful to you.
4. You are angry with a student who is disrespectful to others.
5. You are angry with a student that you have been unable to control.
6. You are discouraged or frustrated with a student that you have been unable to motivate.
7. You do not believe what a student is telling you.
8. A student does not appear to like you even though you have made many attempts to build a relationship.
9. A parent or a student communicates in an angry or accusatory way with you.
10. A parent is emotionally upset at a parent–teacher conference when you tell her that her daughter has been skipping class and is receiving a letter grade of D for the quarter.

SUPPLEMENTARY QUESTIONS

1. High school students sometimes complain that teachers treat them disrespectfully. Which of the communication tips in this chapter do you think teachers are violating?
2. Some teachers say that they are too busy to communicate through listening and that it is not realistic to expect them to take the time. What do you think? How will you decide when you must take the time and when it is not as necessary?
3. Think about a teacher in your past who was a positive influence on you and your peers. What were his or her communication skills? Was communication the most important skill, or were there other reasons that prompted you to select this teacher?

SUPPLEMENTARY PROJECTS

1. Record or videotape your interactions with others to see which of Ginott's communication no-no's you use. Write scripts to replace your current messages and provide evidence of rehearsal. Critique new tapes that show improvement.
2. Use the same tape to listen to your communication skills and gauge your use of body language, listening, and sending spoken messages. Do your predominant communication skills match the philosophical and theoretical beliefs that you identified in chapter 1? Justify your response.

REFERENCES

Aiello, J. R., & Jones, S. E. (1971). Field study of the proxemic behavior of young school children in three subcultural groups. *Journal of Personality and Social Psychology, 19,* 351–356.

Anderson, L. M., Evertson, C. M., & Emmer, E. T. (1979). *Dimensions in classroom management derived from recent research.* Austin: Texas University, Research and Development Center for Teacher Education. (ERIC Document Reproduction Service No. ED175860)

Barker, K. (Ed.). (1985). *The new international version Bible.* Grand Rapids, MI: Zondervan Corporation.

Baron, R. M., Tom, D., & Cooper, H. (1985). Social class, race and teacher expectations. In J. Dusek, V. Hall, & W. Meyer (Eds.), *Teacher expectancies* (pp. 251–269). Hillsdale, NJ: Erlbaum.

Bernard, M. E. (1979). Does sex role behavior influence the way teachers evaluate students? *Journal of Educational Psychology, 71,* 553–562.

Charles, C. M. (1996). *Building classroom discipline.* White Plains, NY: Longman.

Connors, E. T. (1981). *Educational tort liability and malpractice.* Bloomington, IN: Phi Delta Kappa Educational Foundation.

Conoley, J. C., & Conoley, C. W. (1992). *School consultation: Practice and training.* Boston: Allyn & Bacon.

Cooper, H., Baron, R., & Lowe, C. (1975). The importance of race and social class in the formation of expectancies about academic performance. *Journal of Educational Psychology, 67,* 312–319.

Cooperman, M. L. (1975). Field-dependence and children's problem-solving under varying contingencies of predetermined feedback. *Dissertation Abstracts International, 35,* 2040–2041.

Cotton, K. (1990). *Schoolwide and classroom discipline* [School improvement research series]. Portland, OR: Northwest Regional Educational Laboratory.

Dweck, C. S. (1975). The role of expectation and attributions in the alleviation of learned helplessness. *Journal of Personality and Social Psychology, 25,* 109–116.

Gay, G., & Abrahams, R. D. (1973). Does the pot melt, boil, or brew? Black children and White assessment procedures. *Journal of School Psychology, 11*(4), 330–340.

Gilliam, H., & Van Den Berg, S. (1980). Different levels of eye contact: Effects on Black and White college students. *Urban Education, 15,* 83–92.

Ginott, H. (1971). *Teacher and child.* New York: Macmillan.

Gordon, T. (1974). *Teacher effectiveness training.* New York: Wyden.

Grossman, H. (1984). *Educating Hispanic students: Cultural implications for instruction, classroom management, counseling, and assessment.* Springfield, IL: Thomas.

Grossman, H. (1995). *Classroom behavior management in a diverse society* (2nd ed.). Mountain View, CA: Mayfield.

Heider, F. (1958). *The psychology of interpersonal relations.* New York: Wiley.

Heller, K. A., & Parsons, J. E. (1981). Sex differences in teachers' evaluative feedback and students' expectancies for success in mathematics. *Child Development, 52,* 1015–1019.

Iverson, A. M. (1996). *Preservice educators' self-reports of communication skills.* Unpublished manuscript, University of Northern Iowa, Cedar Falls.

Jones, V. F., & Jones, L. S. (1995). *Comprehensive classroom management: Creating positive learning environments for all students.* Boston: Allyn & Bacon.

Kounin, J. S. (1970). *Discipline and group management in classrooms.* New York: Holt, Rinehart & Winston.

Multon, K. D., Brown, S. D., & Lent, R. W. (1991). Relation of self-efficacy beliefs to academic outcomes: A meta-analytic investigation. *Journal of Counseling Psychology, 38,* 30–38.

National Education Association Committee on Professional Ethics. (1975). *Code of ethics of the education profession.* Washington, DC: National Education Association.

Nguyen, T. P. (1987). Positive self-concept in the Vietnamese bilingual child. In M. Dao (Ed.), *From Vietnamese to Vietnamese American: Selected articles.* San Jose, CA: Division of Special Education and Rehabilitative Services, San Jose State University.

Reeder, M. A. (1996). *Acceptability across disciplines of attribution retraining alone and combined with learning strategy instruction.* Unpublished (Ed.S.) thesis, University of Northern Iowa, Cedar Falls.

Sprick, R., Sprick, M., & Garrison, M. (1993). *Interventions: Collaborative planning for students at risk.* Longmont, CO: Sopris West.

Tom, D., & Cooper, H. (1986). The effect of student background on teacher performance attributions: Evidence for counterdefensive patterns and low expectancy cycles. *Basic and Applied Social Psychology, 7,* 53–62.

Tom, D., Cooper, H., & McGraw, M. (1984). The influences of student background and teacher authoritarianism on teacher expectations. *Journal of Educational Psychology, 76,* 259–265.

Wei, T. D. (1980). *Vietnamese refugee students: A handbook for school personnel* (2nd ed.). Urbana: Illinois University, Midwest Organization for Material Development. (ERIC Document Reproduction Service No. ED208109)

Wiley, M. G., & Eskilson, A. (1978). Why did you learn in school today? Teachers' perceptions of causality. *Sociology of Education, 51,* 261–269.

Wong, M. C. (1980). Model students? Teachers' perceptions and expectations of their Asian and White students. *Sociology of Education, 53,* 226–246.

Building a Classroom Management Plan

AN AUTHORITATIVE ORIENTATION

Step 1: State beliefs and expectations.

_____

_____

_____

_____

_____

Step 2: Make a list of:

Nonassertive Behaviors (to avoid)	Hostile Behaviors (to avoid)	Assertive Behaviors (to cultivate)
_____	_____	_____
_____	_____	_____
_____	_____	_____

Step 3: State rules that govern responsible conduct; that is, conduct that enables us to get work done and get along with one another.

1._____

_____

_____

(*Note:* Use this format for each additional rule.)

Specify behavior expectations covered by this rule.

1. _____
1.1 _____
1.2 _____
1.3 _____
1.4 _____

Step 4: State unacceptable requests that you find difficult to refuse:

1._____
2._____
3._____
4._____

State the assertive way you will handle each of these requests.

1._____
2._____
3._____
4._____

Step 5: Identify key activities or methods used to deliver instruction, and specify the directions students need to follow when they are participating responsibly in these activities.

Activity

1._____

_____

(*Note:* Use this format for each additional activity.)

Directions

1.1 _____
1.2 _____
1.3 _____
1.4 _____

Step 6: Select several low-profile techniques you will use to prevent problems.

_____

_____

_____

_____

Identify situations in which these techniques may be most appropriate.

_____

_____

_____

_____

Step 7: Select a hierarchy of consequences that will be applied when students disobey the rules.

Least Severe: _____
_____
_____
_____
_____
_____

Most Severe: _____

Select severe consequences that will be used when a student's behavior is absolutely intolerable and/or is not well managed by the regular plan.

Consequences that can be administered without cooperation of others:
_____
_____

Consequences that require assistance:
_____
_____

Step 8: Identify common sidetracking tactics students use to avoid negative consequences or obedience.

_____
_____
_____
_____

Identify assertive communication techniques to counteract these student tactics.

_____
_____
_____
_____

Step 9: Select consequences that will be used to support good behavior; that is, to reinforce behavior that helps us get work done and get along well with one another.

Social (Verbal/Nonverbal)
_____
_____
_____

Written/Spoken
_____
_____
_____

Public/Private
_____
_____
_____

Activities and Privileges
_____
_____
_____

Individual
_____
_____
_____

Classwide
_____
_____
_____

Tangible (if any)
_____
_____
_____

Individual
_____
_____
_____

Classwide
_____
_____
_____

Token (if any)
_____
_____
_____

Individual
_____
_____
_____

Classwide
_____
_____
_____

Step 10: Select noncontingent (quality-of-life) reinforcers that will be made contingent.

_____
_____
_____

_____
_____
_____

Step 11: Identify people and roles essential to the implementation of your plan.

Person _____   Role _____
Person _____   Role _____
Person _____   Role _____

Step 12: Identify ways to document behavior to evaluate the effectiveness of your plan.

_____   _____
_____   _____
_____   _____

Resources

Canter, L., & Canter, M. (1976). *Assertive discipline: A take charge approach for today's educator* (Chaps. 1 and 2). Los Angeles: Lee Canter and Associates.

Dobson, J. (1970). *Dare to discipline* (Chap. 1). Wheaton, IL: Tyndale House.

Rosemond, J. (1989). *Six-point plan for raising happy, healthy children* (Part 2). Kansas City, MO: Andrews & McMeel.

York, P., York, D., & Wachtel, T. (1982). *Toughlove* (Part 2). New York: Doubleday.

A DEMOCRATIC ORIENTATION

Step 1: State beliefs and expectations.

_____

_____

_____

_____

Step 2: Make a list of your management behaviors (use Nelsen's behavior categories to identify examples).

Object: "Done to" (excessive control) behaviors (e.g., demanding, punishing, lecturing)	*Recipient:* "Done for" behaviors (excessive pressure) (e.g., rescuing, indulging, overprotecting)	*Asset:* "Done with" behaviors (firmness with dignity and respect) (e.g., involving, inviting, encouraging)
1._____	1._____	1._____
2._____	2._____	2._____
3._____	3._____	3._____

Step 3: Engage students in a discussion to identify the conditions that make school a good place to be.

1._____

2._____

3._____

4._____

5._____

(*Note:* Use this format for each additional rule.)

Identify the behaviors of teachers and students that contribute to these conditions, and formulate rules to state these as behavior expectations.

1._____

1.1 _____

1.2 _____

1.3 _____

1.4 _____

Rule: _____

_____

Step 4: State unacceptable requests you find difficult to refuse.

1._____

2._____

3._____

4._____

State the 'I' messages you will use to handle these requests.

1._____

2._____

3._____

4._____

Step 5: Identify key activities or methods used to deliver instruction, and specify the directions students need to follow when they are participating responsibly in these activities.

Activity

1. _____

_____

(*Note:* Use this format for each additional activity.)

Directions

1.1 _____

1.2 _____

1.3 _____

1.4 _____

Step 6: Select several low-profile techniques you will use to prevent problems.

1. _____
2. _____
3. _____
4. _____

Identify situations in which these techniques may be most appropriate.

1. _____
2. _____
3. _____
4. _____

Step 7: Select a behavior manifestation for each of the four mistaken goals (Dreikurs) that would be most troublesome for you.

1. _____
2. _____
3. _____
4. _____

Identify natural and/or logical consequences (use Nelsen's "Three R's for Logical Consequences") for each mistaken goal.

1. _____
2. _____
3. _____
4. _____

Step 8: Identify specific teacher behaviors that undermine the development of responsible children (use Glenn and Nelsen's "Five Barriers").

1. _____
2. _____
3. _____
4. _____
5. _____

Identify specific teacher behaviors that affirm and validate responsible behaviors (use Glenn and Nelsen's "Five Builders").

1. _____
2. _____
3. _____
4. _____
5. _____

Step 9: Identify ways to win cooperation through encouragement (use Gordon's active/reflective listening; Nelsen's "Four Steps for Winning Cooperation" and "The Three R's of Recovery;" or Dinkmeyer and Losoncy's "Differences Between Praise and Encouragement").

_____

_____

_____

_____

Step 10: Demonstrate the way to use a class meeting to improve the quality of life and decision making in the classroom. (Employ the "define, personalize, and challenge" format for applying Glasser's group arrangement and process guidelines, and Dinkmeyer and Losoncy's group leadership skills for facilitating these meetings.)

_____

_____

_____

_____

Step 11: Identify people and roles or functions essential to the implementation of your plan.

Person_____   Role/Functions _____

Person_____   _____

                                             Role/Functions _____

                                             _____

Step 12: Identify ways to evaluate the effectiveness of your plan.

_____

_____

_____

_____

Resources

Dinkmeyer, D., & Losoncy, L. E. (1980). *The encouragement book: Becoming a positive person.* Upper Saddle River, NJ: Prentice Hall.

Dreikurs, R., Grunwald, B. B., & Pepper, F. C. (1982). *Maintaining sanity in the classroom: Classroom management techniques* (2nd ed.). New York: Harper & Row.

Glasser, W. (1969). *Schools without failure* (Chaps. 10–12). New York: Harper & Row.

Glenn, H. S., & Nelsen, J. (1989). *Raising self-reliant children in a self-indulgent world.* Rocklin, CA: Prima Publishing & Communications.

Gordon, T. (1974). *Teacher effectiveness training.* New York: David McKay Company.

Nelsen, J. (1987). *Positive discipline.* New York: Ballantine Books.

Model Solutions to Three Prototypical Classroom Management Problems

REFLECTING ON CONDUCT MANAGEMENT

Problem

Bill and Mark are inseparable inside and outside of school. Ms. Wenzel is not surprised when they ask for permission to be seated next to each other. Although another teacher who has both boys in class has expressed her consternation about their outrageous behavior, Ms. Wenzel, not wishing to be unduly influenced by her colleague, agrees to give them a chance to prove that they can be responsible while they are seated in adjoining desks. The boys prove worthy of her trust for several days. However, following a period of exemplary behavior, they begin to whisper back and forth and persist in this behavior after being asked to be quiet on numerous occasions. On this particular day, Ms. Wenzel loses her patience and angrily tells the boys to shut up or get out. Bill stands up at his desk, glaring belligerently at the teacher, and storms across the room. He deposits his textbook in the wastebasket as he exits through the back door. Mark remains at his desk and stares out the window for the remainder of the class period. What should Ms. Wenzel do now?

Solution

This problem originated in the ineffective use of legitimate power and should be dealt with as a conduct management problem. Ms. Wenzel does have the right to determine where students are seated in the classroom, a right to which Bill and Mark acceded when they sought her permission to take adjoining seats. She also has the responsibility to set standards for social and work relationships in the classroom. Unfortunately, Ms. Wenzel acted as though the boys could be trusted to behave properly, despite information to the contrary, and permitted them to sit next to each other on a noncontingent basis. We do not have a clue to her motives, but her behavior might be traced to a nonassertive response style.

Had Ms. Wenzel been assertive, a leadership stance that is suggested by the circumstances, she would have at a minimum instituted several preventive management measures. She would have told Bill and Mark that they could sit next to each other if they agreed to certain terms. The terms would have been expressed as specific behaviors: "You may sit next to each other on two conditions. First, you begin work promptly and continue without reminders during independent study time, and second, you confine your socializing with each other to the period before class begins and after the bell rings." An affirmative response to these two conditions would have served as a contractual agreement.

Ms. Wenzel would have used supportive management techniques to help the two boys honor their agreement. At first, these would have consisted of proximity control and generous use of positive reinforcement for on-task behavior. She would not have assumed that they could responsibly manage their behavior; without some external forms of support, the temptations to socialize are too great for such close friends. She could have created incentives to behave appropriately to counterbalance tendencies to disregard the rules and engage in inappropriate behavior.

Finally, Ms. Wenzel would not have tolerated unacceptable behavior to the point of becoming angry. Her hostile response followed a series of requests for appropriate behavior, requests that were not accompanied by a statement of the consequences for failure to comply with the rules. Had Ms. Wenzel stated what would happen if the boys persisted in misbehaving, her corrective management decisions might have saved the day. Prompt and decisive action might have reinstated the conditions of the original contract, taught the boys the importance of honoring contractual obligations, and preserved the good feelings that accompanied the initial decision to allow them to sit together.

However, what should Ms. Wenzel do now? At a minimum, she should send a student to the office to notify the principal of the incident. School personnel are responsible for knowing the whereabouts of students during school hours. Mark would be a good candidate for this errand because he would most likely want to extricate himself from the present situation. Going to the office to report Bill's absence from the class would also be a small mark of cooperation. Because it is quite likely that Bill is just down the hall, not really knowing what to do or where to go, Mark is also a prime candidate for securing his cooperation. Mark should be told that in the event he sees Bill, he should tell Bill to go to the office and remain there until he has spoken with the principal. Mark should be instructed to return after notifying the principal or seeing to it that Bill does so, because Ms. Wenzel needs to know what has transpired.

In a well-managed school, the principal will have a procedure for handling teacher–student flare-ups. In this instance, the principal might convene the parties after school and withdraw if the parties believe that they can settle the matter. The principal may remain to arbitrate a solution, if that is deemed necessary.

If Bill cannot be found in the building or on the grounds, his parents should be notified. They should be asked to call the school or a home number of a school official when Bill does arrive at home. Bill's parents should be told to have Bill report to the principal's office before going to classes the next day. Ms. Wenzel and the principal will have had a chance to discuss the next steps.

We see in this episode how a teacher lost an opportunity to teach two young men respect for authority and respect for themselves. They did not learn that a privilege is accompanied by responsibility. The boys' and the teacher's failure to act responsibly led to behaviors that discredited all parties. The teacher can hardly be respected for her part in maintaining control of the class and for her hostile behavior. The boys can hardly respect themselves for violating a trust and provoking the teacher's angry outburst. This disciplinary problem might have been inevitable; however, the final dramatic scene would not have been played out had the teacher used legitimate power and the principles and practices associated with the conduct management function.

REFLECTING ON COVENANT MANAGEMENT

Problem

Marsha is a loner. Each day she enters Ms. Halster's classroom by herself and goes directly to her desk. Social conversations take place all around her, but she is never included. Although she seems to be unobtrusively attentive, she never makes an effort to join these conversations. When assigned to small-group projects, Marsha occasionally shares an idea or an experience, but her contributions are frequently unrelated to the topic and are seldom acknowledged by other group members. Despite the indifference of her peers and her modest success in class, Marsha does not appear to bear any ill will toward her peers, but she does show signs of becoming more and more disinterested in the class. She often daydreams during independent study, frequently seems distant when spoken to, and appears to be content to get by with a minimum amount of work. What should Ms. Halster do now?

Solution

We do not know why Marsha is a loner, but we do know that loneliness is a relationship problem. We also know that relationship problems are best solved with a covenant management model. This choice of models suggests the use of the principles and practices advocated by Glasser, Gordon, Dreikurs, and Nelsen. Glasser believes that some students are alienated and lonely because they do not fare well in a school system that operates according to certainty and measurement principles. Marsha's growing disinterest in school might be attributed to a lack of encouragement for her modest contributions and what appears to be a total disregard for her social and belonging needs. Dreikurs tells us about the faulty logic that drives the behavior of students who cannot find a place for themselves. Marsha's display of inadequacy can be explained by her discouragement.

Marsha needs to experience the encouragement of a person who cares. She needs a role-before-goal teacher who starts by helping her feel like a worthwhile human being. Marsha's discouragement can be ameliorated by giving her a chance to succeed at some small but publicly visible tasks. Every teacher who has attractive power has ways of conferring status on students by giving them responsible roles in the classroom and then making something of their contributions. Preventing Marsha from sinking deeper into discouragement can be achieved through carefully orchestrated success experiences, particularly those that draw her into the classroom group and give her a sense of social significance.

Marsha may make halting progress; she may even resist doing some things because they draw too much attention to her. However, Ms. Halster should not become discouraged. Reflective listening skills can be used to help Marsha achieve insights and become self-directing. Encouragement is another supportive management technique that can be used to help Marsha appreciate her accomplishments and see herself as a lovable, worthwhile human being.

Glasser's problem-solving strategy could be used as a corrective management solution. Making friends with Marsha, by using the previously mentioned preventive and supportive management techniques, would be a good starting point. Recall that a role-oriented student personalizes everything. Marsha must feel differently about herself before she can begin to act differently; behavior starts inside. Having made friends with Marsha and having lessened her sense of discouragement and distrust, Ms. Halster can ask her, "Marsha, what is it you want to happen at school?" or "Marsha, how could things be better for you at school?" And later, "Is what you are doing getting you what you want?" If not, "Are there some better ways?" The questions guide a process that helps Marsha use her full powers for making a difference in her life. She can begin to use Ms. Halster's friendship and encouragement as sources of strength, the personal insights as the tools for changing behavior, and the plans as a means to acquire the knowledge and skills that lead to a more personally fulfilling life.

Marsha provides Ms. Halster a chance to use the personal ideals that drew her to teaching and the opportunity to employ interpersonal relationship skills that enrich the lives of children. All three management approaches—preventive, supportive, and corrective—can be used to forge a plan that can make a profound difference in the lives of students who want only what Glasser has said all students want: to be worthwhile to themselves and to others.

REFLECTING ON CONTENT MANAGEMENT

Problem

Roberta is a very academically able and socially popular student. She is able to complete assigned work in about half the allotted time and is disposed to use the remaining time to socialize with students who have not completed their work. Mr. Anderson decides to control this disposition by giving Roberta additional questions to answer or problems to solve. Initially, Roberta views the additional work as a competitive challenge. She tries to finish her work before other members of the class complete the common assignment, but generally she is not able to do so. After several weeks of this more academically rigorous regimen, Roberta lodges a protest about the extra work by slamming her book to the floor and angrily complaining about the unfair treatment. After all, she asserts, "Why should I have to do more work than everyone else just because I get busy and do the work quickly?" What should Mr. Anderson do now?

Solution

Some preventive management techniques do not work because the teacher does not involve the student in choosing the method or because the teacher neglects to offer the student a convincing rationale for a particular decision. Mr. Anderson obviously viewed the problem from a content management perspective, but he used legitimate power to curtail Roberta's gregarious tendencies. Had he relied on expert power, he might have worked with Roberta to find mutually agreeable outlets for her academic interests and talents.

Additional practice with similar materials might be a suitable alternative in some areas of the curriculum; enrichment materials that go well beyond common class assignments might be the arrangement in other areas of the school program. Or, Roberta might be given some tutorial responsibilities or an opportunity to undertake an independent project. Complete and accurate assignments would be rewarded with time to tutor or to pursue the independent project.

Mr. Anderson might have salvaged his legitimate power—based decision had his preventive management technique been accompanied by some supportive management measures. Had he introduced some ways to recognize Roberta's accomplishments—an occasional report to the class, a special note to her parents, or a specially arranged time to share her learnings with him—she may have been less likely to feel put upon for being a good worker.

Roberta's academic aptitude and esteemed status in the class increase the corrective management options. Beyond planning concrete proposals, such as tutoring and independent projects, Mr. Anderson should be looking for ways to help Roberta maximize her talents while she becomes increasingly less dependent on the teacher and peers for task-sustaining supports. This is a student who should be helped to find intrinsically satisfying ways to express her interests and abilities. She should be given greater latitude to manage her own affairs.

Correcting the problem should be aimed at relinquishing controls and giving Roberta more freedom to be a responsible decision maker. Expert power should be used to create enough structure, in the way of materials, activities, and supervision, to help Roberta select goals, devise ways to achieve these goals, develop self-monitoring progress procedures, and choose ways to report her results. The tangible products of her work and the pride that accompanies accomplishment will be proximate sources of motivation. The ability to think and work independently and to achieve a broad-gauged, meaningful grasp of ideas will be ultimate sources of motivation. Such intrinsically motivated students seldom have disciplinary problems.

Name Index

Abrahams, R. D., 288
Achenbach, T. M., 206
Adler, C. R., 246
Aiello, R. J., 289
Aitken, J. L., 19
Albert, L., 61
Alleman-Brooks, J., 193
Allington, R., 86
Anderson, L., 193
Anderson, L. M., 295
Ausubel, D., 192

Bandura, A., 70
Bany, M. A., 92
Barker, K., 277
Barnhart, C. L., 255
Baron, R. M., 287
Batsche, G. M., 8, 25, 258, 264, 265
Becker, W. C., 62
Bennett, N., 69
Berger, E. H., 6
Bernard, M. E., 287

Berry, K., 246, 281
Black, A., 70
Bloom, B. S., 196
Blundell, D., 69
Brandt, R., 246
Brantlinger, E., 52
Brattesani, K. A., 175
Bridges, E., 7
Bronfenbrenner, U., 5, 10, 11
Brophy, J. E., 7, 175
Brown, S. D., 286
Brubaker, N., 193
Bruner, J., 180
Burbules, N. C., 39

Calderhead, J., 19
Callaghan, T., 177
Cambron, N. H., 162, 217
Cangelosi, J. S., 200
Canter, L., 13, 21, 102, 103
Canter, M., 13, 21, 102, 103
Carlson, C., 235

Subject Index